£80.00
371.10019
22486M

Teacher Thinking and Professional Action

Over the past twenty years, the International Study Association on Teachers and Teaching (ISATT) has become world-renowned as an organisation dedicated to the discussion of current thinking in educational policy and practice. As such, the ideas aired at ISATT conferences are of the greatest significance to today's educational practitioners.

Teacher Thinking and Professional Action aims to satisfy the demand for a lasting record of ISATT's illuminating discussions on the theme. It is based on a selection of papers presented at their third biennial conference and has been updated by each contributor to include their current thoughts and opinions.

The book contains nineteen articles, each an in-depth examination of its topic, and is divided into four sections, entitled:

- Conceptual Frames for Teacher Thought and Action
- Methods and Approaches to the Study of Teacher Thought and Action
- Teacher Judgement and Evaluation of Students
- Teacher Thinking and Teacher Education

Broad in theme, international in scope and thorough in detail, this book is sure to be essential and enlightening reading for anyone with a serious interest in the ongoing development of educational thought.

Pam M. Denicolo is a Professor and Director of the Graduate School for Social Sciences at the University of Reading, UK.

Michael Kompf is a Professor in the Faculty of Education at Brock University, Canada.

Teacher Thinking and Professional Action

Pam M. Denicolo and Michael Kompf

Routledge
Taylor & Francis Group

LONDON AND NEW YORK

First published 2005 by Routledge
2 Park Square, Milton Park, Abingdon, Oxon OX14 4RN

Simultaneously published in the USA and Canada
by Routledge
270 Madison Ave, New York, NY 10016

Routledge is an imprint of the Taylor & Francis Group

©2005 Pam M. Denicolo and Michael Kompf

Typeset in Times by Keyword Group Ltd.
Printed and bound in Great Britain by TJ International, Padstow, Cornwall.

British Library Cataloguing in Publication Data
A catalogue record for this book is available from the British Library

Library of Congress Cataloging in Publication Data
A catalog record for this book has been requested

ISBN 0-415-36223-7 (Hbk)

Sigrun Gudmunsdottir was one of the contributors to the original version of *Teacher Thinking and Professional Action*. ISATT members were greatly saddened when notified of her death during the 2003 meeting in Leiden, The Netherlands. Sigrun's contributions to ISATT, dedication to her students and unfailing good humour stand as inspirations to all of us. It is to her memory that this book is dedicated.

Contents

Contributors

Theo Bergen, The Netherlands
Private address

David C. Berliner
College of Education, University of Arizona
Tuscson, Arizona, USA

Annica Brehmer
Department of Psychology, Uppsala University
Uppsala, Sweden

Jan Broeckmans
Center for Teacher Education
Leuven University
Belgium

Rainer Bromme
Universität Münster, Psychologisches Institut III
Münster, Germany

Alan F. Brown
(Retired) Ontario Institute for Studies in Education (OISE)
Toronto, Canada

Margret Buchmann
The Institute for Research on Teaching
College of Education, Michigan State University
East Lansing, Michigan, USA

Christopher M. Clark
Faculty of Education, University of Delaware
Newark, Delaware, USA

Erik De Corte
Centre for Instrumental Psychology, University of Leuven
Leuven, Belgium

Paul den Hertog
Institute for Teacher Education
University of Nijmegen
The Netherlands

Pam Denicolo
Graduate School for Social Sciences, University of Reading
Reading, UK

Sharon Feiman-Nemser
The Institute for Research on Teaching, College of Education, Michigan State University
East Lansing, Michigan, USA

Steven F. Foster
Institute for Educational Research
University of Groningen
The Netherlands

Manfred Hofer
Universität Mannheim, Lehrstuhl Erziehungswissenschaft II
Mannheim, Germany

Günter L. Huber
Universität Tübingen, Institut für Erziehungswissenschaft
Tübingen, Germany

Michael Kompf
Faculty of Education, Brock University
St Catherine's, Ontario, Canada

Gaea Leinhardt
Learning Research and Development Center, University of Pittsburgh
Pittsburgh, Pennsylvania, USA

Urban Lissmann
Zentrum für empirische Forschung
Landau, Germany

Deborah Loewenberg-Ball
The Insitute for Research on Teaching, College of Education
Michigan State University
East Lansing, Michigan, USA

Greta Morine Dershimer, USA
Private address

Antoinette Oberg
Department of Curriculum and Instruction, Faculty of Education, University of Victoria
Victoria, BC, Canada

Bernard Oliver
Syracuse University
Syracuse, USA

John Olson
Professor Emeritus, Queens University
Kingston, Canada

Sip J. Pijl
RION, Insitute for Educational Research, University of Groningen
Groningen, The Netherlands

Maureen Pope
(Retired) University of Reading
Reading, UK

Hilde Schrooten
Centre for Instructional Psychology
University of Leuven
Belgium

Karin van Opdorp
Institute for Teacher Education
University of Nijmegen
Netherlands

Lieven Verschaffel
Centre for Instructional Psychology
University of Leuven
Belgium

Lucie Vreuls
Institute for Teacher Education
University of Nijmegen
Netherlands

Acknowledgements

This volume would not have been possible without the goodwill, cooperation and patience of the contributors – we thank you. Acknowledgement and thanks are owed to Daniela Brewis for coordinating the flow of paper, Marie Harris for manuscript preparation, Ken Kehl for preparation of the index, Rahul Kumar for scanning in text and preparation of figures and tables, Tony DiPetta for the loan of his laptop and Andrew Short for assistance in proofreading.

We wish to acknowledge the American Educational Research Association and Michael Degnan of the *Educational Researcher* for allowing us to include a paper by Christopher M. Clark.

Thanks and appreciation are owed to Taylor & Francis who took over the project from Swets & Zeitlinger and helped ensure that this important work was preserved to aid teachers and teaching in the future.

We also acknowledge Brock University with thanks for partially funding the preparation of this manuscript through the Research and Development Fund.

Our families near and far are acknowledged and thanked for their patience with our preoccupation. As with the other volumes of ISATT papers we have edited, student travel to ISATT meetings will be assisted through all proceeds of this volume – welcome.

Pam M. Denicolo   **September 2004**
Michael Kompf

Preface

ISATT (then known as the International Study Association on Teacher Thinking) began in Tilburg, the Netherlands in October 1983 and was initiated by Rob Halkes, John Olson, Alan F. Brown, Christopher M. Clark, Erik De Corte and William Reid. In 1985, ISATT met again, this time with representatives from 12 countries. Since that time ISATT has become the International Study Association on Teachers and Teaching; sponsor of the journal *Teachers and Teaching: Theory and Practice*; producer of some 11 volumes of academic writing, research and theory; and mentor to several generations of scholars. The current volume follows on the successful reintroduction of early work produced by members of ISATT in *Teacher thinking twenty years on: revisiting persisting problems and advances in education* (Kompf & Denicolo, 2003). Chapters were drawn from *Teacher thinking: a new perspective on persisting problems in education* (Halkes & Olson, 1984) and *Advances of research on teacher thinking* (Ben-Peretz, Bromme & Halkes, 1986), which in turn were comprised of selections from association meetings held in Tilburg. Interest in the thoughts, research and writing of ISATT members has enjoyed a resurgence accompanied by further requests for materials no longer available. To this end, the current volume *Teacher thinking and professional action* re-presents selections from papers offered at the third biennial conference of ISATT held at the University of Leuven, Belgium in October 1986. The latter part of the ISATT acronym represented 'Teacher Thinking' at that time and is visible through the undercurrents of thought and research in these papers.

Two main resources provided the materials for the current volume. Conference host and ISATT founding member, Joost Lowyck, edited the proceedings – a blue-bound 717-page tome that participants received about 3 weeks before the meeting. From that volume, papers were further selected by editors Joost Lowyck and Christopher M. Clark (also a founding member of ISATT) and published by Leuven University Press in 1989 as *Teacher thinking and professional action*. This volume has not been readily available for many years. Because we were unable to locate some of the contributors to *Teacher thinking and professional action*, we revisited the proceedings and selected additional papers that represent the durability of ideas and the spirit of forward thinking that characterises the ISATT community.

One of the features of *Teacher thinking twenty years on*, as the title indicates, was the inclusion of author comments considering, from the point of view of recent and current work, how well the content stood the test of time and what significance the issues raised still have. Where possible, we have included such comments in this volume and feel that much value has been added by the accumulation of wisdom and experience over the ensuing years.

We include below excerpts from the preface to the original book to set the scene and to honour those who were instrumental in producing it. In particular, we would like to echo the original editors' final acknowledgement to their original publishers who kindly gave us permission to use extracts from that book. We would also like to offer personal thanks to Joost and the other founding members of ISATT who welcomed us so unreservedly to the fold at the Leuven Conference as novice researchers in the field and thus fired our enthusiasm for the intellectual challenge and spirit of international collaboration that ISATT embodies.

Pam M. Denicolo, Reading (UK)   **September 2004**
Michael Kompf, Brock (Canada)

Preface Extracts (1989)

When 'teacher thinking' emerged during the seventies, emphasis was almost exclusively laid on teachers' internal, mental processes. Teaching behaviours and skills were replaced by new concepts like intention, planning, reflection, concerns, constructs, personal theory, pedagogical knowledge, knots, subjective problems, etc. The teacher is no longer perceived as the observable performer of a set of effective but isolated teaching skills: he/she is a problem-solver, professional planner, hypothesis-tester, decision-maker, reflective practitioner. This initial conception of the study of teacher thinking is reflected in the first publication of the 1983 ISATT Symposium: 'In short, what's in the "mind" of teachers could explain classroom processes in one way or another' (Halkes & Olson, 1984, p.1).

Along with the increase of both empirical findings and conceptual refinements, the limitations of a narrowed teacher 'thinking' metaphor has been acknowledged. More action-oriented concepts appear like 'teacher routines', 'interactive thoughts', 'teacher strategies', etc. This evolution has been acknowledged in the 1984 ISATT Conference: 'It is self-evident that research into teachers' thinking runs the risk of excessive "cognitivism". We are witnessing an extension of what is meant by "teachers' thinking". Almost all factors influencing teacher activity are subsumed under this notion. This has led to an over-emphasis on internal and mental control of activity'. (Ben-Peretz, Bromme & Halkes, 1986).

In this 1986 ISATT Conference publication, a tentative attempt is made to avoid a further bifurcation of research on teaching. It seems at least intellectually honest to reflect on the possible integration of different research paradigms and not to accept ... the splitting force of dichotomous choices between description and prescription, teaching and learning, process and product, *teacher thinking and professional action* ... however, this volume will not provide an answer to the complex relationship between teacher thinking and professional action. On the contrary, it invites scholars in the field to reflect carefully upon the possible effects of centrifugal tendencies in research on teaching to look for more integration and cooperation.

It would be impossible to end this preface without an explicit acknowledgement of gratitude to the Editorial Boards of the Studia Paedagogica Series and the Leuven University Press.

Joost Lowyck, Leuven (Belgium)
Christopher M. Clark, Michigan (USA)

Section A

Conceptual Frames for Teacher Thought and Action

Berliner's keynote presentation, entitled 'The place of process-product research in developing the agenda for research on teacher thinking', is included as the first chapter in this book. While he had been asked to provide a comparison of the established process-product paradigm with more contemporary paradigms pervading research on teacher thinking, he produced instead a convincing rationale for recognising the contribution that work in each can make to a functionalist, pragmatic approach that recognises that thought and action are inextricably linked. Having analysed what is required by education and those engaged in it in terms of approaches, methods and foci for research, he provides a set of recommendations to researchers for future practice. In his reflective commentary on his original paper, he notes that he still thinks (Recommendation 1) that more comparative research, for instance examining contrasting groups of teachers, would add to improved understanding of pragmatic problems. He remains unconvinced, as detailed in his paper (Recommendation 2: 'Use more of the best teachers you can find'), that studying 'ordinary' teachers has much to contribute to resolving practical issues. His final recommendation is to focus first on those practical issues deemed important but little understood, and to devise research on how teachers think about them; in essence, reversing the 'figure and ground' in teacher thinking and action. In his reflective commentary, he regrets that much research in the field still fails to address issues of practical relevance.

The second chapter, 'Perspectives on the teaching profession or relative appraisal' by Denicolo and Pope, provides a degree of response to the previous chapter in several respects. In the affirmative, the authors use a method, a Personal Construct Theory technique, which, though firmly embedded in an interpretivist paradigm and using a small sample, includes data amenable to quantitative manipulations to demonstrate pervasive constructs and characteristics within the teaching profession. It also includes a comparison between two groups of teachers – science and non-science teachers. However, these teachers certainly fit into the category 'ordinary' teachers. This was deliberate, for the purpose of the research was to elucidate their views on their professional roles and practices with a particular focus on how these might be both appraised and developed. Since the majority of teachers are 'ordinary', the results of this research alert us to the potential difficulties for government policy implementation in relation to appraisal and staff development. The reflective commentary indicates that these caveats proved to be well founded but also reinforces from subsequent practice the claim in the chapter that the research technique proved useful also as a means of engaging teachers in reflecting on their practice, thereby providing a challenge to improve it.

Bromme, in the third chapter, 'The "collective student" as the cognitive reference point of teachers' thinking about their students in the classroom', addresses the way in which teachers attend to the problems and difficulties that their students have with the subject matter content of their teaching. In introducing an empirical study and a discussion of its results, the author notes that investigations of teachers' perception and interpretation of understanding were quite rare at that time. His current reflection notes that this study preceded a wealth of studies both on teachers' awareness about student difficulties and on students' preconceptions and other factors that inhibit new learning. However, in a way echoing Berliner's attention to solving practical problems in the classroom, he notes that his finding (that teachers, in the complexity of the normal classroom, are forced to work in relation to a notion of the 'collective student') remains currently relevant.

The fourth chapter, Leinhardt's 'A contrast of novice and expert competence in maths lessons', clearly meets Berliner's first recommendation since novice and expert teachers are studied in relation to their competence in weaving together a series of lessons, structuring individual lessons and moving fluidly from one activity to another to reach a transparent goal so that confusion for students is reduced. In her conclusion, Leinhardt addresses the dilemma that arises from her research: that though a detailed mapping of expert procedures has been achieved, nevertheless further research is required to find ways to enable novice teachers to acquire these skills for themselves. However, some useful guidelines on strategies for improving practice for beginning teachers are provided from the results of this research.

Chapter 1

The Place of Process-Product Research in Developing the Agenda for Research on Teacher Thinking

David C. Berliner

Introduction

I was asked if I would discuss the place of, and lessons learned from, an older style of research on teaching, often called process-product research, in developing the research agenda for studying teacher thinking, a contemporary programme of research on teaching. The older research programme has often been linked with the behaviours tradition in psychology; the newer research programme is associated with cognitive psychology in particular, and the exciting new field of cognitive science in general. To carry out my charge, however, means sharing with you my own idiosyncratic view of the two apparently disparate research traditions or programmes. What I offer, then, is a very personal view of these issues in the hope that this will contribute to the dialogue about the future course of research on teacher thinking.

Background

My personal history of involvement in research on teaching began with studies of presumably effective teaching skills, using task analysis as our method, a procedure borrowed from industrial and human factors psychology. Armed with a list of teaching skills we began training teachers to act in ways we thought effective, using microteaching settings and videotape feedback (Berliner, 1969). Then, a few years later I worked on trying to understand teaching by building and empirically confirming models of effective classroom teaching. We believed that our version of the Carroll (1963) model of school learning was so informative that we again worked on ways to train teachers so that they could acquire behaviours that were central to the model (Denham and Lieberman, 1980; Fisher and Berliner, 1985). We wanted teachers to think and act sensibly with regard to variables found to be important predictors of student achievement and attitude. Both of these kinds of research programmes are usually conceived of as squarely in the process-product tradition. They are often criticised as mechanistic in conception, leading to over-prescription for training, reflecting the kind of simple notion of how research gets into practice that is typical of behaviourists. Now I study a group of special teachers – experts – and wonder what they see and remember about classrooms, how they attribute meaning to what they see and do, what kinds of experience they bring to bear on educational issues, how they reason about the future course of events in classrooms, and what explanations they offer for their actions (Berliner, 1986). This work is considered typical of the cognitive research tradition. Supposedly, I have reformed, overcoming my silly behaviourist ideas, which some of my friends saw as my central character defect. I recite my personal history only to provide a background for what I say next, that I personally have not shifted the goal of my research at all, and I believe I work in the same research tradition in which I have always worked. This apparent anomaly is the reason I stated above, that I had an idiosyncratic view. Let me explain.

A Functionalist Psychology

My work and the work of many others that was called process-product is not automatically in the tradition of Skinnerian behaviourism, nor does the new work that is being done necessarily fit clearly within the programme of cognitive psychology. Much of the old and new work is, I believe, in the finest tradition of a much older research programme in psychology called functionalism. The psychological research tradition called functionalism has its roots in Darwin, in the philosophy of pragmatism, and is generally conceded to have been started by John Dewey (and others), around the turn of the century. The Chicago school of psychology, as functionalism was sometimes called, was a loose confederation of people and ideas. The functionalists, therefore, were eclectic. Boring (1957) once labelled functional psychology as 'what a psychologist does when free of systematic compulsions' (p. 559). They borrowed ideas and methods from all their contemporaries: Pavlov, Watson, Thorndike, and the Gestaltists. As applied scientists they were 'pragmatists; they take what works and accept those systems which provide convenient terminology for new general principles' (Boring, 1957, p. 570). Thus, the contemporary research programmes of behaviourism and cognitivism can supply the functionalists with concepts and methods for thinking about how to do the particular kind of work that they want to do. That work is always the establishment of relations between important characteristics of the environment and what human beings do and think about. What should be noted, however, is that one can borrow concepts and methods without taking on the ideology of the programme of research that is doing the lending.

Functionalism was given its most articulate formulation by James Rowland Angell in his presidential speech to the American Psychological Association in the early years of the last century (Angell, 1907). It pre-dated, by six years, Watson's famous paper that announced behaviourism and rejected the study of mental life (Watson, 1913). Watson, by the way, was Angell's student, and a functionalist in outlook. His contribution to the evolution of scientific psychology, however, was to jettison mind as a necessary concept in the determination of functional relationships between an organism and its environment. Watson narrowed the new functionalism that Angell had announced, and by so doing, led psychology down a much narrower path than it needed to go. One consequence of the ascendance of the Watsonian view of psychology was that it paved the way for Skinner and the radical behaviourism associated with that research programme. Like Watson, Angell insisted on using the new indigenous American form of experimental psychology, and avoiding the methods employed by the structuralists such as Wundt or Titchener. Nevertheless, Angell was quite clear about including the study of mental life in the functionalist research programme. The functionalists were interested in the how and why of mental operations, their functioning, more than the what of mental life, the content of conscious experience, which was the concern of the structuralists.

The focus of this psychological position was concern for a person's adjustment to a particular environment. Since environments clearly change, habits that once were successful become inappropriate, thus the problem solving skills and other mental activities used to direct new behaviour that is more relevant, were clearly important for functionalists to study. It was the functionalists more than others who fostered the enormous number of verbal learning studies conducted from the 1930s through to the 1960s. It was the functionalists who fostered the work on transfer and mediation in learning. These areas of psychology, though perhaps not studied in ways we would now consider fruitful, were not at all following the same research programmes that were characteristic of the more well-known behaviourists of that time, such as Hull, Spence, Skinner, or even Tolman. Many functionalists preferred human studies to animal studies. They were concerned with observable verbal behaviour, including meaningful verbal behaviour, and cared much less about movement or act psychology. They were linked to the British associationist tradition that was a simple cognitive psychology as well as a simple learning theory. They saw reinforcement as simply another variable that affects performance, like massed or distributed practice, rather than as a cornerstone of a learning theory. Thus, the functionalists had to be cognitivists, but of a different sort than those of today. They looked for relations between input and output, between stimulus and response, but never denied that what was in between the two was important. In addition, they always believed that the higher cognitive processes were amenable to study. They believed that through correlational and experimental work, reliable relations (including expressions of mathematical functions), would be established between thoughts and actions on the one hand, and measures of adjustment to the environment on the other. Their emphasis on adjustment to environments led them to propagate applied psychology. In this way, they could study the adjustment of people in special environments. Thus, the functionalists promoted educational psychology, industrial psychology, personnel psychology, and mental health professions at the start of the twentieth century. In each area of human concern, say the school or the workplace, the psychologist's job was seen to be the same, namely, to find out what thoughts and actions went with measures of adjustment to the environment.

Functionalism and the Criteria-of-Effectiveness Paradigm

In education and business, the functionalist's goals were very often transformed into what was called the criteria-of-effectiveness paradigm (Gage, 1963). Find a criterion of interest, one representing a good adjustment of the person to the environment (say successful sales in insurance, successful telephone operating, successful piloting of an aircraft, or successful classroom teaching) and find predictors of that criterion of effectiveness. The relations between predictors and criteria of effectiveness can then be used to select people who will fit that environment better than would a sample of individuals chosen at random, or the relations can be used to develop a curriculum for training people to work effectively in that environment, or both. In education, the criteria-of-effectiveness paradigm, an integral part of the functionalist psychology programme of research, became known as the process-product approach. That really is its roots–a special case of the functionalist psychology of an earlier era.

Unfortunately, however, the process-product approach to research on teaching became linked to the mechanistic view of man put forth by the Skinnerian brand of behaviourism, and was linked also to the anti-cognitive view of Skinner and most other behaviourists. A little better luck, a slightly different emphasis, a few different key writers or key works, and process-product research would have been linked to a more purposive view of man as an adjusting organism in the functionalist tradition, where cognition was already seen as a factor in that adjustment and where cognition was also seen as a legitimate area of study. Let us try to put aside the negative connotations associated with process-product research and look instead at what we can learn from the criteria-of-effectiveness research paradigm, stemming from the functionalist research programme.

Functionalism is my research tradition. It always has been, and I see no reason to change. That is what I meant when I said the goals of my research across the years have remained the same. I may be the last living functionalist. I am an unabashedly applied psychologist interested in the selection and training of teachers to be successful in one particular kind of environment, the public school classroom. With that goal, the criteria-of-effectiveness approach seems undeniably sensible to use. In fact, it should be noted that the criteria-of-effectiveness approach to selection and training was considered so successful by Lee J. Cronbach, that in the first edition of the *Essentials of Psychological Testing* (1949) he called it one of the outstanding achievements of social science. Let us use that framework for looking, very briefly, at the bodies of research that fall under the heading of research on teacher thinking: teacher planning, teacher interactive thoughts and decisions, and teacher theories and beliefs. I will use reviews by Clark and Peterson (1986) and by Clark and Yinger (1987) as my primary guides through this literature. Then I will point out a few lessons that were learned in the older research programme that might be worth thinking about for the newer research programme on teacher thinking.

Functionalism and the Study of Teacher Planning

Planning is a central topic of research on teacher thinking. Clark and Yinger (1987) define it as 'a basic psychological process in which a person visualizes the future, inventories means and ends, and constructs a framework to guide his or her future actions – what Yinger calls thinking in the future tense'. Both the focus of the teacher planning studies and the methodology used in these studies would be abhorrent to a radical behaviourist, but are perfectly acceptable to a functionalist. The functionalist, however, would quickly ask: for what purposes and to what ends are planning activities directed? Thus, the descriptive studies of the types of planning that are done by teachers are not valued in and of themselves, but gain their value when the functions of the types of planning activities can be understood. Therefore, learning that teacher planning early in the year focuses on the physical environment and social system of the classroom, or that much planning is not recorded on paper, or that teachers depend on published teachers' guides for planning, or that the activity is the basic unit and starting point for planning, is only potentially important information to those who study teaching from the functionalist tradition.

In the functionalist research tradition one is bound to ask, immediately on the heels of the revelations about the types of planning activities that occur, a very practical set of questions. For example, *why* is the activity the unit for planning? What is its function? Compared with teachers who plan with the activity as their focus, how would people who plan using content, or objectives or the individual student as their focus, fare in the classroom environment? Using the criteria-of-effectiveness approach we would ask: what do different foci of planning yield in terms of different measures of effectiveness, such as student satisfaction, student engagement, smoothness of classroom processes, student achievement, and other easily named and important criteria of effectiveness? For other revelations about the types of planning engaged in by teachers we would ask, early in the development of a research programme, similar questions about what function is served by, say, a reliance on textbooks? Why are plans often not written down? Why do teachers focus on the physical environment and social system of the class at the beginning of the school year, etc.? Using the criteria of effectiveness as a guide for generating practical research, we would propose a correlational and experimental research agenda that enquires whether there is any relation between higher and lower reliance on textbooks as guides, for planning, on the one hand, and such as measures of teacher confidence, student attitude toward the subject, student test performance, and other measures of effectiveness, on the other hand. In like manner, a correlational and experimental research agenda would be built around questions about the relation between plans that vary, say, from unwritten to fully specified, on the one hand, to criteria of effectiveness on the other hand, such as the degree of alignment between curriculum and the tests used as outcome measures, teacher confidence, student knowledge of goals, or teacher spontaneity. The last question was answered, in a way, in Zahorik's (1970) study. He apparently demonstrated the possibility of a reduction in teacher spontaneity as a function of well-specified planning activities. This study receives a great many citations. I think it does so because it is a study in the functionalist tradition, using the criteria-of-effectiveness approach, from which we derive information with patently obvious training implications. Uncovering findings that have training implications for a particular field, is what an applied psychology is about.

The knowledge about the planning activities of the people in a field takes on a special significance when that planning can be related to some criteria of effectiveness. For example, using a different context, we may cite a book by David Halberstam (1986), *The Reckoning,* in which he discusses the decline in the world markets of the American automobile industry. That major, once unthinkable decline in sales (a criterion of effectiveness) is traced to planning activities of a particular type. The American planners pursued short-term goals and profitability for the maintenance of stock prices. The Japanese, Halberstam notes, did long-term planning and picked consumer rather than stockholder satisfaction as their goal. The type of planning done by these business leaders, long- or short-term, concerned with consumers or concerned with stockholders, is certainly worth knowing, as are the types of planning activities engaged in by teachers. But the function of a type of planning activity and the relation of a type of planning activity to a criterion of effectiveness gives it special meaning to policymakers, and to those who select and train business executives or educational personnel.

Some research on teachers' planning has been conducted in this way. These studies provide evidence that such an approach can be useful and would have an appreciative audience. Carnahan (1980) for one has shown that many of the criteria of effectiveness concerned with classroom processes, such things as calling on a broad range of students, or using motivational statements, probably are unrelated to planning activities. Planning does not usually relate to such interactive behaviour, rather, it is related to structural characteristics of the actual lesson, such as the content, teaching activities, grouping patterns, materials to be used, and the like. When we put together our understanding of the functions to be served by planning with this research finding, we have enough of a theory and enough of a relation to be useful. Selection and training could be improved, and that could lead to better fits between persons and environments, which are, after all, an applied psychology and, therefore, a functionalist goal.

Therefore, in education, we should all delight in the new and creative taxonomic work occurring in the study of the teachers' planning behaviour. But the research agenda that has special significance, and should follow closely on the heels of that work, is, I believe, one that analyses the function of this planning characteristic and its relation to measures of effectiveness that we value.

Functionalism and Studies of Teachers' Interactive Thoughts and Decisions

Let us now turn our attention, briefly, to another body of literature that constitutes a part of the programme of research on teachers' thinking, teachers' interactive thoughts and decisions, and see how it might be addressed by a functionalist, using a criteria-of-effectiveness approach. Thus far, we have learned from such studies that teachers' thoughts during interactive teaching are directed primarily towards students. Teachers' concerns about content, materials, objectives, and the like, often fade, or are redirected into concerns about students' learning. The students, as well, provide the major source of cues that give rise to interactive decisions. In this vital research area, Clark and Peterson (1986) suggest the development of a matrix to help guide future research. They suggest crossing certain kinds of cognitive processes that have been found to be used regularly, such as perceiving, interpreting, reflecting, and so forth, with content categories found in teachers' interactive thoughts, such as students, objectives, materials, and so forth. Such a matrix could be used to direct researchers to more fully describe the nature of each process-by-content cell. A functionalist, however, would immediately ask a set of questions about that matrix that others might not ask right away. What is the perceiving for? What does it accomplish? Why are some things perceived and not others? What function is served by this overwhelming concern for students during interactive teaching?

Long before the matrix is fleshed out, functionalist concerns, which are practical concerns, seem to come creeping into this research programme. For example, we are learning from a number of sources that expert and experienced teachers perceive anomalies, or atypical events, quite a bit better than do less expert, less experienced teachers (e.g. Berliner and Carter, 1986). The expert teachers we study simply do not perceive ordinariness at all. It is, apparently, not functional to do so! It seems not to add anything to the teacher's ability to predict the course of events in the classroom, a very important skill, and therefore is of little value to them. Ordinariness, sameness, ongoingness in classroom life requires neither attention nor the making of a decision (except perhaps to stop or change activities). Only the perception of atypicalness, irregularity, or out-of-order events concerning students requires attention and, perhaps, some decision. These studies let us develop a sensible little theory about the function of the perception of cues about student behaviour, explaining why perception is the primary mental process used during interactive teaching and why students are the primary content of thinking during interactive teaching. This theory, however, is laden with ideas whose origins were in information processing and cognitive psychology. Let us keep these ideas in the back of our mind as we cross over to a different research tradition, one that relies on classroom observation, and enter the heart of the process-product research programme, in order to bring to the forefront some work by Jacob Kounin (1970).

Kounin gave us the amusingly named concept of 'withitness', defined, half seriously, as the teachers' ability to perceive events before they happen, that is, to catch events that could blow up into problems, before they mushroom out of control. Kounin related the teachers' measured 'withitness' to student engagement and the classroom's freedom from major behaviour problems. Other researchers went on and related 'withitness' to student academic achievement (e.g. Borg and Ascione, 1982; see also Brophy, 1983). This quintessential process-product finding has been the driving force behind dozens of studies and has fostered many programmes for selecting, identifying and training teachers. The popularity of Kounin's research, I submit, is because it falls squarely in the functionalist camp, using the criteria-of-effectiveness approach, for which there is a great and eager market. Practitioners in applied fields want knowledge about relations between the things people do and criteria of effectiveness so that they can learn to do what they do better. Kounin's little finding does that. Although it comes from the heart of process-product land, it is, in fact, a kind of a cognitive concept. It is the name for the kind of mental activity of teachers we found in that matrix, when we crossed the mental process of 'perceiving' with the content category of interactive thought called 'students'. The function, then, of that kind of thinking is to be 'withit', to perceive anomalies in classroom life early enough to stop them from getting out of hand. I think that the understanding of the functions of such thoughts when melded with replicable relations between that kind of thinking and highly valued criteria of effectiveness, gives that relation special significance.

Those who do cognitive research in the programme of research on teacher thinking may take credit for their part in uncovering the fact that a good deal of teachers' thinking is the perception of student behavioural information; and those in a behaviourist, process-product tradition may take pride in their replications and elaborations of Kounin's finding of a relation. It is the functionalist, however, who takes pride in seeing the two apparently disparate strands of work as a unity, providing all that is necessary for designing better matches of people and environments. We have enough theory to satisfactorily understand the relations that we find and that provide us with enough of the knowledge needed to develop ways to help teachers make better adjustments to the complex and dynamic environment called the classroom. Furthermore, the information can help us design environments in which teachers can function more effectively.

There is no doubt that continued descriptive and taxonomic work to better understand the teacher's interactive thoughts and decisions is highly desirable. This line of research is new, the body of knowledge small and fragile, and thus we all should promote ways that would help this line of research to flourish. However, I believe that it will be the establishment of relations between interactive thoughts and decision making on the one hand, and criteria of effectiveness on the other, that will lead to the greatest growth of knowledge within this field. Functionalism, a concern for the practical, an applied research programme, has a certain valued place in a field of enquiry like education. Such concerns can, and often should, drive the research agenda. The almost inescapable demand for this kind of research is noted when Clark and Peterson (1986) turn to these topics near the end of their review of teachers' interactive thoughts and decisions. They discussed a criteria-of-effectiveness approach in the review, a functionalist way of thinking, and perhaps they could not do otherwise. It is demanded by the field. When building a research agenda in this area it might be desirable to make more conscious efforts to consider these demands.

Functionalism and Studies of Teachers' Beliefs and Attributions

In order to move on to other issues, I will mention only briefly that the third area that constitutes the field of teacher thinking, the area of beliefs and attributions, has had a built-in kind of concern for the usefulness of the data that has accumulated. Attribution training began right on the heels of the discovery of different types of attributions. A programme called TESA (Teacher Expectancy and Student Achievement) has been used in hundreds of school districts, with general satisfaction. It is loosely based on the teacher expectancy literature. The criteria-of-effectiveness approach was built into the original Rosenthal and Jacobson study of expectancy (1968) and it has permeated that field of enquiry. The function of expectancy and its relation to behaviour is now well understood (i.e. Cooper and Good, 1983). This is precisely the kind of information that people want. In this area of research, they get an acceptable theory to surround reliable findings, and this accounts, I think, for the popularity of expectancy research. It is what is expected, I believe, of applied researchers and it is in the mainstream of the functionalist research programme.

The flavour of my remarks about researching on teaching, in general, is now clear. Let me, therefore, move on to recommendations that seem to me to be worth considering in building the research agenda for the study of teacher thinking across a wide variety of areas. I would like to share only three of many possible recommendations. All three, I might add, would bring the process-product and teacher thinking research programmes closer together, as might be expected of a functionalist.

Recommendation 1: Design More Studies Using Contrasting Groups

If one desires, a bit of the criteria-of-effectiveness approach can be incorporated, quite easily, into building the agenda for research on teacher thinking. If the teachers selected for study are simply of contrasting groups we usually learn much more than if they are not. One approach to developing contrasts is to find expert and novice teachers, another is to use experienced and inexperienced teachers, and still another is to use effective and ineffective teachers. After the identification of such groups, one can study the planning of these contrasting groups, or their interactive thoughts and decisions, or their beliefs, attributions, knowledge of students, and so forth. Research on teacher thinking, using stimulated recall and think-aloud techniques, will almost always be done with small samples because it takes so much time to work with a single subject and to analyse that subject's protocols. But even with small samples, contrasts could be useful, as already seen in about 10 per cent of the studies of teacher thinking now done (cf. Clark and Peterson, 1986).

In process-product research, some of the more fruitful studies have used this design. For example, the contrast worked well in classroom studies of management, whereby the behaviour of a small number of teachers who had well-managed classes was contrasted with the behaviour of a few teachers whose classes were chaotic (e.g. Evertson and Emmer, 1982). A small number of teachers who were more or less effective in producing gain scores on achievement tests were studied in the Beginning Teacher Evaluation Study (B TES) to great success, meaning, relations of interest were found even with small samples (Berliner and Tikunoff, 1976). The effective schools literature, from Ron Edmonds (1979) to Michael Rutter *et al.* (1979), has often used the method of contrasting groups. In fact, the whole research programme has its origins in a few contrasts between more and less successful schools that had similar kinds of students enrolled. If contrasts are built into the design of a study, when differences are found, one immediately has a hint of a relation. For aeroplane pilot selection this simple approach has resulted in the savings of millions of dollars. For example, the responses of experienced pilots with high reputations differ enormously from the responses of novice pilots to questions like: 'What do you do when the landing gear won't come down?' or 'Tell me what you think about landings?' The experienced pilot may say: 'When the landing gear will not work I open my emergency procedures book to the right page and follow instructions.' The experienced pilot may also say 'landings are fun'. The novice often says things like: 'When the landing gear won't work, I shut off the pump' or 'I call for help' or 'I prepare for a crash'. The novice reports that landings are 'the scariest part of a flight', or in the words of someone I hope never to fly with, 'landings are controlled crashes'.

Some novices, however, think more like some experts. Those novices have proved to be the best candidates for pilot instruction among the big commercial airlines. Since instruction costs hundreds of thousands of dollars per pupil, enormous amounts of money are saved by a simple, valid, contrast approach that allows a personnel director to hire those who most think like the criterion group. It is hard to talk of this kind of applied industrial/personnel psychology, concerned with pilot selection and training, as process-product research. In addition, it is harder still to attribute to it all the negative connotations associated with such research (behaviourist, mechanistic, anti-cognitive, etc.). I think it is simply an intelligent use of the criteria-of-effectiveness approach for finding people likely to succeed in a stressful, highly responsible working environment. I fail to see why the study of teaching should not also use this approach, when it can.

Research on teacher thinking can profit from this contrasting group approach, and on a basis other than effectiveness criterion, can be used to make the contrast. A basic tenet of process-product research (and, for that matter, all of experimental psychology) is that you should disaggregate data if you expect differences between groups. Gender, IQ and social class are common ways to separate out people because we have found that such distinctions affect performance in a wide variety of tasks. Researchers in the area of teacher thinking should probably also consider these same factors. We already have considerable evidence that a whole set of beliefs about instructions, students, outcomes, etc., are associated with the different kinds of preparation for teaching that occur in different subject matters. Science teachers, as opposed to language teachers, as opposed to teachers of the humanities, show discernible differences in the categories of things they think about, and hold different beliefs about the purposes of schooling and the roles of students (Yaakobi and Sharan, 1985). To combine data from these different groups, when studying teacher thinking, must lead to errors. It would be better, even with small samples, to contrast these groups. I think researchers on teaching will learn more this way than by their current overuse of mixed-sample approaches.

Recommendation 2: Use More of the Best Teachers You Can Find for Studying Teacher Thinking

This recommendation, like the first, is concerned with who would be in the necessarily small samples used to study teacher thinking. Now I want to ask a different question: Why not abandon research on the thinking of ordinary teachers, and devote more effort to the study of people who are more likely to be worth studying? I am embarrassed to admit it, but the thinking of ordinary people usually bores me. Furthermore, it may mislead me if I try to use what I learn from them in selection or for training. Very few people I know want to read any of the thousands of biographies of minor officials of, say, the British Expeditionary Force in the Sudan in the late 1800s.

The Victorian era spawned a great many such biographies, as each minor player in history set out for posterity his views of the heathens and the inevitable wars that were fought. These biographies are, as a group, boring. Worse, yet, I think they are uneducative. Instructive biographies, boring or not, may occur when the person is important, interesting or unique. The biographies of Gandhi, Roosevelt, Khadafi, Hitler and Helen Keller all have a chance to educate. The biography of, say, my mother is much more limited in what it can teach us. So it is, I think, with small studies of teachers' thinking.

The study by Elbaz (1981) comes to mind, since it has recently been so well cited and criticised. I have not been overly worried about it being a study of a single subject, and I consider seriously some of its insights, even though I believe them to be the result of a literary rather than a scientific investigation. Neither of those characteristics of the study makes me reject Elbaz's view of teachers' thinking as having 75 facets. (Elbaz presents us with 75 cells to think about, since teacher thinking is seen by her as crossing five content areas of teachers' practical knowledge, with five orientations to practical knowledge, with three forms of practical knowledge). What scares me more about such studies is that I had no sense that the one and only high school teacher who was studied was anything but ordinary. In fact, the subject of the study quit classroom teaching at the end of the investigation. Should her thoughts be used to launch a dozen confirmatory research studies? I do not think that it is usually a wise expenditure of our minimal resources to do studies of the thinking of ordinary people. They can so easily mislead us. I think of my mother, again, and how she would be described if someone had studied her thoughts about planning to cook, and her thoughts and decisions while cooking. She spent enormous amounts of time in and around the kitchen, shopped carefully and often, talked about recipes with neighbours, carefully watched pots simmer and boil, and served up large portions of food to a hungry family whose individual differences were always kept in mind. Because she was very articulate, she could describe every aspect of the cooking process in detail and with panache. We had a problem with my mother however; she was a terrible cook! She messed up vegetables daily, and she ruined hamburgers and chicken once each week. A record of her thoughts would surely have misled.

In industry, the study of the 'best' executives or 'top' corporations is in the functionalist tradition of trying to use a criterion of effectiveness to think about relations that might exist. The incredible success of that approach was seen in the book *In Search of Excellence: Lessons from America's Best Run Companies* by Peters and Waterman (1982). That book was a hard copy best seller for over a year, and now is a paperback best seller. It has influenced the management of schools and industry worldwide, yet is nothing more than our old, sensible, functionalist, criteria-of-effectiveness paradigm, brought in to study an applied phenomenon of interest. The useful educational version of this approach to research is seen in studies of commonalities among effective schools (where no contrasts with ineffective schools are made) and studies of common characteristics of effective teachers, without necessarily comparing them to less effective teachers. The selection of the 'best' teachers, on whatever criterion one values, is a practice worth considering when preparing to study teacher thinking.

Recommendation 3: Study Teachers' Thinking About Practices We Think Are Important, But Do Not Yet Have Much Understanding About
With this recommendation, I would like to reverse direction. Instead of looking at how thought and action are related, I would like to suggest looking at how action and

thought are related. Process-product research, our indigenous form of the criteria-of-effectiveness approach in research on teaching, has provided a shopping list full of characteristics of teaching thought to be important within that research tradition. Time management, for one, is generally believed to account for at least 10 per cent of the variance in achievement test scores in the public schools, and that is granted even by those who consider time to be a trivial variable in the overall order of things (Fisher and Berliner, 1985; Karweit, 1985). How do teachers think about allocated and engaged time? How do they decide to start or stop activities? In what ways do the clock, the schedule and student attention influence interactive decisions about what to do and for how long? It seems to me that studying the thinking of teachers with regard to issues of apparent importance is a worthwhile endeavour.

Another example is easily found. We know that mastery programmes, in research study after research study, when compared to traditional instruction, show enormous positive effects on achievement and student attitude (e.g. Block and Burns, 1976). We hear as well that, in practice, in grades K-12 in the public schools, mastery programmes often fall apart. My belief, though yet untested, is that teachers' beliefs about their role enter in here. The teachers' conceptions about what is 'proper' student behaviour are challenged, as their capacity to manage heterogeneity – groups of 30 individuals – is also strained. In short, I think the research from process-product investigations of mastery, which is so positive at first glance, needs to be understood not in terms of its effect on students' performance, but rather, in terms of its effect on teachers' thinking! Teachers' thoughts about mastery, and its associated characteristics, are what probably need to be investigated more thoroughly. We need least in our field another experimental study demonstrating that mastery is effective. We need most in our field some knowledge of teachers' thoughts while doing mastery programmes. That would be much more helpful.

There is an example of what happens when the recommendation to study things we already know are important is followed. A team at Michigan State University (Schwille et al., 1983) studied teachers' content choices, a cognitive concern, related to the well-established process-product finding that content coverage is a constant predictor of achievement (e.g. Berliner and Rosenshine, 1977). This research is noteworthy because it is one of the few examples I know of that blends the two traditions of research so well.

Teachers are often given the opportunity to learn apparently important and useful skills, methods and concepts, but make personal decisions to use or not to use them. Why? We do not yet know. Why is it, for example, that a dozen years after Mary Budd Rowe (1974) revealed the fascinating findings associated with wait-time during recitation, that we have no knowledge of why teachers ignore this simplest of all process-product findings? Dozens of replications have occurred (e.g. Tobin, 1987) and still there is scant evidence that practitioners will implement this reliable finding. My point is that many process-product findings are not implemented when learned. They apparently are not functional, or, I would assume, they would be used more often. A set of studies, therefore, of great utility, could be designed to work back from process-product relations to teachers' thoughts about the context and other variables associated with the empirical relations that were found. This would satisfy the functionalist who needs to know how certain behaviour is interpreted by the performers of the behaviour, in order to better teach (or abandon teaching) those behaviours.

I have been told that some of my research on instructional time is trivial, because time is an empty vessel. It is what fills time that is important to study, say such critics. The same partially silly, partially true criticism can be levelled at those who study teacher thinking. Thinking must be about some thing! It is like an empty vessel without an object of thought. Therefore, I suggest that one of the things to study is teachers' thinking about phenomena that have been found to be important, at least found to be important from the perspective of the process-product research programme.

The source of the information, the process-product research programme, should not cause a researcher concerned with teachers' thinking to reject the information about a relationship between teachers' actions and some criterion of effectiveness. Dewey, in *Democracy and Education* (1916, p. 120), points out that to act purposefully, to act with an aim, is the very essence of intelligence. He then says, 'A man is stupid or blind or unintelligent – lacking in mind – just in the degree in which, in any activity, he does not know what he is about, namely, the probable consequences of his acts. A man is imperfectly intelligent when he contents himself with looser guesses about the outcome than is needful'. Process-product research, even with its defects, provides some information of value about how things might turn out. It is, as Dewey notes, a sign of imperfect intelligence to merely guess about the outcomes of events when reasonably reliable information about relations is available. The relations from the process-product research programme can be used to inform a planner so that a reasonable estimate can be made of the probable consequences of actions A or B or C. The functionalist, armed with the criteria-of-effectiveness approach to the world, tries to provide the relations that decision makers can use, so that mere guesses about the outcomes of certain actions are not always needed when attempting to act purposefully. Learning how people think about the relations that are uncovered changes those relations from mere empirical findings to findings embedded in webs of meaning. Moreover, in that way we know so much more about them.

Conclusion

Process-product research is the way that the criteria-of-effectiveness approach is carried out in research on teaching. Its roots are in functionalism, and should not automatically be considered a radical behaviourist research programme, or inherently anti-cognitivist. What process-product research reveals, with all its shortcomings, is worth thinking about. In fact, it is not sensible to maintain the split between the two research traditions based on some partially true conceptions of what the other is about.

I was told of a wonderful interchange that illustrates this point. It is said that N. L. Gage, a key figure in the process-product research tradition, was talking to Lee Shulman, a key figure in the programme of research on teacher thinking. Gage worried that Shulman's teachers were 'too often lost in thought'. It took some time for Shulman to reply, but eventually he noted, 'It is better for teachers be lost in thought than missing in action'. I would enter this agreement between my two dear friends and colleagues by pointing out that thought and action are so inextricably linked that it is really a fiction to maintain their separateness.

Functionalism, concerned as it is with the reasons behaviour occurs, has recognised the inseparability of thought and action since it began as a psychological system. Dewey's (1896) famous reflex arc paper pointed out the indivisible nature of the stimulus (which could be a thought or an action) and the response (which also could be a thought or an action). In a complex serial process, extending over minutes or months, what is stimulus, what is response? What thoughts stimulate actions, what actions stimulate thoughts? How can one really wrench apart ongoing behaviour? Thus, functionalism as a research tradition would attempt research in teacher thinking with research in teacher action, since from its inception it could not distinguish between the stimulus and response, seeing behaviour, instead, as ongoing and purposeful. That teachers' thinking and actions are inseparable is also recognised by the title of the 1986 meeting of the International Study Association on Teacher Thinking. The title of this year's meeting is not the Third Conference on Teacher Thinking, as I originally thought it was. It is called, officially, and for the first time, a Conference on Teacher Thinking and Professional Action. If you will pardon some playfulness with words, that was appropriate behaviour, I think.

Author Reflection 2004

The functionalist movement described in this chapter is alive and well in contemporary America. The US government is currently demanding 'evidence-based educational research'. That means the scholars to be supported, and the schools to be praised, are those that have accepted the criteria-of-effectiveness paradigm, whose long history in psychology and education I noted. The supporters of the government's directives are not theory-oriented people, seeking understanding, as social scientists prefer. They are practical people asking the pragmatist's question, will it work? They seek to predict and control effects, caring less about understanding them. The sensibility of this approach will always be appealing to educators and the public.

Since publication of the original 1986 volume, the research on teacher planning has diminished greatly. Perhaps that is because, as I predicted, it led nowhere that a practical person would find useful. It was descriptive and taxonomic, and both the educators and the politicians of the world need practical knowledge about relationships between thought and action. Other kinds of research are of little value.

Teachers' interactive thoughts and decisions are still studied, and as a scientist, I find these of interest. We know a good deal more about how teachers' knowledge is directed by beliefs, is person- and context-bound, action oriented, and often implicit or tacit. However, we still have little knowledge of what that means for designing teacher education programmes. As a community of scholars, we pass the scientific test of finding out interesting things. Nevertheless, we may still be failing the practical test of what it all means for Ms Williams in the Roosevelt school, on Monday morning. A little more attention to the criteria-of-effectiveness paradigm might prove beneficial.

I continue to believe that we need more comparative research on thinking (expert vs. novice; suburban vs. inner city teachers; mathematics vs. social studies teachers). I also would like to know more about the thinking of unique individuals – exemplary teachers, teachers who drop out of the profession, teachers who do not adjust to changing demographics, and so forth. I remain unconvinced that useful lessons are learned from studying ordinary, run-of-the mill teachers.

Chapter 2

Perspectives on the Teaching Profession or Relative Appraisal

Pam M. Denicolo and Maureen Pope

> "O wad some Pow'r the giftie gie us/ To see oursels as others see us!"
> R. Burns 1759–1796 (*To a Louse*)

Currently it would seem that teachers worldwide are receiving the gift of seeing themselves, at least in their working role, as others (society and its alter ego, government) see them. None perhaps more so than UK teachers, who seem in imminent danger of having this, as an unsolicited gift, thrust upon them from without in the form of criteria for appraisal of their professional practice. Parkes (1985), writing an appraisal in the Further Education sector, proposes:

> There appears to be little doubt that what goes on in education is
> going to come under growing scrutiny from outside agencies.

While discussion rages about the appropriateness, or otherwise, of these criteria and about the viability of various forms of appraisal, it would seem expedient to ascertain the teachers' own views of their professional roles and activities. It is recognised that this would be a complex task for it would encompass teachers' own views in conjunction with, or contaminated by, a second-order perspective (Marton, 1981), i.e. how teachers perceive others' perceptions of themselves. In addition, it is likely that individual teachers or groups of teachers differ in perspective, e.g. across cultures, within culture, across experience and within discipline. From the UK point of view, Stenhouse, as early as 1975, noted that at that time morale in British schools was often low, while at the same time suggesting that morale is founded on professionalism. In the interim period, a protracted dispute between teachers and government cannot have increased morale and has increased the urgency for a study of professionalism in education.

Thus, this chapter represents an initial foray into the domain of investigating teachers' constructs about their profession and its activities, reporting on a small pilot study conducted in the UK. The data from this study is in the process of being coordinated with data from a similar study conducted in Israel by Ben-Peretz and Katz. Both studies are grounded in the philosophy and theory of Personal Construct Psychology and use repertory grid methodology in order to illuminate teachers' thinking in this sphere and to suggest implications for initial teacher training and in-service staff development.

The rationale for the methodology is detailed in Ben-Peretz (1984b), a flavour only being given here:

> Kelly's theory as a general theory of thinking and action provides us with a framework for viewing professional thinking and action as one instant of a general paradigm... The theory of personal constructs provides us with a large army of research questions related to the nature of teachers' thinking. Appropriate research instruments and data processing procedures have been developed. The theory permits in-depth investigation of the construct system of individuals as well as comparisons between individuals and groups.

Further detail of the philosophical and methodological basis for this research may be found in Pope and Keen (1981) and a description of the rationale for, and the methods used for, grid analysis may be found in Shaw (1980).

The implicit assumption so far in this chapter has been that 'teaching' is a profession. Certainly some sectors of the public see it time-honoured as such. Teachers themselves also appear to support this view in that, preliminary to the main part of the study, teachers from a wide spectrum of education included 'Teachers' when asked to devise lists of categories of persons that they would designate as belonging to the domain of an element set called professions. These lists were used to devise a common set of elements for the first grid exercise, those professions being included which were most commonly identified as such by the participants. This first grid was then used to elicit from teachers their constructs about the various professions, using the triadic method (Pope and Keen, 1981). This method allows for comparisons to be made on several dimensions between teachers' views on their own and other professions. In so doing, it also allows some of the constructs that constitute the teachers' professional lore to be set in relief.

While the first grid encouraged teachers to contemplate their own profession *in relation* to others, the second grid engaged them in considering their unique professional practice and in making a critical analysis of it. The elements for this set of grids were obtained in a similar way to the first element set, i.e. teachers were asked to identify activities which were part of their professional practice and which constitute their professional role. It was hoped that this grid would begin to tap what it means to teachers to adopt a professional stance vis-à-vis teaching activities.

Some commentary on the practical use of the grids is necessary for, although a wealth of data was derived from them, it did prove time consuming both for the administrators and for the participants. The first grid elements (*professions*) generally provoked a large number of constructs, the teachers apparently having little difficulty in construing the rather 'concrete' elements. This is in contrast to the elements in the second grid (*activities*), which the teachers found difficult to construe, at least in terms of time required to articulate constructs and rate the elements. However, they did find the exercise stimulating. All requested extra time to devote more attention to the second grid, reporting their interest in being enabled to contemplate their activities in such depth, albeit this being something which they had not systematically done in the past. The often-explicit addendum that they seldom had the time/opportunity to do this is important in itself, since, as Ben-Peretz (1984b) advocated, part of professional activity should be to review constructs about the job. The value that they finally gained from the activity will be discussed later, with the results of the study, in relation to professional development.

The data from the UK study derives from ten participant teachers, all experienced teachers in the comprehensive system. Five of these teachers teach science/maths subjects while the remaining five teach other subjects including social sciences, languages and craft subjects. All participants were given a brief verbal synopsis of the nature of the enquiry, i.e. an interest in teachers' views about various professions and about the activities that constitute theirs, and about the nature of the method. Before completing their own individual grids, they were given instruction and practice in the techniques involved using an example unrelated to the topic of current enquiry. Each teacher was given grid forms on which the elements, either professional persons (set 1) or activities involved in teaching (set 2), were provided along with indications of triads, randomly assorted, to be used to elicit up to 20 constructs for each grid. After producing a construct for each triad, the participants were asked to rate *each* of the elements on the grid on a 5-point scale to reflect where each element lay between the two poles of the elicited construct.

Data Analysis and Results

Using the Planet Suite computer package FOCUS (Shaw, 1980), each grid was analysed separately to produce tree-diagrams that indicate degree of match between elements and between constructs. The initial data in the 'raw' grid is focused to display the pattern of relationships inherent in the ratings used. The Sociogrid package allows comparisons to be made as to similarity between each person's grid and the Modegrid displays the most 'common' constructs/ways of ordering the elements found within the group (Shaw, 1980). Modegrids were produced for the science and non-science group for both 'profession' and 'activities' and finally two combined sets of grids were made, i.e. for all the teacher participants, one concerned with professions and one concerned with activities.

We will first discuss the area of 'professions', starting with the more general findings and moving then to look at the case of one teacher in more detail. The same pattern of commentary on general findings and then one case will be used when we turn our attention to activities, using the same teacher in each case study to illustrate the nature of the data.

Commentary on Combined Grid on Professions

Only the first 15 of the ranked constructs (which emanate from several members of the teachers' groups) are used here to give an indication of those which show the highest level of agreement across all participants in the pattern of rating of elements. In addition, a content analysis of general ideas conveyed by construct wording was undertaken for this set of grids especially with respect to their application to the teacher element.

Although there may have been variations in rating of these constructs, it is noteworthy in this context that, from a total of ten teachers, the following general ideas were elicited as constructs: (the description is given in terms of the pole nearest to which 'teacher' fell in rating).

'occupation demands emotional involvement'	9 teachers
'occupation requires high level of creativity'	7 teachers
'occupation involves playing a role to an audience'	6 teachers

'occupation receives poor pay in comparison to others'	6 teachers
'occupation commands little public/media respect'	5 teachers
'occupation is ill-defined/has complex definition'	5 teachers

In addition, most of the teachers conveyed some notion related to a family of ideas that their occupation has 'long or unlimited working hours' and that it 'impinges on family and/or social life'.

The element tree for the combined grids (Figure 2.1) contains three main clusters that are clearly separated. To focus on the one containing 'teacher' (elements 5, 1, 9, 2, 3, 10), we observe that 'teacher' is closely related to the pair 'nurse' and 'clergy' and to 'social worker' with other members of the health professions, i.e. 'doctor' and 'dentist', next closely linked. The next nearest link is to 'actor', which is itself well separated from its neighbours in the next cluster.

The construct tree (Figure 2.2) has one predominant cluster containing eleven constructs (11, 3, 8, 14, 12, 5, 13, 7, 1, 2, 15), all of which, with the exception of 13, convey ideas about a *humanitarian, people-centred, altruistic perspective* to a profession as opposed to a *profit-making, materialistic* and *self-interested* perspective.

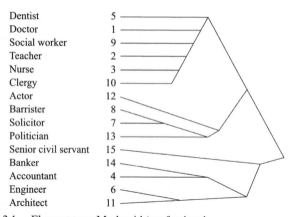

Figure 2.1.   Element tree: Modegrid 'professions'.

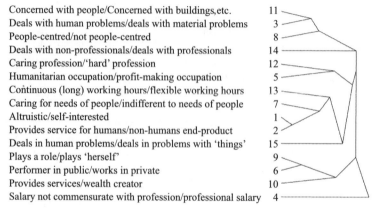

Figure 2.2.   Construct tree: Modegrid 'professions'.

In these constructs 'teacher' rates well towards the former poles whereas it is centrally placed on construct 13 that is *continuous, (long) working hours/flexible working hours.* The tree also contains a small cluster composed of a pair, 9 and 6, concerning *degree of playing a role and performing in public* and a single construct – *provides services/wealth creator.* The profession of teacher is rated towards the role-play, public performance and service provision poles of these constructs. The two clusters are linked together and the final construct (4) links to all of these, but at a much lower level of correlation. Again, 'teacher' comes towards the elicited pole of *salary not commensurate with profession/professional salary.*

The separate grids for the group of science teachers and the group of non-science teachers are very similar in pattern and type of constructs to the whole combined grid with only minor differences in detail. For instance, non-science teachers introduce a construct *high status/low status* whereas science teachers include *known to 'Joe Public'/not well known.* While science teachers include *generally a non-numerate activity/generally a numerate activity,* non-science teachers use *involves a lot of paperwork/ involves little paperwork!*

Commentary on Case (Professions)
The teacher whose tree diagrams are displayed here (Figures 2.3 and 2.4) is an experienced science teacher. The grid is chosen as being representative of many of the general points made by the sample set of teachers.

From the element tree (Figure 2.3) we can see that 'teacher' (2) is closely linked with 'social worker' (9) both being in the cluster that includes the health professions (1, 5, 3). Linked with this cluster is 'clergy' (10) but this whole group is clearly separate from the other professions. 'Politician' (13) and 'actor' (12) are separate from the whole body of professions and we can assume that this teacher construes these last two professions in very different terms to the rest. This teacher was able to produce 20 constructs about professions.

The first main cluster (constructs 13, 5, 15, 3 and 14) seems to concern general features of the profession that are public knowledge. Linked to this is a construct concerned with the *day-to day satisfaction from the job* (16) and one concerned with the *social background of members.* The next main cluster (18, 1, 17, 10) gives more job detail as does the following cluster (11, 19, 4, 2, 9, 7), the second perhaps concerning more intimate details. These last two are linked together and are then linked

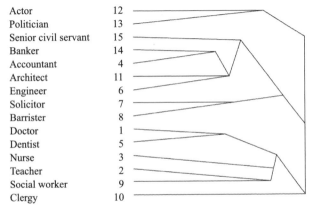

Actor	12
Politician	13
Senior civil servant	15
Banker	14
Accountant	4
Architect	11
Engineer	6
Solicitor	7
Barrister	8
Doctor	1
Dentist	5
Nurse	3
Teacher	2
Social worker	9
Clergy	10

Figure 2.3.   Element tree: case study 'professions'.

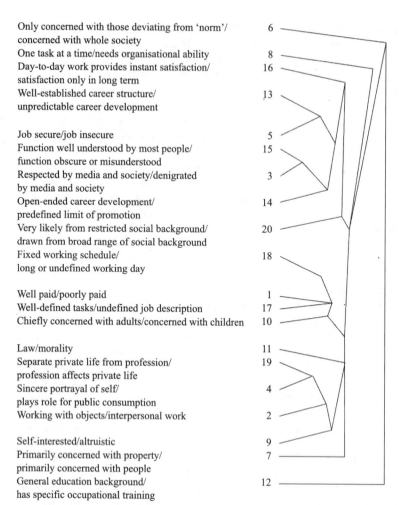

Only concerned with those deviating from 'norm'/   6
concerned with whole society
One task at a time/needs organisational ability   8
Day-to-day work provides instant satisfaction/   16
satisfaction only in long term
Well-established career structure/   13
unpredictable career development

Job secure/job insecure   5
Function well understood by most people/   15
function obscure or misunderstood
Respected by media and society/denigrated   3
by media and society
Open-ended career development/   14
predefined limit of promotion
Very likely from restricted social background/   20
drawn from broad range of social background
Fixed working schedule/   18
long or undefined working day

Well paid/poorly paid   1
Well-defined tasks/undefined job description   17
Chiefly concerned with adults/concerned with children 10

Law/morality   11
Separate private life from profession/   19
profession affects private life
Sincere portrayal of self/   4
plays role for public consumption
Working with objects/interpersonal work   2

Self-interested/altruistic   9
Primarily concerned with property/   7
primarily concerned with people
General education background/   12
has specific occupational training

Figure 2.4.   Construct tree: case study 'professions'.

to the first-mentioned group, making one overarching cluster to which three other con-structs are added sequentially: (8) *one task at a time undertaken*, (6) *only concerned with those deviating from the norm* and (12) *has specific occupational training*. It would appear that these three constructs show increasing variety across the professions, rather than fitting a pattern of association.

It is notable that on only two constructs (16 and 13) does the teacher fall close in rating to the elicited pole. Therefore, the results will be discussed in terms of the contrast poles of the constructs. Thus, for example, this teacher would seem to describe his profession in these terms: *misunderstood by most people; denigrated by the media and society; limited career development; longer undefined working day; low paid; undefined job description; profession affects private life; involves playing a role for public consumption; altruistic; primary concern is the people*. In spite of the negative tone to many of these, this teacher does see his job as *providing instant sat-isfaction in day-to-day working*. These tensions appeared in several of the teachers' grids.

Commentary on Combined Grids for Activities

When the activity grids for participants were combined we found that activities (7, 3, 1, 5) and (2) were very closely linked (Figure 2.5). These are activities dealing with the selection and organisation of topic material: what might be considered the elements of forming lesson plans/schemes of work. Linked to this main cluster are elements (6, 10, 4), i.e. *construction of aids, evaluation* and *time allocation* that gives the impression that, although necessary to the above, they are of second-order consideration. Linked to the main group, but with decreasing similarity and not forming clusters, come elements (8, 12, 11, 9), i.e. *identification of pupil difficulties, strengthening of pupil motivation, classroom management* and *assessment of pupils*; i.e. the focus has moved from *content of lessons* to more pupil-centred activities. Finally, elements (14, 13, 15) are quite separate from the rest, the first two being concerned with developing relationships, with parents and with other colleagues, and the last being participation in staff development activities.

This grid also gives us some indication of generally used constructs about these activities (Figure 2.6). These fall into two main groups with subdivisions in each. The first contains a construct cluster (3, 8, 5, 12) noting the importance and pervasiveness of activities but including *takes place in the classroom*. There are also two pairs, (10) with (1) and (2) with (13), the first linking the description *interesting* with lesson-centred activities and the second showing a comparability of rating between *intellectually demanding activities* and those *usually performed in a solitary manner*. The second main group contains a cluster (15, 6, 11, 4, 14, 9) that demonstrates a strong link between activities which are seen as emotionally demanding or stressful, and those that involve cognitive skills and are educational in nature rather than administrative. These are also activities that the teachers see themselves as doing on their own with little support available.

In view of the potential of linking appraisal with staff development and our interest in such links we found it illuminating to reflect on the rating of *staff development activities* on the constructs presented here, which suggest that although support for these is perceived as available, the activities themselves appeared to be currently perceived as trivial, neither intellectually nor emotionally demanding, intermittent and mainly concerned with administration. Such views have implications for attempts to encourage teachers to see staff development, especially if based upon an appraisal system, in a more positive light.

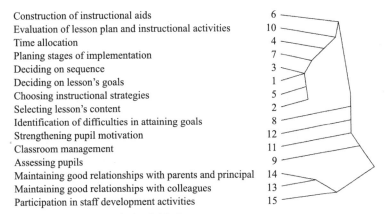

Construction of instructional aids	6
Evaluation of lesson plan and instructional activities	10
Time allocation	4
Planing stages of implementation	7
Deciding on sequence	3
Deciding on lesson's goals	1
Choosing instructional strategies	5
Selecting lesson's content	2
Identification of difficulties in attaining goals	8
Strengthening pupil motivation	12
Classroom management	11
Assessing pupils	9
Maintaining good relationships with parents and principal	14
Maintaining good relationships with colleagues	13
Participation in staff development activities	15

Figure 2.5.   Element tree: mode 'activities'.

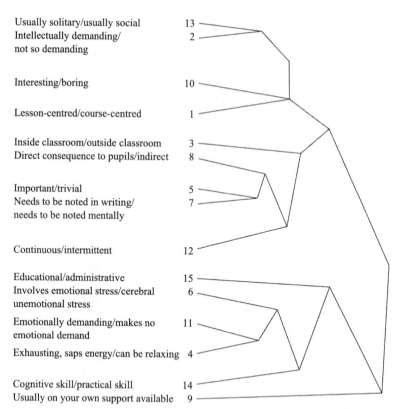

Figure 2.6.   Construct tree: mode 'activities'.

When the grids of the two groups, designated as scientists and non-scientists, are compared, we find that the general pattern is similar but with some differences in detail. For instance, elements (10, 6) i.e. *evaluation* and *construction of aids* are more closely linked together and to the main cluster for the non-scientists, and their main cluster subsumes *identification of student difficulties* (8) and *strengthening of pupils motivation* (12). *Assessment of pupils* (9) is more clearly separate for this group also, whereas *classroom management* (11) is more separate for the scientist, as is (4) *time allocation*.

The construct tree on the combined scientists' grid strongly echoes the theme concerning the link between emotionally demanding educational activities and those with little support. It is noteworthy that the activities rated as pupil-centred also tend to be considered as not relevant to career development, being also rated as required by the teacher rather than subject to wider requirements. This grid also contained three constructs of an 'objective'-descriptive nature, being focused on the 'planning' rather than 'doing' nature of activities.

In contrast, the combined non-scientists' grid contained three constructs related to the degree to which activities promote relationships (with pupils, parents and colleagues) and one which rates activities along a continuum of whether they require more self-analysis or are more 'outward-looking'. Again, though, there is a stress on pupil-centred classroom activities that are under teacher control, rather than external control, as being the most important and interesting intellectually.

Commentary on Case (Activities)
The tree diagrams for the science teacher are shown in Figures 2.7 and 2.8. Again, the pattern of content focus is discernible as a cluster separate from the other elements. It is of interest here to note that *staff development activities* (15) is linked in finally with this group before the other activities, and that *assessment of pupils* (9) and *classroom management* (11) are very separate activities from the two clusters which might be labelled respectively content orientated and management orientated.

There are several clusters of constructs that seem to have face validity. The first (9, 2, 5, 7) deals with the degree of essentialness of activities, but, interestingly, also includes the construct *satisfying*. In contrast is the group (13, 15, 8, 12, 20) that deals with external constraint on activity, and includes *can involve emotional stress*. A third group (17, 4, 11, 10, 16, 3) contains ideas about involvement of attitudes and natural skills and abilities, along with how pupil-centred the activity is and how dependent it is on class size.

Although there are many points worthy of discussion in this grid, the focus here will be on how participation in staff development activities (15) fared on the constructs. For this particular teacher, such participation seems to be viewed as: *tends to be omitted under pressure of work* (9); *optional rather than essential* (2); *required for full career development* and *for personal satisfaction* (5, 7); *subject to external constraints* (15, 8) and would be one in which *additional, external help would be useful* (19).

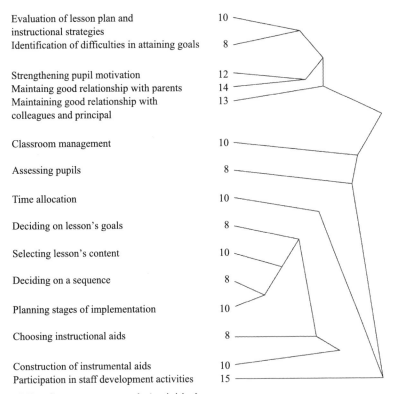

Construct	
Evaluation of lesson plan and instructional strategies	10
Identification of difficulties in attaining goals	8
Strengthening pupil motivation	12
Maintaing good relationship with parents	14
Maintaining good relationship with colleagues and principal	13
Classroom management	10
Assessing pupils	8
Time allocation	10
Deciding on lesson's goals	8
Selecting lesson's content	10
Deciding on a sequence	8
Planning stages of implementation	10
Choosing instructional aids	8
Construction of instrumental aids	10
Participation in staff development activities	15

Figure 2.7.   Construct tree: mode 'activities'.

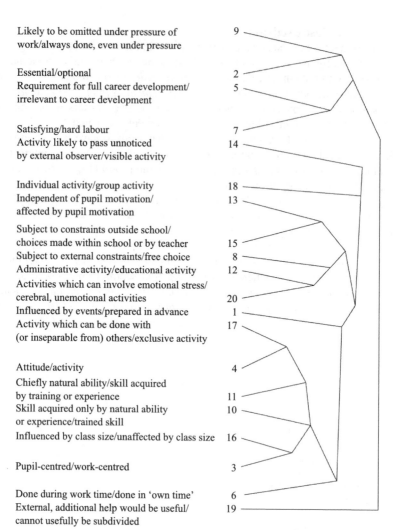

Likely to be omitted under pressure of   9
work/always done, even under pressure

Essential/optional   2
Requirement for full career development/   5
irrelevant to career development

Satisfying/hard labour   7
Activity likely to pass unnoticed   14
by external observer/visible activity

Individual activity/group activity   18
Independent of pupil motivation/   13
affected by pupil motivation

Subject to constraints outside school/
choices made within school or by teacher   15
Subject to external constraints/free choice   8
Administrative activity/educational activity   12
Activities which can involve emotional stress/
cerebral, unemotional activities   20
Influenced by events/prepared in advance   1
Activity which can be done with   17
(or inseparable from) others/exclusive activity

Attitude/activity   4
Chiefly natural ability/skill acquired
by training or experience   11
Skill acquired only by natural ability   10
or experience/trained skill
Influenced by class size/unaffected by class size   16

Pupil-centred/work-centred   3

Done during work time/done in 'own time'   6
External, additional help would be useful/   19
cannot usefully be subdivided

Figure 2.8.   Construct tree: case 'activities'.

Discussion of Results and Implications

The results of this study indicate that for this group of teachers in the UK the profession of teacher has much in common with the 'caring' professions, being most closely linked with the social worker and the pair nurse and clergy. The link with clergy is interesting, given the history of education in the UK that had its roots in the religious training of disciples and missionaries. From these beginnings 'church schools' developed and it is pertinent to note that even today the only compulsory subject in primary schools is religious education. The constructs produced which indicate a commensurate level of altruistic commitment demanded either by society or teachers' own expectations of themselves are noted by Stenhouse (1975):

> people working in schools tend to invoke ideological, judgmental,
> or moralistic bases for making decisions... society has commonly

endorsed this stance historically by demanding particular moral standards of teachers.

The degree of commonality of role with the clergy is echoed in the links with the roles of both nurse and social worker, stressing the humanitarian, 'client-centred' nature of their occupation. However, pupils cannot be comprehensively described as 'patients' or 'cases' and thus the teacher's professional concerns cannot be limited to effecting a cure or solving the problem of a case. The intricate meshing of role elements of all three of these professions seems to be well recognised by these teachers, who produced constructs which suggest a complex and ill-defined job description, lengthy hours of commitment which impinge on private life and the necessity of a degree of creativity in day-to-day working.

Two other dominant constructs for these teachers with regard to their profession are that it is under-supported in terms of both salary and perceived status. This is not surprising given the context of a long-drawn-out dispute between government and teachers over salary and the imposition of standards from outside the profession. This latter is in opposition to the generally held view that professionals, as a collective, have the right to determine their internal codes of practice, policies and procedures. It would not be far-fetched to relate to this the numerous individual constructs on the activities grids which indicated some activities are subject to some form of interference from without. One form of this is the production of curriculum packages with texts for students and scripts for teachers, which may also relate to the linking of 'teacher' with 'actor' on many grids.

It seems appropriate to link this with the constructs produced about both professions and activities that mentioned degree of stress involved in or produced by the various elements and the emphasis on emotional involvement apparent in the combined activities grid. This suggests that the inherent difficulties of the job, which is perceived as demanding commitment, etc., may currently be exacerbated by the antagonistic perception that it is largely devalued in terms of financial compensation, accredited status and professional standing with regard to locus of control. (Further reflections on this may be possible when the data from a different cultural context (Israel) is combined with this data.)

Another repercussion of these negative constructs may have been an effect on the construal of *taking part in staff development activities.* It was noted earlier that this activity, or rather the teachers' experience of it to date, was not valued greatly by them. This in spite of the fact that, albeit in another cultural context (Canada), Common (1984) notes:

> The system is based on the assumption that the desire for growth is latent in everybody and that individuals look to the work place to grow personally and professionally.

Additionally, a DES (1985) paper by H. M. Inspectorate suggests:

> There is however an equally important responsibility for teachers themselves to ensure that they remain academically and professionally well-qualified for their jobs by undertaking private study and reading, by seeking opportunities to improve their knowledge and skill, and by taking part in further training where appropriate.

It may be that the participants in this study fulfil this responsibility by the first method identified in the above quotation, although, with the perceived pressures of work indicated as experienced, this may not be likely. This would only be resolved by an extension of this study to incorporate interviews with teachers about reasons why certain ratings were given. However, another suggestion might be that the 'further training' involved in staff development activities is deemed 'inappropriate' by them, perhaps because of this current popular link with appraisal. We have already noted a somewhat negative stance portrayed towards staff development activities in Figure.2 6.

Pennington and O'Neil (1985) noted that appraisal belongs to a family of concepts that includes 'evaluation', 'assessment' and 'monitoring' and is frequently perceived as being synonymous with these in contexts where accountability is the dominant value. It is also perceived as being unilaterally imposed from above to reveal weakness and 'to weed out incompetents'. Such perceptions frequently lead to the closing of professional ranks because autonomy is threatened, as is the professional right to determine standards and ethics.

This suggests a need for collegiate, or peer, appraisal linked with self-appraisal, as has been proposed by several studies as more appropriate (e.g. Parkes, 1985; Makins, 1985) because:

> attempting to import an appraisal system based on an industrial model is no solution since it grossly underestimates the complexity of teaching in its assumption that there is an easily identified end-product.

and

> criticism of teachers' performance is not beneficial unless they are aware of more effective teaching methods, and are capable of implementing them (personally and within the context). (Murray 1979)

The issue of context is an important facet of peer appraisal, in-service teacher training and staff development activities for it allows account to be taken of restrictions on resources, unfavourable environments, special community, student needs, etc. and also permits appreciation of the teacher's unique contribution to the school. This can engender a feeling of being valued, and of belonging to a community of professionally developed staff as well as providing an opportunity for career counselling. All of these in turn facilitate stress reduction.

The maintenance and improvement of personal occupational standards not only is necessary for professional respect but also for self-respect. However, this is difficult to achieve without some method of continuing self-appraisal.

> Such self-direction or self-organisation can only come about if the individual makes an effort to explore his viewpoints, purposes, means for obtaining ends and keeps these under constant review. (Pope, 1978)

There is little doubt that the teachers involved in this study made an effort during the course of it to explore their own viewpoints, purposes and means for obtaining ends. Indeed, they reported to us that they had enjoyed and valued being encouraged to reflect more deeply on their professional roles and practices. This finding echoes reactions to similar research with teachers by Denicolo (1985), with teachers and student teachers by Pope (1978) and with student teachers by Diamond (1985). The latter reported:

> This awareness of the personal process of construction enabled them to experiment with and to change, in self-chosen ways, their own views of teaching.

And so we come full circle, for this brief UK pilot study has allowed us to highlight some perceptions and concerns of some UK teachers with regard to their profession and practice, only a few of which it has been possible to discuss in any depth here. However, it has also allowed us to further investigate a method, the compilation of repertory grids, which could be usefully incorporated into staff development and self-appraisal programmes to alleviate some of the difficult areas identified by teachers during the course of the study.

> If teachers can be helped to *open their eyes*, they can see how to choose and fashion their own version of reality. By repacking their past for whatever needs arise, *they can travel ahead in their own devices for observing and appraising*. (Diamond, 1985, our emphasis)

Author Reflection 2004

The data described in this chapter has served us well over the years as an illustration for education research students of the versatility of the repertory grid method of exploring teachers' understanding, especially when used in conjunction with the data from the parallel study in Israel by Ben-Peretz, mentioned in the text, and a similar one in Italy. One of the notable differences between teachers' constructs about their professions in those countries and those described in the text from UK teachers is that UK teachers saw their profession as involving creativity and flexibility. Our study took place before the advent of the National Curriculum in the UK whereas Italy and Israel had had such a policy for some time. If the study were replicated now we might well find UK teachers' constructs in this respect converging with those of their overseas colleagues.

Another change that has taken place over the years is the increasing acceptance of 'continuing professional development' for all professions, though whether the courses provided are viewed more positively than fifteen years ago requires some further research. Certainly, those teachers were resistant to external appraisal, though it was far less pervasive and intrusive then, as were the dreaded 'league tables', than is commonplace now.

On a more positive note, in our conclusion we advocated the use of repertory grids for helping professionals to reflect on their professions and its practices. Since then, our doctoral students and we have used them and other constructivist techniques to do just that to very good effect. Many of these projects are described and discussed in our recent books, (Pope and Denicolo, 2001; Denicolo and Pope 2001), which were written to introduce others to the techniques but mainly to celebrate the perceptive work of those students.

Chapter 3

The 'Collective Student' as the Cognitive Reference Point of Teachers' Thinking about their Students in the Classroom

Rainer Bromme

Introduction

In order to teach successfully, teachers must pay attention to the problems and mistakes of their students. In accordance with this need, students' cues are important for teachers' decisions. However, how is this related to the students' relationship to the subject matter content which is the main concern of learning in schools, and what is the nature of the students' cues that are considered?

Research results about the cues, which are important for teachers' interactive decision making, are rather puzzling. On one hand, several studies show an extensive reference to the so-called students' cues (Clark and Peterson 1986, p. 269). But teachers' activities during instruction consist (to a large degree) of presenting and discussing subject matter content. When do teachers think about that? Moreover, how do teachers refer to the relation between students, their activities and the subject matter content? These questions are even more puzzling when taking into account other findings.

It will be argued that students during instruction fulfil different roles. They are individual learners, but also they are contributors to the (more or less cooperative) process of knowledge construction during instruction. Because it is the teacher's task to initiate and steer this process of cooperative knowledge construction, he/she does not refer cognitively to the student as an individual learner. Instead, she/he refers to the student as a member of a cognitive unit, which we call the 'collective student'.

Parts of this chapter have been adapted from 'Teachers' assessment of students' difficulties and progress in understanding in the classroom', which appears in: Calderhead, J. (Ed.) (1987) *Exploring teachers' thinking*. Eastbourne: Holt, Rinehart and Winston.

We assume that teachers refer to the 'collective student' instead of the student as an individual learner, when they think about ongoing classroom instruction.

A Study on Mathematics Teachers' Recall of their Students' Understanding

Teachers' cognitions about students' understanding have been investigated quite rarely. Although the encouragement of students' understanding is probably one of the most important tasks of the teacher, there have been very few investigations of teachers' perception and interpretation of understanding in the classroom. There are, however, many studies on teachers' general perceptions of students (e.g. Hofer, 1986; Brophy and Evertson, 1982). Although these studies differ in some details, they demonstrate that the students were perceived according to traits and behaviours that were functional for the teachers' tasks (Cooper, 1979).

There are also many studies on the validity of teachers' judgements and predictions of students' learning outcomes. But there are almost no studies – with a few exceptions – of teachers' cognitions about the process which is the 'heart' of the teacher's task, namely students' understanding of subject matter.

One of these exceptions is the important study by Shroyer (1981). By means of stimulated recall, she showed that three mathematics teachers seldom thought about the sudden insights – we would say: 'understanding of subject matter' – made by their students. Only a very low percentage of all student errors that were observed by the researcher were also perceived by the teacher as being problematic for the ongoing instruction.

This leads us to ask: what is the nature of the students' cues that have been reported in studies of interactive decision making as being so important for teachers' decisions?

Why do so few investigations focus upon teachers' understanding of their students in the classroom? In the early days of research into teachers' views of their students, it was assumed that teachers' concepts of their students were situationally invariant. As long as one supposed a stable number of cognitive categories by which students are perceived (for a long time, a total of 3–5 categories was considered empirically proven), there was no need to describe situation-specific teacher perspectives on their students. Since then, it has been shown that the assumption of a fixed number of student types is possibly an artefact of the data analysis procedure (factor or cluster analysis; e.g. Oldenburger, 1986), and that the differentiation of the teacher's view of students depends on the situation in which students are perceived (e.g. Morine Dershimer, 1978/79).

Both methodological and cognitive psychological reasons support the idea that one should investigate the teachers' situation-specific views of students.

In order to analyse teachers' situation-specific views, we made two specifications of the situation. We investigated the teachers' recall of students' understanding in the *classroom* (and not in any other situation) and their general picture of their students, regarding their *understanding* (and no other behaviour).

Our study was concerned with the following two main questions:

(1)   How many and what problems and progress in students' understanding are remembered by teachers if they are interviewed immediately after the lesson?

If it should emerge that there is little memory of instances of understanding and of problems, then we must ask:

(2)   Who or what is the focus of the recall?

As part of a larger project on the teaching of probability in secondary schools, we observed the teaching behaviour of mathematics teachers and interviewed them after the lessons. All teachers taught the same subject matter, namely an introductory course on probability. For this, they were given curriculum material developed by the project team. This consisted of a system of mathematical tasks, out of which the teachers could freely select the tasks of their choice.

Interviews with 19 teachers were analysed in this study. The teachers taught students between 11 and 14 years old in five different comprehensive schools. The average length of professional experience was about eight years. All of the teachers volunteered for the study. Each teacher was observed and interviewed on at least four occasions, in addition to earlier 'warm up' observations. One lesson per teacher was chosen that occurred relatively early in the series, as at this stage the lesson content was most similar in all classes.

The interviews were carried out in the teachers' next free lesson or, at the latest, before their lunch break.

At the beginning of the interviews, the tasks that had been used in the lesson and the lesson phases (individual work, group work, discussion of homework, etc.) were entered on a sheet of paper in their order of occurrence. Then questions were presented on teaching goals and the desired motivational effect of the methods the teacher had chosen. After the course of the lesson had been called into memory by these questions, the questions relevant to our investigation were presented, namely:

(1)   Do you remember any subject-oriented learning progress made by individual students or groups of students, i.e. single questions or comments that made it clear to you that the student or students had learnt or understood something? (Question *on progress* in understanding.)

(2)   Do you remember any subject-oriented mistakes or misunderstandings from individual students or groups of students, i.e. single questions or comments that made it clear to you that the students had made a mistake or misunderstood something? (Question on *problems* in understanding.)

(3)   Were there deviations and differences from your plan, and why? (Question on the *plan* of the lesson.)

The construction of the interview was designed so that recall of individual students' understanding was encouraged as much as possible. However, we did not use lists of names in our questioning, as this would have destroyed the natural structure of the recall. We were much more interested in keeping the interview as freely structured as possible, so that we could then analyse the structure of the reports (What was recalled? What was the sequence of recall? How many students were recalled?).

In carrying out an interview that was only backed up by a single written record of the course of the lesson, we naturally did not obtain such a complete picture of the perceptions and considerations in the classroom as would have been provided by the joint viewing of a video recording, as described for example by Calderhead (1981b). However, it is likely that only those events would be recalled that were subjectively important for the teacher, and to which he or she paid conscious attention during the lesson. In our study, this has one advantage compared to the video-stimulated recall design, namely that the teacher is unable to make discoveries and interpretations of students' mistakes, based on the viewing of the videotape. This can occur without teachers having any conscious intention to deceive.

On the other hand, one must be aware that the semantic integration effect causes a blurring between the perceptions of understanding in the classroom and the teacher's existing knowledge. The semantic integration effect refers to the fact that new information is integrated into old knowledge, and that it is often no longer possible to separate the new information that was actually perceived (Bransford and Franks, 1971). We must therefore assume that the teachers' reports can, in some circumstances, distort the actual events. However, it is assumed that this subjective structuring of observations on understanding that teachers perform is not an arbitrary process, but reflects the teachers' concepts of understanding. In this sense, the teachers' recall on their students presents us with information about the teachers themselves. In other words, the selection of events through memory processes is not a hindrance to our investigation. Thus, with our method we do not obtain the immediate perceptions of the teacher during the lesson, but an application of existing knowledge to the classroom situation. However, this is exactly what we wished to reveal with our questions.

Data Analysis

The answers to the questions were transcribed, and comments made by the teachers on other occasions during the interview that concerned the learning progress and problems in understanding of their students or class were included in the analysis.

For the content analysis, a system of categories was formed for *events, protagonists* and *causes*, concepts borrowed from story understanding research.

These categories show similarities to the most important elements of stories (Thorndyke, 1977). Our interviews had in fact requested verbal presentations of short stories about understanding. As verbal protocols are texts, it is at least heuristically meaningful to relate the construction of the content analysis to the instruments from research into the production and understanding of texts (Bromme, 1983).

The categories for events describe individual activities in the learning and application of concepts and procedures in probability, the construction of which is based on a rational task analysis of mathematical tasks. Operating with subject-related concepts requires either observable activities (for example: Drawing up a table for a tree diagram is difficult for the students) or mental inferences or insights (for example: Comparing chances between different random generators is difficult for students).

A large proportion of the answers contained an element that could be regarded as the cause of the event. To cover causes in the analysis, a list was constructed that included the important variables of the instructional process taken from recent research models of teaching and learning; for example, variables that refer to student characteristics, the task and the instructional quality. The concepts and skills in the lesson unit were listed in order to record the teachers' mentions of the subject-related knowledge and abilities of their students as causes of understanding.

There were mentions of progress and problems, which were so global that it was not possible to code an event. Also sometimes events were recalled without any statement that could be coded as cause. Table 3.1 presents the list of all categories. All these categories about events and causes could be used to record cases of successful understanding or difficulties as well as deviations from the lesson plan. Rating was performed by a coder who was familiar with the content of the lesson unit. Each statement in which at least one cause or event was given was regarded as one coding unit. Then the protagonist for each unit was ascertained. Six interviews were selected at random and coded by a second rater in order to assess rater reliability. Agreement between raters was 79 per cent, which is sufficient for our descriptive purposes. For the following discussion of selected results, it is important to point attention to the categories for *protagonists*, which discriminate between teachers' recall of a single student, a group, or the whole class.

Results of the Study

In reply to the question on the progress of understanding of individual students or groups of students, there were 83 cases; an average of 4.4 per teacher in a 45 minute lesson. The protagonists named in these cases were: 64 per cent named individual students, 23 per cent the entire class and 13 per cent groups of students. Table 3.1 gives the frequencies for all teachers.

The question on problems of understanding produced 69 cases; an average of 3.6 per teacher. Teachers named 39 cases in reply to the question on deviations from the lesson plan. The mentioning by name of individual students per teacher was on average only 3 for the question on progress in understanding (one teacher mentioned a maximum of 6 students). There were very few individual differences. For the question on problems in understanding, each teacher mentioned on average 2 students by name, with a maximum of 6 students by 2 teachers. Individual differences were larger in this question; 8 out of the 19 teachers mentioned no individual student by name as having a problem in understanding!

There is not enough space to cover all the results of the study here (see Bromme, 1987); instead we will focus on the following question: Which protagonist was in the focus of teachers' recall: the individual student or the entire class? This question arises because the number of recalled student problems and progress is surprisingly low. However, observer notes from the lessons indicate that a lot more than an average of two or three individual students had problems in understanding. However, these were hardly mentioned by the teachers in their reports. This leads to a first impression that only a few observations were important enough to be remembered by the teachers afterwards. This is not to say that nothing at all was remembered. Instead, the teachers recalled the problems and progress of the class as a whole. It would seem that our study has produced a disappointing picture of teachers' memory for individual students' understanding. However, it also contains indications that something completely different was the focus of recall (and as we infer, in the focus of teachers' awareness during instruction), namely: an artificial, but in a sense quite real protagonist, whom we call the 'collective student'. This alters the impression of apparent blindness toward the learning process in the classroom.

There were always only one or two episodes in the lesson that contained problems and progress. However, these were the episodes in which a new step in the presentation of the curriculum took place. In this respect, they were key episodes from the teacher's perspective. This inference is also supported by the sequence of the recall of problems and progress.

In most reports, the subject-related activities of the entire class were described first. Then, individual students were mentioned whose comments had indicated that the class had not yet understood something, or that articulated the insight that was desired for the entire class. The position of episodes in the course of the lesson was determined by the subject-related course of the lesson discussion, and not by the time of their occurrence.

Three teachers could even recall long verbal dialogues. One teacher began his account with a question from a student, and was then able to reconstruct the subsequent answers. He commented, 'This answer helped a great deal'. The remembered

Table 3.1. Frequencies of protagonists, events and causes for all teachers (n = 19)

| | Interview questions | | | | | |
| | Deviation from lesson plan | | Progress in understanding | | Problems in understanding | |
	Frequency	%	Frequency	%	Frequency	%
Protagonist						
Not specified	7	18	-	-	-	-
Group of students	4	10	11	13	11	16
Entire class	24	62	19	23	19	28
Named student	4	10	53	64	39	56
Total	39	100	83	100	69	100
Event						
No event (but cause mentioned)	5	13	27	30	22	32
Task not treated	4	10	-	-	-	-
Organizational event	6	15	-	-	-	-
Subject matter activities	12	31	28	35	32	46
Subject matter insights	12	31	28	35	15	22
Total	39	100	83	100	69	100
Cause						
No cause (but event mentioned)	10	26	39	47	29	42
Task difficulty	4	10	4	5	1	1
Students' knowledge and skills	-	-	8	10	6	9
Quality of teacher planning and knowledge	4	10	-	-	2	3
Pacing and course of the lesson	9	23	-	-	-	-
Instructional quality	8	20	9	11	9	13
Students' giftedness	-	-	6	7	5	7
Students' engagement	2	5	3	3	8	12
Self-confidence or anxiety of students	-	-	-	-	-	-
Motivation of students	1	3	13	16	5	7
Global characterization (good vs. bad student)	1	3	1	1	4	6
Total	39	100	83	100	69	100

situation occurred at the point where it was necessary to understand the new and really difficult task in the lesson. Sometimes only a single word was remembered: 'Frank gave a key word at the beginning that indicated that he had made great progress'.

In the case of the questions on problems, descriptions were often given that were very exact in their reference to the subject content, but not in their reference to the protagonist or the time of their occurrence. For example, I quote: 'The main difficulty in chance comparisons was that the students had to compare fractions'. 'The greatest difficulty was with the comparison of tables (on the results of dice throws)'.

In summary, we can note that student contributions were remembered when they had a strategic value. By strategic value, we mean that they occurred at the moment when the lesson 'had got stuck' (as one teacher expressed it) from the teacher's perspective, or where the actual transition from old to new knowledge was supposed to occur.

During classroom interactions, a notion of 'collective student' was assembled from the many varied contributions of individuals. All teachers showed good recall for the problems and difficulties of this 'collective student' but only about half of them did so for any of the individual students' problems.

One could argue that these results are not that surprising, given the amount of information within a classroom. Can we expect recall for more than a few students' progresses and problems? It is no wonder – one could argue – because they have to reduce cognitively the complexity of the classroom.

However, the mere statement of cognitive reduction of complexity is not very satisfying and has never been very fruitful within research. It is more interesting to ask: Which are the teachers' professional concepts that are used to overcome this complexity, and which are the elements of the teacher's task which lead to the focus on the so-called collective student and not on the student as an individual learner?

The 'Collective Student' and the Collaborative Construction of Knowledge in the Classroom

In the following, it will be argued that the apparent blindness of teachers is due to an inadequate focus on their task in the classroom, i.e. the task of initiating and organizing the subject matter – knowledge flow.

The task of the teacher during instruction is to organise the more or less cooperative process of subject matter construction. The subject matter that should be understood by the students has to be presented. It cannot be presented and discussed by the teacher alone. Therefore, she or he needs students' contributions to generate the flow of knowledge within a lesson.

This task of cooperative knowledge construction makes it understandable that problems of students are not remembered as events of their individual learning, but as events of the more or less collaborative development of knowledge within the classroom.

Therefore, a model of the collaborative construction of knowledge can help us to interpret functionally the apparent blindness of teachers against their individual students' learning.

What are central elements of the teacher's task of constructing subject matter knowledge as an opportunity for students' learning within the classroom? To know those elements could be useful as a backdrop for interpreting data about teachers' interactive thinking as well as our data about recall (Bromme and Brophy, 1986).

Or to put it in other words, what are the constraints of the teacher's task to generate and develop the process of knowledge construction? This is now to be discussed. We shall refer to two issues.

(1)   The understanding of subject matter requires activity, i.e. it is more easily achieved by self-contained working on tasks than by simply listening to instruction. This fact of knowledge acquisition has also altered the view of

the role of the teacher. While in earlier research on teaching a direct effect of the teacher on learning was assumed and investigated, the role of the teacher is currently viewed differently (Harnischfeger and Wiley, 1977; Denham and Liebermann, 1980). The teacher only indirectly influences the students' learning, and can only directly influence activities in the classroom. By stimulating these activities, he or she can provide learning opportunities, but neither learning nor understanding. Learning and understanding only occur because of the student's own activity, while the educational environment supports this process (Bereiter, 1985).

This is a well-known insight within process-product research, but it is necessary to think through the consequences for research on teaching thinking of this insight. If the teacher only indirectly influences students' learning, but directly influences activity within the classroom, it becomes explainable when teachers do not recall much about individual students' learning and even if they do not perceive individual students' learning.

(2)   Students already have preconceptions of what a new concept could mean for at least the majority of subjects dealt with in the classroom. Thus, learning and understanding mean a restructuring of knowledge that is already present (Romberg and Carpenter, 1986; Davis, 1984). In mathematics lessons, a practical problem is caused by the fact that the student is not aware that his or her old knowledge is mathematical knowledge; it is not organised according to the curriculum.

The student has everyday concepts of 'number', 'equal', or 'probability' that the teacher is not able to simply exchange for the mathematical meaning of these concepts. Therefore, teaching does not only require the imparting of mathematical skills and concepts, but also the conveying of a mathematical meta-knowledge or philosophy. This enables the student to understand the mathematical nature of concepts such as 'number', 'probability', etc.

However, it is impossible to teach this meta-knowledge explicitly, it is taught implicitly. This implicit teaching of knowledge occurs by the students mutually observing each other's handling of mathematics and the teacher's comments about students' ways of handling mathematics. This is true not only for mathematics. Therefore the teacher's task of knowledge construction is not only the teacher's task, it requires also the students' contributions. In our study, some student comments were very precisely recalled as *problems in understanding*, as they formulated the incorrect construction of meaning and misunderstandings that were the object of the lesson discussion. The teacher needs an instructional presentation of these incorrect constructions in order to consider students' preconceptions. It is ineffective and sometimes impossible for the teacher to anticipate all misunderstandings when planning their lessons. Therefore, by letting students explicate their understanding, the problems can be dealt with in the classroom. In that sense, students' problems are part of the knowledge construction and not only indications of individual students' misunderstanding.

So far, one can summarise that the constraints of teachers' task to generate and to steer a collaborative process of knowledge construction can be helpful to explain findings showing a lack of teachers' recall and awareness of students' understanding.

The concept of a 'collective student' and of collaborative knowledge construction within the classroom can be helpful as a background for analysing data about teacher thinking. However, is the 'collective student' more than an artificial construct? Is it a reality within teachers' thinking?

Of course, the contributions of the 'collective student' are a combination of the answers and questions of individual students, and therefore they may contribute to the teacher's picture of the individual student. It must also be recognised that not all students participate to the same extent, and they do not all receive the same amount of attention. Therefore, not all students are equally important for the forming of the 'collective student'. There are spatial zones of different teacher activity in relation to their students (Adams and Biddle, 1970). Lundgren (1972) has shown that the pacing of instruction is directed by the teacher's orientation toward a so-called steering group. He found that teachers oriented toward those students who lay between the 10th and 25th percentile of the ability distribution.

The cognitive focus on a 'collective student' makes it possible for the teacher to deal with 'the class' instead of with 24 different persons, which is necessary to avoid mental overload.

However, the concept of the 'collective student' does not only reduce information in the sense of neglecting details. It also provides cognitive possibilities which are not available if one thinks about students only as individual learners.

In order to talk about knowledge, to recall knowledge and to think about knowledge, one always needs more than concepts about the subject matter itself (e.g. mathematical concepts). Knowledge in schools always requires an agent or subject who deals with it, who applies it, who processes it. One can say that the idea of knowledge is not possible without the idea of a subject or an agent dealing with it.

Therefore, if a teacher does not have the cognitive capacity to perceive anything about individual students' understanding of knowledge, he or she cannot dispense with the idea of an agent for this knowledge, which can be abstract like the 'collective student'.

Up to now, the concepts of collaborative knowledge construction and of the 'collective student' are as yet no more than a possible background for analysing that which is in the foreground of our daily work: the data. Nevertheless, they may help to uncover the mysteries of teachers' professional thinking and knowledge, which are so apparent in the reality we have to deal with.

Author Reflection 2004

When this chapter was written not much research was available on teachers' cognition about students' understanding. Since then, many interesting studies on teachers' awareness about students' difficulties and progress in understanding have been published. This very interesting research has inspired research on the student side: students' preconceptions, subject matter-related attitudes, systematicity of errors, etc. are in the focus of present research, and findings on such issues raise questions on teachers' views and knowledge about the complexity of students' minds.

The very inspiring increase in research on individual students' understanding might also lead researchers and teacher educators to expect elaborated professional knowledge on such issues from expert teachers. They might overlook that teachers who have to deal with whole classes are also in need of knowledge and awareness about an issue which is an entity of its own, not simply a sum of individual students. From this perspective, notions like the 'collective student' are still important.

Chapter 4

A Contrast of Novice
and Expert Competence
in Maths Lessons

Gaea Leinhardt

An approach to the study of teaching is to consider it as one of the more interesting and complex cognitive processes in which human beings engage, and to analyse the tasks, resources and constraints in which teachers are enmeshed. With this perspective, one stands figuratively behind the shoulder of the teacher and watches as the teacher juggles the multiple goals of script completion (Putnam, 1985), tactical information processing, decision making, problem-solving and planning (Leinhardt and Greeno, 1986). In studying this cognitive skill, we attempt to identify the elements of expertise that are involved. One method for doing this is to contrast experts' performance with that of novices. Although there are limits to the expert–novice research paradigm, such contrasts provide a useful beginning in the quest for information about the nature of expertise (Voss *et al.,* 1986). Novice–expert contrasts have proved fruitful in the study of complex cognitive tasks such as playing chess (Chase and Simon, 1973), solving physics problems (Champagne, Gunston and Klopfer, 1983; Chi, Feltovich and Glaser, 1981) and note taking (Hidi and Klaiman, 1983). To highlight the dimensions of competence in elementary mathematics teachers, we have contrasted the performance of experienced and highly competent or expert teachers with that of new or novice teachers. In so doing, we hope to characterise the dimensions of competence in terms

An earlier version of this paper was presented at the annual meeting of the American Educational Research Association, San Francisco, California, 1986. The revised paper was presented at the Psychology of Mathematics Education Conference, East Lansing, Michigan, 25–27 September, 1986, and at ISATT, Leuven, Belgium, 14–17 October, 1986. The research reported herein was supported in part by the Learning Research and Development Centre's Centre for the Study of Learning, which, in turn, is supported in part by funds from OERI, United States Department of Education, and by a grant from the National Science Foundation (Contract No. MDR-8470339). The opinions expressed do not necessarily reflect the positions or policies of OERI or NSF, and no official endorsement should be inferred. The author gratefully acknowledges the helpful comments and research support of Joyce Fienberg, Gwendolyn Hilger, and the technical support of Patricia Carswell Flannagan.

of not only what experts do well, but also what function each competency serves. The ultimate goal is to understand expertise well enough to develop instruction for novice teachers which will make their early performance more expert-like, and, eventually, to move the performance of all teachers into the expert range.

In examining the teaching and thinking behaviours of experts and novices over the last five years, we have become interested in the specific locations of their competency differences. We have identified several dimensions in which competency differences are likely to occur: planning actions, managing actions systems consistently, and building explanations of mathematical material.

The complex cognitive skill of teaching involves:

(1)   assembling known pieces of organised behaviours, namely, action systems or schemas,[1] into effective sequences that meet particular goals;
(2)   assembling appropriate goals to meet larger teaching objectives; and
(3)   doing both of these in a way that attends to specific constraints in the total system.

We refer to this collection of skills as planning. Planning is ongoing, interactive and dynamic, occurring both before and during any specific teaching activity (Hayes-Roth and Hayes-Roth, 1978). As such, this notion of planning differs from the solely preactive (before instruction) and out-of-class planning described by Jackson (1968), Clark and Peterson (1986) or Yinger (1980).

The task environment that the teacher faces is both complex and dynamic. A teacher faces a classroom of 20 to 30 children, each of whom is in a unique emotional, motivational and subject-matter competence state. The teacher must teach in a flexible, responsive and consistent fashion balancing responsiveness to student needs with the need to stay on course so material is covered clearly. The resources are the teacher's own knowledge of teaching the subject, knowledge of the particular students, text material and time.

The teacher is constrained by the time of year, month, week and day that a lesson occurs, and by the curriculum that has to be taught within that subject. Topics that naturally fall into blocks of anywhere from 3 to 6 weeks may collide to some extent with the natural calendar, which has interruptions such as national holidays, Christmas, spring break and standardized testing (Clandinin and Connelly, 1986). Thus, we see that the teacher is involved in a specific task context that is fixed within the total environment in terms of the time it occurs and in terms of its context within the intellectual sequence of the material to be covered. However, there is also flexibility for the teacher. The crafting of specific lessons is completely up to him or her. It is this crafting of lessons and the differences between novices and experts in constructing and teaching lessons that will be the focus of this chapter.

The Nature of Lessons

Effective lessons in mathematics are not homogeneous masses of teacher or student activity. Lessons are segmented into discernible parts such as homework check, presentation and monitored practice that are recognisable to both the students and the teacher (Leinhardt and Greeno, 1986; Leinhardt and Putnam, 1987). These parts serve different and important functions, and each segment requires different kinds of actions from the students and teacher. In general, effective maths lessons move from a teacher-based presentation or exploration of new content towards independent student practice of the material. (Although, in less teacher-centred, more enquiry-based approaches, quite the opposite may be the case.) Teachers must assemble these action segments into scripts that are effective teaching sequences (Putnam and Leinhardt, 1986). It is the plans for these lessons that form the teaching agenda. The presentation segment is perhaps the most important teaching segment and the one that must be most carefully constructed, because that is where the explanation of new mathematical material usually takes place.

There are aspects to effective instruction other than the structure, content and execution of lessons. These more global, non-subject matter structural characteristics have been reviewed by many (Berliner, 1986; Rosenshine, 1983; Brophy and Good, 1986). It is critical to note that in order for the effects of competence in crafting mathematics lessons to become visible, these other more global features of effective instruction must be under control. Our research builds on established knowledge from classroom process studies and on our own analysis of what an effective lesson looks like, and why it looks that way in terms of the functions of particular structures and the cohesiveness of a series of lessons (Leinhardt and Greeno, 1986; Leinhardt and Smith, 1985; Leinhardt, Weidman and Hammond, 1987). We will analyse the nature of lessons with respect to two key features of a lesson: the agenda, and the nature of explanations.

Agendas

An agenda is a unique operational plan that a teacher uses to teach a mathematics lesson. It includes both the objectives or goals for lesson segments and the actions that can be used to achieve them. As the teacher's own mental note pad for the lesson, it includes not only the major action schemas that will be used (see Leinhardt and Greeno, 1986, and Sacerdoti, 1977) but also markers that indicate the need to obtain specific information about students at different points in the lesson. Implied in a teacher's agenda, but not always explicitly available, are the goals that the actions will help meet. In previous analyses of teachers we have noticed that the action schema for each lesson segment (homework checking, for example) is itself a miniature plan that has specific goals and that incorporates well-known routines and other actions into it (Leinhardt and Greeno, 1986; Leinhardt, Weidman and Hammond, 1987). Evidence of these agendas is not visible in the written lesson plans of either novices or experts but exists in the teacher's mental representations of the lessons. We can tap these agendas by interviewing teachers immediately before their lessons, asking them what they are going to do and what they expect will happen. In general, the verbal trace of the mental agenda (i.e. the teacher's response) is a relatively brief list of topic and action segments that correspond roughly to lesson segments (discussed below).

Model of an Explanation

We turn now to a second lesson component, the *explanation* that is usually given during the presentation segment. Figure 4.1 shows a theoretical model of an explanation for a set of elementary mathematics lessons. The formalism used to express the model is that of a planning net (Leinhardt and Greeno, 1986; VanLehn and Brown, 1980). In this formalism, action schemas and goal structures are combined in ways that permit across-level access of action schemas. Thus, a higher order goal state may be partially achieved by means of an action schema embedded in another goal system. In this formalism, goals are in hexagons and actions are in rectangles. At the top of Figure 4.1, there are three main goals: *clarifying, learning* and *understanding* the concept or procedure. These goal states are achieved as direct and indirect consequences of action systems and sub-goals, only some of which are shown.

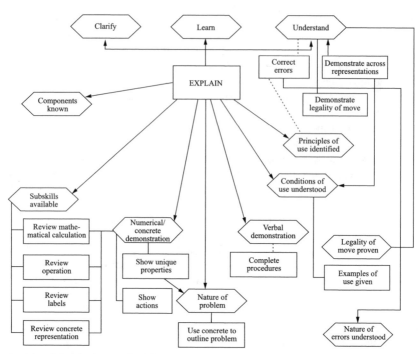

Figure 4.1. Model of an explanation.

The action of *explaining*, shown in the dominant rectangle immediately below the top three goal states, has as a consequence the complete or partial achievement of one or more of the top-level goals. Explaining has a prerequisite goal state, namely that the *components* (i.e. the salient features of the referents or representations) to be used in the explanation are already known by the students. If a teacher or instructor attempts to explain something new by using an analogy or a new representation which itself must be learned, the explanation is unlikely to be of any major benefit to the hapless student who will likely lose sight of the principal objective.

Another prerequisite for the explanation is that the *sub-skills* (i.e. other mathematical procedures) to be used in the performance of the new procedure be available – some might even argue that they must be available in automatic form. If these skills have already been taught, they can become available for use in the explanation process merely by asking for them, or activating them, or taking them out of cold storage, so to speak. The performance of one or more of these retrieving actions results in meeting the goal of having sub-skills available.

The actions that support the goal of having sub-skills available can also be seen as prerequisites for the goal of having the necessary *numerical* and *concrete representations* described. Further, each demonstration must include the action of identifying the particular feature of the representation that makes it unique with respect to the solution. A good explanation will refer to this uniqueness.

Another prerequisite for an explanation is to have the students realise what the *nature of the problem* is and, if appropriate, to locate the contradiction – the particular mathematical circumstance – that requires this solution. This can be done by actions that constrain the solution path so that students 'bump into' the problem. For example, in subtraction problems that require regrouping, the *problem is* only apparent if there is some inherent 'binding of the tens' in the representation used, such as that in place value or felt strips. A set of 26 loose chips will not point up the 'problem' in solving 26 minus 8.

In the process of explaining something, a teacher should provide a *verbal demonstration* that goes through all of the key moves. Often, this is accomplished simultaneously and is yoked with the numerical and concrete demonstrations.

A constraint on the explanation is that the *condition* and *circumstances* of use be identified. That is, the procedure (or concept) needs to be recognised as one that does not get used all the time but only under some specific circumstances. Finally, the *principles* that permit the procedure to be used need to be identified and the *legality* of the procedure needs to be proven. The intentional production of *errors* is often a key move in an explanation – it is an action that can be used to accomplish the goal of understanding and identifying principles of use. Not all explanations contain all of these elements, but for each mathematics topic a competent teacher is able to access specific action schemas that support these goal states, to a greater or lesser degree.

In summary, we propose that these three components of teaching – agendas, lesson segments and explanations – are not only critical ingredients for expert teaching, but also dimensions along which a novice–expert contrast will shed considerable light. In the study described below, agendas were assessed by examining and analysing teachers' brief answers to the question, 'What are you going to do today?' Lesson segments were assessed by looking at the amount of class time spent on four important segments – transition, presentation, guided practice and monitored practice. Explanations were assessed by checking whether the teacher achieved each of the explanation goals in the model.

Methods

The sample consisted of four expert teachers and two novices (student teachers who were in their last semester of school and were actively engaged in student teaching). Experts were initially identified by reviewing the achievement *growth* scores of students in the district and selecting the teachers at each grade whose students' growth scores were in the top 15 per cent for at least 3 years in the 5-year period.[2] From this select group, teachers with high growth classrooms in which the *final achievement* was in the top 20 per cent were ultimately chosen. The student teachers were chosen from an available pool of 20 and were teaching fourth grade in two integrated middle class schools. These student teachers were among the top four teachers in their cohort, as nominated by their supervisors. They had full responsibility for the mathematics instruction of their students and had been teaching in the classes for at least 4 weeks.

The teachers were observed for a 3.5-month period, which included classroom observations, interviews, and videotapes of up to 25 hours of mathematics classes. In addition to interviews to assess their mathematics knowledge, all teachers were interviewed before and after each videotaped lesson. The pre-class interviews were transcribed and analysed for agenda information. The videotaped lessons were transcribed and analysed in terms of lesson segments and lesson content. Two pre-class interviews with each of the four experts (n=8) and four pre-class interviews with each of the two novices (n=8) generated the data for the analysis of agendas. Videotapes of experts' and novices' lessons were analysed for structure by identifying the lesson segments and calculating the time spent in each. Measures of time were based on anywhere from 9 to 79 occurrences of each activity. Two lesson videotapes for each teacher were examined in depth to generate the database for analysing eight expert and four novice explanations. An example of one novice and one expert explanation were analysed more closely by constructing semantic net diagrams that displayed the content of the lessons. (For details of semantic net construction, see Leinhardt and Smith, 1985.)

Results and Discussion

To understand teachers' agendas we studied their responses to the first pre-class interview question, 'What are you going to do today?', looking at their productions in five different ways. First, we measured the overall quantity of the first unprompted verbal response by counting the number of typed lines. Second, we counted the number of references to *student* actions that occurred in this initial response. Third, we looked for instances where the teachers indicated some planning for 'tests', that is, checkpoints or midstream evaluations of student understanding or of lesson progress. Fourth, we examined the entire pre-class interview for items that could be classified as 'instructional' actions. These actions referred to both physical moves and content coverage. For example, one expert said, 'I'm going to introduce the *unit on fractions*, the *terminology*, numerator, denominator. We're just going to work on *what part of a region is shaded...* we're going to use the *overhead*. We're going to *fold paper.*' Within this statement, five instructional actions were counted. From a novice, we have the following: 'I'm planning on *going over the homework* that I gave yesterday on fractions. I'm planning on going over it on the board.' Within the novice's statement, one instructional action was counted. (The novice's use of the phrase 'on the board' referred to the location of the homework checking activity – it was not a separate move. The expert's mention of using the overhead (cited above), however, was counted as a separate instructional move because it referred to the use of a concrete representation such as chips to demonstrate a fraction concept in a different way from the other action, paper folding.)

Finally, we examined the entire pre-class interview for the level and explicitness of instructional logic and flow. We were trying to determine the degree to which any particular action preceded or followed another by some overarching rule. Rules that guided this logical flow could be content driven (e.g. moving the presentation from concrete to abstract or moving from the problem situation to solution) or child driven (e.g. extending the lesson because one group needs extra practice, or controlling the lesson pace until the whole class reaches mastery). We scored the presence of this logical flow for each unique instance within an agenda. The importance of instructional logic is that it acts as a general posted constraint for the next probable move a teacher could make. This constraint becomes crucial when a teacher's particular move has been poorly or inadequately specified in the plan.

The results of the novice and expert agendas are shown in Table 4.1. The experts produced twice as many mean numbers of lines of response as the novices. This difference could mean that the experts were simply more verbal than the novices were; but in other situations (such as stimulated recall interviews), this was simply not the case. We think this difference represented the experts' richer plans for their lessons, plans that actually contained more detail and displayed that detail when verbally presented to others. Two other aspects of an agenda may be related to this notion of richness: the use of explicit references to student actions in the agenda statements and the mention of planning for a test point (or several) within the lesson. The mention of a student action suggested that the teachers kept parallel plans going, namely, the teacher's action and goal

Table 4.1. Means and standard deviations for characteristics of agendas

Characteristic	Novice (n=8)		Expert (n=8)		
	Mean	SD	Mean	SD	t
Lines of response	13.6	5.2	26.4	8.1	3.76*
Student actions	0.9	0.8	1.8	1.5	1.45
Tests	0.0	0.0	0.8	0.7	
Instructional actions	2.9	1.2	6.5	1.2	5.90*
Instructional logic elements	0.1	0.4	1.4	0.9	3.54*

*$p < 0.005$, one-tailed.

sequence and the students'. This parallel planning is a difficult but necessary part of being an effective teacher. References to student actions within the teacher's agenda occurred twice as often for experts as for novices; however, the high standard deviations for both novices and experts indicate that the difference was not significant.

The data on number of references to 'tests' in the teachers' agendas were gathered by scrutinising the interviews for any mention of a plan for checking on lesson progress. A test was usually referred to in terms of checking on the students' understanding or on their performance, with some indication that this would influence the teacher's decision about whether or not to go on to the next instructional segment. Although this type of action was frequently mentioned in the stimulated recalls of both novices and experts, it was less frequently mentioned in the agendas. In fact, for the novice teachers, such a test point was not mentioned in any of the eight pre-class interviews; however, every expert mentioned a test at least once in their agendas.

A mathematics lesson consists of a series of instructional moves. All of the teachers reported a topic or lesson title; for example, 'fractions and fractional parts', 'review equivalent fractions', 'problem solving skills', or 'word problems on time and money'. After looking for the presence of a stated lesson topic, we counted the number of separate mathematical instructional actions that were reported in the agenda. Here again, the novices reported half as many planned instructional actions as the experts.

Finally, we scored the instructional logic that seemed to drive the flow of the lesson. In all but one case, the novices' agendas failed to show any indication of a guiding logic to the instructional actions. However, in all but one of the experts' agendas, there was at least one systematic statement that indicated the flow of the lesson. In three cases, there were two statements: one about content, and one about the students and their level of control (i.e. moving from teacher-led action and pacing to students' independent action and pacing).

To capture the flavour of the differences let us look at excerpts from one novice and one expert agenda. A novice is first:

Novice: Uh, we're going to work on uh, multiplication as uh, using sets...

Interviewer: Okay.

N: ...you know, as in two sets of, and that way multiplication...

I: And you're actually using the overhead?

N: Yes, the overhead and chips.

(Coding: one instructional action, no student action, no test, no instructional logic)

In this protocol, there is no mention of a test point, student action or instructional logic. We are told only that the lesson topic is multiplication and the approach will be through sets with chips. In the above agendas there seems to be little from which the teacher may work. It may well be that by writing out a detailed lesson plan (something required from the novices); they failed to build representations that were very strong or accessible. In essence, they 'dumped' their knowledge into the lesson plan and made no accessible long-term memory set.

In contrast, the following is one expert's agenda:

Expert:	Okay, now first of all, yesterday we used at the end of the period, we used a feltboard.
Interviewer:	Mm-hmm.
E:	...to show uh, tens and ones and then to change a ten to ones.
I:	Mm-hmm.
E:	Okay, so we're going to continue with *that... (First instructional action)*
I:	Okay.
E:	And the kids will be recording some of the information on a piece of paper that they saved from yesterday. *(Second instructional action, student action)*
I:	Mmm.
E:	And then I'm going to uh, write that on the board in long form, renaming five tens and two ones as four tens and twelve ones. *(Third instructional action)*
I:	Right.
E:	Okay, and then I'm going to wean them away from the regular name like five tens and two ones and just go to the one line... *(Fourth instructional action, instructional logic)*
I:	Mmm.
E:	Just rename it, and then I'm going to go to, uh, just putting the number on the board and showing them how to cross out. *(Fifth instructional action)*
I:	Mmm.
E:	...And narrow it down. And then I'm going to go to uh, uh, their fooler problem. *(Sixth instructional action)*
I:	Mmm.
E:	And show them how they can rename the top number and then subtract.
I:	Mmm.
E	So, that's the logical way I want to do it. *(Instructional logic, content: move towards algorithm)*
I:	Yeah, okay.
E:	And I'll go to the pace they let me go at. *(Test).*

(Coding: six instructional actions, one student action, one test, one instructional logic)

Not only were the elements that we noted in the expert's agenda clearly different from those in the novice's, but also, overall, the expert's agenda was richer and more detailed. The topical segments were clearly differentiated and noted. The expert's agenda had goal statements and actions. The expert also had a specific overarching goal that ordered the actions so that the lesson moved from the broad, general procedures to the focused, narrow algorithm. This meant that not only was there a more complete action list with each action supported by more complete sub-plans and routines (Leinhardt and Greeno, 1986), but there was a conceptual road map that kept the lesson flowing in a particular direction, 'weaning away', and 'narrowing it down'.

Finally, a note: all of the experts always started their planning statements by telling what they had done the day before, whereas none of the novices did so. The experts saw lessons as connected and tied together as a pattern. The expert agendas were richer in detail, in connectedness, and in constraints (tests for continuing, logic for flow, and student actions). The expert's explicit and available plans were more powerful than the novice's were. The novice may very well have had much more elaborate plans than the one she at first told us about, but the plans were not accessible in the moments just prior to teaching or seemingly while teaching.

In the second contrast of experts and novices, we move to a key element within the presentation segment: the explanation of new material. Table 4.2 reports the percentages of expert and novice explanations that reached each of the major goal states depicted in Figure 4.1. Bear in mind that there were fewer cases of novice lessons that contained explanations (four out of eight) because, in general, the novices were considerably less likely to actually explain something. (For example, novices frequently lost the opportunity to present an explanation because they never finished correcting and handing out homework.) Because there was no variance in eight of the nine contrasts, either among the experts or among the novices, no inferential statistics were calculated.

The first row in Table 4.2 contrasts the degree to which experts and novices gave explanations in which the salient features of the components being used to explain the phenomena were already known by the students. 88 per cent of expert explanations had this characteristic whereas none of the novice explanations did. For example, in two of the novice explanations for multiplying by 9, both the number line and an overhead with chips were used. Although the students may have seen a number line before, they clearly did not know how to use it for counting or

Table 4.2. Percentage of explanations reaching each goal state

Goal state	Novice ($n=4$)	Expert ($n=8$)
Components known	0	88
Sub-skills available	50	100
Numerical and concrete demonstration	50	100
Verbal demonstration	25	100
Procedure completed	25	75
Unique features shown	0	25
Nature of problem	0	50
Circumstances of use	0	13
Principles of use	0	50

adding; thus, when it was used to distinguish between 3 times 9 and 9 times 3 (3 steps of size 9 versus 9 steps of size 3), the novice had to teach both the substance and the number line simultaneously. Therefore, it was less likely that the students could learn from it than if they were already familiar with the number line as a representational system. A similar problem occurred with the use of chips displayed on an overhead projector (a representation that was used in all four lessons given by the novices). What was being shown and how the chips showed it were totally unclear.

The experts, in contrast, tended to use well-known representations and to use the same representation for multiple explanations. For example, one expert fourth grade teacher taught the number line in a lesson on numeration at the beginning of the year and then was able to use it for lessons on adding, multiplying and fractional equivalence. An expert second grade teacher used bundles of ten popsicle sticks to teach subtraction with regrouping after she had already had the students assemble the bundles several weeks earlier for use in a lesson on adding with carrying. Experts, in general, tend to use something familiar to teach something new while novices often use something new to teach something new. (Note that novices often seem to give demonstrations without having tried them out in a dry run so that they simply do not work a certain percentage of the time.)

The second row in Table 4.2 refers to sub-skills. These are procedural skills that the student needs to have in order to handle the components or steps of a new procedure in either a concrete or abstract domain. With respect to this goal, 100 per cent of the experts' explanations incorporated already existing skills while only 50 per cent of the novices' explanations had this feature. As an example, in reducing fractions, one expert required the students to factor the numerator and check each factor against the denominator. This procedure hinged on the availability of students' factoring skill and their knowledge of multiplication tables organised in a particular way in order to call up the factors. It is perhaps worth noting that there was no lesson on factoring in the textbook being used; so, the expert, knowing she would use factoring in this and other lessons, taught it while teaching multiplication. In contrast, when a novice was teaching reducing, she simply asked the students by what number to divide. Not only did the novice neglect to give a procedure, but also she was clearly in trouble when she asked the students for common 'multiples' instead of factors, and they were unable to come up with any. Her solution was to have them try different numbers (2, 3, etc.) until they managed to find a factor that worked.

The next two rows of Table 4.2 refer to the completeness of the numerical and concrete demonstrations of a procedure or concept and to the completeness of the accompanying verbal presentation. Although it is theoretically possible to simply present an example with little or no verbal accompaniment, it is rarely done as a teaching technique in mathematics. Likewise, although it is possible to follow a purely verbal description without any demonstration using numbers or another representation, it is unusual. For the experts in this study, both of these goal states were reached in every explanation, whereas for the novices, these goals were achieved much less often. The experts tended to give a complete and usually well-connected explanation of the phenomena whereas the novices not only did not do this, but they frequently made serious mistakes. For example, during one of the novice's lessons on the 9 times table, she tried to teach another teacher's version of the 'trick' that the digits in the product always sum to 9. She became hopelessly entangled and simply could not do it. In some sense this illustrates the role that a good, well-rehearsed and well-understood script plays in teaching (Putnam, 1987; Putnam and Leinhardt, 1986). The novice in this lesson was trying to teach the 9 tricks from someone else's script. It was not her own.

A subtler mistake occurred on the number line for this same lesson. The novice teacher asked a child to demonstrate 3 times 9 on the number line. The purpose of this part of the lesson was twofold: to teach that 3 steps of 9 each were different from 9 steps of 3 each in terms of the size of step; and to show that these two expressions were the same in terms of result. She did not explicitly show this. When she asked the first student to show 3 times 9 on the number line, the student showed 9 steps of size 3. The novice erased the student's work, said it was wrong, got another student to show 3 times 9 the 'right' way, and then called a third student to show 9 times 3 with the same drawing that had been wrong when done by the first child (see Figure 4.2). This must have been incredibly confusing to both the first student and the rest of the class because it was very hard to see what the difference was between the first and third student attempts.

The next row in Table 4.2 deals with the rather trivial issue of whether the entire procedure to be learned is ever given in the lesson. The two occasions when the experts failed to teach a complete procedure in one lesson occurred in lessons that focused on underlying concepts before a procedural lesson. This was not the case for the novices; they simply started teaching procedures and did not finish them.

In the remaining four rows of Table 4.2, we see that the novices did not engage in the behaviours that would achieve the goals whereas the experts did, although less than half of the time. These goals are ones that derive from a theoretical analysis of what a good mathematical explanation would contain. Thus, the action of demonstrating the unique features of a problem would include actions that somehow differentiated one arithmetic circumstance from others that might at least superficially resemble it (such as subtraction with and without regrouping, or adding fractions versus adding whole numbers). Only one teacher did this. This cluster of actions is connected to understanding the nature of the problem. Identifying the nature of the problem refers to pinpointing the need for a particular representation (such as fractional notation) or procedure (producing equivalent fractions for what?), and closely related to it are identifying the circumstances in which the notation or procedure will be used: Does one always borrow? Is re-grouping like modifying the multiplication procedure or is it done only under specific circumstances? Again, only one explanation included this goal. Principles of use refer to the mathematical laws that permit the transformation or reorganization of the mathematical circumstances that cover the problem. (For example, negative numbers are an extension of the natural number

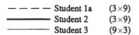

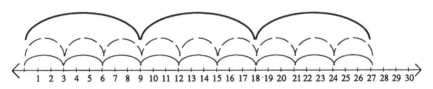

* Erased as wrong by teacher

Figure 4.2.   Demonstration of multiplication on the number line.

system that closes the operation of subtraction.) One half of the expert explanations included some actions related to this goal.

The experts gave better explanations than the novices did. The experts' explanations contained features that are more critical and less likely to contain errors; and when errors did occur, they were not as serious. Furthermore, the experts were more likely to simply complete an explanation than novices were. My colleague, Ralph Putnam, and I have described at least one reason why this may be the case, in our analysis of curriculum scripts (Putnam and Leinhardt, 1986). Two other reasons suggested themselves after we watched the videotapes of the explanations. First, the novices did not seem to have a cohesive schema for a lesson, one that differentiated between an introductory and a review lesson. They did not seem aware of the different components of lessons and what the goals are for each. Second, they did not seem to know the subject matter well enough to be flexible while teaching it.

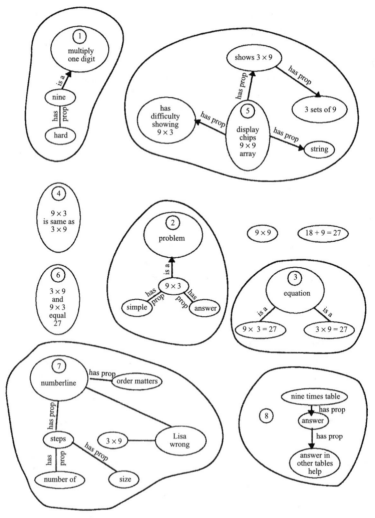

Figure 4.3.   Novice's explanation of multiplying by 9.

As part of the analysis of explanations, we constructed semantic net diagrams of the first major portions of one novice and one expert explanation (Figures 4.3 and 4.4). The nodes in the diagrams show the concepts that were presented and the lines between nodes show how the concepts were connected and organised. The novice was teaching a lesson on multiplying by 9 and the expert was teaching subtraction with regrouping.

In Figure 4.3, the novice's explanation is shown with numbers that indicate the order of presentation of each information cluster. The novice started directly with the statement that the lesson would be about the 'last two one-digit numbers that you're gonna learn to multiply by: 8 and 9. Nine is the harder of the two, so we're going to work with 9 a little more'[3]. The novice then flipped on an overhead projector that was crammed with a 9 by 9 array of 81 chips. A child interrupted and said he knew the answer, to which the novice replied that that was impossible because there had not been a question. One might presume that the student assumed that the 'question' was either what is 9 times 9 or what is 9 times 8, depending on how the opening statement was interpreted. However, the student's enthusiastic reaction to a challenging display was treated as wrong, whereas it was more the act of calling out that was wrong. Using a student to tell how many chips were in the display would not have been a poor instructional move; and finding a way to graciously incorporate unexpected student input might have been a useful strategy, one which we have noticed often in experts' lessons.

The novice's next statement was that she would start with a 'simple' problem, 3 times 9. In 60 seconds of dialogue, the novice had mentioned the numbers 2, 1, 8, 9, 9 by 9, 1, 2, 3, 4, 5, 9, 9, and then 3 times 9, with *six* different meanings (one digit, last two numbers of the times tables, 9 by 9 array, counting 1 to 5, skipping to 9, and the 'problem' 3 times 9). She then introduced sets as a label and talked while standing at the overhead, having one child rope off 3 groups of 9 chips while she simultaneously got another student to verbally answer 3 times 9 as an addition problem. Here is the dialogue:

Teacher:	That means we have 1, 2, and 3 (columns of 9). What's the answer, Robin?
Student:	(No response.)
T:	If there's 3 sets of 9, what's the answer?
S:	What?
T:	All right, Robin, what is 9 plus 9?
S:	—
T:	No, what is 9 plus 9?
S:	(No response.)
T:	What's 18 plus 9?
S:	—
T:	Twenty-five?
S:	Fifty?
T:	How much, Tom?
S:	Twenty-seven.

During this exchange, the display was abandoned as a possible source for the answer. The novice then proceeded to an 'equation' to show equivalence of 3 times 9 and 9 times 3, but could not show it on the overhead and proceeded to the number line example described earlier. As shown by the separate clusters in Figure 4.3, each piece of the novice's explanation lacked a connection to any other piece and was often at

odds with it. For example, the chips display and the number line showed the difference between 3 times 9 and 9 times 3, whereas the equations and problem solutions
showed the identity of both expressions. Of course, these two attributes are both correct but showing both and making a clear distinction between them is difficult and was
not accomplished.

    Figure 4.4 shows a semantic net of the expert's lesson on subtraction with
regrouping in which she introduced the regrouping concept and procedure. The first
and most noticeable feature of the diagram is the degree to which everything is connected; the lesson had the feeling of being integrated and, in fact, actually was. The
second feature to note is the set of three parallel strands of smaller nets extending from
the representation node. The expert presented three iterations of the same regrouping
algorithm, one using sticks, another using felt strips, and a third using numerals with
two versions of a written procedure. Although the expert did not choose to connect
the representations explicitly (this one stick is like this one felt square, etc.), the par-
allelism of the presentations highlighted the connections. A third feature to note is the
degree to which the expert's explanation was denser with actions than the novice's,
just as experts' agendas were found to be denser or richer. Although the lengths of

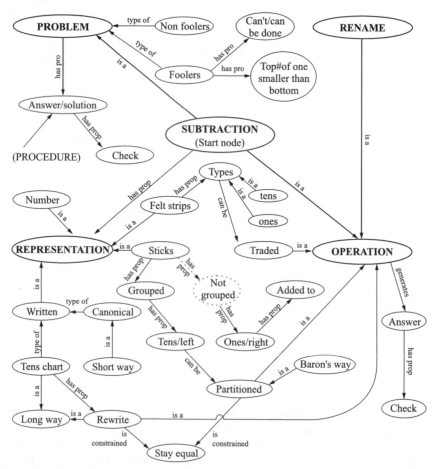

Figure 4.4.   Expert's explanation of subtraction.

these two analysed explanations were not identical, the novice was clearly covering less content in a less integrated way than the expert was. (If the analysed portion of the novice's explanation had been extended to equal the length of the expert's, the addition would have consisted of only a prolonged erroneous piece of explanation in which the novice attempted to teach the 'rule' of digits summing to nine, but forgot it in mid-lesson.)

An additional comment on the difference between the expert and novice explanations concerns what they were each trying to explain. The expert was trying to explain the procedure, concept and legitimacy of trading or regrouping tens in order to calculate the answers to a specific set of subtraction problems. The novice was trying to explain the similarities and differences of 3 times 9 and 9 times 3, and to teach the 9 times facts. The novice's explanations were to some extent incompatible. It seemed as though one part of the lesson had nothing to do with the other, but that the novice was trying to make it appear that it did.

Expertise is characterised by speed of action, forward-directed solutions, accuracy, enriched representations, and rich elaborations of knowledge in terms of depth and organisational quality. Expert mathematics teachers weave a series of lessons together to form an instructional topic in ways that consistently build upon and advance material introduced in prior lessons. Experts also display a highly efficient within-lesson structure, one that is characterised by fluid movement from one type of activity to another, by minimal student confusion during instruction, and by a transparent system of goals. These goals are consistently met by the application of cohesive well-rehearsed action systems. In addition, some experts display considerable sophistication in the subject matter presentation portion of their lessons. This is characterised by a careful selection of multiple representation systems (such as numbers, blocks, drawings and verbal chains), by a logical rule-bound explanation of new material that connects well with previous material, by a careful parsing of the total topic into manageable pieces introduced over time, and by skilled judgement of how much repetition and practice are needed. Not all of these skills are explicitly recognised by the expert, and their existence, therefore, has been inferred.

Novice teacher's lessons, on the other hand, are characterised by fragmented lesson structures with long transitions between lesson segments, by frequent confusion caused by mis-sent signals, and by an ambiguous system of goals that often appear to be abandoned rather than achieved. In our interviews of novices, they showed signi-ficant subject matter competence but did not seem to access that knowledge while teaching. Their lessons did not fit well together within or across topic boundaries. From interviews based on stimulated recall, we know that novices are aware of these problems while teaching, at least to some extent. However, novices lack the analytic skills to understand where failures occurred or when goals that were implicit in certain actions were not achieved.

Conclusion

The research reported here has helped us to go beyond mere lists of teachers' successes and failures, and to trace a path from planning, to actions, to the heart of teaching explanations so that we could begin to see what it is that expert teachers possess. We can and should go further in understanding their active available plans by mapping specific verbal components in the agenda onto specific actions within a lesson and then annotating that map with the teacher's own lesson commentary.

Such a mapping would provide us with a clearer picture of how lessons are built and modified. We also need to begin to stockpile the procedures used in effective explanations so that novices can see how to weave pieces of their action strings together. Finally, it seems that having novices build more cohesive and script-like lessons and rehearsing them might be a helpful way of getting them over the hump of early teaching.

It is clear that we cannot simply provide novices with goals of what we want – namely, lessons that are open, flexible, responsive, problem-based and intricate; nor can we simply show videotapes of what experts already do and expect this expertise to transfer. We need to study the process of acquiring expertise. As McIntyre (1987) and Ball and Feiman-Nemser (1986) have shown, teachers seem to grow from being structured and somewhat rigid, to being introspective, flexible and responsive. They acquire this flexibility after they are confident in their mastery of the pedagogical subject matter knowledge that they need to operate in a somewhat conservative and well-structured environment. Beginning teachers need to build more efficient strategies for keeping mental notes about the lessons that they teach – how one lesson connects with others, what the key point of a lesson is, what students need to experience in order to build meanings for themselves, and how long it will take students to do that. Beginning teachers also need to design routines for simple actions, both managerial and instructional, that will save time and energy, and they need to understand what each part of a routine will buy them. Further, beginning teachers need to craft simple but effective scripts for teaching key topics. These can and should be modified by the teacher over time, but starting with a core of critical scripts is important and can help alleviate the tremendous time pressures they feel. As part of developing these scripts, beginning teachers need to study, design and revise explanations, deciding whether the explanation should be discovered, guided or directly given, and orchestrating the critical components of referent and demonstration so that they (the teachers) do not 'forget' to point out the new or interesting features of a mathematical concept or procedure.

Notes

1. An action schema is a 'general representation of an action (at some level) that an individual can perform' (Leinhardt and Greeno, 1986, p. 77).
2. Classroom growth scores are developed by taking the spring standard achievement scores (scaled) from the target year and subtracting those students' prior year's scores, and then averaging. This produces a ranking identical to a residualised gain.
3. This expert lesson on subtraction was chosen for closer analysis because of its display of virtually all the idealized goal states for an explanation. None of the novice teachers recommended for this study taught this lesson, however, so we chose for this comparison a lesson that contained most of the features of interest. When we match novices and experts on identical topics (see Leinhardt, 1987), the novices perform even more poorly.

Author Reflection 2004

The invitation to reconsider both the contents and the stance of one's own work nearly twenty years later could make one feel old, proud, or in my case bemused. There are parts of the work that I did not remember and am pleased with and other parts that seem to get in the way. My task here is to distinguish between the two and to share with the reader what seems to remain of value and what feels dated.

I approached the original work as a part of a much larger effort designed to tease apart what distinguished novice or new teachers from expert or highly successful teachers in terms of their actual practice. The stance was decidedly respectful of what excellent teachers already knew and understood even if that knowledge was apparently tacit. I am pleased with that respect; and also that I recognised then, as now, that teaching is an enormously complex intellectual endeavour. At the general level, I think that the distinction between immediate plans – plans in action – and enactments of explanation goes to the heart of the instructional dynamic in mathematics. I have continued to find that newer teachers, as well as those struggling after several years, have great difficulty imagining the full stage on which learning is played out – they can see themselves and their intentions, but not the intentions and competencies of others. Excellent teachers 'hear' the competencies of their students and build from them instead of struggling against them. In terms of explanations, with respect to both core structure and intellectual coherence, the competency of excellent teachers resides with their having coherence and explicitness as a goal, and with their ability to move around a central idea and cover it from many angles – generating examples and counter examples, deep questions, rephrasing and extending the students' ideas to meet an explanatory goal.

What has changed? What rings less true? The major feature so strongly present now is the explicit recognition of the classroom as a social system in which students have personal and collective histories that contribute to and define the actions that take place. While it might still be reasonable to 'stand behind the shoulder of the teacher' to view the classroom it would be imperative to consider the entire system as such. Thus, agendas are always negotiated, explanations are only complete when all of the explainers reach a consensus that it is so, and coherence is built by the engagement of all of the actors. If I had a magic wand and could not merely reconsider but rewrite I would focus on finding a different and perhaps more useful set of formalisms to express the core ideas. I would find a way (have been struggling in current work to do so) to build in the role of the student voice so that the reader is not left with the erroneous impression that the actor of explanations is only the teacher. I would talk about the development of patterns of practice and activity instead of scripts – because the word script that means so much to me as a child of generations of actors means something so very different to the larger educational community. Finally, I share an uncertainty. One goal of the original work was to inform those concerned with the computer modelling of learning and of teaching. By using semantic and planning nets as formalisms, there was the possibility that designers of intelligent tutors might make use of these ideas. However, the core goal was to support the learning of new teachers in explicit and powerful ways. I am still unclear as to whether the two goals can be met, or, if they are in some profound ways in conflict.

Section B

Methods and Approaches to the Study of Teacher Thought and Action

Huber begins this section with a chapter titled 'Strategies and methods in research on teacher thinking'. He approaches research on teacher thinking as promised in the title in two main sections – methods and approaches. Huber suggests that a framework for research is necessary and that systems theory may provide a heuristic principle. He acknowledges that such an adoption is not without difficulties and may further emphasise existing or budding areas of theoretical and methodological differences. He illustrates a number of possibilities beginning with epistemological reorientation and the effects of summative and formative strategies of research followed by a discussion of nomological versus quasi-paradigmatical research. Huber proposes models with the acronym ART (action–reflection–transformation) and its reverse as a dynamic that would provide a conceptual formulation for thinking about teacher thinking. He goes on to discuss the problems of research design and explores statistical methods and the advantages and differences of experimental and field studies as well as data types (i.e. qualitative and quantitative).

The second chapter by Oberg deals with 'The ground of professional practice' and begins with the question 'Why do teachers teach the way they do?' Oberg observes that this question is of more interest to educational researchers than educational practitioners and is usually aimed at improving practice by bringing it in line with current theory or prescribed policy. Her purpose in this chapter is to empower practitioners to become better educators rather than influencing practice to a predetermined outcome. She argues that the ground of teaching practice is definable through the actions and reasons for actions and may be articulated by examining taken-for-granted assumptions having to do with meaning, commitment, and definitions of learners and sense of purpose. She discusses a conception of ground, ground as beliefs and intentions, and illustrates the ground of practice theoretically by describing it as a system of personal constructs by drawing on the work of George Kelly (1955). She explores the methods chosen along with alternatives and describes a set of research procedures that included conversations and observation of teaching practice. Her data-organising scheme included a variety of roles in collaboration with teachers, confirming previous research.

Olson contributes a chapter titled 'Case study in research on teaching: a ground for reflective practice'. He begins with a caution about the tensions between technological rationality and reflective practice as ways to express faith and beliefs in experience and research. Olson feels the distinction between these two ideas may be too firmly drawn and exclusive. He addresses the matter by describing the positive values of case studies in educational research and how validity and generality might be maintained. The movement towards improving teaching needs to look seriously at disclosures teachers make and the clues they contain for understanding teaching actions, thus providing a basis for developing and using action research models. Contrasted with the problematic grounding of historical research, lived experiences reported by teachers have currency and vitality because of their existence in the moment. Olson advocates beginning with teachers' understanding of their own actions from a deeper perspective that might help explain classroom behaviour and the diversity of approaches that might eventually affect policy making.

Kompf and Brown contribute Chapter 8, 'Teachers' personal and professional ideals about practice'. In this chapter, the idea that teachers might have ideals about practice is supported through reference to William James, John Dewey and George Kelly. A construct of ideal/least ideal is explored as a superordinate dimension through which teachers conceive of direction and action that might lead to desired educational outcomes. Ideals may be personal or professional, or both. The process of idealising is discussed and described and opportunities for re-conceptualisation and reformulation considered after testing out such ideals in practice. Further ideas are explored regarding the change in ideals because of experience in teaching.

De Corte, Verschaffel and Schrooten contribute the final chapter in this section, 'Computer simulation as a tool in studying teachers' cognitive activities during error diagnosis in arithmetic'. They provide a theoretical background for studying teachers' cognitions and the effects that understanding such processes might have on the subsequent instruction of students. Lack of procedural correctness and teachers' understanding of it had not been systematically explored at the time of this research and a computer-assisted approach was developed. The use of computer programs to assist in teacher understanding, while not providing full insights into the cognitive structure and thinking process of student teachers, provides a basis for an elaborate set of questions that will provide insights and a basis for further discussion and investigation. While limitations in computer applications at the time of this research precluded in-depth pursuit of this problem, the authors acknowledge that subsequent sophistication has not found its way to further study of this worthwhile idea.

Chapter 5

Strategies and Methods in Research on Teacher Thinking

Günter L. Huber

Introduction

Methodological approaches to teacher thinking should be discussed within a general frame of reference for educational research. As the root *hodos* in 'method' tells us, we are dealing with a way – a way that leads us from some place to some goal. Considerations about the right way or about the adequacy of procedures thus are dependent on an analysis of the state or knowledge we start from, and from decisions about the state at which we aim.

Therefore, this chapter has two parts. In the first part, under 'Strategies in Research on Teacher Thinking', it will approach the question of methodology by asking about general ways of devising research on teacher thinking; in the second part it addresses specific tactical questions about procedures in use or about methods necessary for specific goals.

Relying partially on Klauer's (1980) work on *Experimentelle Unterrichts-forschung* the first section deals with (1) questions of theoretical orientation, (2) the dichotomy of summative versus formative research, and (3) nomological versus quasi-paradigmatical research strategies. This part is summarised (4) by drawing conclusions for research on teacher thinking from the point of view of a seriously challenging critique from behavioural approaches to teacher training.

The second part starts (1) with methodological implications. Focusing on lines of development, (2) experimental designs versus field studies are considered, concentrating on an aspect shared by both approaches, i.e. the construction of meaning by subjects. This is connected finally (3) with the relation of qualitative and quantitative methods, pointing at the promising role of computers for the practical use of qualitative methods.

Strategies in Research on Teacher Thinking

Theoretical Orientations

The discussions during earlier ISATT conferences were at least partially centred on several dichotomies. This repeatedly activated the participant to look for solutions that would avoid the threat of a bifurcation of research endeavours. Lowyck (1984) chose a well-fitting metaphor. These seemingly contradictory tendencies are represented in metaphors such as the teacher as decision-maker versus the teacher as problem-solver; the teacher as information-processor versus the teacher as user of subjective theories; teaching as rational activity versus teaching as making use of routines. This list could be enlarged by additional dichotomies on different levels such as structural versus functional research; cognitive versus emotional/ motivational processes; thinking versus acting and so on.

Differentiations like these and the foundation of camps among the scientific community seem to be symptomatic of scientific approaches in search of a paradigm. Under conditions like these the request for theoretical orientation, at least for a conceptual frame of reference for different aspects of teaching, emerges repeatedly; to develop such a frame of reference is not an easy task – we can only agree in this respect with Halkes (1985) in his overview of the ISATT conferences of 1983 and 1985. Nevertheless we should look for a framework, and I dare to suggest at least an orientation for further discussions: the frame of reference of systems theory, which has already proven its adequacy in other areas of educational psychology. Nevertheless, here too we immediately meet a serious problem: *The* system theory as *one* body of knowledge does not exist. There are differing conceptions in biology, physics, geology, sociology, communication theory, etc. Therefore, we may easily go from bad to worse, bartering a meta-theoretical bifurcation in addition to our conceptual-methodological differences.

If we tentatively use systems theory as a heuristic principle, how would we then perceive research on teacher thinking? Systems are conceived as wholes which consist of elements between which there are interactive relations, as Miller (1978) in his monumental, all-encompassing work on living systems wrote, or there is interdependency as a fundamental characteristic (Parsons and Shils, 1954). Which advantages are supplied by this orientation, and which disadvantages do we have to put up with? Referring to different areas of psychological research, Brunner (1986) has drawn five conclusions for practical research. For the area of research on teacher thinking, we can formulate them as follows:

(1)   System orientation leads to changes in epistemology: Elements are not isolated from their context, they should not be abstracted of their relations, but interrelations of teachers' activities are to be studied. In this connection, the category of patterns is of central importance. These changes in epistemology can put into operation a shift from a view of isolated elements which are to be studied (mechanistic-reductionistic paradigm) towards an implicit viewpoint of ecosystems. Though linear thinking is most familiar for all of us, we should keep in mind that it is based on an implicit epistemology, too; or, as Keeney (1979, p. 188) quoted from Bateson (1977):
All descriptions are based on theories of how to make descriptions.
You cannot claim to have no epistemology. Those who so claim have nothing but a bad epistemology.

(2)   From the feature of interrelations it follows that we give regard to the principle of holism: It must not be concluded that empirical access to single elements or single relations is forbidden, but instead of unilateral cause-effect relations we have to look for transactional dependencies.

(3)   Interdependency of structure and process: Structure and processes have to be studied in interdependent relations. Existing structures provide a framework for possible processes, whereas structures can be changed by means of

specific processes. On the other hand, processes may determine the development of structures.

(4)   Cyclic structure of models: Linear models have to be replaced by cyclic models.

(5)   Researchers as elements of the system: Investigators can no longer insist on the idea of being neutral observers, because they and their activities in the process of research become elements of the system under question, too.

What could a theoretical orientation like this one mean, for instance, if we have to deal with the dichotomy *rational activity versus use of routines* in interactive teaching? We could perceive existing rational activities and routines of a teacher as elements of his/her pattern of professional actions. We also have to take into account the context of his/her teaching, and not concentrate on the system *teacher* alone. Then we will see that under differing conditions tendencies for the testing of hypotheses or for spontaneous reaction are prevalent. We also have to look for cyclic interdependencies: What has been the result of a rational analysis finally becomes a routine; in order to change routines they must become objects of reflective processes as Olson (1984) pointed out or as Wahl, Weinert and Huber (1984) tried to take into account in the development of a programme for teacher training. In order to deal with the dichotomy *information processing versus use of subjective theories* we could derive integrative heuristics from principle 4, which claims the inter-dependency of structure and process. These two examples may be sufficient.

The metaphor of systems is dangerous, as Brunner (1986) accentuates. Despite the danger that ontic qualities are attributed to the model there could be a serious misunderstanding of the holistic principle: Empirical approaches and their necessary strategy of dissecting transactional relations could be avoided, and the principle of circularity could seduce some researchers to formulate circular models in a way that they no longer could be used in empirical research. Finally, the principle of non-neutrality could lead to the abandonment of observational methods – instead of a search for methods that are suited to the control of observers' influences. More important are the advantages of this orientation, even if only the more comprehensive system of the classroom is chosen as the object of research. Findings of research on teacher thinking which take into account only cognitive structures and processes of teachers are necessary elements, and they are important especially for teachers. However, there are two major shortcomings:

(1)   It was shown many times that teachers are in danger of learning nothing from their everyday experiences, because they interpret stimuli they are used to in such a way that these stimuli match their experiences. What counts for instructional research in the end is the meaning of the findings for the students. The stress on the principle of functionalism in Berliner's chapter at the start of the book was as well aimed as important. Just one empirical example as illustration: Shavelson and Stern (1981) reported findings about the complexity of teachers' decision-making. Of special interest are teachers who are ready to consider alternatives or even to change their strategies during interactive teaching. Such behaviour is fitting into the picture of teachers as problem-solvers: They show flexible, adaptive behaviour. What does this very behaviour mean for their students? The correlation between complexity of the teachers' decision-making and the students' achievements was negative!

(2)   Even if we insist on concentrating primarily on teachers only, their verbally
          reported cognitions are not too revealing if isolated from the context of the
          teachers' professional actions. Teacher thinking should always be understood
          as a part of ongoing activities. Let us finish these considerations with three
          conclusions:

    (a)   Research on teacher thinking should include the whole field in
              which a teacher's activities are embedded, at least the system of the
              classroom.
    (b)   Research on teacher thinking should take into account the principle
              of cyclic interdependencies. Maybe in our example just the more
              difficult, lower-achieving students caused teachers to carry out more
              complex decision-making.
    (c)   Descriptive studies are necessary but not sufficient. We need more
              complex, experimental designs.

Summative versus Formative Strategies

Scriven's (1972) differentiation between strategies of evaluation was used by Klauer
as a heuristic for recommendations of specific designs in educational research. I want
to concentrate here on the general strategic line. A strategy is called summative if it
gives access to global effects; in our last example, the students' achievements were
global effects. On the other hand, a strategy is called formative if it gives access to
stepwise effects and interrelations of teacher thinking and teachers' professional activities. Whereas summative strategies seem to ignore the often-complained-about gap
between cognition and action by a daring jump, formative strategies on the other hand
seem to grasp the details and deficits of the bridge needed. Using a formative strategy
we would, for instance, follow the line of a teacher's judgements about different students to his/her lesson preparations, to decisions and routines during interactive teaching, to effects on different students – and back again to this teacher's judgement about
students, and so on. Of course, it is not necessary always to use all-encompassing
research strategies. However, a formative strategy should be advantageous also in
studies including only single elements of a teacher's activities, for instance in research
on teachers' questions.

       As a prerequisite for a formative strategy of research, we should understand
research on teacher thinking as applied research; more specifically as action-oriented
research. (Formulated bluntly: What follows from our research for teachers and teaching, for students and learning?) For this reason four points have to be taken into
account (Huber, Krapp and Mandl, 1984):

(1)   As a basis, we need a body of descriptive-explanatory knowledge about
          teacher thinking.
(2)   This – hopefully action-relevant – basic knowledge does not per se change
          instructional practice. The transformations into rules of action, at least rec-
          ommendations for action, have to be provided, too. This means we have
          to tell teachers under which conditions, for which goals, which sequence
          of considerations, decisions, actions seem to be suited best (cf. Herrmann,
          1979; Heiland, 1984).
(3)   For natural settings, e.g. real classrooms, we cannot formulate recommenda-
          tions for all possible situations. That is why we have to consider what we can
          tell teachers in order to teach them to accomplish a productive reduction of
          complexity (Herrmann, 1979); this means we have to teach teachers how to

create the conditions in their classrooms, at home at their desks, etc., under which our rules or recommendations for action are still valid. As an example: The flexible, but less efficient decision-makers, whom we have heard about, may not have taken into account that their students too have specific expectations with regard to a pattern of teaching activities, for instance a need for structure, reliable consequences, etc. How can teachers reduce complexity productively? As a prerequisite for alternative planning, teachers should try to communicate with their students about their subjective perceptions of lessons and lesson plans. At least this is one point that could lead to positive conditions of change, and which, if not taken into account, is a cause of failure of approved and technically well-practised sequences of action. Selvini-Palazzoli *et al.* (1978) have shown this in more than 25 case analyses from the field of school counselling.

(4)   In addition, we have to teach this knowledge to teachers. We have to do this job in such a way that scientific knowledge is not stored in isolation by the teachers, but that they can connect it with their experiences, tacit knowledge and so on (Heckhausen, 1976; Weinert, 1977). This is the point where the metaphor of subjective theories (Bromme, 1984) is of special importance. Teachers must become ready to question their experiences, and to consider more differentiated concepts. This strategy of research on teacher thinking could meet the demand to do educational research as instructional research.

Nomological versus Quasi-paradigmatical Research

Regarding descriptive-explanative tasks in research on teacher thinking. Herrmann (1976, 1979) differentiates – among other types – between strategies that aim at the elucidation of problem areas, i.e. the search for means of explanation, and testing the adequacy of available means of explanation.

The first type, also called scientific domain programme, is nomological in the full sense. An interesting phenomenon, for instance what is in a teacher's mind before, during and after teaching, is defined by a set of core assumptions, and is conceived of as something that needs to be explicated or explained by something else.

The second type – quasi-paradigmatical research – starts with specific explanatory means in search of phenomena with which they might match. It seems we do not lack such quasi-paradigms in want of application to teacher thinking and professional action. I suppose this is reflected in many of the dichotomic topics of earlier discussions. I guess in some of our colleagues' understanding research on teacher thinking is a domain programme, whereas others feel they have at their disposal some indispensable means of explanation that they want to have applied to the field of teacher thinking. If we at least try to reach an understanding about each other's positions, many problems in our discussions would disappear. However, something more should be brought about. To give an example: Both lines could be merged in this specific area of teacher thinking where teachers' perceptions of situations, appraisals of action alternatives, expectations and evaluations of consequences are of central interest; this is the case in a number of studies on teacher planning, coping with problematic situations during interactive teaching, dealing with conflicting goals, etc. A domain programme could try to get hold of explanative constructs, and in parallel quasi-paradigmatic efforts could investigate the effects of systematically varying explanations of teachers' professional activities. A promising theoretical orientation for this end seems to be supplied by instrumentality theory, as Krampen has shown (1986) in a summary of his studies.

Conclusions

An agreement about fundamental research approaches seems to be necessary, because I have a hunch that there is a development under way which could deprive us of our business basis – at least if we understand our endeavours as a programme of applied research: The relation of thinking and professional action is in question as the central element of our research domain. In the *Educational Researcher* Guskey (1986) proposed a behavioural approach to staff development (Figure 5.1) as an alternative to, as he claims, inefficient reflective approaches. Referring to Doyle and Ponder's *practicability ethic* the author demands teacher training orientating to practical questions and classroom behaviour. A contradictory and inefficient way – according to Guskey – starts by altering teachers' attitudes, expectations, opinions, perceptions, etc. Both approaches share the same set of elements, but they make use of them in totally different sequences:

For Guskey changes in teacher thinking are not antecedent conditions for changes in their professional actions, but a consequence of the teachers' experiences that due to new ways of interactive teaching their students' achievements change. In other words: Principally positive changes in teacher behaviour have to precede changes in opinions and attitudes. Obviously, the author does not trust his linear behavioural model too much; so he suggests providing assistance for teachers even after the initial training, because otherwise some of them may never reach the final step of cognitive changes. So in line with the system-theoretical orientation proposed, we change Guskey's unilateral causal sequence into a cyclic sequence (Figure 5.2). For its representation, I also changed the labels of the main stages, borrowing the new concepts (and the nice acronym ART for the cycle) from discussions in 1978 at the OISE with D. E. Hunt.

By this delineation, it appears equally biased to claim reflection on practice as the one and only way to change teachers' professional activities. 'Professional practice is more than the correct application of knowledge and skill' – as Oberg and Field (1986) claimed. Referring to Galperin's (1979) action-based theory of learning and teaching with its sub-processes of orientation, execution and control, every professional's *basis of orientation* has to exceed the actual demands of everyday

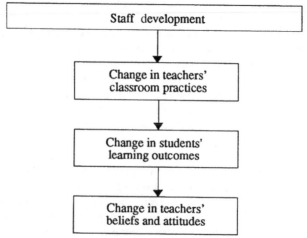

Figure 5.1.   Model of the process of teacher change (Guskey, 1986, p. 7).

professional situations. So an improvement cycle of teaching can be represented as in Figure 5.3, even if the acronym RAT sounds much less inviting. The two models are not mutually exclusive, but seem to be complementary in nature. Let me summarise the conclusions that were already drawn implicitly:

(1)   A system-orientation seems to be valuable at least from the point of view of heuristics.

(2)   It seems to be necessary not to apply too readily a handy quasi-paradigm for a domain where a lot of basic research has still to be done.

(3)   The system-oriented cyclic conception of teacher improvement easily opens the way to a more comprehensive, transactional model including students and their activities.

As a final remark, a broader orientation could be helpful to avoid an undue concentration on cognitive aspects of instruction – as the label teacher thinking programmatically suggests. Shulman and Carey's (1984) model of limited rationality may be a warning,

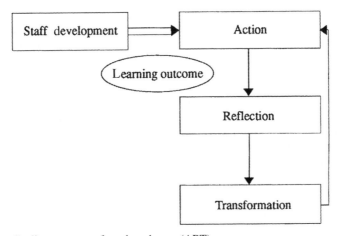

Figure 5.2.   Cyclic processes of teacher change (ART).

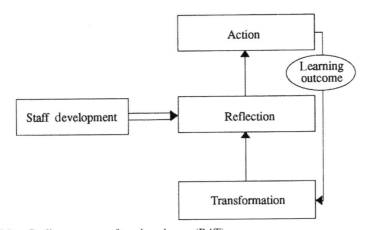

Figure 5.3.   Cyclic processes of teacher change (RAT).

and Prawat's (1985) findings about affective goal orientations of teachers is a promising step to enlarge the perspective. Though Prawat (1985) symptomatically studies 'teacher *thinking* about the affective domain' (italics added by me), I agree with him that this domain 'deserves more attention from researchers than it has hitherto received'. I only would like to include teachers' affects, motivations and values, especially in coping with stressful situations.

Methodological Perspectives

Implications of a System Orientation

What are the methodological implications of attempting the application of a system orientation to research on teacher thinking? Here we must concentrate on three areas. We start with the most important and at the same time the most problematic one:

(1)   One could conclude from the holistic principle that nothing should be analysed because otherwise relations are dissected, and even a following synthesis of analytically derived results is insufficient to grasp the whole phenomenon (cf. Brunner and Huber, 1983). Angyal (1969, p. 22; cf. Brunner, 1986) explained: 'In a system the members are, from a holistic viewpoint, not significantly connected with each other except with reference to the whole'.

A position like this opens an aporetic blind alley for empirical research. Brunner (1986) suggests, nevertheless, one does not drop the advantages of a system approach but studies the relations between elements of the system, and then draws careful conclusions about the whole system. The result may be imperfect, even distorted – but not a priori reduced to linearity! I hope the reader will allow me, an analogy from the area of mechanics: The example of computer-aided construction shows that characteristics and behaviours of complex systems can be approximated satisfyingly enough by dealing with just a limited number of elements. Complex parts of an engine, for instance the system of a crank-shaft and its bearings, are studied as an assembly of subsystems; their behaviours under various conditions can be computed, the system can be altered and checked again – until the whole system functions as required, above all until no weak element endangers the total functionality.

Brunner and Huber (1983) formulated several proposals for this process in research on teaching and learning. We recommended beginning with a definition of the systems' constituent elements; then elaborating an overview of relations between these elements (with reference to the whole), not forgetting the check of empirical accessibility. After the administration of the study, deduction of conclusions for the whole system is possible.

(2)   Structures and processes have to be regarded as interrelated. It is insufficient to describe only the hierarchy of elements, because such a static analysis does not master the dynamic characteristics of social systems. Empirical studies must succeed in comparing the states of a system at different points in time, and inferring the critical conditions of constancy and variability.

(3)   Access to the dynamics of a system is impossible if we stick to the model of linear-causal relations. But we should keep in mind Brunner's warnings against a-empirical circular models.

From these three points, further considerations can be deduced with regard to design, statistical procedures and validation of findings. It is not intended to elaborate on the most complex approaches, but to outline some rather simple procedures that nevertheless lead beyond structural descriptions and/or linear relations.

Problems of Research Designs

In order to have a chance to gain access to the system's dynamics, studies on teacher thinking cannot rely only on collecting data at a single point in time. Assessments should be scheduled at least at two points in time. Though this is a less-than-ideal design – surely a more prolonged time series design would be preferable – measurement on two occasions of course is better than on one (cf. Rogosa, 1979).

Even the minimal demand of one repetition would allow controlling for the often deplored side-effects of approaches to teacher thinking, above all the reactivity of research methods on ongoing processes. As a further advantage of repeated measures, we have occasion, even on a correlational-descriptive level, to draw conclusions about the direction of influences and interrelations between variables. The least sophisticated model for this goal is the *cross-lagged panel design* or *two-wave-two-variable (2W2V) panel* (Rogosa, 1979) (Figure 5.4). To be sure, this is a quasi-experimental approach, as Petermann, Hehl and Schneider (1977) point out. There are well-known limits, but this design seems to be superior to more sophisticated approaches, for instance path-analytical ones; there are no restrictive suppositions referring to exogenous and endogenous variables. However, Rogosa (1979) cautions against enthusiastic claims for the adequacy of the method of cross-lagged correlation related to 2W2V designs.

If the difference between the cross-lagged correlations R (x1, y2) and R (y1, x2) is positive and statistically significant, then it is attributed that X is causing Y (and vice versa). However, there are assumptions implicit in the model: that there is no simultaneous causation, that measurement was error-free, and that disturbing influences on X2 and Y2 are uncorrelated. Relying on the results of the re-analysis of several studies, Rogosa (1979, p. 278) concludes that '... the difference of the cross-lagged correlations does not provide unambiguous evidence as to the predominant direction of causal influence', though the application of the method is widely recommended. On the other hand, Rogosa (1979) accentuates the specific value of this design, if the goal of

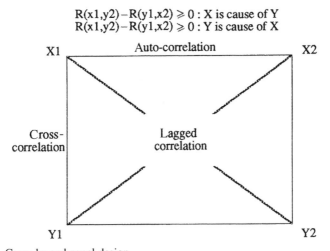

Figure 5.4.   Cross-lagged panel design.

research is the identification of reciprocal causal relations – which is a core assumption of systemic approaches. He describes a relative measure of the strength of the reciprocal causation by determining the relative incremental lack of fit of the 2W2V data to a restricted model, where the critical causal parameters are constrained to be zero (1979, p. 299). Taking into account the warnings, this design provides a function not to be underestimated: it mediates between correlational analysis and specific experimental methods that always afford the manipulation of causal variables (Petermann, Hehl and Schneider, 1977).

Statistical Procedures

If we have a complex set of data, with results from *structural* variables at several points in time or from different persons, we can also analyse *process* interrelations just by identifying the frequencies with which one event follows another one. We could for instance assess the probability of a teacher pondering about the idea X whenever he/she showed the behaviour Y. If time as well as variables are assessed discretely, an especially simple method for this analysis is provided by the model of Markoff processes (cf. Leistikow, 1977). A Markoff process is any sequence of events that contains data of the same variable, and where the sequential dependency between immediately following data is maximal, and shows a decline towards zero for greater distances of data within the sequence. Because of the demand for discrete data, this procedure seems to be especially apt for qualitative approaches. There are many highly interesting applications in the literature on psychotherapy (cf. Revenstorf and Vogel, 1979), and some in research on teacher thinking. Bromme (1981) analysed teachers' thinking during lesson preparation (using a think-aloud technique) by means of the Markoff procedure of computing the probabilities for all dyadic sequences of preparation categories (see Table 5.1). He found remarkable sequential dependencies in lesson planning, for instance a high probability that one decision (cat. 4) is followed just by another decision ($p = 0.55$), or that the expectation of a specific event is followed only rarely by pondering about alternative possibilities for action or problem-solving (cat. 3; $p = 0.08$) – but mostly by decisions ($p = 0.52$). The matrix of probabilities for a switch from one state to another can be analysed under quite a variety of aspects:

•   Are there sequential dependencies (data of one person)?
•   Do the data meet a priori valences or are probabilities for different persons comparable? (aspect of homogeneity)
•   Are the probabilities stable over time? (aspect of stationarity)

Table 5.1.   Dyadic sequences in teacher planning

The following categories precede	1	2	3	4	5	6
1. Statement of facts	0.31	0.10	0.07	0.45	0.05	0.06
2. Problems or questions	0.24	0.12	0.13	0.42	0.04	0.08
3. Alternative actions	0.11	0.10	0.21	0.53	0.02	0.06
4. Decisions	0.21	0.10	0.06	0.55	0.04	0.07
5. Expectation of events	0.18	0.10	0.08	0.52	0.12	0.04
6. Self-instruction	0.35	0.12	0.06	0.34	0.05	0.11

From Bromme (1981, p. 206).

- Are two series of observations interdependently related, for instance teacher/student behaviours? Because of the sequence in time, we can also decide about the direction of effects.

We see again that it is not necessary to indulge in fancy statistical procedures if we want to analyse more complex relations than linear causality.

Validation Procedures

Discussions of validation procedures in research on teacher thinking very clearly reflect the problems of non-systemic orientations. In our contribution to the 1983 ISATT conference, Heinz Mandl and I discussed the significance of

- Communicative validation, which means to reconstruct a teacher's thoughts and validate them by consensus, using the criterion of adequacy-to-reconstruction, and
- Action validation, which means to assess relations between reconstructed thoughts and actions, using the criterion of adequacy-to-reality (Treiber and Groeben, 1981).

We then criticised the fact that validation procedures according to the criterion of adequacy with respect to reality obviously are based on a static conception of relations between teachers' thinking and their professional activities. Relying on data about dynamic interrelations between thinking and acting, we proposed a procedure of prognostic validation together with adequacy-to-prognosis as criterion as shown in Figure 5.5.

In studies of pre-teaching thoughts, both researcher and teacher may take the prospective stance, whereas other timings of cognitive assessment lead researchers to interpret teacher thinking retrospectively. In doing so the advantages of reactive methods in teacher thinking are missed: teachers expressing thoughts about their thinking do not report detachedly, but they start to structure or restructure their experiences, intentions, evaluations thus formulating new expectations which may gain influence on their later activities.

We tried to assess these reactive effects with a small sample of student teachers. We had them solve problems and talk afterwards about what went through their heads during the task. A week later, they had to solve a set of similar problems. Out of five subjects in a control group where subjects did not talk about their thinking, only one changed her problem-solving strategy during the second trial. In three

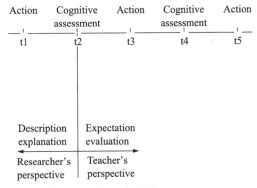

Figure 5.5.   Retrospective and prospective orientations.

experimental groups (Recall, Stimulated Recall, SR together with probing questions) 12 subjects out of 17 altered their strategies – in line with their thinking after the first trial – even for the worse if they reported thinking about their inability to solve tasks like those used in the experiment. The difference between control and experimental groups is statistically significant.

The clinical literature shows (cf. Kendall and Hollon, 1980) that the influences of talking about thinking on later activities are most remarkable if a person is convinced of his/her statements, if a person believes in what he/she is telling. What seems to be a fundamental disadvantage from the perspective of retrospective validation changes into a particular advantage of research on teacher thinking if one makes use of the prognostic criterion within a framework of dynamic relations between thinking and acting. The appraisal of findings about teacher thinking therefore should not depend on information about whether a teacher indeed has acted as he/she said, but on data about the way he/she will act.

A prospective stance with respect to validation includes *not* insisting on the neutral position of researchers in the domain of teacher thinking but to include or to take into account the investigator's influences within the design of a study.

Experimental Studies versus Field Studies?

Is this a question at all? Is it possible, if we appreciate a system orientation, to justify the 'artificiality' of experiments, their lack of external or ecological validity – to name just the major points of criticism? Well, I already mentioned the threat of methodological one-sidedness. In order to elaborate on this aspect, let me quote from Herrmann (1979). He summarised the points of view of critical rationalism, and advocated with reference to Feyerabend (among others) what he calls *pluralistic liberalization* of methodology (p. 62):

> The heterogeneity of efforts to define psychological problems and to solve them, and the heterogeneity of means used to solve those problems (strategies, methods, procedures, theories, hypotheses etc.) must no longer be conceived of as a disadvantage: heterogeneity, repeated starts, and change may contain progressive forces, which compulsive verificators of small details as well as the great reductionists with their stance of 'nothing – but' rarely can dream of.

This quotation should not be misunderstood as an invitation to methodological anarchy or the laissez-faire point of view of 'everything goes'. Instead, we should appraise the specific contributions of different methodological approaches – and we should try to relate these contributions. What is the essence of the contributions, and how could the task of relating them be approached?

The actual state really looks like a bifurcated one – at least many informal discussions with colleagues have given me this impression. What I want to collate under the heading 'experimental' are methods that render it possible to create, to control, to vary conditions critical for the study of the interesting phenomena. This presupposes knowledge, at least assumptions about the setting. That is why cognitively oriented critics would say – as we also did on a specific occasion: The investigator imposes his/her pre-structured suppositions on the situation, the subjects, etc., for instance in defining the units of analysis during or after observing a lesson.

Field approaches, on the other hand, try to avoid just these impositions, and to capture instead the subjects' perspectives. Under headings like ethnomethodology, biographical approach, access to personal constructs and so on, a broad variety of methodological approaches is in use already in research on teacher thinking. However, do the users of both differing methodological orientations take notice of each other's findings? As I stated at the beginning: Methods are ways to a specific goal – are we all looking for the same goal? If we can find a least common denominator, then the fences should not be insurmountable.

A contribution by Berkowitz and Donnerstein (1982) seems to be especially important for our situation in my eyes. The authors call their readers' attention to comparative reviews of experimental and field studies in the area of organizational psychology: between about 200 experimental findings and about 300 findings from field studies there was no difference in the degree to which one can generalise from either of these two kinds of investigations! Of course, as the authors say, experiments are not necessarily as externally valid as are field studies conducted in natural settings. However, the generalisability of findings should be understood as an empirical issue! I cannot see yet what we have to offer in our field of research to answer the demand implicit in this statement. In addition, I suggest that we do not try to generate answers along a line that is characterised more by competitive than complementary tendencies of methodological orientation. At least we met reactions like these to our own considerations about meaning and validity of verbal reports. I would classify many of these reactions as biased by specific presuppositions. Instead, I propose the following:

(1)   Berkowitz and Donnerstein (1982, p. 249) formulated what they declared to
        be the central thesis of their article:
        The meaning the subjects assign to the situation they are in and
        the behaviour they are carrying out plays a greater part in determin-
        ing the generalizability of an experiment's outcome than does the
        sample's demographic representativeness or the setting's surface
        realism.

I think this is our central interest too. Whether within experimental designs or field approaches we try to get access to the subjective perspective of our subjects. At the same time, this interest fosters understanding as it urges investigators and subjects to develop a common language.

(2)   Then both approaches can supplement each other, whether we compare them
        under a viewpoint of levels or of steps in research. In the first case, there
        is a complementary relation between data gained by field or experimental
        approaches on a phenomenological, functional and structural level. In the
        second case, we can start with field studies or we can use other investigators'
        field results, which give us an overview or call our attention to phenomena
        that otherwise we would have overlooked completely. Therefore, field stud-
        ies play an absolutely necessary role in explorations of our research domain.
        A good example for this role is Chapter 6 in this volume by Oberg. She
        reports on teachers' grounds of practice, which are those personal constructs
        about teaching that make a teacher's actions understandable. Oberg and
        colleagues have conceived and revealed the ground of a teacher's practice
        in a way that did not impose their perspective and terminology; they
        understand their study as an 'explorative project, aimed at the description
        and analysis of a complex phenomenon'. A second step could be a series of
        experiments which vary or influence important ground elements systemati-
        cally by studying contrasting groups, by matching or mismatching personal
        grounds and external conditions, etc. The explorative results could be used for

the construction of a questionnaire, just as an example, and with this instrument one could study changes of attitudes, effects of thinking on action, etc. in
the process of repeated occasions of interactive teaching under differing conditions, with different teachers, etc. An example of an approach like this is the
study by Killian and McIntyre (1986) on preservice students' attitudes towards
pupil control. Another example is Krampen's (1986) study on action-guiding
cognitions of teachers.

(3)   Finally, as step three, I'd like to suggest looking at natural settings again in
order to find out about the conditions for application of our findings – for
instance, as Killian and McIntyre asked: How can we educate teachers who are
trustful, accepting, and optimistic in their view of children? The message in one
sentence: We should notice more often each other's findings, independently
of their methodological descent.

Quantitative versus Qualitative Data

The threat of a polarisation according to fundamental methodological presuppositions
seems to be of an even larger import with the question of the nature of data. The suspicion that there may be differing aims of research behind preferences for different
types of data is reinforced if one recalls the discussion of recent years, especially in
the *Educational Researcher*: obviously representatives of different epistemological
orientations are gathering in two camps. The contact between investigators oriented
towards principles like realism or positivism or objectivism on the one hand, and
researchers with idealistic or relativistic inclinations on the other hand are so often
limited to mutual rejection, attributing labels like storytellers versus number crunch-
ers or variable scientists to inhabitants of the other camp. Nevertheless, a great number of examples from practical research, in our proceedings too, show an explicit
readiness both to reconstruct subjective world-views and to reduce data in objective
ways. These seem not to be incompatible contradictions. Obviously it is possible to
gather qualitative data – 'based on the point that reality is made rather than found', as
Smith and Heshusius (1986) wrote, and then try to analyse these constructs using
quantitative methods. For instance, think of studies from the tradition of personal construct theory which use structure-analytical procedures. Or think of dimension-analytical
reductions of the results of a content analysis of an interview. With this in mind, I was
very surprised to find the following statement in an American journal – and not in a
German one:

> ...if a quantitative inquirer disagrees with a qualitative inquirer, is it
> even possible for them to talk to each other? The answer, for the
> present anyway, is a qualified no. An appeal that one must accept a
> particular result because it is based on facts will have little impact on
> one who believes there can be no uninterpreted facts of the case. On
> the other hand, the idea that facts are value-laden and that there is no
> court of appeal beyond dialogue and persuasion will at the very least
> seem unscientific and insufficient to a quantitative inquirer.
>
>   (Smith and Heshusius, 1986, p. 11).

This dangerous dichotomy may be founded on the mistake that objectivism is
restricted to quantitative data whereas interpretative science can only make use of
qualitative data. Practical research seems not to be too much infected by such thinking in terms of closed drawers or boxes. Even if I do not want to go as far as Miles
and Huberman (1984b) who proclaimed an epistemological ecumenism, I strongly

recommend their pragmatic orientation regarding the questions and aims of research. I also can easily identify myself with their self-characterisation; Miles and Huberman (1984b, p. 23) write:

> We strongly believe in being systematic about inquiry and favour the development of substantive and methodological consensus among researchers. Perhaps we are right-wing qualitative researchers, or only 'soft-nosed positivists'. We offer our ideas to qualitative researchers of all persuasions, including the mostly resolutely interpretative, and believe they can be useful. One reader of this article understood us as 'advising idealists to be more like realists'. That may be true, but we also encourage realists to attend to the importance of their own personal visions in constructing meaning in data, or in deciding what to consider 'data' in the first place, and to remember that understanding and portraying the unique individual case may be more important than 'generalizations' and 'variables'.

In this context I want to call the reader's attention to a development which may be a real encouragement for realists but may be rejected as ultimate perversion by resolute interpretationists: the use of computers for gathering, reducing and displaying qualitative data. Indeed this tool can help to communicate, to reconstruct, and to control processes and results of qualitative research more easily, to say nothing about its effects on the mechanical tasks of the qualitative investigator him/herself (e.g. coding, sorting information by categories, scanning for specific patterns, etc.). The computer can structure naturalistic approaches, and it can systematise rigorous interpretations.

Shelly and Sibert (1985) introduced the software package QUALOG which is based on Polinson and Sibert's (1981) LOGLISP; this package seems qualified to fulfil even exacting expectations. A number of examples from educational research seem to prove this statement. Shelly and Sibert (1985, p. 4) describe the language environment as well suited to the requirements of qualitative research:

(1)   LOGLISP allows the researcher to work directly with symbolic information, including prose text, with no necessity for numeric encoding;
(2)   the researcher easily enters and records arbitrary information (e.g. interview transcripts, field notes, observer's memoranda, codes, line numbers) without extensive advance planning or special programming;
(3)   LOGLISP provides extremely flexible means for retrieving such information, for studying relationships in the information, and for testing hypotheses about the relationships.

In addition the request by Miles and Huberman (1984a) seems to be dischargeable, as Sibert and Shelly (1985, p. 3) say; the necessary operations no longer stay strictly implicit, they can be documented, and they can be reported. So procedures and thinking used in qualitative research can be made explicit. Shelly (1986) gives a convincing example from her own study of teachers' conceptions of reading (p. 30):

> Sharon's responses to my questions about reading as a specific subject or as a general concept focused back to her thoughts about students, classes, materials, and constraints. Based on my analysis of the data, I concluded that I could not identify Sharon's conception of reading. The data did not support such an analysis. Rather, they supported the work of researchers such as Brophy and Good (1974) who suggest broadening the definition of 'teacher expectation'.

I guess this approach and its recent results are very promising for the task of bringing people from the qualitative and quantitative camps together. If they do not develop some other way of mutual understanding and sensitivity for the importance of each other's findings for their own work, maybe QUALOG can provide the common language needed as the basis for understanding.

Acknowledgement

I wish to thank David Berliner, Rainer Bromme and Ewald J. Brunner for their helpful comments on the first draft of this chapter.

Author Reflection 2004

Over the years, the accumulating results of research on teacher thinking have contributed essentially to bridging the notorious gap between knowledge acquisition about teaching and routines of classroom practice in teacher education. Moreover, the approach and its findings proved to be useful generally wherever people are trained to put theoretical considerations into practice, above all, if this implies modifying everyday experiences.

The general topics of theoretical orientation and design addressed in the first part of this chapter are still subjects of controversial debates today, whereas in the field of specific methodological implications complementary approaches have been developed in recent years. Particularly the formerly predominant controversy between proponents of quantitative versus qualitative methods has been overcome by an understanding of the importance of 'mixed methodologies'. Thus, for instance, the discussion of 2W2V designs and the analysis of cross-lagged correlations will no longer draw too much attention. On the other hand, reconstruction of meaning in practitioners' actions and explanations with the support of computer programs is not an exotic approach today, but everyday practice in larger research projects, and researchers meanwhile can choose from a variety of software tools.

Based on the results of studies on teacher thinking, interest in implicit theories of practitioners has grown in a broad variety of areas of education, training, and adult learning at large. Therefore, the strategic and tactical questions of studies on implicit theories discussed in this chapter are still meaningful in applied social research. At least, this is true if these studies take into account that it is not sufficient just 'to give away' scientifically approved knowledge and expect that the recipients will change accordingly their personal (as, for example, in the case of health education) or professional routines.

Chapter 6

The Ground of Professional Practice

Antoinette Oberg[1]

Introduction and Purpose

Why do teachers teach the way they do? The answer to this question preoccupies an increasing number of educational researchers (see for example Halkes and Olson, 1984; Ben-Peretz, Bromme, and Halkes, 1986) but surprisingly few educational practitioners. The desire to answer this question most often stems from a concern to improve practice, which usually means to bring practice in line with prescribed policy and/or current theory about effective teaching. In this chapter, however, the concern is not to influence practice to bring it closer to a predefined outcome, but rather to empower practitioners themselves to become better educators.

We were ultimately interested in good professional practice. It follows from our conception of educational practice[2] that its goodness is judged not only by looking at the results of teacher actions, but more importantly by looking at what the actions are an expression of. Teaching actions are understood as an expression of teachers' ideas of the educational good and their ideas of how to move towards that good in the present circumstances. These ideas constitute what we called the ground of practice. Teachers become better educators as the ground of their practice is refined. Ground is refined through careful consideration or reflection, a process through which what has been previously taken for granted is questioned. For example: What do I mean by education? To what am I committed and what do I stand for as a teacher? Who are these learners? What am I striving for with these learners? How can I contribute to their education?

In answering such questions, teachers not only reveal their view of their practice, but also reconstrue that vision. They get more closely in touch with the ground of their practice while at the same time remoulding and changing that ground. In order that we might eavesdrop on some part of this essentially private and personal process of change with a number of different individual teachers, we needed a way of objectifying some components of ground. We required some heuristic devices, both conceptual and methodological, for creating texts that spoke of the ground of teachers' practice to both teachers and researchers.

We conceived ground to be multi-dimensional, complex, abstract, evolutionary, personal, understandable only in part, accessible only in concrete cases, and because of this last feature understandable to us only in collaboration with teachers. We were less interested in the origins and structure of ground than in what the reality of it was and how practice was informed by it. The key questions for the research became: What is the ground of teachers' practice? How can it be conceptualised and represented?

A Conception of Ground

The preliminary pre-understandings of what was being studied and of the questions being asked revealed the borders of a path that we hoped would provide access to the ground of teachers' practice. The path was further defined by our pre-understandings of what would count as answers to our questions, that is, of what underlay teaching practice. We believed that while some acts of practice are consciously considered, others are routine and still others are intuitive. When problems arise and time and circumstances permit, teachers can act like model decision makers, casting about for alternative solutions to the problem and lighting on one alternative that suits their goals and their understanding of the situation. If we cared to ask teachers about such a decision-making episode, they would likely be able to explain it in terms of what problem they were trying to solve and how their actions were expected to contribute to its solution. This type of considered decision-making characterises a relatively small proportion of teachers' practice. In much of teaching, time is so compressed and circumstances so complex that teachers act routinely on the basis of unexamined precedent or habit. While the initial establishment of patterns of actions that become routine may be a conscious decision, the repeated use of routine behaviours is automatic.

The more significant and major part of practice is more appropriately characterised as practical activity, which occurs on an intuitive level and proceeds from a holistic awareness of the situation. Those things stand out which are relevant to teachers' concerns at any given time. These concerns are not isolable 'problems' but rather part of the ongoing project to do what is educationally right in the light of how teachers understand their situation. Beneath deliberate, routine and intuitive teaching acts we expected to find teachers' understandings and beliefs about their particular situations and their intentions to accomplish some project related to education or schooling.[3] We presupposed the major components of ground were beliefs and intentions, defined as follows.

Ground as Beliefs and Intentions

As professional educators, teachers have certain *beliefs* about what is real and what is relevant with respect to their learners, learning, their own teaching, the subject matter of the curriculum, and the contexts, both immediate and remote, in which these exist. These beliefs are commonly called teachers' professional knowledge. They also have ideas about what present or future states of affairs are desirable with respect to their learners. These are their values or goals, their ideas of the educational good. Furthermore, they have ideas about what actions or arrangements might help these desired states to come about. Daniels (1971) calls these linking beliefs. Teachers' abilities to execute these successfully are usually called their teaching skills. Out of these kinds of ideas arise intentions to act in particular ways for particular purposes. These elements are shown in Figure 6.1.

Getting at the ground of conscious and possibly even routine acts of practice could be done by asking teachers about their beliefs and intentions, that is, asking them why they did what they did. In answering, teachers would give reasons for their

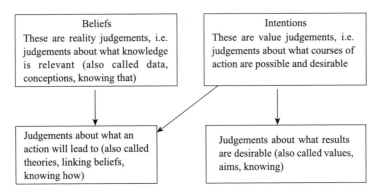

Figure 6.1.   The ground of practice.

actions. For example, they might say that they allowed a child to look after the video equipment because they believed he/she was sufficiently mature and reliable to be trusted with it (a reason as a belief), or, in order to reward and reinforce, and therefore said to be on solid ground.

Getting at the ground of the unreflective everyday practice of teaching required a different approach and a modified conception of what the ground would look like. It is nonsensical to ask directly for the reasons behind pre-reflective actions. Practical activity is a way of being as well as a way of doing. Its essential character is semantic or textual rather than abstract or causal (Packer, 1985). Understanding why it is the way it is requires understanding the purposes the action serves and the context in which it occurs; in short, understanding the actor's point of view. Looking for a way to get at and represent teachers' implicit views of the nature and purpose of their activities as economically as possible, we examined personal construct theory.

Ground as Personal Constructs

Personal construct theory was attractive on at least two counts. It was consistent with many of our presuppositions about ground, and in addition, well-established methods existed for identifying and displaying people's constructs. Personal constructs, as defined by Kelly (1955), are qualities and characteristics attributed to the elements that make up a person's world. Each construct is seen as having a bipolar opposite. One pole of a construct is valued positively and the other negatively. A teacher who values maturity will try to encourage and reward it, while a teacher who believes maturity should wait for adolescence to pass will simply compensate for its absence.[4] Constructs that teachers use to understand and deal with their world encompass all the components of ground described above, namely, beliefs about what characterises and what is relevant to the elements in their world; and intentions to act in a certain way based on these beliefs and their valuations of them, and based on beliefs about how to affect those elements that are the focus of their attention.

Methods for studying constructs include repertory grids, personal character sketches, and dialogue. We expected at least some of these to be suitable to our purposes. Our deliberations about these are described in the following section.

The crucial question which determined the suitability of personal construct theory for our own evolving conceptualisation of the ground of professional practice was whether or not it threatened our conception of practical activity as immediate, unreflective and prior to any abstraction or interpretation. Kelly (1955) saw constructs as real entities which existed in the natural world and 'channelised' human actions. In contrast, we preferred to view constructs as *post hoc* theoretical interpretations of practical actions which exist in the immediate present prior to any notion of how actions are structured. In our formulation, interpretation follows action and makes it intelligible, rather than preceding and directing it. Aside from this subtle difference, the fit of personal construct theory with our preconceptions, noted above, was quite good. Its particular appeal was that it explicitly accommodated unreflective action. Constructs are neither necessarily conscious nor fixed. They are like exchangeable goggles through which the mind's eye sees the world. In this sense, they are similar to the idea of the good that brings certain features of a holistically perceived situation into focus.

Therefore, we sought to represent the ground of practice as constructs, that is, as sets of descriptive terms that embodied teachers' implicit and explicit beliefs and intentions with respect to the important elements of their practice. For example, we sought to understand what teachers believed about and intended for learners in their classes. We also wanted to represent links between beliefs and intentions, and actions as concretely as possible. In terms of personal construct theory, the link between ground and actions was clear (Mischel, 1964, p. 189). We were uncertain how this link would appear in practical terms. Its discovery would have to wait until we had begun to build a preliminary description of a teacher's ground.

Evolution of a Method

As in all research studies, the accounts of the conceptual framework and the method given here are separate ex post facto reconstructions of deliberations that actually occurred simultaneously. In the account of method, we begin with the purposes and presumptions that influenced our decisions.

From the outset, we presumed the inquiry would be collaborative between teachers and researchers, dialectical in shape, and free from technical terms. Collaboration built on trust and respect would be necessary in order to achieve a shared understanding of teachers' practice. The process would be dialectical, moving between descriptions and interpretations of events, between teacher interpretations and researcher interpretations, between conversation and written text. The language we used would have to be the everyday language of teaching and thinking about teaching, because it is appropriate to the study of practical actions (Daniels, 1975), and because it could be owned by teachers as much as by researchers.

We anticipated using conversational interview as the primary method, perhaps supplemented by observations in teachers' classrooms. We knew from earlier experiences (Oberg and Tucker, 1985) that structured interview questions were likely to feel artificial and unnatural, hindering rather than facilitating the communicative understanding we hoped to achieve. We were convinced by Buchmann's (1985) persuasive case for conversation as the mode of talk most appropriate for understanding and improving education, and we were further encouraged by Yonemura's (1982) account of conversations in which teachers came to understand their own and each other's beliefs and perspectives on teaching.

Finally, and perhaps most importantly, we presumed that we would have to begin by asking teachers to describe actual events of practice rather than how or what they thought about their practice, because the ground we sought is meaningful only in the context of the practical activity it supports. The route to understanding beliefs and intentions, whether conscious or subconscious, was through the actions that constituted the everyday practice of teaching. Ground would become accessible to the researchers only as the teachers themselves became aware of it by reflecting on the experiences that were an expression of it.

Alternative Approaches

Approaches were suggested by the theoretical frameworks that had enriched our conception of the ground of practice. Personal construct theory offered a specific and well-developed method for gathering and analysing data called the repertory grid. The grid is a two-dimensional display of a person's system of personal constructs, with important elements of the person's world (people, events or things) along one axis and characteristics attributed to the elements along the other axis. There are precise techniques for eliciting characteristics or constructs and for calculating the degree of association among constructs and elements. While the use of teachers' own language and the efficiency of representing beliefs and intentions as constructs were attractive features of the repertory grid method, we had two serious reservations. We were uncertain how to elicit elements that would represent the entire compass of teacher practice. Studies which had utilised repertory grids successfully had focused on particular aspects of practice, for example, curriculum guides (Ben-Peretz, Katz and Silberstein, 1982), personnel decisions (Rix, 1982), a particular instructional innovation (Olson, 1980). Attempts to encompass all of practice had yielded mixed results (Munby, 1984). Moreover, we felt such mechanistic treatment of personal meanings was unsuitable to our phenomenological stance, a sentiment shared by Yorke (1985).

Intrigued by Kelly's less frequently encountered suggestion that constructs could be elicited through dialogue (Diamond, 1982), and predisposed to more natural and authentic ways of entering teachers' worlds, we sought guidelines for capturing personal meanings through discussions of a more conversational nature. Conversation is the method used in hermeneutics to seek a common understanding between researcher and subject. The building up of a common language coincides with the art of understanding (Gadamer, 1975). Hermeneutic conversation is characterised by open-ended dialogue in which participants are authentically present to each other and questions arise naturally in the discourse.

Questions are asked and answered out of a true desire to understand the human being's direct experiences of the world (Douglas, 1985) rather than out of adherence to a predetermined interview schedule. The requirement of hermeneutic conversation, that teachers describe their own immediate experiences in their own language, was consistent with our aims and likely to be comfortable for teachers. However, we were hesitant to use this method because of time constraints. We felt we had insufficient time to build the relationship with teachers that would permit authentic dialogue, to share individually unique research experiences among three researchers, and to build accounts of these experiences that could combine to enhance our understanding of the ground of practice. Moreover, our intended future use of the method was likely to be similarly constrained by lack of time.

With multiple researchers and a desire for efficiency in our method, we sought more precise discussion guidelines in the methodological literature of ethnography. The fit with our intentions was not perfect. Ethnography seeks a generalised understanding of the shared beliefs by which members of a culture structure their reality. Although in contrast we were interested in individual teachers' beliefs and intentions, we found the form of questions suggested for ethnographic interviews (Spradley, 1979) helpful.

Research Procedures

The plan which resulted from melding these three methodological traditions called for three open-ended conversational interviews interspersed with classroom observations and collaborative exercises in data interpretation. As might be expected, this plan was modified soon after data collection began. Beginning with teachers' narration of the day's events in their classrooms,[5] and aiming to end up with a shared understanding of how they construed the key elements of classroom life, we expected to go through at least five intermediate steps: (1) rudimentary analysis of the narrations for key questions to ask teachers in subsequent conversations, (2) observation of teachers in their classrooms to augment teachers' verbal descriptions, (3) teacher analysis of their own practice in our presence using a grid-type exercise, (4) further interpretation to develop organised accounts of actions and beliefs which fit each teacher's practice, and (5) presentation of results to teachers for modification, clarification and extension.

The methodology that evolved in the course of 16 weeks of data gathering was both simpler and more fruitful than we had anticipated. In the initial interview, the length and detail of teachers' responses to the opening grand tour question (Spradley, 1979) requesting a narration of the teaching day, greatly surpassed our expectations, making most of the planned probe questions and the second probing interview unnecessary for this preliminary study. To our pleasant surprise, each of the researcher/teacher pairs felt sufficiently comfortable to engage each other in authentic dialogue that developed a spirit of its own. Transcripts of these first conversations contained such rich descriptions and such an abundance of teachers' own interpretations of their practice that we were able to take on ourselves the task of identifying the structure of practice implicit in teachers' accounts. Accordingly, the purpose of observational field notes shifted from gathering additional descriptive data to corroborating, refining and extending our analyses: and the intermediate interview was dispensed with, making the validating interview the second and final one.

Participants

Three researchers worked with eight experienced (more than five years) elementary teachers, half of whom had undertaken graduate work in Curriculum Studies and were known personally by us to be confident professionals, verbally fluent, and receptive though not accustomed to reflecting on their practice. We chose these kinds of people to see what our method might yield under ideal circumstances. The other four participants, who had not done any graduate work, were unknown to us and presented a more challenging test of the efficacy of our method. We talked with each of the eight teachers and observed two of the graduate teachers and two of the baccalaureate teachers.

Revealing Ground

Identifying the constructs implicit in teachers' practice required that we move backwards, so to speak, from literal descriptions of everyday activities, to teachers' interpretations of why they did what they did, and then to an understanding of how these activities were structured in terms of teachers' beliefs and intentions. By taking advantage of the economy of form offered by constructs, we hoped to be able to represent teachers' beliefs and intentions in a way that made their connection with actions clear. As we understood constructs, they should be expressed in the form of adjectival phrases denoting qualities attributed to or desired for important elements in teachers' practice.

Themes and Categories

Our initial analysis of the transcribed descriptions of a classroom day yielded long and unrelated lists of items and themes, such as learner self-direction, diagnostic use of data, marking, and use of peer learning arrangements. Unable to categorise these under our anticipated element headings of actors, events, objects (Kelly, 1955), time and space (Dobbert, 1982), we sought some alternative organising scheme. We eventually decided to use as macro-organisers the often-encountered commonplace categories of curriculum (Schwab, 1973), which had been used successfully for a similar purpose in an earlier study (Oberg, 1987). These were *Learners, Learning, Teacher Role, Teaching, Subject Matter* and *Schooling.*

Although these were not sufficiently specific to function as the elements (persons, objects, things) construed according to construct theory, they subsumed what construct theorists call elements, for example, individual learners, separate subjects, teaching techniques, materials, the school as an institution, and so on.

Next, we required a language in which to express what we understood about teachers' interpretations of learners, learning, and so on. Other studies of educators' constructs had used descriptive phrases that were unidimensional, for example, talkative, high motivation (Ritchie, 1982), or bipolar, for example convergent/divergent, expository/inquiry (Ben-Peretz, Katz and Silberstein, 1982). Our data were ripe with similar phrases, most unidimensional, and so we undertook to translate our themes into constructs of similar form. In the data from Gerry, one of the teachers participating in our study, the theme 'learner self-direction' became the two constructs 'self-directed/requiring direction' and 'capable of being self-directed'. These fell under the heading *Learners.* Under *Learning,* the same theme yielded the construct 'requiring self-direction and good work habits'. Similarly, what had at first been identified as the theme, 'use of peer learning arrangements', became the construct, 'learning as facilitated by learner–learner interaction' (see Table 6.1, left column).

Reworking the data in this manner paid handsome rewards. Reformulating themes into constructs, we could see all the elements of ground shown in Table 6.1. For example, Gerry's sample constructs indicate that he saw learners as varying in the degree of self-direction they exhibited (a belief about reality with respect to learners), but capable of becoming more self-directed (another reality judgement about learners, in which is implicit an intention to foster more self-direction). He believed that successful learning required that learners develop self-direction and good work habits and that learners could help each other to do this (linking beliefs).

Linking Constructs and Actions

Gerry's beliefs and intentions captured in the few phrases noted above made a large portion of his practice intelligible both to him and to us. They made clear why he

Table 6.1. The structure of action: Gerry

Constructs	Principles of practice	Examples from practice
LEARNERS AS: Self-directed or requiring attention	Let self-directed learners work independently and monitor those requiring direction	Six children who 'continue to pass at the 80 percentile level... require ten minutes instruction and two minutes monitoring compared to 20 minutes instruction over four days and half an hour monitoring of the other group'
	Form temporary groups so as to ensure a more independent learner in each group	For proof-reading stories, separated children into high, medium, low and then formed groups with one member from each category
Able to take responsibility for each other's learning	Arrange for top students to monitor slower peers	'I use some of my fast readers who finish the work to provide oral reading experience with the slower children. As time will allow, I use the fast group as monitors for correcting procedures'
Capable of being self-directive	Allow self-directed learners to structure their own activities	D made his own video A child convinced teacher he could read a whole book by picking out certain sections
LEARNING AS: Facilitated by learner–learner interaction	Provide for peer learning arrangements	Library assignments, social studies stations, proof-reading in language all happen in groups 'when there is interaction, I really want to see them interacting...' Suggested one child help another organise her notebook
Requiring self-direction and good work habits	Monitor closely children who cannot work independently; let those who can, work on their own	'If you were in that (fast) group you were there because you can function independently'
	Give less capable learners a chance to try learning on their own	'...those students who require... repetitive correcting... drift in excess of the average... if the atmosphere remains... a little bit laid back,... I'm hoping that... eventually their talking will transform into something written'

TEACHER AS:		
Monitor of learning	Monitor learners' work, especially work of those who lack self-direction	Constantly checking on individual children; has list of those whose work is to be collected; names of those not finished on the board to be removed when finished; helped oral reading group from wherever teacher was in the room whenever there was a pause or mispronunciation
Orchestrator of learner interactions	Arrange for different forms of learner–learner and learner–teacher interaction depending on nature of learning intended and maturity of learners	Reading skills must be mastered individually; 'spelling is an individual task'; in social studies stations, 'they are encouraged to exchange. If someone discovers the answer, they are to exchange, provide each other with peer guidance'

The teacher plays his role like a restrained symphony conductor. He is there to direct the performance of his students.... The teacher's goal is to help each student learn as much as possible, and in order to do that, they must become proficient performers in the classroom.... Some students are good enough to be solo performers, while some will always require the security and direction of a group under a conductor. The good students are allowed to work independently, in a group or individually, with occasional monitoring by the teacher. The others require more teacher supervision... all of these various arrangements are orchestrated by the teacher.

grouped learners for library assignments, social studies stations, and proof-reading activities in language arts, and at other times let some children work alone. They accounted for the constant task-oriented talk among learners and learners' feelings of personal responsibility for the quality of their work. They made intelligible variations in the pace and intensity of instruction and in the supervision of learners' activities. They made it easy to understand why Gerry gave privileges only to some learners and why he controlled his class with rules and expectations rather than with verbal directions. All of these actions made sense in light of Gerry's understanding of each learner's capacity for self-direction, his belief in the efficacy of peer learning arrangements, and his desire to increase learners' self-direction as much as possible.

Constructs not only made intelligible specific actions, but they also enabled us to discern patterns in the actions that constituted teachers' everyday teaching practice. For example, Gerry arranged to permit self-directed learners to work independently and to structure their own activities while always ensuring less independent learners were closely monitored. Often he used peer-monitoring arrangements. He also used peer-learning arrangements. Phrased in the imperative, these practices sound like 'practical principles' that Gerry adhered to in his work: Let self-directed learners work independently and monitor those requiring direction; arrange for top students to monitor slower peers; allow self-directed learners to structure their own activities, provide for peer-learning activities; and so on (see Table 6.1, middle column). We called these 'principles of practice' as had Elbaz (1983), although as soon will be evident, we might also have used Halkes and Deyker's (1984) term, 'teaching criteria'. They described the ways Gerry generally expressed his beliefs and intentions (constructs) in action.

Good Practice

We sought principles of practice in our data because of our concern about teachers becoming better educators. Teachers cannot know whether they are contributing to the educational good of learners unless they stop to reflect on their practice. What is revealed in the act of reflection is the beliefs and intentions implicit in practice. Practice is judged against these criteria. More accurately, the basic moral principles implied by beliefs and intentions are the criteria for judging practice (Simpson and Jackson, 1984) along with public and professional norms (Buchmann, 1984). The principles of practice we identified in our data were early forerunners of teachers' moral principles or theories of the educational good, which defined the essence of their teaching practice.

The Tone of Teaching

Table 6.1 shows some of what Gerry and we together came to understand about his practice through reflection and analysis. Columns one and two of the table are sets of interpretations two or more steps removed from the practical activity in which they were expressed. Only snippets from Gerry's actual daily practice are recorded in column three to show where the interpretive task was begun. Missing is a sense of what Gerry' s practice felt like, its pace, tone and character. The three-column format of the chart fails to communicate Gerry's way of being as a teacher. In a somewhat meagre effort to remedy this shortcoming, we composed a few short paragraphs to illustrate what each teacher's practice was like. Where possible we constructed the paragraphs around a unifying metaphor. Some excerpts describing Gerry's practice are included beneath the charts in Table 6.1.

Teachers' Reactions

We may have been too heavily influenced by our preconceptions that teachers would be disinterested in anything other than the most economical display of the ground of their practice. When we handed them back the charts and paragraphs we had prepared, they pored over them avidly, partly to answer our questions about accuracy and completeness, but mostly out of the keen interest human beings have in any reflections of themselves. As in the first conversation, our carefully pre-planned questions were pushed into the background as conversations that are more natural developed. We had approached the teachers to hear their reactions to what we had written with some trepidation, wondering what they would think of these rather sterile encapsulations of the welter of beliefs, frustrations, joys, failures and accomplishments that made up their own professional lives and the school lives of their students. Would they see anything of themselves in our written interpretations? We were relieved to find our fears unfounded. The teachers reacted to our accounts with surprise and appreciation. They were surprised at the amount we had gleaned from our brief conversations and observations, and they appreciated seeing laid before them aspects of their own practice to which no one had ever given voice. Gerry's comment was revealing: 'The whole document was something I never had to say out loud before and had never seen in print before... the fact that it is written down instead of just spoken about, that in itself is a very commanding thing'.

As became evident in later analysis (Oberg and McElroy, 1987), reflecting with us on their practice to identify the beliefs and intentions in which it was grounded was a significant revelatory experience for all of the teachers. As was to be expected, teachers were convinced that both practice and ground were affected by the experience. Teachers felt differently, thought differently and acted differently in their professional practice after examining its ground. In most cases, they and we suspected that 'differently' meant more educationally, but confirmation of this suspicion awaits the next stage of this study.

Conclusion

The teachers' evaluation of the charts and paragraphs we prepared suggested that our data did represent significant aspects of the ground of practice we sought. They encompassed the teachers' idea of the good, beliefs about what is, and what is not possible in the education of their learners, and beliefs about how to achieve that. They showed the link between teachers' beliefs and actions. They attempted to capture some of the tone that was part of each teacher's practice. They were at least a beginning in all these respects.

The methods we finally settled upon were more fruitful than we had expected. Researchers and teachers both were surprised at the depth of understanding achieved in the first conversation. The observations added to this understanding, but whether or not they were essential is unclear. They certainly permitted the researchers to develop an intuitive grasp of teachers' ways of being with learners that was missing from the interviews alone.

It is important to note that we make no claim to have captured all of the ground of practice. We knowingly neglected the social and organisational context of schooling, the politics of teaching, and the autobiographical and historical influences on teachers' perspectives. What we portrayed, however, matched remarkably well with teachers' understandings of their practice. We were seeking to understand both the explicit and the implicit in practice, much of which in the beginning was unclear to both teachers and researchers. In order for us to come to understand the ground of practice, teachers themselves had to come to understand it. Ultimately, we hope to create conditions under which teachers on their own can develop reflective understanding of the ground of their practice.

Notes

1.   The contributions of Cynthia Chambers and Roger Field, graduate students and co-researchers with me in this study, are gratefully acknowledged. The first person plural pronoun used throughout this paper refers to the three members of the research team.

2.   Following MacIntyre (1981), we defined educational practice as a complex set of interrelated activities directed toward the attainment of the educational good. The concept of the 'educational good' is an abstract idea that takes shape only when acted upon (Grundy, 1982). To have an idea of the educational good is to be predisposed to seek out or attend to those things in the present situation that are in the educational interests of learners. The educational good is not a set of predictable outcomes, but rather the upshot of acting in ways that are consistent with one's educational ideals.

3.   There are varying formulations of how people act on their beliefs and intentions. In theories of action, the nature of the link between thought and action is instrumental and somewhat problematic. It is seen as a logical connection, alternately explained as causation, volition, or meaning derived from fit with context (Davis, 1979). We believed the move from thought to action could entail logical reasoning *or* a deeper form of understanding that is expression of teachers' being-in-the-world. Teacher action is purposeful, though its proximity to goals varies. Teachers may intend that they or learners achieve a task that has a particular predefined behavioural result, for example, to close the door or to pronounce some words correctly. Often, such immediate goals are part of a longer-term intention such as creating a comfortable learning environment or developing language competence. Intentions such as these, which aim at states or capacities, do not have behavioural signs of achievement that can be predetermined. What counts as their accomplishment depends on the circumstances and cannot be known until after the fact (see Daniels, 1975). Determining what to do to contribute to such goals requires a disposition to further the educational good of learners and the ability to discern learners' experience of the situation and what is the right or educative thing to do at any given time for any given child. These capacities have been called pedagogical tact (van Manen, 1984) or pedagogical wisdom (for example, Oberg and Field, 1987).

4.   This is not to say that a construct is necessarily bipolar, only that an assertion of the way a thing or person is implies a negation of the way the thing

or person is not, within a particular context (Bannister and Fransella, 1971, pp. 24–25). Generally, we defined only one pole of a construct.

5.   We prompted teachers to consider their teaching simply by asking them, 'What did you do today?' Questioning what has formerly been unproblematic begins the interpretive process that eventually reveals the practical understanding that operates in everyday unreflective practice.

Author Reflection 2004

Since the original publication of the article in this collection, I have ceased using the languages of both psychology and phenomenology, which were then dominant discourses in the study of teacher thinking, and have been seeking to use language in a way suited to what the radical hermeneutic philosopher John D. Caputo calls 'radical thinking', thinking that resists the desire for definitive answers and instead stays open to the question of how to live in relationships respectfully.

When I began to study teacher thinking, as described in this chapter, I was interested in understanding teachers who were able to make ordinary classrooms into places where extraordinary transformations were commonplace. Intent on dissecting the complexities of such teaching, I worked out a conceptualisation of what I called 'the ground of teaching practice' using terms like *beliefs*, *intentions* and *judgements*, and the methodology of construct theory. While researchers continuing in this vein developed ever more detailed and precise ways of studying teaching and learning, my own work reached a bifurcation point at which I adopted a classical holistic systems view of learning environments. I came to view teaching and learning as a dynamic set of co-productive relationships. In other words, I came to view learning environments as places where the interactions of teacher and student transformed both. I was strongly influenced by the particular kind of learning environments where I spent the majority of my teaching time, namely, graduate student inquiry courses. Here was a ready-made laboratory where students took up often-intractable questions about what really mattered to them both personally and professionally, and subsequently observed continuous transformations in the ways they lived their lives. Guiding and witnessing students' inquiries and simultaneously immersed in my own, I too noticed continuous changes in my style of living and teaching. Using the languages of chaos and complexity theory, interpersonal ethics, and Maturana and Varela's cognitive epistemology, in my recent work I articulate my own experience, alongside graduate student co-inquirers, of such autopoietic transformations.

Chapter 7

Case Study in Research on Teaching
A ground for reflective practice

John Olson

Introduction

It is now common to hear people speak about the 'reflective practitioner'; equally, it is common to hear people refer to the 'practical knowledge' of the teacher.

These ways of talking about teachers are set in opposition to the idea that practice ought to be a form of applied 'science'; that is practice should be regulated not by reflection but by scientific enquiry, and by a concept in which ends are settled and means selected on the basis of assured knowledge.

So the lines are drawn: technological rationality versus reflective practice and theoretical versus practical knowledge. We are called to rally to either side and so express our faith in experience, or our faith in research.

I think, now, that these lines are too firmly drawn. Of course, we ought to be suspicious of principles of teaching derived from a limited understanding of what is happening in classrooms. Often these researches are really evaluations of practice (which teachers usually fail) based on what research says about how teachers 'ought' to practice, but of course, we ought to recognise the limits of reflection and personal experience. In the former case we cannot do without the insight of the insider, in the latter we cannot do without the perspective of the outsider. Commandments for practice as tablets from the scientific gods seem absurd, but so does practice eternally bounded by the limits of personal reflection. How can we escape from this fractured perspective? With this question in mind, I want to re-consider the special value case study has for the study of teaching. As Shulman (1986a) has pointed out recently, case studies are ways of knowing things. They include all the detail that helps us understand what is going on, but they are also cases of *something*. That something can be seen from the perspective of social science in order to understand what is recurring and why it recurs. That something can be seen against a background of what ought to occur: a moral framework. Thus, a case has a rich potential to help us understand, explain and do better. It is not for nothing that the study of cases has been so widespread in the social practices of history, of economics, business, law and now education.

Not everyone would say that cases could do the work claimed for them. Not everyone is satisfied that doing case studies is a 'respectable' form of educational research. Not everyone thinks that claims based on case study can be trusted; for how can the truth be warranted without some step-by-step method?

Given the significant potential, and the many doubts that exist about the scientific status of case studies, I think it is worth considering in some detail how a study of cases can contribute to improved practice. In the first part of the chapter, I draw on work from the philosophy of history to illuminate certain epistemological and methodological issues to do with cases, and in the second part I illustrate how case study can be useful in the improvement of teaching.

Positive Values of Case Study in Educational Research

The rationale for case history is often given as a reaction against the reduction of complex episodes to quantifiable variables; or against behaviourist assumptions of research; or against the formalism of research designs. Here I would like to reconsider *positive* reasons for conducting case study, and to discuss a number of methodological issues related to the study of teaching that I believe deserve attention.

What are the positive contributions case researchers might make to understand educational problems? First, it should be said, there is a substantial body of scholarship in this area, especially in history, that is germane to educational problems. The texts I propose to draw on (the historian Collingwood (1946) and his student Dray (1957)) are examples taken from this literature.

Case study rescues teachers' actions from being reduced to an unwanted determinism without having to give up the possibility of general knowledge. For as we shall see later, cases can be used for making general statements about teachers and teaching.

Case study is less liable to the pitfall of presenting normative assessments based on 'implications' of research as if they were descriptions of teacher behaviour, since cases start with what the teacher is trying to do, not with what the teacher might be construed as doing in order to be able to subsume behaviour under scientific laws. By starting with what the teacher is trying to accomplish one is forced to attend to behaviour that the teacher considers important, rather than to behaviour to which the theoretical framework points. In short, the case approach demands that one recognises the larger context of the teacher's behaviour, rather than isolate elements of it so that a causal law can be made to apply. This in itself provides a remedy for a major problem in educational research, which is the reduction of the richness of the classroom to simpler terms in order to explain behaviour. Teachers who read educational research often complain that they cannot recognise their purposes and actions in the accounts of their work. Teacher educators cannot draw easily upon these accounts to help them work with people whose situations are resistant to simplification and reduction. Case study, on the other hand, helps one understand oneself, and because of this, it is a significant basis for reflective practice.

Validity and Generality in Case Writing

With these positive values of case study in mind, let us turn to two methodological questions that deserve further attention: they are validity and generality.

What makes a study about teaching significant? Which is another way of saying: What makes it valid? First, we need to keep in mind that research in education is conducted within a critical, constructive perspective given by an educational framework. This framework controls the direction of research in a much looser way than does commitment to social/psychological theories, but it controls nonetheless. It is against this framework that the validity of the cases chosen for study can be assessed. Second, the way that the problem is posed must also share some organic connection to the work of the people being written about. This is a significant issue for case study.

Let me give a personal example. I am interested in how teachers use microcomputers in their classrooms and am looking at their behaviour in connection with certain problems to do with the process of innovation. There is a connection between what they are doing and what I want to learn about, but what they are doing is important to them and to their school board. They are the first group of teachers in that school system to explore in a systematic way how to use microcomputers.

What makes *these* cases valid? It is that they deal with problems that teachers consider significant. They treat matters that emerge from experience and are brought into focus against a background of teacher purpose. It is the relationship of the cases to those purposes that makes them valid.

Even if we have chosen educationally significant cases, what is to say our interpretation of them is justified? This is yet another way of raising questions about validity. Dray (1957) provides useful advice in his discussion of this issue. We have already considered the matter of significance (what he calls the *pragmatic* test of validity). He suggests that another test be applied to our cases as a way of further assessing their validity.

The reason for the behaviour must be something under human control; so that either something done or undone could matter in the kind of case being written. There is an essential link between assigning responsibility to agents and attributing casual status. Dray (1957) says that 'Unless we are prepared to hold the agent responsible for what happened, we cannot say his action was a cause'. This test is called the *inductive* test of validity; it assures us that there is some justification for singling out the reasons we have.

Beyond the issue of validity, there is a matter of the generality of the case findings. Dray (1957) notes, for example, that in many case studies of accidents excessive speed has been implicated as a cause. Although excessive speed cannot be predicted to be a cause in advance based on covering laws, it is a likely potential cause of an accident. Given the frequency with which excessive speed is a factor in accidents we can generalise about the place of excessive speed in accidents. It is on this kind of basis that we can accumulate knowledge through case study.

How might we apply this idea to cases involving teaching? Again, I would like to use a personal example. Having talked to some twenty teachers about their work at considerable length as part of a number of research projects (Olson, 1981, 1982, 1986), I find that in order to understand the way these teachers have construed the relationship between teaching and the curriculum, I have had to look at the 'expressive' dimension (Harre, 1982) of their behaviour; that is, at what they are saying about themselves as teachers through their teaching behaviour. Argyris and Schon (1974) call these purposes 'governing variables', and it is particularly those affective dimensions of teaching such as control of anxiety, self-esteem, and other aspects of the presentation of self that seem very much at issue in understanding especially the fate of innovations in classrooms. We have found, for example, that teachers are concerned with being 'modern', with being effective guides to the 'system', with being good at selecting and 'editing' material which will be externally examined, with being quick to unravel classroom problems, with being 'on track', and so on.

However, what hinges on this sort of general knowledge about teaching? In the next section, I argue that such knowledge can be the basis for a more effective practice. Normally research on teaching focuses on instrumental matters: gain scores; teacher and student attributes of one kind or another; or personality measures. However, I want to claim that certain kinds of expressive purposes are heavily implicated in understanding how teachers enact the curriculum and how they affect their students. We cannot predict teacher behaviour based on our understanding of these expressive issues in teaching, but we now know to look for them when writing our cases in order to understand what causes it.

Case Study and the Improvement of Teaching: The Ground for Effective Action-Research

How can case studies contribute to the improvement of teaching? Shulman (1986b) suggests that the interpretation of cases become an important part of the education of teachers so that they might learn how to make judgements in the face of complex and incomplete information, and in the light of conflicting principles. It is the same education that Schon (1983) would have for practitioners in other professions. What is it about the interpretation of cases that yields such potential? In teaching we are not at all sure how it can be improved, yet prescriptions for action derived from knowledge gained under very highly simplified assumptions about human action and context are used to govern highly complex and ambiguous situations. How would a study of cases be an improvement?

Without knowledge of past practice in particular cases, we have no way of understanding what might happen in the future if people were to try to change their teaching approach. Cases tell us about why people do what they do and why they persist in doing it. Collingwood (1946) characterised case study as a way of 'knowing ourselves'. As we become the subject of case study, an opportunity for self-knowledge is created through the critical interpretation of our actions by another and through that to critical self-interpretation to autobiography.

Such a practice lies at the heart of Argyris and Schon's (1974) approach to professional self-education, for example. Their method asks individuals to subject experience to causal analysis to find out why they do what they do. Based on many cases of professional behaviours, Argyris and Schon have concluded that much of professional behaviour is systematically sealed off from critical appraisal. The status of this claim, by the way, is no different from Dray's 'speed kills' or my look for the expressive aspects of teaching when explaining the fate of innovations.

How do case studies contribute to opening up behaviour for critical study? The case study of one's own practice is subject to one's own critical analysis as well as that of the researcher. Researchers are contemporaries and share an understanding of the events at hand that are given significance in terms of the setting. The relevant features of this setting and its boundaries are open for discussion. Neither teacher nor researcher alone can isolate episodes for case study because each is conditioned and shaped by some significant problem of his/her own that depends on what educational issues are taken to be important.

Considerable attention needs to be given to the way problems are identified. In historical case studies, no one is present to comment on how the important issues are defined: one doesn't care because one isn't there; but teachers are there and they do care because they have a stake in the way cases are written about them. The cases are being written for purposes in which they share, and thus researchers have a special task in defining the research problem; because a judgement presupposes certain values that researchers and teachers hold about what is educationally important.

The point is that the past is recent and the testimony is live and our critical interpretation of that testimony has special features; we can talk to the person whose case we are considering. This gives our contemporary case studies an additional resource, because we researchers can probe the testimony directly and we can control how the testimony is obtained; we can ask for comments on it and we can get behind it. Our enquiries are not limited to considering the behaviour of teachers in terms of their purposes, but they cannot avoid those purposes. I take this to be the lesson that Shulman (1986b) draws from Collingwood's (1946) discussion of causes in historical research.

There is yet a further educational potential of case study as action research. Teachers do things for reasons of which they are not always aware. They are subject to social pressures and constraining forces with which they cope, but on a relatively unconscious basis. It is here that cases become subject to analysis in terms of social forces and unconscious causes, but not to the extent of saying that the teacher has no part in his/her behaviour; only that the behaviour is relatively less controlled by conscious processes and relatively difficult to construe. Having made every effort to understand the teacher's behaviour in terms of purposes, we might want to consider the forces that shape the context in which teachers act.

As researchers we are interested in why people really did what they did, but they may not know very well why they did what they did; sometimes what they did seems not to be in their interest. What are we to make of this? In this regard, Theodore Mischel's (1964) analysis of the logic of clinical activity is helpful. He suggests that the researchers try to construe relatively unconscious motives, as reasons for action as a basis for making apparently odd behaviour seem less odd. In terms of these odd intentions the researcher can construct a 'calculation' which shows that seen from the person's point of view, apparently odd behaviour would seem justified; would seem the right or appropriate thing to do; and the person can at least ideally be helped to see that he/she has really been operating in terms of a rationale whose nature is hidden. In other words, we should do everything possible to see how behaviour might make sense from the agent's point of view even though the agent is relatively unconscious of it. Difficult-to-understand actions can be understood in the same way as more easily understandable actions. This is a critical point to consider when writing case studies. Of course, there are limits to this. Let me illustrate this point by again citing a personal example.

To return to the example I gave earlier of the teachers using computers in their classroom, we found in most of the eight cases that well-tried classroom routines did not work well, yet teachers professed satisfaction with them. At first, we could not understand their satisfaction. We found it odd that they were satisfied with what looked to us to be a flawed teaching strategy. With probing, we found that the teachers saw that students enjoyed the new subject in spite of the difficulties of the classroom routines they had adopted, and the teachers felt that the difficulties were worth enduring because they enjoyed the children's pleasure at having a computer in their room. We think that the teachers construed their own work with the computer as a way of being 'modern', of expressing something about the kind of teacher they are. This purpose seemed to overrule the concern about classroom routines that did not work at all well so that teachers could claim that their students *were* becoming literate. Seen this way, one has to wonder what the teachers meant by literate, and so the process would continue.

Our understanding of the way teachers construed the impact of computers in their classroom is that they value the computer as a symbol to be used *expressively* (Harre, 1982) by them to enhance their standing in the eyes of the students, parents and principal. The *instrumental* outcomes – gain in understanding and skill – could be ignored for the time being since they were not immediately part of the expressive process. In the end, of course, expressive and instrumental purposes are linked, and as teachers work their way through the expressive dimensions of their task, it is likely that instrumental issues will receive more attention. How quickly the process occurs and how it might be facilitated are important further questions for research and policy in the field of innovation and teacher education.

I do not want to suggest here that often teachers do odd things; only that at times we may not understand their behaviour, and that teachers may not be aware immediately of the reasons why they act as they do, or not aware of all of the reasons. Thus examining their behaviour is a complex process of reconstructing as fully as possible their real reasons for doing what they are doing – of rendering their behaviour as intelligible. Thus, their cases become a basis for critical reflection as they and we engage in an evaluation of them. What looked to us as 'odd' behaviour became understandable in the light of the purposes of the teachers we believe we have uncovered. Of course, the further question remains: Are these purposes justifiable? That is yet another issue to which an examination of cases gives rise. Another question also remains: What if a calculation for the teacher's behaviour cannot be rendered? Here we have to look for causes beyond the reasons of the teacher, and we enter the domain of pathology.

What these teachers did is an outcome of a complex set of purposes that give causes (reasons) for their actions without their constantly considering them. In fact, our analysis of their action does not depend on saying anything about the psychological processes that may have gone on; we simply need to look at the causes (reasons) that can be used to explain what went on from the evidence we have. We try to give a coherent account as far as we can. Nor should we assume that the explanatory calculation we create must have been recited by the teachers in propositional form either aloud or silently. Not all high-grade actions are performed deliberately in the sense that they are undertaken with a plan consciously formulated (Polanyi, 1958; Ryle, 1949). Whatever the level of conscious deliberation, there is a calculation that can be constructed for it and it is by producing some such calculation that we explain the action. Of course, nothing stops us from asking how it is, for example, that certain kinds of causes recur; nor from asking whether or not they ought to occur.

Conclusion

If the teacher is to understand his/her own actions after the event, he/she may have to do so by constructing a calculation, although at the time of the action no propositions were consciously recited. Nonetheless, not any reconstruction will do. As Dray (1957) says, 'When we do consider ourselves justified in accepting an explanation of an individual action it will most often assume the general form of an agent's calculation'.

We are not going to be especially satisfied with a calculation that the teacher does not recognise, and the researcher must probe behind the initial construction of events to see if there are any motives that have not been articulated. Since the subject of our case is alive, we can do that. Dray (1957) points out that we may have to accept some odd principles of action, and we may not agree with these and yet be able to see the rationale from the agent's point of view.

Now this account of research differs considerably from common approaches to research on teaching that stress information processing theory. One suspects that some of that research involves applying assumptions about how norms derived from information theory 'ought' to operate to control action. The disguised norm appears to be this. Teachers ought to plan their actions by making use of certain available information and they should process that information systematically, and act on the answers the processing yields moment by moment; and thus they act rationally. It appears that research which begins as an *explanation* of teacher behaviour can easily end up by being an *evaluation* of it in relation to certain rational and mechanical norms of a model prescribing what information teachers ought to think about and how their minds ought to process that information. It is not surprising that teachers have failed to live up to these norms.

It is also a mistake to concentrate only on what teachers *say* about what they are doing. Just as loudly do their *actions* speak about what they are doing, and it is often the case that what people espouse concerning action and what they 'say' in action are different (Argyris and Schon, 1974). In the end we are interested in how teachers teach, that is in how they act in their classrooms, and in understanding why they act this way. However, this does not mean that we are not interested in how teachers talk about what they do.

Accumulating views that people have about their work helps us appreciate the range of perspectives they bring to that work; yet one doesn't only want to know *what* people think, one wants also to understand *why* they approach problems in the way they do. We want to explain their behaviour in classrooms. As a student of teaching, one's puzzle is that teachers do not seem to solve problems according to official norms; or even as they say *they* would act. Indeed, there seems to exist a wide variety of ideas among teachers about how these problems can be solved, but these ideas are expressed or not expressed in practice itself; that is the key point.

What might one do about this apparent diversity of approaches? I would suggest that each teacher become a problem of biography. Why did this or that teacher solve this or that problem as he/she did? To understand that, we have to understand how the teacher solved the problem, and once we can work the teacher's calculation metaphorically and literally we can understand why the teacher tried to solve it in such a way. We have to engage in a biography of that teacher, and having done that, there may be common features in the accounts that teachers give of their approach to these problems from which we can generalise, and features of their thinking which might alert us to look for this or that element in the beginning phase of our subsequent biographical studies.

From the kind of studies we have been discussing can come a body of general knowledge which can be shared; which can become the basis of an increasingly sophisticated awareness on the part of *researchers* of what to look for in their study of teachers, on the part of *policy makers* as they commission and interpret research; and, most importantly, on the part of the *teacher* as he/she engages with these others in considering practice. This is the hope for a 'new order' of research into teaching.

Author Reflection 2004

This chapter was written at a time when research on teachers was moving from the behaviourist paradigm to the cognitive one: indeed, concern about such a transition was much in evidence in keynote addresses at the ISATT Leuven conference. Quite outside those concerns was Philip Jackson's analysis of a poem about teaching: what the poem said about the moral universe in which teachers work. As it happened, the present chapter addressed such concerns as well. One theme of the chapter is that if we want to understand why teachers act as they do we ought to consult their purposes as they arise in particular settings. Those purposes, as they and we come to understand them, allow researcher and teacher to see what the framework is that informs and directs those actions, including the moral grounds of the action. Those frameworks can be traced back to traditions of teacher practice. Case study brings those frameworks into view and such traditions, as Charles Taylor reminds us, have moral force but are not immune from change and improvement.

Case study provides for these possibilities by creating a relatively sharp focus on some process of teaching and directing enquiry to understanding that process. In my own case, the interest was in how teachers cope with innovation. This led me into the world of teacher hopes and fears about change and ultimately into what teachers thought was worth doing and what the risks were. Behind what teachers told me about adapting to change was a tension between wanting to change and be successful, and protecting zones of security provided by well-tried routines: routines often derided in the literature. This tension, I concluded, explained much about what the teachers said and did. This advocacy of case study I see more clearly now was a reaction against a number of trends in research. Teachers were said to resist change and lack an adequate scientific basis for their work. The bureaucrats said they were resistant and the social scientists said there were naïve. Both in effect denied any claims teachers might have to being professionals. My research convinced me that both sets of critics were wrong. Teachers' work was far more sophisticated than the critics knew, and what the critics wanted the teachers to do was often regressive. Subsequently I came to see that evaluative nostrums based on cognitive science were masquerading as descriptions of what teachers did: the *expert* teacher (Olson, 1992).

The bureaucrats had pragmatic, political concerns; the scientists simply thought they knew the answer to achieving the outcomes desired by the bureaucrats: train teachers to act and think correctly according to the theory, and later perhaps reflect on the thoughts which at least introduced a pause to put the action into some kind of context. That context increasingly is the professional framework of teaching and its traditions that provide sources for explanation and justification. This sophistication is thanks to a much-increased exploration by researchers of the moral universe of the teacher. ISATT has been instrumental in this process of exploration. Case study has played a role.

Chapter 8

Teachers' Personal and Professional Ideals about Practice

Michael Kompf and Alan F. Brown

Summary

This chapter reports on a form of teacher thinking that bears directly on professional action: their personal ideals about practice. We attempt to set out the process and structure of ideals held by six schoolteachers. The ideals are limited to those that are both personal and professional and were elicited from the teachers with a reptest adaptation. Initial interviews were conducted to discover general and more abstract ideals that prompted the choice of teaching as a career. Responses were considered by examining perceived change in the status of ideals over ensuing years of practice. The reptest, by creating a superordinate dichotomy of ideal/least-ideal gave participants an opportunity to construct, for further discussion, their representations of significant others comprising their professional environment. Representations of ideals-in-abstract (initial interview results) and ideals-in-use (operational constructs from reptests) were synthesized in a final interview through guided structured reflection brought out in researcher–participant discussion.

Background

William James (1890) and John Dewey (1963) defined and discussed their notions about the origins and dynamics of individuals' ideals. James felt that ideal conceptions came about through perceived incongruities between internal and external realities, thus allowing individuals to envision a preferred state of affairs representing for them a sense of true order. Dewey (1939) extended this line of thinking by differentiating between the desired and the desirable. Desires arise from raw impulse and are mediated by foresight and the communicated experience of significant others. The ends-in-view that are formed because of a mediating process constitute an effective-ideational activity, i.e. a union of prizing and appraising. Competing desires and interests draw the distinction between the desired and the desirable by contrasting the:

> object of desire as it first presents itself… and the object of desire
> which emerges as a revision of the first appearing impulse, after the

latter is critically judged in reference to the conditions which will decide the actual results. (Dewey, 1939, pp. 32–33).

This reflection acts in concert with Dewey's recurrent theme of the educational process acting for teacher and taught as an end in itself rather than as a means to an end. Dewey's larger view of education and learning saw them as opportunities and possibilities leading to something better.

Kelly (1955) extends the ideas of Dewey and James through his position of person-as-scientist. By examining the generation and testing of hypotheses about events, much of Personal Construct Psychology (PCP) may be used to account for the origin, posting and testing of ideal conceptions as defined and discussed by Dewey and James. Further to this, the characteristics of superordinate constructs (permeability, consistency, organisation and integration) provide an adequate framework for the discussion of the conceptual and research implications of an ideal/least-ideal construct subsystem.

Ideal/Least-Ideal as a Superordinate Construct for Teachers

Our adaptation of Kelly's role construct repertory test has the usual construct poles. The construct or emergent pole (ideal) indicates a system with elements represented by a conjunction of ideals about educational practice that are both personal and professional. The contrast pole (least ideal) similarly represented elements that were personally and professionally least-ideal, resulting in a construct–contrast dimension of: personal, professional ideals / not personal, not professional ideals (PPI / not PPI).

For a notion about the practice of education to be considered as ideal, it must represent a desirable state of affairs that emerges as a result of a felt incongruence between inner, preferred situations and an external situation that is perceived as less desirable, and possibly restrictive, indicating a striving towards true order or perfection as James or Dewey thought. Idealising contains elements of hopefulness and optimism providing directions for anticipation of things that are better or more desirable. The juxtaposition of internal and external perceptions of reality may bring about value-based choices or preferences, i.e. what ought to be, underpinning the personal and the ideal.

The internal act of determining incongruencies and their implications for becoming self indicates a process of idealisation defined as purposive, order-concerned notions representing a striving towards resolving a felt incongruence in a manner consistent with personal constructions of that which is better or more desirable. This is not to say that ideals as the product of idealisation are, in fact, better or more desirable, but that they are the construing person's approximation, based on available perceptual resources at that time.

An ideal can be thought of as personal when it arises from and unifies associated aspects of individuality as a function of personality. Personality represents a bastion of individuality, identity, intentionality and purposiveness. All persons strive towards the definition, maintenance and extension of self. Mere existence in society indicates greater or lesser degrees of success in this endeavour. The nature of shared uniqueness has similarities in process with diverse results attributable to content. Two persons acting on the same external information or content may construct, or reconstruct, their anticipations in very different ways, yet maintain consistency with their internal frames of reference. Such processes may or may not be subject to articulation or be rational but are distinctly personal and meaningful, adding to and embracing the differences that enhance and complicate all persons' interactions. Ideals are not only personal, but are unique and actively constructed connotative subsystems.

Ideals that are personal may or may not be professional. Professional for our purposes has a twofold frame of reference. First, it refers to practical aspects of education such as ideals-in-practice, or ideals-in-use. The connotation here emphasises an applied link between the outcomes of personal idealising and the conceptualising of what could be termed 'giving to teaching that which is teaching's'. The second meaning of 'professional' considers the pragmatic aspects of distinctly personal ideals. For example: Do they work, and are they functional and worthy of maintaining a teachers purposes for developing self-as-professional within the confines of the educational process?

The contrast pole of the PPI / not PPI construction (things that are not personal, not professional and not ideal) is dealt with in a manner similar to its emergent pole. A conception that is not ideal will not have been processed through a person's perceptual systems for consideration of its fit (or lack of fit) with their conception of true order. Such a not-ideal may be an assumption that is not warranted, not examined or that is simply taken-for-granted.

Seizing and acting upon an inclination in this manner is akin to Dewey's notion of desired or unexamined impulse. Such responses have not been subjected to the critical mediating processes that render preferred personal states of affairs into thought-out desirable purposes or ends-in-view. PCP views such anticipations as inappropriate or faulty constructions that may be too tight (restrictive) or too loose (apathetic or ambivalent) that could threaten the integrity of that construct system, leading to eventual invalidation and necessitating reformulation and retesting. Such an occurrence need not throw an entire system into jeopardy, but may merely indicate that reconstruction or abandonment of those constructs in use is warranted.

The choice of PCP methods to assist the development of personal themes is useful because not only can the reptest method serve as an ice-breaker for the purposes of starting an investigative conversation (Kompf, 1983), but resultant reptest conversations are able to reveal more about the research participant than those persons whom she or he chooses to discuss (see Hastorf *et al.,* 1970; Brown, 1957)

Ideals as Preferred Constructions

By extending what seems like a Pollyanna hypothesis, several researchers (Adams-Webber, 1979, is one example) have shown that there is not only a tendency for persons to use 'evaluatively positive words more frequently, diversely and facilely that evaluative negative words' (Adams-Webber, 1979, p. 162), but the usage of such a distinction repeatedly conforms to a predictable Golden Section ration of 0.62 positive to 0.38 negative. Although support for this notion was not the intent of the current research, participants did represent ideal and least-ideal significant others on personal constructs by the use of ratings of intensity that approached the same Golden Section ratio. This tendency indicates, to some extent, that persons use positive descriptors (constructs) to discriminate and organise their perceptions of ideal others in ways that are more meaningful and/or more familiar than are negative constructs (see Warr and Coffman, 1969; Kuusinen, 1972; Bender, 1974). Such findings indicate a level of cognitive literacy or fluency with the specific subsystem of personal, professional ideals that have positive and arguably optimistic sets of anticipations. Indeed, some recent studies are finding the level of cognitive literacy of schoolteachers to be highly correlated with their stated levels of quality of life in teaching (Brown, 1986).

Positive constructions of others were also apparent during interviews where participants, in general, discussed ideal/least-ideal others only as they provided contrast to, and not conflict with, their preferred conceptions of order. Constructions of ideals (positive and negative) were maintained until they failed to provide grounds for consistent successful anticipations of ideal related events. Subsequent reconstructions emanated from perceived dissonance within the participant's organisation and integration of ideal-related constructs in attempts to provide a sense of order and predictive facility about their interaction with the educative process.

Figure 8.1 represents the theoretical setting for this research, with a display of the larger problematic, positing a tentative investigative framework that provides a conceptual foothold from which the content and process of teachers' ideals may be viewed. In this way the researcher may look at teacher ideals from the outside and the teacher as co-researcher may look at his/her ideals from the inside, resulting in the mutual development of a plan for categorisation and evaluation. This is quite similar to Hill's (1986) 'reciprocal conversation' that progresses between client and consultant as a loop process.

As Figure 8.1 indicates, Stage 1, the process of idealising (the setting of ideals through felt incongruence, striving to make something better, or Dewey's (1938) notion of impulse) gives rise to some level of conceptualisation of ideals (that which is desirable) at Stage 2. Such ideals, as indicated in Figure 8.1, may exist at a sub-verbal level and may be unarticulated or unavailable for articulation. Ideals may progress from this stage to becoming articulated ideals visible through being publicly

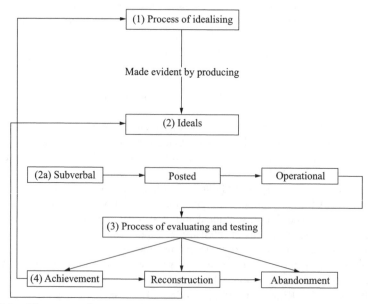

Figure 8.1.   The structural process of personal idealising.

or privately discussed as outcomes of felt incongruence and represented as a desired state of affairs.

These ideals, when acted upon in an attempt at realisation, become operational ideals or ends-in-view, visible through actions and words directed at bringing existing states of affairs more in line with the perceiver's conception of true order. In Stage 3, having operationalised ideals, the teacher must evaluate and test the possible outcomes and, in light of environmental or perceptual feedback, assess the chances for beneficial developmental additions to his/her process of becoming self. Stage 4 shows that at some level a process of reckoning must occur allowing teachers to come to terms with their ideals and make sense of their fitness, adaptability and ability to survive. Achieved ideals may lead to further processes of idealising. Reconstructed ideals that have been revised in light of posting or operationalising re-enter the process as anticipatory ideals wanting evaluation and testing. Abandoned ideals may dissipate or continue to exist dependent on previous emotional investment. Consider the following participant interview synthesis:

A new teacher of English literature, with a love of classical writing, emerges from teacher training (often a process of idealising in itself) supposing and/or hoping: (1) the subject matter he is dealing with is vital and will enrich and benefit his students; and (2) his beliefs in the subject matter will act in concert with his teaching abilities in the transmission and reception of the vitality of English literature.

The development of this teacher's mindset of optimism or hopefulness about infusing his love of English literature most likely occurred before and/or during his teacher training. He desired to provide insights and exposure to an area he felt would be desirable for and by students' experience.

During the first months of teaching he finds that: (1) students 'couldn't care less' about classical literature; (2) apathy and boredom are the only visible effects of his teaching methods; and (3) classroom management and discipline demand most of his time, detracting from the content and process of teaching.

This scenario examined through the stages of Figure 8.1 will illustrate further considerations and implications:

(1)   Process of idealising

(2)   Ideals

(2a)   Sub-verbal   Posted   Operational
         These ideals most likely existed at a sub-verbal level until the opportunity arose for the posting and operationalising of such a construction in a classroom setting.

(3)   Process of evaluating and testing
         In light of the student response to the posting and operationalising of his ideals about English literature the teacher must evaluate the data from such a testing procedure. His findings, in this example, must indicate to him that his ideals for this agenda will not be achieved or realised in their present form in this setting.
         In fact, persistence in pursuing his present course of action may prove detrimental or dysfunctional to his development as a teacher or in maintaining his identifying factors as a teacher-type with a valuable message.

(4)   Achievement   Reconstruction   Abandonment
           Achievement having been overruled in light of the deleter-
           ious results of the present course of action presents the
           teacher with at least two options. (1) He may reconstruct
           his notions about: (a) the actual importance of English
           literature as he views its reception by modern students; or
           (b) his abilities of teaching such an agenda in the manner
           he has chosen causing a re-hypothesising and return to the
           stage of idealising in light of environmental information.
           (2) He may abandon his ideals about both English litera-
           ture and teaching – leaving the choice of changing his
           subject area, teaching other students, or pursuing an alter-
           native livelihood to teaching.

Although simplistic, such an application and extension of this model may promote
deeper interpretations of an example of teaching, and the reception of both that act and
the subject being taught, thus producing outcomes that can be fed back into a teacher's
perceptual and actual process of educating. Further examination of actual constructs
in use and constructions that gave rise to the anticipations and subsequent behaviours
could reveal issues that are more telling.

Personal and Subjective Theories about Education

Throughout many discussions pertaining to Kelly's (1955) theory of personal
constructs, the implicit notion is carried that persons build over time construct systems
and subsystems that are prearticulate, articulated and testable theories about their
interactions with the world around them. Highly subjective, personal theorising is
validated and updated by the constant process of revision through construct
testing.

Development and articulation of personal theories of education have caused
many teachers discomfort in stepping outside of familiar, traditional academic discourse about teaching. Sensed discomfort seemed largely attributable to the necessity
of reaching into personal belief systems about education and educating by discovering elements of meaning in what teachers did or wanted to do in their classrooms and
why they espoused that view. Some teachers found that substantial portions of their
actions and beliefs about education were taken-for-granted. A common reaction during shared reflection was 'I never thought about it like that.' More rigid reactions of
teachers encompassed indignation about approaching a topic with other than the professional distance that had played a large part in their academic and practice lives to
that point. Certain discussions and subsequent analyses had to be investigated from
the game-like aspect of 'acting-as-if-it-really-mattered' leading to a teacher-as-
philosopher stance through that of teacher-as-scientist.

By treating new personal conceptions and theories in this way a more global
process of integration seemed to occur wherein overall personal and professional
systems of values, beliefs and ideals fell under scrutiny. Incongruence and incon-
sistencies became the focus of active and articulate examination rather than acting
as a source of philosophical numbness or apathy. Common metaphors for describing
the process were those of map building and testing a circuit board for faulty
connections.

Some Observations

The posted results of this process presented themselves as ideal conceptions that were highly personal and distinctly practical. All teachers seemed to possess to greater and lesser extents ideals about educating and education that acted as filters or ways of processing and/or justifying what they did and needed to do in their schools and why they adopted and maintained specific stances towards those ideals in practice.

We noticed two benefits to our teachers from the process of this study. First, as it was hoped, teachers gained access to perceptual windows allowing them a new look at their environment in scientific, aesthetic and pragmatic ways. Second, exploring through this process allowed new meanings to emerge that assisted teachers to develop better understandings of the influences that shape, guide and lead their ideal-directed (and sometimes not-ideal-directed) behaviours and attitudes. Some benefits may be passed on to students in the form of teacher enthusiasm and commitment. In the larger sense, education as a way of helping people to learn how to learn may become more of a doing-with activity than a doing-to process. A teacher on literate terms with their personal, practical ideals and the way in which they are constructed may be more willing to share them in theory and in practice with his/her students that a teacher who is not. Such a stance supports the Inviting Approach advocated by Purkey and Novak (1984) wherein teachers and students are seen to be valuable, able and responsible, and should be treated accordingly.

However this study did not demonstrate whether this process is good for teachers or not, but only examined as fully as possible the personal, practical ideals teachers use in their daily practice from a personal perspective.

The PCP view may be extended to consider the dynamic interplay of competing aspects of the organisational press in educational practice. Figure 8.2 illustrates some possibilities for dissonance.

If the various aspects of these spheres of influence are examined or considered out of context with the rest, accurate perceptions of *what exactly teachers do and why they do it* may be distorted or at least incomplete. The ways in which teachers

A Broad View

Ideological decisions	A Narrow View	Personal decisions
	Coping	
Structural decisions	Teaching	Curriculum decisions
	Disciplining	
	Surviving	
Procedural decisions		Political decisions

Figure 8.2.   The role of the teacher (Simpson & Jackson, 1984, p. 5).

choose courses of action and attitude in response to situationally specific events neces-
sitates high-level ordering of personal constructions about educating and the role of
the teacher. Ideal conceptions of persons and events may alternate in a field–ground
relationship in providing teachers with simultaneous perspectives of what actually
occurs in real-life educational circumstances and the ideal conception of what is a
desired or desirable circumstance.

Some Extensions

As a person's perceptual world is personally constructed, so are the common, shared
senses of social reality constructed and explicit in their goals and implications (Berger
and Luckmann, 1966). In both personal and social constructions there are ongoing
processes of: construction-evaluation-testing, and where necessary or desired, reformulation and reconstruction. This process is best described further by a synthesis of
three theoretical positions.

Piaget, Kelly and Kuhn (cited in Nystrand, 1977) may be considered through
their theoretical overlap vis-à-vis the public and personal epistemological dynamics
used to articulate, test, revise and extend knowledge. Nystrand discusses the similarities of Piaget's schema, Kelly's construct and Kuhn's paradigm. He states: 'There is
nothing static or fixed about a schema, construct or a paradigm. Each may be said to
undergo assimilation and accommodation; elaboration and reconstruction; or investigation, crisis and revolution. Each may be looked on as an essential participant in a
fluid, ongoing process of development involving a personal commitment and tension
between individual and world... experience is conceived as a spiral regulated by the
need for order and the potential for equilibrium or a coherent, open and reversible
system' (p. 9).

As Britton (cited in Nystrand, 1977) states: 'Every encounter with the actual
is an experimental commitment of all I have learned from experience' (p. 41). The
mechanism by which experiences are processed, and thereby provide cues for action
and meaning, may be considered as constructs, schemas or paradigms. All processing
and subsequent conceptual frameworks have evolved in a uniquely personal way
taking into account the similarities and differences between actual events and the
meanings the events contain for the perceiver in her or his attempts to anticipate the
outcomes of similar events in the future. As successful anticipations are a fundamental
goal of self-preservation and extension, the best, most accurate or ideal representations
of these events necessarily underlie the personal search for meaning and knowledge.
Therefore, what teachers do and why they do it can be viewed as having elements of
the cognitive, affective and physical domains contributing interactively to an ongoing,
dynamic psychological and philosophical process that is personal, professional,
practical and ideal.

Author Reflection 2004

The approach to understanding teachers' ideals derived from personal interest reflecting school experiences. Why teachers do what they do connects with how they think
about what they do and what the origins of those thoughts might be. Ideal conceptions,
and the cognitive dynamics of how they change, help practitioners consciously adapt
to circumstances through socialisation, familiarisation awareness. These ideas have

helped continuing research into how teachers experience personal and professional development throughout the career span. The 'ideal' embedded in education, e.g. the concept of a university, can also be considered as a subject of change in response to perceptions of changing circumstances and definitions of what education and learning mean and represent.

The basis in constructivism and the foundation laid by George Kelly has been sustained and runs as a consistent theoretical theme in much current work. The ISATT meeting in Leuven was Kompf's first exposure to this community, with the encouragement and support of Alan F. Brown, one of the co-founders of the organisation. The freedom of discussing ideas in a collegial, congenial, yet constructively critical forum was more formative than the content of the paper – the feeling has endured.

Chapter 9

Computer Simulation as a Tool in Studying Teachers' Cognitive Activities during Error Diagnosis in Arithmetic

Erik DeCorte, Lieven Verschaffel and
Hilde Schrooten

Introduction

Research on teaching undertaken over the past decades has mainly focused on subject-matter-independent teaching behaviours and skills, such as management of classrooms, the cognitive level of questions, allocation of time, etc. This is certainly true for the vast amount of process-product studies (see e.g. Brophy and Good, 1986; Gage, 1985; Rosenshine and Furst, 1973), but it also holds for the more recent strand of research on teacher thinking (see Clark and Peterson, 1986; Shavelson and Stern, 1981). In this respect, Shulman (1986b) has rightly remarked that questions about the *content* of teaching are lacking in the available research. Commenting more specifically on the work on teacher thinking the same author (Shulman, 1986a) writes:

> Where the teacher cognition programme has clearly fallen short is
> the elucidation of teachers' cognitive understanding of subject mat-
> ter content and the relationship between such understanding and the
> instruction teachers provide for students (p. 25).

The obvious lack of attention in the study of teaching for the content of what is taught is the more remarkable, because in research on children's learning and problem solving the focus has already since the late seventies shifted towards subject-matter areas and the role of domain-specific knowledge in performance and in the acquisition of cognitive skills (see e.g. Resnick, 1983). In between, several researchers (e.g. Berliner, 1986; Leinhardt and Smith, 1985; Putnam, 1985; Shulman, 1986b) have started work aiming at an analysis of teachers' actions and cognitions in relation to the content being taught. For example, using extensive protocols, Leinhardt and Smith (1985) explored the content and organisation of expert teachers' knowledge of fractions. Putnam (1985) studied how teachers structured subject-matter content while tutoring individual students in adding whole numbers. The present study is related to Putnam's investigation, and aims at analysing teachers cognitive activities while diagnosing systematic errors in the algorithms of addition and subtraction in a simulated environment.

Research has obviously shown that children's errors on arithmetic problems are mostly the result of very systematic but wrong procedures (see e.g. Brown and Burton, 1978; DeCorte and Verschaffel, 1985; Resnich, 1982). At the same time, it has frequently been argued that effective instruction and remediation in mathematics requires that teachers have substantial knowledge and understanding of those incorrect procedures. Being able to diagnose them seems therefore a very important teaching skill. However, in spite of the attention on those incorrect arithmetic procedures in recent research, and the frequent claims for the importance of skill in diagnosing them, the way in which teachers determine what students know and how they operate internally has not yet been systematically explored. Consequently, we are also ignorant of how teachers use such knowledge to adjust the content of their instruction to the needs of children. Finally, we know very little about how to teach effectively the skill of diagnosing errors.

Theoretical Background

The present state-of-the-art cognitive instructional psychology and educational computing research provides us with the necessary tools for developing computer programs that simulate systematic errors on arithmetic tasks. The starting point of the present study was our assumption that administering such an error-simulating program offered an interesting environment for studying student teachers' cognitive processes during diagnosis. Moreover, we hypothesised that such a simulation program can be useful and efficient for training student teachers in the skill of diagnosing errors in the algorithms of addition and subtraction.

The basis of the computer simulation program used in this study is twofold. First, there is the work of Brown, Burton and VanLehn on procedural bugs in basic arithmetic skills (Brown and Burton, 1978; Brown and VanLehn, 1980, Brown and VanLehn, 1982; Burton, 1982). The term 'bugs' refers to erroneous but systematic procedures that are often a variant of a correct one. An example of a common subtraction bug is called 'smaller-from-larger': instead of borrowing in a column where it is necessary, the pupil subtracts the top digit, which is smaller, from the bottom one, which is larger. Using computer simulation Brown, Burton and VanLehn have constructed an extensive catalogue of bugs; furthermore, they have developed a generative theory of those procedural bugs, called the repair theory. Starting from the catalogue of bugs of those investigators, computer programs can be written in which a sample of errors is represented for diagnostic purposes, i.e. the user of such a program has to discover the simulated bugs.

Second, a rather global process model of competent diagnosing of errors was used as a frame of reference in developing the computer program. The model involves two main phases, namely a hypothesis-generating and a hypothesis-testing phase. In the first stage, the user of the program tries to generate a plausible assumption concerning the erroneous procedure underlying a given error. In the second phase, the hypothesis is verified by predicting the wrong responses that would be obtained on a series of problems if the buggy procedure were applied.

Description of the Computer Program

The computer program used in the present study is based on VanLehn's 'Buggy Game'. It is written in Basic, runs on an Apple IIe or IIc computer, and simulates fifteen frequently occurring, incorrect procedures in addition and subtraction. A description of the program in the form of a flow chart is given in Figure 9.1.

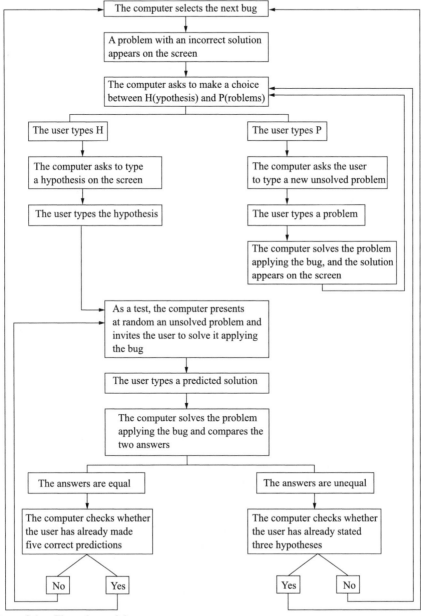

Figure 9.1.   Flow chart of the computer program.

Method

The computer program has been administered individually to ten student teachers during the last semester of their training. Each student worked about 2 hours on the computer. To allow a detailed qualitative analysis of their diagnostic processes, all the students' reactions typed on the screen were registered by a video recorder connected directly to the monitor.

One day after all ten students had finished the computer simulation program a collective paper-and-pencil test was administered to this experimental group and to a control group; the experimental and the control groups were matched based on a rating of their overall capacity by the teacher who was mainly responsible for their training. The test was specially designed to assess student teachers' diagnostic skill of arithmetic bugs, and consisted of nine items representing nine bugs: two of these errors were also represented in the computer program (no transfer), four related to addition and subtraction bugs not trained in the program (near transfer), and three others were multiplication and division errors (far transfer). Each item presented the subjects with five incorrectly solved problems, and they were asked first to define their hypothesis concerning the underlying bug, and then to predict the answers to three unsolved problems that would be obtained because of applying this bug.

The following procedure was used to score the test. The statements of the hypotheses and the predictions of the answers on the unsolved problems were treated separately. The hypotheses were scored as correct (2 points), incomplete (1) or incorrect (0). The intersubjective agreement between two independent judges who scored all the statements of hypotheses ($n = 150$) was $r = 0.94$. For the predictions of the answers on the unsolved problems, a severe criterion was applied: 1 point was given if the three predictions were correct; the score was zero in all other cases.

In line with the general hypothesis stated before, we expected that the average score on the post-test for the statements of hypotheses as well as for the predictions of the answers on unsolved problems would be significantly better in the experimental group than in the control group.

Process Results

As said before we collected all the reactions of the student teachers typed on the screen using a video recorder connected to the monitor. An analysis of these three reactions was carried out after a hypothesis was rejected. Qualitative data revealed several aspects of the cognitive activities of the subjects during diagnosis. We will briefly report some results relating to the following aspects: (1) hypothesis-generating in the beginning of the diagnostic process; (2) the quality of the hypotheses and their relationship with the results on the prediction tests.

In view of the presentation of the findings, it is useful to mention that no one subject attained the end of the computer program that contained 15 bugs. Most student teachers did not go beyond the tenth bug, and only two reached the eleventh one. Furthermore, note that the student teachers were given at the maximum three opportunities to state a hypothesis with respect to each bug (see Figure 9.1). In all, 137 hypotheses were formulated: They were distributed as follows over the three consecutive opportunities: 95, 31 and 11.

After a hypothesis was stated a prediction test was given: The computer presented at random a series of maximum of five problems asking the user to predict the answers applying the assumed bug. The hypothesis statements were scored in the same way as on the post-test. For the prediction tests the procedure was also similar: 1 point if the five predictions were correct, zero in all other cases.

Hypothesis-Generating at the Beginning of the Diagnostic Process

The flow chart of the computer program shows that with respect to each bug the subjects were first given a problem with an incorrect solution, followed by the question to either state a hypothesis (H), or to type a new problem (P). A careful hypothesis-testing phase would be characterised by typing some additional problems trying to collect more information concerning the bug before stating a hypothesis. The results show that the choice between H and P was student- as well as bug-dependent.

First, there was an obvious trend towards more careful hypothesis testing as one progressed through the program. However, this effect is difficult to interpret because of the confounding of the difficulty level of the bugs with a possible learning effect. Indeed, the sequence of the bugs was based on their difficulty level, starting with the easy ones.

Second, as shown in Table 9.1, the student teachers seemed to use consequently one of two approaches, namely either typing a hypothesis immediately after the presentation of the incorrectly solved problem (six out of ten subjects), or typing one or more additional problems to collect more detailed information on the underlying error (four subjects).

The finding that the choice between H and P at the beginning of the diagnostic process was student- as well as bug-dependent also explains why there was not a strong relationship – as one might expect – between the P-choice, indicating that a subject looks for more detailed information on the bug, on the one hand, and the quality of the subsequent hypothesis statements and scores on the prediction tests, on the other. Indeed, the average performance on those two measures following an H-choice was only slightly but not significantly lower.

Quality of the Hypotheses and Results of the Prediction Tests

The results concerning the quality of the hypothesis statements and of the prediction tests are summarised in Table 9.2, in which the relationship between the two measures is also shown.

Table 9.2 reveals that only 30 per cent of the hypothesis statements were scored as correct, while almost 50 per cent were definitely incorrect. On the other hand,

Table 9.1. Reactions of the subjects after presentation of the problem with an incorrect solution

					Subject					
Reaction	1	2	3	4	5	6	7	8	9	10
H	8	2	10	0	9	5	1	7	3	10
P	2	8	1	10	0	2	9	2	8	0

Table 9.2. Relationship between the quality of the hypothesis
statements and the results of the prediction tests

Scores on the prediction tests	Scores for the hypothesis statements			Total
	2	1	0	
1	38	24	18	80
0	4	5	48	57
Total	42	29	66	137

more than 60 per cent of the prediction tests were solved entirely correctly. This shows that in a number of cases the subjects made five correct predictions with respect to a bug, although their hypothesis statement concerning the underlying error was wrong, or, at least, incomplete. The point-biserial correlation between the two measures was: r pbi = 0.57. If the two measures tap subjects' understanding of the corresponding bug, one would expect a higher correlation. However, several factors had a depressing impact on that correlation: (1) the student teacher understood the bug, but the hypothesis was faulty or too specific (this happened frequently when a subject formulated a hypothesis based only on the initial problem with a incorrect solution); (2) the student teacher stated a correct hypothesis but made a typing or counting error in the prediction test which was not discovered afterwards; (3) the student teacher had initially typed an incorrect hypothesis but adapted it mentally during the prediction test; (4) the student teacher succeeded by chance in the prediction test.

Reactions after a Hypothesis was Rejected

When a subject did not succeed in the first prediction test with respect to a bug, the corresponding hypothesis was rejected, and the subject could make a second (31 out of 95 cases), and possibly a third attempt (11 out of 31 cases). The subjects' reactions following the rejection of a hypothesis were of two kinds: rigid perseverance and flexible revision.

In the case of rigid perseverance, the student teacher stuck to his or her first hypothesis negating counterevidence. Consequently, the subject generated new problems – mostly only one – that confirmed the initial hypothesis, and ended with typing it again on the screen. This led to a new failure on the prediction test. Flexible revision, on the other hand, started with accepting that the hypothesis was wrong, followed by an attempt to change, adapt, refine or generalise it.

Post-test Results

Table 9.3 shows that the experimental group obtained a better average result on both post-test scores. A t-test revealed that in each case the difference was significant: t (18) = 2.12, p < 0.05 for the statements of hypotheses, and t (18) = 2.43, p < 0.05 for the predictions of answers. These findings confirm the hypothesis concerning the favourable effect of the computer program on student teachers' diagnostic skills.

Table 9.3.   Post-test results of the experimental and the control groups
with respect to the statements of hypotheses and
the predictions of answers

Group	Statements of hypotheses (max. score = 18)		Predictions (max. score = 9)	
	Mean	SD	Mean	SD
Experimental	11.6	2.5	6.2	0.9
Control	9.4	1.8	5.1	1.0

However, this effect seemed to be rather specific. Indeed, a further analysis of the data showed that the experimental group outperformed the control group significantly only on the items relating to bugs trained in the computer program. On the near and the far transfer items the results were in the expected direction, but not significant.

The specificity of the learning effect can probably be accounted for by the short duration of the training, in which, moreover, only a restricted set of bugs were presented to the subjects.

Discussion

A first goal of the present study was to explore the usefulness of the adapted version of Buggy Game as a simulation tool for studying teachers' thinking and decision-making processes while trying to understand children's errors in arithmetic. In our opinion, the investigation has yielded positive results in this respect. By providing a task environment involving some important features of a natural setting but at the same time permitting careful control and automated recording of the subjects' reactions, Buggy Game constitutes a valuable context for research.

However, the diagnostic computer environment alone does not provide us with full insight into the cognitive structures and thinking processes underlying student teachers' performances. The program informs us about the kinds of problems adminis-tered to the child by the student teacher, his or her hypothesis concerning the child's underlying bug, predictions about the child's answer on a series of unsolved problems, etc. The data collected do not allow answers to questions such as: Why did the student teacher choose these problems during the hypothesis-generating stage? Why did it take so long before he or she was able to state a hypothesis concerning the bug? Why was there a discrepancy between his or her hypothesis and predictions on the test problems?

With regard to answering these kind of questions, it seems possible to increase the richness of the data by making some extensions and alterations to the present program. For example, the (student) teacher could be given an opportunity to restate his or her hypothesis about the underlying bug after the prediction test and before moving on to another bug; a more well-thought-out generator of the test prob-lems could be developed, etc. Undoubtedly the most straightforward way to improve the richness of the empirical data lies in the collection of thinking-aloud or retrospec-tive protocols of subjects working through the program.

In summary, it seems to us that the combined application of self-reporting techniques and the registration of teachers' reactions while using the computer program can lead to a more comprehensive picture of the cognitive processes underlying diagnostic activities.

A second purpose of this investigation was to explore the program's usefulness as a device for teacher training. Two kinds of data represent positive indications in this respect: the program's face validity as evidenced by the enthusiastic reactions of teacher trainers during previous presentations of Buggy Game, and the positive empirical evidence found in the present study. However, there remain some critical remarks relative to the value of the program for training the skill of diagnosing errors in algorithms. Two major criticisms are respectively based on Putnam's (1985) study of teacher thoughts and actions in live and simulated tutoring of the addition algorithm, and on Resnick's (1982) distinction between the syntax and the semantics of arithmetic operations.

Putnam (1985) explored the thoughts and actions of experienced elementary teachers and non-teachers (mathematics students and prospective elementary teachers) as they tutored individual children in whole number addition in both a live and a simulated situation. The major goal of the study was to discover the goals and strategies teachers use to infer the state of student knowledge and to adjust their instruction on this basis. More specifically, Putnam (1985) wanted to test the popular idea in educational and research circles that a detailed model of a student's knowledge, including his or her misconceptions and faulty procedures, is a prerequisite to successful remediation. This viewpoint underlies also the diagnostic computer environment used in our investigation.

Putnam (1985) showed that there is little empirical evidence for this so-called diagnostic-remedial model. Indeed, one of his major findings is that the experienced teachers did not try to construct highly detailed models of the child's wrong procedures before attempting remedial instruction. In other words, they rarely had the sub-goal of determining the exact nature of a student's errors. Indeed, only seven per cent of children's errors and deficient responses were followed by presenting more problems and allowing the pupils to continue working incorrectly in order to reveal more about their wrong procedures or knowledge. On the other hand, in most cases the teachers appeared to move through a predetermined set of skills and concepts that they expected the child to know. This predetermined set of skills and concepts, along with problems, activities and strategies for teaching the material, is called the 'curriculum script' and constitutes a teacher's pedagogical knowledge about addition.

To summarise, Putnam's (1985) study suggests that the diagnostic-remedial model underlying Buggy Game does not correspond to an expert elementary arithmetic teacher's approach to errors and their remediation. However, one first could criticise the way in which teaching expertise was operationalised in this investigation, namely using as the only criterion having at least ten years of teaching experience at the elementary level. Second, even if a descriptive study with 'real' expert teachers were to reveal that they operate according to the curriculum script rather than the diagnostic-remedial model, this would not immediately justify the conclusion that teaching diagnostic skills is inappropriate at any stage during in-service or pre-service teacher training. For example, the diagnostic computer environment can probably be very useful in making (student) teachers aware of the systematicity in many of the learners' errors. Moreover, the question can be raised whether remedial teaching would not be more effective if based on the diagnostic-remedial model instead of the curriculum script approach.

The second major criticism of Buggy Game relates to its restricted scope for the diagnostic process. In this respect, Resnick's (1982) distinction between the syntax and the semantic of arithmetic operations is relevant.

According to this author written addition and subtraction 'can be analysed as an algorithm defined by a set of *syntactic* rules that prescribe how problems should be written, an order in which certain operations should be performed, and which kinds of symbols belong in which positions' (Resnick, 1982, p. 137). On the other hand, there is the conceptual or *semantic* basis on which these rules and procedures are based, such as the ten base system and positional notation.

In line with the preceding distinction, instructional interventions can focus either at the syntactic (or algorithmic) or at the semantic (or conceptual) level (Resnick, 1982; see also Putnam, 1985). An algorithmic intervention is an attempt to describe or demonstrate the procedures of addition and subtraction without explaining explicitly the reasons for the various steps, or without linking these procedures to the underlying conceptual knowledge. A conceptual intervention, on the other hand, aims at helping children to understand the arithmetic procedures by linking them to mathematical concepts, e.g. with concrete materials.

In term of this distinction, Buggy Game can be described as a simulation program that is almost exclusively focused at the algorithmic aspects of the arithmetic procedures. Indeed, there is little or no attempt to deal with the concepts on which they are based: The insight into the nature of the child's errors necessary to predict his or her answers on the test problems, is restricted to the superficial, syntactic level of operating. However, recent research on elementary mathematics learning and teaching has convincingly shown that appropriate instructional interventions involve providing appropriate links between the semantics and the syntax of the written algorithms (Resnick, 1982).

Again, the preceding remarks do not imply that using Buggy Game in teacher training is useless or even harmful; nevertheless, they show that the present diagnostic computer environment represents a restricted approach to the remediation of errors. Therefore, it should be complemented by the development of diagnostic and remedial teaching skills focusing on the concepts underlying the algorithmic procedures and on the multiple links between the syntactic and the semantic knowledge base.

Author Reflection 2004

Major remarks on the study that were made in the Discussion section of this chapter at the time of publication almost twenty years ago are at present largely still valid.

First of all, we think that an error-simulating program like the one developed in the study can still today be a worthwhile and useful tool in training (student) teachers in diagnosing and reflecting on systematic errors that children make in algorithmic procedures for basic computational operations (for an extensive overview of procedural misconceptions or 'bugs' that cause such systematic errors, especially how they develop in children, see VanLehn, 1990). In particular, the fact that the user has the possibility of testing his/her predictions about the underlying bug by constructing carefully chosen items and having them solved by the 'virtual' pupil with a particular bug, is an extremely powerful learning experience that is difficult, if not impossible to achieve otherwise.

Second, because the simulation program as such cannot fully unravel the cognitive structures and processes of the user of the program during error diagnosis, some alterations and extensions were suggested in the chapter. At present, we are not aware of any research that has attempted to follow up the suggestion to revise the program along these lines. However, even today it would be relevant to do so, for instance by combining the use of the simulation program with the collection of thinking-aloud data or retrospective protocols of subjects working through the program.

Third, and probably most importantly, it was observed that the approach to error diagnosis involved in the simulation program is restricted to the syntactic aspects of the arithmetic operations at the expense of the semantics. Therefore, it was argued that it should be complemented with and linked to a semantic component. This is very much in line with current thinking about learning and teaching arithmetic operations in which the integration of conceptual and procedural knowledge is considered as the basis for acquiring computational fluency, i.e. skill in computing efficiently, appropriately and flexibly (Baroody and Dowker, 2003; National Research Council, 2001).

Section C

Teacher Judgement and Evaluation of Students

Chapter 10, Hofer's 'Goal-dependent perception in relations between teachers and students', begins by reviewing studies of perception, particularly person perception, and the phenomena of selective attention as a prelude to descriptions of experimental studies concerned with selection by relevance. He specifies four theoretical categories of relevance: criterially, prognostically, conditionally and instrumentally relevant. The results of his experiments demonstrate that theoretical explanations derived from previous work on object perception are inadequate for the inter-personal perception that occurs between pupils and teachers. Various possible influences are considered as contributory factors to this result. While it is noted that the complexity of the situation within a student–teacher encounter mitigates against experimental manipulation of independent variables, the author, in his original paper, contends that these preliminary studies indicate a need for further investigations, a suggestion he reiterates in his current reflection on the paper. Thus newcomers to the field might like to take up this challenge.

The next two papers, presented as Chapters 11 and 12, are concerned with assessment as a particular example of making judgements through perception. The first is by Brehmer, entitled 'Grading as a quasi-rational judgement process'. This author explores two hypotheses: that grading controls learning, or that emphases in teaching and grading influence learning. Brehmer starts from the premise that grading is a judgement process that can be studied using methods derived from psychological research on judgement and by drawing on Social Judgement Theory, explicated in the text. The results of the investigations described by her support that premise, with models of grading being deduced, but they also provide comparisons to other studies on teachers' teaching criteria, suggesting that further research is required in both domains. The grading process is described in the discussion as a quasi-rational one, a description that might well apply to other aspects of teacher cognition. The author argues that quasi-rational thinking may be a blend of routines and analytic thinking, so this paper carries implications for other research on teacher thinking. Of particular interest is her discussion of the models extracted from the judgements in the data that predict teacher behaviour more accurately than do their verbalisations of the process.

The following chapter, again concerned with evaluation of student performance, is provided by Lissmann: 'Analysing teachers' thoughts prior to student assessment'. Following a review of previous studies, Lissmann poses five questions about teachers' thoughts related to assessment that have been neglected by those investigations. A pilot study to provide grounded information in response to these questions is recounted in the text. This study, using three school types and addressing a range of disciplines, thus yielded data suitable for comparative analysis, as Berliner in the first chapter recommended. In Lissmann's Author Reflection 2004, the results of further analysis of the original data are provided, which further illuminate her former contentions. Further, this commentary also notes the changes in nomenclature used in literature databases that have appeared in the interim years; in general, the word 'thinking' has been replaced by 'cognition'. This observation may help current researchers to explore more of the history of research in this still germane topic.

Chapter 13 is contributed by van Opdorp, den Hertog, Bergen and Vreuls and is titled 'Teachers' causal attributions in problematic situations'. These authors, like the previous ones, are also concerned with teachers' thinking about the success and failure of their students, in particular how, and to what effect, cause of failure/success is attributed. The review of previous research cited recognises that little attention has been paid previously to teachers' perceptions of their own behaviour and performance in conjunction with that of their learners. A critique of the methods used in previous work is used to further inform the research questions and enquiry method, an open inventory study, documented in this paper which focuses on attributions in problematic situations. Again the data elicited from participants lends itself to comparative analyses along various dimensions and across categories. In summary, the authors conclude that personal, rather than impersonal, factors are generally attributed as causes of problematic situations and the fine detail of the findings will be of interest to reflective teachers and researchers alike.

Another decision-making or judgemental task required of teachers in the Special Education sector is the focus of the last paper in this section by Pijl and Foster: 'Teachers' need for pupil information in special education'. The authors investigate why teachers do not make use of potentially helpful information from entrance tests to Special Education. As did the previous authors, they refer in part of their literature review to published research on teachers' attributions for the causes of achievement levels, finding it wanting. Details of their own research methods and the resulting data precede a synthesis of the participant teachers' need for certain forms of information and why those forms are critical for their practice. In the Discussion section, it is posited that teachers prefer advance information that will aid them in the activities taking place in the first few days of the student's enrolment in the school, such as fitting them in to an appropriate social group with other students. However, teachers thereafter prefer to make decisions about ability, etc., based on their own experience with the student. In their 2004 Reflection, the authors provide cogent comment on the implications of the original research results for contemporary efforts to develop inclusive schools.

All of the papers in this section add a few more tiles to the mosaic of our understanding of how teachers make judgements and decisions. Together they provide today's researchers with an excellent entry to previous research on the topic but, importantly, they also highlight areas that still require further investigation.

Chapter 10

Goal-Dependent Perception in Relations between Teachers and Students

Manfred Hofer

What Constitutes Relevance in Person Perception?

There seems to be no fundamental difference between the perception of inanimate and of animate objects. Perception does not begin with the reception of stimuli. Subjective factors are present before they can affect the perception of other individuals. A judge will perceive witnesses according to their credibility, bankers their clients according to their solvency. We tend to assume that this holds true also for the teacher, who will perceive students mainly on those characteristics that he or she considers as 'relevant' for his or her actions. The influence of attitudes on person perception has been investigated with differing results (Cohen, 1961; Jones and De Charms, 1958; O'Neal and Mills, 1969; Zajonc, 1960). In each case, however, cognitive inferences functioned as dependent variables, rather than variables for sensory experience as the result of the perception process. The two experiments described in this study investigate the influence of interactive goals on the sensual processing of visual stimuli; here, selection is taken as an effective mechanism for the choice and control of actions.

Most recently, perception and attention have been considered more intensively under a functional aspect. In all species, perceptual systems have evolved as a means of guiding and controlling action. Prinz (1983) considers that criteria for action are present in an organism. These criteria provide the information conditions according to which an action is performed. If the perceived stimuli correspond to the present information elements, the action is initiated. Allport (1987) argues that the segmentation of the phenomenal world in terms of objects is conditioned by the demands of coherent action. Structural relations among object attributes need to be represented temporarily for the immediate guidance of action. Some of these properties are encoded more durably and can be used to guide actions on subsequent occasions. Not all the information available to the senses appears to be encoded. What is encoded depends on attention. Unattended objects and relations are not encoded. The criterion for successful attention to an environmental event depends on the subject's will to act selectively in response to the event. Allport terms this criterion selection-for-action.

Jones and Thibaut (1958) propose a systematic approach to the influence of role characteristics on interpersonal perception. A cognitive structure is derived from the goals that an individual pursues in an interaction, and it is presumed that this structure influences the perception of the other individual. The following study attempts a more precise depiction of what constitutes the 'relevance' of objects/aspects/events to which an individual pays particular attention. Reference is made to the view about the cognitive determinants of teacher behaviour described by Hofer (1986). In a given social situation, a person will assume a role. A person in a role wants to achieve something specific, namely role-related goals with or over the other person (subjective goals). Thus, certain pressures are put on the protagonist to act in a specific way (demands of action). This makes it necessary for the protagonist to gain information about the other person in order to make judgements for those categories that are required in planning the action. The number and content of categories that a person activates in the social role forms the cognitive structure. The cognitive structure contains slots. They state dimensions about which information is required. The person is 'adjusted to' this information. This adjustment has an effect on perception. Those characteristics are expected to be relevant for a protagonist that stand in *functional relation* to the fulfilment of the goals or aims the protagonist wants to achieve.

Now I should become more specific about what might constitute relevant characteristics for a teacher. I will derive theoretically four distinct categories of relevance using action theoretic concepts.

1. Action has its point of departure in the teacher's ascertainment of a discrepancy between the actual state of affairs and his or her notions of how students should behave and what they should achieve. In my theoretical terms, the Is-condition must be perceived with regard to the goal dimensions of the protagonist. Action is only necessary when the discrepancy between the Is-condition and the Shall-condition exceeds a tolerable proportion. Thus, perception performances are necessary with regard to the subjective goal dimensions. I term *criterially relevant* those characteristics that enable the protagonist to make a diagnosis of the goal variables.

2. The theory states that individuals have a tendency to attribute the behaviour of others to causes. This serves to enable them to form an expectation about the further course of the interaction (see Hofer, 1986, p. 213). The protagonist can recognise factors that will enhance or impede an action even before it is performed, and thus be able to assess the foreseeable success of the activity. Dimensions having such a function are to be termed *prognostically relevant*. Prognostically relevant characteristics are those that are cognised as external causes for the achievement of the goal.

3. A further assumption in the theory is that, in order to select suitable strategies for action, it is essential for the teacher to determine conditions for an appropriate intervention. I term perception performances that are expedient in this sense *conditionally relevant*. Teachers will find relevant those characteristics of their pupils on which they can base differential treatment. We have evidence from our investigations that teachers tend to group their students cognitively according to their activity and anxiety. These characteristics of pupils could be meaningful for the teacher if they produce differing strategies of action in pupils who differ in these characteristics.

4. For the most part, actions cannot be considered as consisting of a single stage, but must be divided into sub-stages. Additional units, related to interim goals rather than the final goal, are also part of the action. Thus, it is important

for the teacher to produce discipline as an interim goal for teaching behaviour in the lesson. I term the dimensions that are supposed here to be as of *instrumental relevance*.

From this starting point, social roles were manipulated by instruction in two experiments and the perception of personal characteristics, as presented in written or pictorial form, registered. The roles were varied in relation to a pupil. On one occasion, the role of a teacher was assumed (Experimental Group 1). In Experimental Group 2 the role of a fellow pupil was assumed. Subjects were allocated at random to the two experimental groups. For the cognitive structure of a teacher the following five dimensions were taken: 'effort', 'ability', 'conduct', 'social activity' and 'anxiety'. For the implicit personality theory of a pupil about another pupil the categories 'emotion', 'community spirit' and 'initiative' were taken (Jones and Thibaut, 1958). The hypothesis in every experiment was that a subject in Experimental Group I would be more likely to perceive characteristics from the structure allocated to the teacher's role. In contrast, it was expected that a subject in Experimental Group 2 would select more characteristics from the structure allocated to the pupil's role. The two experiments are distinguished by the operationalisation of the independent and dependent variables. In the first experiment, words representing character traits were used as independent variables; in the second experiment, drawings. In the first experiment, the direct memory was taken to determine perceptual selection; in the second, the length of time spent on viewing was used to measure the focusing.

Experiment 1

The reproduction method was used to examine the hypothesis that those personal characteristics are processed selectively that constitute the cognitive structure of a person in a given social situation. It was assumed that the quality of reproduction would reflect the extent of selective perception.

Method
The subjects were 144 trainee teachers at a teacher training college and 64 elementary school teachers. They were told that the task would be to put themselves as well as possible into two different roles. Half of the subjects were allocated first the teacher's role, then that of the pupil; for the other half, the order was reversed. The instruction ran: 'Please put yourself in the role of a teacher (pupil). A new pupil, Carl (Peter) joins your class. Here I have a list of personal characteristics used to describe pupils. Please read and memorise them. Later, you will be required to describe Carl using these words.'

After receiving these instructions, the subjects were given a list of 16 characteristics. Eight were from a teacher's perspective (e.g. intelligent, diligent, obedient), eight from that of a pupil (e.g. humourless, courageous, comradely). The subjects were given thirty seconds to read the list and then asked to write all the characteristics down on a sheet of paper distributed previously in order not to forget them. Subjects had two minutes to complete this task. Inevitably, it was not possible to note all 16 characteristics equally in this time. Subjects were thus compelled to divide their attention.

In addition, subjects were asked to record on a four-point scale how important they considered the respective teaching goals 'imparting knowledge', 'conveyance of problem-solving attitudes' and 'cultivation of the overall personality'. A four-point scale was also used to record how important they considered the eight dimensions for each of the three goals. This was intended to determine the subjective estimate of relevance.

Results

Table 10.1 shows the mean values under both experimental conditions. The significances were reached by means of a t-test for correlated samples.

When the subjects were asked to assume the teacher's role, significantly more characteristics from the set presenting a teacher's perspective were reproduced than from that representing the perspective of a pupil. Correspondingly, significantly more characteristics from the set of words describing a pupil's attitude were reproduced when the group assumed the role of pupil than the role of teacher.

The overall differences can be attributed above all to the dimensions 'ability', 'effort', 'discipline' (teacher) and 'emotion' (pupil). The characteristics functioning as individual goals had no significant influences on the direct reproduction of different characteristics. Neither was there any relation between the estimated goal-related relevance and the frequency of the reproduction of corresponding characteristics.

Overall, the results affirm the hypothesis with respect to the most important categories of the perspectives of each social role. However, perception was measured according to memory performance. To a greater or lesser extent, empirical criteria affecting perception usually involve memory performance. The longer the time between the moment of perception and the measuring process, the greater the effect of memory and the easier it is to prove the effects of existing attitudes. In the second experiment, therefore, the result of perception was registered more immediately.

Experiment 2

In the second experiment, the form of the independent and the dependent variable was derived in a different way. The perception of the behaviour of others in social interaction is portrayed only inadequately by the perception of words representing character traits. Newtson (1976) investigated the perception of continuing behaviour using the technique of interruption. He showed subjects short films on which a person was performing an action. They were to press a button whenever one meaningful action was completed and another began. He was able to establish that subjects undertook a reliable segmentation of action sequences. According to the instruction and situation, a differing level of segmentation was established: Individuals can divide sequences of behaviour into either large or small units. Evidently, perception of behaviour arises

Table 10.1.   Mean value of student characteristics from the
              individual perspectives reproduced under both
              experimental conditions

Characteristics	Role instruction		Significance
	Teacher	Pupil	
Teacher perspective	3.90	3.14	0.01
Pupil perspective	2.93	3.72	0.01

from the attention being directed to specific characteristics. There is much evidence that individuals infer characteristics or dispositions of another person from perceived behavioural data (Jones, 1979). It follows that it must be possible to simulate the natural situation by means of pictorial illustrations that arouse the impression of completed sequences of behaviour and invite the deduction of specific characteristics.

As stimuli, illustrations of fourteen characteristics were used. Each picture showed the same boy undertaking some activity that expressed or indicated a certain characteristic. In order to examine the dependence of perception on specific goals within an adopted role, a second independent variable was conceived. Half the subjects were to put themselves into a role in which they wanted to achieve high performance results in their relations with the fictive pupil. The other half was to aim more at social achievements. Presentation time of each stimulus was 20 seconds. To measure the variable attentional selection, the eye movements during the viewing of the pictures were registered.

Method

The subjects were a group of 42 students composed mostly of student teachers. They were divided at random into four groups. A total of 14 illustrations were drawn, showing a pupil doing some activity or in a certain state of mind. For example, a drawing showing the pupil sitting concentrating at a desk was used to express 'diligence'. Another example: the pupil sitting on a moto-cross bicycle indicated the characteristic 'active'. The drawings were modified until it was certain that they suggested the characteristics intended to describe the pupil clearly enough. In these preliminary experiments, student subjects were asked to characterise each drawing according to trait qualities. A drawing was then selected if it gained high results in the relevant characteristic and low results in the others. Seven drawings represented qualities from a teacher's perspective ('modest', 'diligent', 'polite', 'intelligent', 'concentrating', 'shy', 'sensitive') and seven qualities from a pupil's perspective ('active', 'imaginative', 'cheerful', 'sociable', 'helpful', 'companionable', 'self-assured'). Two characteristics, one each from the teacher and pupil perspectives, was simultaneously presented on a slide. Two series of slides were assembled at random, and one was presented to each subject. Each slide was shown for 20 seconds. The equipment used to measure the eye movements was a computer-driven DEMEL DEBIC 80. The dependent variable was the number of units of measurement per drawing, with one unit equalling 1/50 second.

The investigation was explained to the subjects as an experiment about role adoption, which required them to adopt the role of teacher/pupil to the best of their ability. After this, a five-minute video film was shown the subjects to put them into the right frame of mind for their respective roles. There were two versions of the video. The teacher's version showed how, at the end of a conversation, the headmaster of the school asked the teacher to observe a new pupil joining the class as a report was required. In the pupil's version, a visit to a sick classmate was shown from the pupil's perspective, in which the sick pupil also requested a report about the new pupil.

The independent variable 'goals' was introduced in two steps. The condition 'achievement goals' was produced by informing the subjects in the role of teacher that, although there was a good atmosphere in the class, there were gaps in the pupil's fundamental knowledge. The principal concern of both headmaster and teacher was to fill in these gaps. Correspondingly, the subjects in the role of pupil were instructed that it was important that their collaboration with their new classmate should result in academic achievement.

As far as the experimental condition 'social goals' was concerned, the class was described to the subjects in the teacher role as 'running wild' and the instructions were above all to minimise conflict and aggression. The subjects in the pupil role were instructed that the new pupil could be included in leisure activities. After assessment, the subjects were requested to describe the drawings that they could recall and to state which of these were particularly significant for the description they were to submit.

Results

For the analysis of the experiment only those subjects were included for whom measurement was successful and for whom at least 70 per cent of the total units of measurement per slide were valid. The results of 42 subjects out of a possible 55 were valid. After the experiment most subjects stated that their success in putting themselves into the role was 'quite good' (29 per cent) to 'average' (34 per cent). Twenty-one per cent 'hardly' succeeded in identifying with their respective roles. An analysis of variance with repeated measurements on one factor showed that the interactions A ('role') × C ('characteristics') and B ('goals') reveal the expected tendency but are not significant.

Discussion

The hypothesis of the dependence of selective perception on cognitive/motivational factors resulting from the behavioural demands of a certain social situations can only be partially affirmed by the results of the two experimental investigations described. In Experiment 1, the subjects could better recall characteristics relevant to the experimentally constructed situation. But the subjects did not look at different characteristics for different periods of time (Experiment 2). First of all, then, the assessment made by Haber (1966) cannot be reaffirmed, namely that the effects of existing attitudes can be proven more easily the fewer memory effects there are involved. Furthermore, it could prove useful to consider the process of selection-for-action in detail that is more precise. On what level could selection occur? If the classical filter theory were used (Broadbent, 1971) – regardless of the fact that this was developed using simple experimental tasks – it would be expected that, after the early stage of simultaneous processing of stimuli, subjects would move into a stage at which only successive processing is possible. There are, however, indications that, in a massively parallel system, selective enhancement provides a possible mechanism of selective cueing that need not entail the exclusion from further processing of the non-cued information. Sensory-motor communication proceeds in many parallel, specialised channels (Allport, 1987).

One reason for the only scant confirmation of the hypotheses, contrary to the results of social-perception research, could be put down to a further point. In the experiments, no particular expectations were aroused by the instructions about the roles or goals to be assumed. Instead, cognitive slots were activated. These state that information (e.g. about ability) is required for certain dimensions, but not what form this information will take (e.g. whether the level of ability is high or low). The hypotheses provided did not specify quantitative values within a category, but they provided whole categories to decode the stimuli.

The theoretical explanation of expectation effects is more complicated in the case of the perception of individuals than of inanimate objects. If, as in the case of this investigation, an approach is used based on the theory of action (Hofer, 1986), then a number of assumptions of unproven legitimacy must be introduced. Our approach first assumes that perception of another individual depends on those aims an individual pursues in a given situation. The effective induction of a social role is no guarantee that the proposed goals will be activated. In the experiments, controls were used to test the expression of the individual goals without the predicted effects being established. It was assumed further that the goals activate a cognitive structure that is composed of categories regarded as relevant with respect to goal-oriented actions. In the first experiment, individual goal-related judgements about relevance were made for each of the given dimensions without these judgements having a regular relation to the perception data. In addition, Experiment 2 indicated that the structure assumed was not clearly activated, as supposed, and as would have been necessary had this had a significant effect on the process of perception. Lastly, it was assumed that the activated structure would partly depend on representations of behavioural tasks that are seen as necessary to reach the goals. This element was not assessed or controlled at all in these experiments.

Finally, specific aspects of the way the experiments were conducted must be examined. It is conceivable that the cognitive structures of the pupil and teacher perspectives overlap to too great an extent. The shared school context could possibly lead to a strong measure of agreement and emphasis of variables such as ability, effort and conduct. It is also conceivable that the subjects could have failed to adopt each perspective in a realistic way. The assumption that student teachers would have easy access to both perspectives may also be inaccurate. Admittedly, the use of teachers and pupils as subjects inevitably entails forgoing the possibility of experimental manipulation of the independent variables. In addition, doubt might also be cast on the assumption that the measurements used are capable of making a valid record of the dependent variable. This concerns the artificiality of the experimental situation. Durations of eye fixations on pictures presented on a screen may or may not be valid indicators of people's attention to attributes of individuals in interpersonal situations.

Overall, the results and conclusions of these two experiments give rise to the need to investigate in greater detail cognitive mechanisms that are assumed during an individual person's perception when using an approach based on the theory of action.

Author Reflection 2004

In this chapter, the cognitive mechanisms which are assumed to occur during a teacher's perception of pupils are studied using the theory of action approach. Two experiments are described, in which subjects are required to take the role of a school teacher and a fellow pupil vis-à-vis other school students in random order. Starting from concepts of person perception, it was assumed that a person playing a known role activates typical expectations regarding attributes and behaviour of the respective role partner. When perceiving a new pupil, teachers and pupils should direct their attention to different characteristics relevant for their specific goals. Therefore, role players should remember attributes presented to them to characterise students differentially (Experiment 1). They should direct their eyes longer on those behaviours which are relevant to deciding on actions leading to the goals associated with the respective role (Experiment 2). At the time this study was published, cognitive experimental investigations like this were highly unusual in teacher research. They probably were regarded as not taking into account the complexity of the teaching situation. Instead, most studies were directed either towards the process of classroom teaching or towards the effects of teaching. Even today, these studies seem to be rare. As my own research interests shifted away from the teacher area, I can only guess that experimental social psychology and research on teaching remained two disparate and disconnected fields. However, as we can infer from Milgram and Zimbardo's studies, teachers' behaviour is strongly influenced by how teachers interpret their role, the goals they strive for and the strategies they judge as effective. Therefore, the study of cognitive processes active during teaching and mediating between societal roles and behaviour in the classroom is still of interest.

Chapter 11

Grading as a Quasi-rational Judgement Process

Annica Brehmer

Introduction

The goal of research on teacher thinking should be to find and study those hypotheses and theories/beliefs that govern how teachers practice their work to be able to understand better what happens in the classroom (Clark and Peterson, 1986). One way of meeting this goal would be to focus upon the process of grading. The point of departure is the hypothesis that grading controls learning (Marton *et al.,* 1976; Snyder, 1971). In support of this hypothesis, Snyder (1971) showed in a well-known study that university students are actively involved in finding out what their teachers consider important to know and adapt their learning to this.

A relation between grading and learning is, however, not proof that grades actually control what pupils learn. An alternative interpretation is that teachers emphasise the same aspects in their teaching and their grading, and that the pupils concentrate on what is emphasised in the teaching. In both these cases, the question of what the teachers emphasise in grading will be of central importance for understanding the results of teaching. If this could be uncovered, we would have a basis for predicting what the results of the teaching would be. It would then be a problem for later studies to reveal what the nature of the causal relation between learning and grading might be.

Grading as Judgement

The general assumption here, then, is that grading expresses the operative goals of teaching. One way of ascertaining what these operative goals are is to investigate how teachers believe that pupils with good grades differ from pupils with poor grades. The dimensions used to order pupils should express the goals of the teacher's teaching, and the order of the pupils should express the extent to which pupils fulfil these goals.

This study was supported by a grant from the Sector for Teaching Professions, Uppsala University. The author is indebted to Berndt Brehmer for his comments on earlier versions of this manuscript.

This order should be most clearly expressed in the grading. This raises the question of how grading can be studied. The present chapter takes, as its point of departure, that grading is a judgement process and that it can be studied using the methods developed within psychological research on judgement.

Frame of Reference

The general frame of reference is the Social Judgement Theory (SJT) (see B. Brehmer, 1987). SJT defines judgement as the process whereby a judge applies his/her general principles to make inferences about individual cases. SJT is especially concerned with situations that require people to make inferences from uncertain information when they cannot, or do not, obtain an answer through an analytical scheme (B. Brehmer, 1987). This seems like an accurate description of grading: Grading clearly requires the teacher to infer the pupils' real knowledge from the more or less uncertain information that can be obtained from observations of the pupils' performance and behaviour.

Results obtained within SJT suggest that under the abovementioned circumstances judgement tends to be a quasi-rational process, consisting of both analytical and intuitive elements (Hammond and Brehmer, 1973; Hammond, 1982). Such a process can only be partially recovered. That is, people cannot give precise descriptions of how they arrive at their judgements. Consequently, we need indirect methods to study people's judgements. Within SJT linear statistical model are used for this purpose. This kind of model makes it possible to infer a number of characteristics of the judgement process (see e.g. B. Brehmer 1987 for a full discussion).

Results from a number of studies (for reviews see Slovic and Lichtenstein, 1971; Libby and Lewis, 1982; see Shavelson, Webb and Burstein, 1986 for a review of results on teachers) which have used a variety of judgement tasks and many different kinds of experts as judges show that:

1.   *Judgement processes are relatively simple:* judgements are based on a few cues (3–5) only, and the information from these cues is integrated in a simple additive way.
2.   *Judgement processes are inconsistent,* that is, the judgements for one set of cases cannot be fully described with only one rule, and the judgements for a given example may differ from time to time.
3.   *There are considerable inter-individual differences,* both with respect to the information used and the way in which information is combined, and this applies also when the judges are experts with years of experience of the actual judgements.
4.   *People have poor insight into their own judgement processes,* that is, it is not possible to predict the actual judgements from the verbal reports about how the judgements were made.

Hypotheses

The results referred to above form the basis for a number of hypotheses regarding grading and its function. Thus, we should expect that:

1.   The operative goals will be few.
2.   There will be considerable differences among teachers with respect to how they grade.

3.   Lack of consistency in teachers' judgements will give pupils a blurred picture of what the goals for teaching actually are. This means that there will be limits to the possible steering effects of grading.
4.   Lack of insight into how grading judgements are made means that the operative goals in teaching will be different from what the teachers think they are, i.e. part of the curriculum will be hidden also for the teacher.

The remainder of this chapter will report some of the results from a series of studies on grading. These studies are part of a larger project on the role and function of handicrafts, and thus the grades of concern here are grades in textile handicrafts (see Lindgren-Rydberg, 1982 and Brehmer, 1986a, 1986b, 1984; Brehmer and Lindfors 1986 for earlier reports from this project). The results presented here are concerned with the three general problems:
1.   Is it possible to describe the grading process as a quasi-rational judgement process?
2.   Is the grading done in the same way in different age groups?
3.   Do the pupils know how they are graded?

The first question concerns the value of the judgement approach to grading, while the second and the third questions provide a basis for deciding whether there is any possibility for grading to influence learning. Thus, the second question concerns the problem of whether grading creates a curriculum that is constant throughout school that pupils could adapt to, and the third question concerns the problem of whether the pupils have detected how they are graded.

Method

As already mentioned, these studies use the general method developed within judgement research, i.e. a number of cases is presented, subjects are asked to judge these cases, and a mathematical model is then fitted to the subjects' answers.

Subjects

All participants in this series of studies were women; there are no male textile handicrafts teachers in Sweden. The teachers worked in the public school system in and around Uppsala and were between 30 and 63 years of age. All were qualified textile handicraft teachers and had worked at least 4 years after their degree certificate. They worked, or had previously worked, in all grades of the public school system. A total of 18 teachers and 10 pupils participated in the studies reported here. The pupils participating in the study came from the public school grade 9, and were 15–16 years old.

Judgement Task

All subjects judged fictitious pupils on a scale ranging from 0 to 20 from information about five characteristics:
        The quality of the product, i.e. the extent to which the product is well-made, has no loose threads, keeps in one piece, and can actually be used or worn as intended.

Independence, i.e. the extent to which the student shows initiative, can plan his/her own work, and is not bound to what peers think, as well as his/her ability to use earlier knowledge.

Social ability, i.e. the extent to which the student is able to collaborate with others when needed, functions well together with peers and teacher, and helps others when possible.

Creativity, i.e. the extent to which the student has new and usable ideas and is able to find new areas for old knowledge.

Working style, i.e. the extent to which the student carries out the planned work in reasonable time without the teacher having to supervise him/her.

The factors were taken from a study by Brehmer and Carnmark (1984) in which 20 textile handicraft teachers participated in a structured interview. One of the items asked them to write down what they paid attention to when grading.
These answers form the basis for the aforementioned factors.

All subjects were given information about each 'pupil' in the form of a bar graph presented on a CRT. In the graph the height of the bars indicated values of the cues: the quality of the pupil's products, the independence of the student, and so on, on a scale from 0 through 10. The factors used were orthogonal, that is, the intercorrelation between each pair of factors was r = 0.

Procedure

Subjects were seated in front of a computer terminal. An interactive program, COGNOGRAPH, presented information about each 'pupil', accepted the answers from the subject and analysed them. (See Hammond and Brehmer, 1973, for a discussion on this method.)

The subjects were asked to form an overall impression of each pupil from the factors presented and to give their judgements on a scale from 0 through 20, where 20 was the highest possible value.

Each subject made 50 judgements divided into two blocks of 25 judgements each, where the two blocks consisted of identical 'pupils' presented in a different random order.

When a subject had completed the 50 judgements she was asked which factors she had given weight and which factor had received the highest weight. Furthermore, the teacher was asked if she missed any factor that she usually paid attention to when grading.

Data Analysis

For each subject a regression analysis was made for all judgements, where the beta-weight for each factor and the multiple correlation was computed. Only beta-weights significant at the 0.01 levels were used in the analyses. In addition, the correlation between the two replicates was computed. The correlation between the replicates, r_{tt}, is an estimate of the proportion of systematic variance in the judgements. The squared multiple correlations, R^2, express the proportion of variance accounted for by the regression model. If r_{tt} and R^2 agree, it is reasonable to conclude that the regression model captures the systematic variance in the judgements and that these follow a linear model.

Results

Can grading be seen as a judgement process? The results showed that there was indeed a close correspondence between r_{tt} and R^2. For the three groups of subjects the results were: teachers judging grade 4 $R^2 = 0.88$, $r_{i2} = 0.84$; teachers judging grade 9 $R^2 = 0.81$, $r_{12} = 0.73$; pupils $R^2 = 0.87$, $r_{12} = 0.83$; all values are mean values for each group. The regression model thus gives a good description of the judgements. Consequently, we conclude that the judgements follow a linear model. This means that the subjects combined information from the different factors in a simple additive way. Moreover, it means that the judgements are compensatory, that is, a low value in one factor, e.g. social ability, can be compensated by a high value in another factor, e.g. creativity (for further details see A. Brehmer, 1984). It is important to note that both r_{ig} and R^2 are below 1.0. Thus, the judgements are not fully systematic, i.e. the subjects are inconsistent.

As is shown in Tables 11.1 and 11.2 the teachers did not use all of the information available to them. They only used between three and four factors. The tables also show that there are considerable inter-individual differences among teachers with respect to which factors they used in their judgements, as well as with respect to the relative weights they gave to different factors.

It is important to note that another study in which each individual teacher was allowed to define her own factors gave very similar results (Brehmer and Brehmer, 1986a). Thus, the present results are not because the experimenter has selected the cues.

These results correspond closely to the results usually obtained in studies of judgement processes. This, together with the finding (reported elsewhere: see Brehmer and Brehmer, 1986b) that teachers have limited insight in how they grade, supports the general view that grading can be seen as a quasi-rational judgement process.

Studies of the Validity of the Judgement Models

Two different attempts at validating the results from the analyses above have been made (A. Brehmer, 1984). Both are attempts to predict real grades of the analyses

Table 11.1. Teachers judging fictitious grade 4 pupils

Teacher	Quality of product	Independence	Social ability	Creativity	Working style
			Factors		
1	0.57*	0.62*	0.16*	0.30*	0.17*
2	0.60*	0.42*	0.03	0.57*	0.12
3	0.33*	0.83*	0.18*	0.25*	0.07
4	0.50*	0.36*	0.28*	0.35*	0.10
5	0.58*	0.55*	0.08	0.18	0.05
6	0.51*	0.23*	0.52*	0.47*	0.25*
7	0.72*	0.09	0.11	0.55*	0.12
8	0.38*	0.49*	0.19	0.52*	0.29*
9	0.33*	0.28*	0.41*	0.58*	0.30*

*Significant at the 0.01 level.

Table 11.2.   Teachers judging fictitious grade 9 pupils

	Factors				
Teacher	Quality of product	Independence	Social ability	Creativity	Working style
1	0.64*	0.10	0.29*	0.19	0.20
2	0.31*	0.54*	0.28*	0.49*	0.29*
3	−0.10	−0.31	−0.06	−0.21	−0.19
4	0.40*	0.39*	0.42*	0.46*	0.35*
5	0.43*	0.46*	0.52*	0.29*	0.12
6	0.73*	0.38*	0.22*	0.28*	0.26*
7	0.45*	0.40*	0.39*	0.42*	0.25*
8	0.88*	0.29*	0.07	0.19*	0.09
9	0.62*	0.45*	0.21	0.25*	0.11

*Significant at the 0.01 level.

from judgement analyses. The first study departs from the result that the factor 'quality of the product' got the highest weight from most of the teachers. Therefore, it should be possible to predict grades with great accuracy from the students' products only.

To test this, the products from one semester in one grade 9 classroom were collected. These products were then judged by ten teachers who were asked to grade to justify their grades for each pupil. The results show first that there was very high agreement among teachers, and second that it was possible to predict the pupils' actual grades from their products with almost perfect accuracy. It is not surprising that there is a relationship between the quality of the product and the pupils' grades. However, that the grades can be predicted with such high accuracy is not trivial and supports the results from the judgement analyses.

In the second study, two teachers judged their pupils on the five factors used in these studies. These judgements were then used to predict each teacher's pupils' actual grades by means of the policy obtained for the teacher from judgement analysis. The results showed that 96 per cent of the variance in grades could be predicted by means of these policies. While limited to two teachers, these results nevertheless suggest that the results of judgement analysis have considerable validity. Data from additional teachers are now being collected.

Do Teachers Grade in the Same Way for Different Grade Levels?

Tables 11.1 and 11.2 show the results from the judgement analyses for teachers in grade 4 and grade 9.

The factors 'quality of the product', 'independence' and 'creativity' are the three most important factors for grading in textile handicraft for grade 4. All teachers pay attention to the quality of the product in their judgement, eight pay attention to the pupils' independence and eight pay attention to the pupils' creativity. Turning to the factor 'social ability', we find that five teachers use this factor in their grading. A similar result is found for the factor 'working style' where four teachers feel that it is an important factor when grading. The teachers who use one or both of these latter factors use at least one of the factors 'quality of the product', 'independence' and 'creativity' as well.

In Table 11.2, there is one teacher (no. 3) who is different from the rest in that she seems to be completely random in her grading. As can be seen in Table 11.2 none of the factors are significant in her judgement. Why she is different is not known. Except for this case, the results correspond well with the results from Table 11.1.

These results demonstrate that the operative goals for textile handicraft are the same in grades 4 and 9. This suggests that the pupils are exposed to a constant 'curriculum' from grade 4 and onwards. This means that there is a good basis for the pupils to adapt their learning to this 'curriculum'. The question is whether the pupils actually discover what is expected of them. We now turn to this problem.

Do Pupils Discover What Is Expected of Them?

Table 11.3 shows the results of the analyses of ten pupils from grade 9 who have graded fictitious pupils in textile handicraft in the same way as the teachers. The first impression is that there is considerable resemblance with the textile handicraft teachers. The pupils have on the average 3.4 significant factors that are about the same as the teachers'.

All pupils have 'quality of the product' as the single most important factor for the grade. No other factor has received as much, or more, weight from the pupils. Independence and creativity is second in importance as it is with the teachers, but the weights are relatively low. Further, we note that social ability and working style are considered only if at least two of the other factors receive weight. Thus, the pupils seem to have understood the grading policy of their teachers, but they seem to have a simplified picture of teachers' grading; they exaggerate the importance of the most salient feature so they end up with what is almost a caricature picture of how grading is done. This is not surprising. If their teacher is inconsistent it will be difficult to

Table 11.3.   Pupils from grade 9 making judgements about fictitious pupils

	Factors				
Pupil	Quality of product	Independence	Social ability	Creativity	Working style
1	0.56*	0.44*	0.37*	0.35*	0.30*
2	0.67*	0.32*	0.09	0.41*	0.23*
3	0.67*	0.45*	0.19	0.18	0.16
4	0.97*	0.04	0.04	0.06	−0.01
5	0.77*	0.25*	0.19*	0.32*	0.13
6	0.68*	0.27*	0.21	0.24*	0.24*
7	0.71*	0.35*	0.21*	0.26*	0.23*
8	0.68*	0.12	0.35*	0.39*	0.14
9	0.67*	0.30*	0.36*	0.22	0.00
10	0.72*	0.13	0.30*	0.26*	0.17

*Significant at the 0.01 level.

detect anything but the most salient features of her grading. These results are, of course, limited. They come from only one class, but this class is especially relevant because it has had several textile handicraft teachers. Thus, the pupils have had the chance to form a picture of grading based on many teachers. However, future studies should relate the pupil judgements to the teacher they actually have rather than to an 'average' teacher.

Conclusions and Discussion

Three aspects of these results need emphasising. The first of these is that the results support our general point that grading can be studied by means of the methods developed in the psychology of judgement. Thus, the results show that it is possible to extract models of the grading process by these methods, and that these models then predict actual grades.

The second set of results concern what the teachers actually emphasise in their grading, i.e. the content of their grading, and, according to the present hypothesis about the relation between grading and learning, what the pupils will actually learn. Here, the strong emphasis upon the quality of the product suggests that the teachers are mainly concerned with imparting knowledge, and that other kinds of goals, such as social goals, are not so important to the teachers. These results differ from the results on teachers' teaching criteria, i.e. research into the goals teachers try to pursue when teaching (e.g. Halkes and Deijkers, 1984). There is some commonality; both our studies and the studies on teachers' criteria emphasise social development, and work ethos, but the results on grading suggest that these aspects may be of little importance compared to subject matter aspects that lead to a good-quality product. To investigate which kind of method gives the best predictions of teachers' classroom behaviours is an important problem for future studies.

The present results suggest that pupils are evaluated in the same way throughout school. This is important because it indicates that they are subject to the same operative goals. They thus have a chance to actually adapt to this curriculum. It is therefore not surprising to find that the pupils know how they will be graded. That is, they know the actual curriculum, even though their picture seems to be somewhat simplified. This suggests that the opportunity for grading to have an effect upon what the pupils will learn is there, and that this effect will be to cause the pupils to focus on the subject matter aspects of the classroom activities, rather than upon other kinds of aspects, such as developing cooperation and social skills. This provides an interesting hypothesis to be tested in studies of what the pupils are actually concerned about in the classroom.

A third important result is that the grading process exhibits all the marks of a quasi-rational process. If grading has these characteristics, it seems reasonable to assume that much of teacher thinking in other respects will have a quasi-rational nature also.

Quasi-rationality provides an alternative to the distinction between thinking and routines in the study of teaching (e.g. Lowyck, 1984; Olson, 1984), and suggests that this distinction may not be very useful. Instead, if teacher thinking is quasi-rational, we have to think of it as a blend of analytical (i.e. thinking) aspects and experience (i.e. routines). This suggests that it is not useful to focus exclusively on either the analytical aspects or the routine aspects of teaching. Both have to be considered together. Analysis of teacher judgement does precisely this.

The notion of teacher thinking as quasi-rational also has the important implication that we cannot expect to get the whole truth about this process from verbal descriptions from the teachers. This shows that the concerns of, e.g. Huber and Mandl (1984) about the use of verbalisations, and the need for actual validation of teachers' verbalisations, are well placed. In this connection, it is important to note that the teachers' verbal descriptions do not agree with the models extracted from their judgements but that the models actually predict their behaviour (Brehmer and Brehmer, 1986b). Thus, these models seem to provide more useful descriptions of actual teacher thinking than do the teachers' verbalisations.

The quasi-rationality concept also leads us to share Bromme's (1984) concern about the usefulness of the theory metaphor in describing and analysing teacher thinking. If teacher thinking is a quasi-rational process, it cannot be fully described as a set of propositions, as Bromme pointed out. Whether the descriptions of teacher thinking emanating from judgement analysis will provide the kind of psychological concepts that Bromme asks for as a substitute for the theory metaphor is an important question for the future.

The present results are, of course, limited: only one subject, that of textile handicrafts, has been studied. Yet, the form of the results does not seem to be specific to this particular subject. The same kinds of factors could be used for evaluating pupils in other subjects also. To extend the present work to other school subjects is, of course, the most important problem for future studies.

Chapter 12

Analysing Teachers' Thoughts Prior to Student Assessment

Urban Lissmann

Introduction

Research on teachers' thoughts has rapidly expanded during the 1980s, 'as it has become increasingly recognised that much of teachers' professional activity is cognitive in nature, and that a large portion of teachers' classroom behaviour is the product or accompaniment of some form of thinking' (Calderhead, 1986, p. 1).

The rapidly growing relevance of research on teacher thoughts is shown, first, by the fact, that the journal *Educational Research Quarterly* edited a volume that focused on teacher thinking (Joyce, 1978–79). In addition, the number of empirical studies has grown rapidly as well as the number of research reviews (Clark and Yinger, 1979a; Shavelson and Stern, 1981; Borko and Shavelson, 1983; Mandl and Huber, 1983; Calderhead, 1984) and research proceedings (Halkes and Olson, 1984; Ben-Peretz, Bromme and Halkes, 1986). Special areas of research include the teaching process under naturalistic conditions, decision-making processes, judgement processes and lesson planning. Furthermore, research is guided by two theoretical positions. The group associated with Joyce understands teaching as an information processing approach, and the group associated with Shavelson as a decision-making process.

Although teacher thoughts concerning judgement of student performance have been examined in empirical research, little is known about them. Relevant research concentrates on the implicit personality theory of teachers (Mandl and Huber, 1983) and the accuracy of the estimations of intellectual capability, motivation and social behaviour (Shavelson and Stern, 1981; Helmke and Fend, 1981). Teacher judgements 'appear to be the basis for their decision making ... selecting content, tutoring, handling behaviour problems, and grouping students...'. Furthermore, ' research on human judgement and decision making has found that people are generally unaware of the nature of their judgement policies' (Shavelson and Stern, 1981, p. 475). The following two studies illustrate our topic.

Rapaille (1986) used a thinking-aloud method to access the mental processes in a naturalistic correcting and assessment situation. The verbalisations of the Belgian

This research was supported by a grant from the Deutsche Forschungs-gemeinschaft, D-5300 Bonn 2, Az.: Li 379/1-1.

teachers on audiotape were transcribed and submitted to five content analyses. Macro-analysis is used to highlight the general structure, e.g. if teachers correct pupil-by-pupil or question-by-question. The second content analysis consists of coding teachers' thoughts into 16 categories, e.g. referring to an objective, a task or an information pick-up. It is called functional analysis. After the functional analysis, a sequential analysis is done to discover behaviour patterns that occur repeatedly. The aim of the analysis of enunciations was to look for characteristics of teachers by counting linguistic data, e.g. personal pronouns, persons' names and possessive pronouns. Microanalysis examined students' answers to find explanations of wrong answers. Although data analysis is still going on, each content analysis explores a specific facet of the complex assessment process.

Baumeister (1986) wanted to reconstruct the subjective achievement-assessing theory of German teachers of special education. At first, the judgement categories were derived from daily judgements in school. Therefore the judgement behaviour of 10 teachers was audio-taped (over several weeks), and coded with help from the teachers. Second, 20 teachers answered a questionnaire which contained 16 of the judgement categories. Similarity of the subjective theories of teachers was expected, but not found.

This is, in summary, the knowledge about teachers' thoughts of student assessment. There is a lack of grounded information, e.g. thought processes themselves, and their connection to student, teacher and context variables. Some of the problems should be ameliorated by our pilot study.

The purpose of the study was to investigate from a qualitative research perspective teachers' thought processes before the correcting and assessment situation. The focus was on five questions:
1.   Which thoughts will be reported by teachers?
2.   What frequencies of specific teachers' thoughts are found?
3.   Did teachers' thoughts depend on written examinations?
4.   Did teachers' thoughts depend on the school system?
5.   Do correlations between teachers' thoughts and student assessment exist?

Method

Sample
The sample was 46 teachers from different school systems and between 1034 and 1243 written examinations in different subjects.

Thought Listings
At the time the teachers start to correct the students' written examinations, they have to report what they are currently thinking about the individual. There are several assumptions underlying this procedure.

First, we refer to teacher 'thoughts' to express the idea that there are not only cognitions but also feelings, hopes and wishes. Second, the writing method was chosen. However, the writing process requires time, and as Ericsson and Simon (1980) stated, slow processes are subject to a greater degree of cognitive control, and therefore may be less valid as representations of rapid thought processes. To weaken this critique, teachers were instructed to write down briefly what they really think, and not what experts would think. Moreover, teachers could choose the method. Although they had the option to speak on tape or to write down their thoughts, all except one preferred the writing mode. Third, a pre-actional access to thoughts has been chosen (Huber and Mandl, 1982).

Written Examinations
Students' work in German dictation, German composition and mathematics has been considered. It is part of our strategy not to influence the natural setting; therefore, the topics of the examinations are not restricted. We only wanted to look at German and mathematics – two main subjects in Germany. In addition, the curriculum is restricted to the seventh grade.

School System
Thoughts of teachers from German 'Hauptschule' (vocational track), 'Realschule' (mixed track) and 'Gymnasium' (university track) will be reported below. For a better understanding, some details concerning the German school system will be given.

In Germany, all children attend 'Grundschule' (primary school) for the first four years. Thereafter their parents have the option of choosing, in principle, from four different school systems to continue their child's schooling.

In the traditional school system, the children have the possibility of continuing from grade 5 upward at either a 'Hauptschule', 'Realschule' or 'Gymnasium', according to ability and previous performance in school. The Hauptschule is vocational-oriented and includes schooling until grade 9 or 10. Graduation from Realschule at the end of grade 10 entitles the student to continue schooling at certain special schools, e.g. 'Fachhochschule', technical high school, vocational high school. Graduation from the Gymnasium takes place at the end of grade 13 ('Abitur').

In addition to the traditional school system, the 'Gesamtschule' (comprehensive school) was established in 1968. The fourth graders need not decide at which school they would like to continue. All students attend the same school until grade 10 or 13, instructed separately in courses of different standards.

Pupil Assessment
As an indicator of scholastic achievement teachers stated four different marks: the expected mark, an expected mark under the assumption of optimal preparation, an expected mark under the assumption of minimal preparation, and the actual mark received. The scale of marks given in German schools ranges from 1 to 6. A '1' is given for excellent performance (letter grade 'A'); '5' and '6' are unsatisfactory ('F'). Usually grades are given in an undifferentiated and norm-referenced manner, although they are supposed to be curriculum-oriented.

In addition to the expected marks, two new variables are defined. One is called expectation accuracy. It is the difference between expected and actual marks. The other new variable is called effort scope. This is the difference between the expected mark under optimal preparation and under minimum preparation. Effort scope is an indicator of the teacher's perception of student effort.

Procedures
The teachers were instructed to correct and assess in the following way: First the teacher takes the first written examination. Second, the teacher write down catchwords of his/her thinking. Third, the expected marks are stated. The fourth step consists of the correcting process. Then the same procedure is repeated with the second written examination, the third, and so on, until the whole class's work is corrected. The last step requires calculating the actual marks, and reporting those marks.

Analyses of Data

Analyses of the written teacher thoughts were done by computer-based content analysis (Textpack; Mohler and Zuell, 1984). It is the aim of computer-based content analysis to transform the alphanumerical data into numerical data by certain rules. The rules have to be defined by the researcher and gathered in a dictionary. In general, the word is the unit of analysis.

Coding was done in three steps by a teacher, a student of education and the senior researcher. First the traditional grammar coding was done, where nouns, verbs, comparatives, conjugation and declination were summed up. The word 'trained', for example, is coded together with 'to train, (he) trains, (the) training, to exercise, the exercises'. There were 5090 different words in the thought data. By this way of coding, they were condensed into 760 categories. The second step consisted of summarising the synonyms and words with similar expression, e.g. 'trained' together with 'working expenditure, fighter, endurance, to pull one's weight'. By this coding there are 121 categories left. The third and last step used the frequency of occurrence of the categories. After eliminating the categories with 3 per cent or less, 54 categories remained (see Table 12.1). They consist of 20 sub-categories, e.g. one-word categories, and 34 broader categories like the following: Character traits: arrogant, fair, charming, cheeky, sanctimonious, dreamer, reliable. Effort: (he) tries hard, fighter, skilled, perseverant, prepared, and so on.

The method used also had its limitations. Word analysis did not distinguish between 'effort/little effort/much effort/no effort at all'. If one wanted to count the word 'effort', the computer counted it regardless of the context. Word analysis also did not discriminate between addresses, e.g. whether teacher or student is 'pleased, disappointed'. Therefore, we had to make such distinctions manually.

To ensure the validity of coding, the experts not only decided how a category is defined, but also looked at the key-words (categories) in text context. In future research, it seems to be worthwhile to let the teachers participate in coding their own thoughts. This method is referred to in the literature as communicative validity (Lechler, 1982).

Analysis of numerical data consisted mainly of cross-tabulations. The main problem is that the cues, i.e. students, and responses have not been constant across teachers. Therefore, data analysis is done twice, with unweighted and weighted data. In the weighted case, the number of students per classroom served as a denominator. Since the results of weighted and unweighted data largely coincide, only unweighted data are reported.

Results

Frequency of Particular Teacher Thoughts

In answer to the first two research questions, Table 12.1 presents 54 thought categories, and the percentage of nomination of particular thoughts as opposed to non-nomination. The categories are listed in alphabetical order.

The 10 most frequently reported thoughts are described in detail. 'Task references' (63.7 per cent) refer to about two-thirds of the students. Not only do different actions belong to the task references (to interpret, to cross out, to articulate, to write, to calculate), but also different task requirements (basic calculation, construction, punctuation, curriculum, objective), and materials necessary to complete the tasks (work sheet, exercise-book, close tests, i.e. tests with missing words).

The category mentioned second in frequency is achievement references (person) (45.6 per cent). About half of the students were referred to by this category. The concept relates in any way to achieving persons, e.g. a good student. (Other examples: to decrease, to increase, inclination, success, failure.)

Ranges 3, 4 and 5 are defined by the frequency of nomination of 'character traits' (28.5 per cent), 'work habits' (28 per cent) and 'positive remarks' (27.4 per cent). About one-quarter of the students were labelled by these terms.

Mathematics is difficult to characterise because of the heterogeneity of the teacher thoughts. Most frequently used, as opposed to the other written examinations, are the categories 'instruction', 'illness' and 'handicaps'. In contrast, 'effort, work habits, school-related interest and motivation, and task-specific achievement references' are seldom used concerning mathematics.

In summary, across written examinations there are many characteristics. German dictation, for example, is associated with concentration and home environment. It is less associated with teacher expectations. German composition is seen as a matter of intellectual and character traits. Finally, yet importantly, dictation together with composition evokes thoughts of effort, good work habits, and interest in school.

Teacher Thoughts and School System

As shown in Table 12.1, the number of significant differences across tracks, i.e. Hauptschule (vocational track), Realschule (mixed track) and Gymnasium (university track) is enormous (43.7 per cent).

The vocational track is labelled by thoughts of 'effort' and 'work habits' because teachers did report these categories more frequently in the vocational track than in the mixed track or in the university track. In particular, the vocational track is characterised by the subcategories 'diligence, concentration' of work habits. In the vocational track, teachers most often, spoke of 'task reference: essay, dictation', and of lower achievement (failing grades). 'Grade level 4', and some other categories are as often cited in vocational track as in the university track.

The university track is characterised by thoughts of 'character traits, parents and family, social references (social behaviour), development and maturity, and emotions'. The categories refer to the general personality of students, whereas the following categories refer to achievement-related affairs: 'task reference: test achievement reference (person): marks, learning, and classroom'. The third pattern of thoughts characterises the teacher–pupil interaction. In the university track, teachers report most frequently positive or negative remarks ('remarks: positive, negative'), thoughts or ideas ('thought, idea'), things they had to look at ('teacher: task references') and expectations ('teacher: expectations'). In addition, teacher thoughts in the university track are more differentiated than in the vocational track, whereas teacher thoughts in the mixed track are not at all striking.

Teacher Thoughts and Student Assessment

Mark Expectations
Mark expectations are divided into three groups at the 33rd and 66th percentiles. The three groups of 'mark expectation high, medium, and low' are analysed separately for

Table 12.1. Percentage of teacher thoughts, total and by school system (Hauptschule, HS; Realschule, RS; Gymnasium, Gy), regarding dictation (D), composition (C) and mathematics (M)

	Total	D	C	M	p	HS	RS	GY	p
Sample size	1034	374	325	287		573	292	135	
Ability	13.9	14.4	16.3	8.7	0.02	14.3	13.7	14.8	
Ability (absence of)	4.3	4.8	3.7	4.2		3.0	5.8	5.9	
Achievement references (person)	45.6	46.8	45.5	42.9		45.7	43.5	54.8	
Achievement reference (person): achievement	11.6	10.2	13.2	12.9		11.2	14.7	8.9	
Achievement reference (person): mark	7.7	8.6	9.5	3.8	0.02	7.7	5.8	14.1	0.01
Achievement reference (person): mistake	5.5	11.2	3.4	1.4	0.0	5.6	4.5	8.9	
Achievement reference (person): to produce	5.2	2.7	9.5	3.8	0.0	5.1	5.5	5.2	
Achievement reference (person): weakness	4.1	2.7	4.9	5.2		4.4	3.1	5.2	
Achievement reference (task)	11.2	13.9	13.2	5.2	0.001	12.4	8.9	14.1	
Character traits	28.5	28.1	34.8	17.1	0.0	27.2	25.7	42.2	0.001
Character traits (negative)	3.9	3.2	3.7	4.2		3.5	4.8	3.7	
Classroom	7.7	7.2	8.6	5.2		5.2	9.2	17.0	0.0
Development and Maturity	10.2	11.8	11.1	4.9	0.01	11.3	5.1	17.8	0.001
Difficulties (school)	7.4	8.3	5.5	7.7		6.8	8.2	9.6	
Effort	12.5	15.8	14.2	7.0	0.002	15.4	9.2	9.6	0.02
Emotions	11.3	12.3	10.2	8.4		10.6	9.6	18.5	0.02
Grade levels 1 + 2	7.1	8.0	7.1	5.6		7.9	5.1	9.6	
Grade level 3	7.4	5.9	10.2	6.6		7.7	6.8	9.6	
Grade level 4	3.2	1.3	4.6	3.8	0.03	4.4	0.3	4.4	0.004
Grade level 5 + 6	3.2	4.0	1.9	3.8		4.7	1.0	2.2	
Illness and handicaps	4.0	2.9	3.1	6.6	0.03	4.5	4.1	2.2	
Instruction	8.0	5.1	8.0	10.5	0.03	7.5	7.5	11.1	
Interest, motivation (school)	11.5	12.6	13.5	6.3	0.01	12.6	9.2	13.3	0.01

Learning	4.9	3.7	4.9	4.5	0.0	4.5	3.4	8.9	0.04
Nationalities	3.5	6.4	3.1	0.7	0.02	3.8	3.8	2.2	0.01
Outward appearance	6.5	8.8	5.8	3.5	0.01	7.5	3.4	10.4	0.0
Parents and family	18.0	20.3	12.3	13.2		20.8	9.9	26.7	0.0
Participation	7.0	4.8	7.7	7.0		6.6	6.5	9.6	
Remarks, negative	7.3	8.6	5.5	5.2		5.9	5.8	17.8	
Remarks, positive	27.4	28.3	25.8	26.8		25.7	26.7	36.3	0.04
School, related	4.8	5.1	5.5	2.4		4.4	6.5	4.4	
Social references, behaviour	17.6	19.5	15.7	12.9		18.3	12.7	26.7	0.02
Task references	63.7	59.9	68.0	61.7		64.6	63.7	63.0	
Task reference: Dictation	4.6	8.8	4.3	0	0.0	6.6	1.7	3.7	0.005
Task reference: Essay	6.0	3.7	14.2	0	0.0	9.8	0.3	3.7	0.0
Task reference: German	3.8	4.3	5.8	0.7	0.003	4.0	3.4	4.4	
Task reference: handwriting	7.2	10.2	6.5	4.2	0.01	9.1	4.5	6.7	0.05
Task reference: mathematics	3.4	2.4	0.3	7.7	0.0	2.8	4.1	5.2	
Task reference: spelling	6.3	11.5	6.2	0	0.0	7.7	4.8	5.2	
Task reference: test	17.5	9.1	17.5	23.7	0.0	10.6	21.9	31.9	0.0
Task reference: too busy o.s.	3.7	2.9	4.6	3.5		3.7	3.8	3.7	
Task reference: writing	9.3	9.4	12.0	4.5	0.005	11.2	4.8	11.9	0.01
Teacher: emotion	3.9	3.7	4.6	3.1		3.8	2.7	7.4	
Teacher: expectations/presumption/hope	18.2	13.6	18.8	18.1		16.6	16.8	26.7	0.02
Teacher: expectation	3.8	1.9	5.5	4.5	0.03	3.3	5.1	3.7	0.03
Teacher: hope	9.1	8.8	6.2	8.0	0.0	8.0	7.5	14.8	0.02
Teacher: task references	5.4	4.3	10.8	0.7		5.9	3.4	9.6	0.001
Teacher: thought, idea	3.2	1.9	4.3	3.5	0.01	2.4	2.4	8.9	
Thought, idea	3.5	2.7	5.8	1.4	0.002	3.3	2.7	5.9	
Work habits	28.0	31.6	31.4	20.2		33.7	19.2	25.9	0.0
Work habits (absence of)	5.1	4.0	4.6	6.3		6.5	2.4	5.2	0.04
Work habit: diligence	3.4	4.3	2.2	3.1		8.2	4.1	2.2	0.01
Work habit: concentration	3.5	5.3	2.5	1.4	0.01	3.8	2.4	5.2	
Work habit: cleanness	6.0	8.3	5.8	4.2		4.7	1.4	0.7	0.01

each written examination. Significant results together with the direction of influence have been summarised in Table 12.2.

With respect to German dictation, German composition and maths, there is a dependency between achievement-related thoughts and mark expectation without exception. Reference to 'grade levels 1 + 2' corresponds to a high mark expectation, whereas reference to 'grade level 3' is followed by a medium mark expectation. Reference to 'grade level 4' or 'grade levels 5 + 6' leads to low mark expectations, too, but without becoming significant ($p = 0.05$). These results show that judgement-related thoughts would result in a concrete mark expectation.

A second judgement policy, which is followed by action, consists of teachers' positive remarks. Without exception, teachers' positive thoughts are connected with high mark expectation in German dictation, German composition and maths. 'Negative remarks' do not follow the (opposite) direction; therefore, they have been omitted from Table 12.2. Table 12.2 represents many results which are specific to a certain written examination. In German dictation, 'diligence' is associated with a high mark expectation, 'character traits' with a median, and 'lack of ability' with a low mark expectation. In German composition, characteristics are restricted to a high mark expectation, e.g. 'diligence, character traits, and teacher expectancy'. The only exception is found in mathematics, which is seldom affected by thoughts.

With respect to German composition, there is another interesting result. If the mark expectation is high, teachers prefer to name the task references 'dictation' and 'essay'. It is reasonable that teachers compare different achievement domains. They report thoughts of 'dictation' if the achievement expectation in composition is high. The generality across situations is referred to as 'distinctivity information' in the literature (Heckhausen, 1980). In contrast, teachers report thoughts of 'essay' if their achievement expectation in dictation is high. Though significant, this result is not displayed in Table 12.2 because an assumption of chi-square testing is not met.

Expectation Accuracy

Three groups of students are distinguished: At first, if the mark is worse than the expected mark, the student is labelled 'overestimated'. Second, if the mark is better

Table 12.2.   Mark expectations as affected by teachers' thoughts based upon written examinations

	Dictation	Composition	Mathematics
High mark expectation	Grade levels 1 + 2 Positive remarks Diligence Task reference: spelling	Grade levels 1 + 2 Positive remarks Diligence Teacher expectation Character traits Task reference: dictation Task reference: essay	Grade levels 1 + 2 Positive remarks Task reference: test
Median mark expectation	Grade level 3 Character traits	Grade level 3 School	Grade level 3 Task reference: test
Low mark expectation	Lack of ability Task reference: spelling Grade levels 5 + 6	Task reference: German Achievement reference (person): weakness	

than the expected mark, the student is labelled 'underestimated'. Third, only if the mark equates with the expected mark, do we call the estimation 'proper'.

The proportion of students who are estimated properly is 35.3 per cent for dictation, 26.4 per cent for composition and 31.9 per cent for maths. It is astonishing that the proportion of proper estimations is not higher. We also know that there are many personal and situational factors influencing the actual marks given by teachers (Ingenkamp, 1977).

Table 12.3 presents the summary of significant results. If significantly affected, the most frequent nomination is indicated by listing the thought category. If a thought category is listed twice, frequency of nomination is about equal in two of the three estimation groups. The most striking results are the differences between the written examinations, and the differences between proper and wrong mark expectations.

German dictation yields most of the differences. If the estimation of the mark is proper, teachers have reported a quite negative image concerning their students, as is shown by 'grade levels 5 + 6 and absence of task references'. With respect to wrongly estimated marks (underestimation together with overestimation of marks) 'teacher expectations, teacher hope, social references (behaviour) and averaged achievements' ('grade level 3') are dominant thought categories. Moreover, and with respect to over-estimated dictation marks teachers report most frequently 'negative character traits', in an emotionally affected way ('teacher emotions'). Lastly, 'effort' is a characteristic of underestimation.

Although teacher thoughts have been reported prior to mark expectations, there are some lines of communication that teachers probably do not remember, but which make sense: if students put more effort into the task, their achievement will increase to an unexpected extent. This would result in underestimation. If negative character traits (unsteady, restless, lack of self-concern) are reported, there is

Table 12.3. Expectation accuracy as affected by teachers' thoughts based upon written examinations

Dictation	Composition	Mathematics
Proper estimation	Grade levels 5 + 6 Lack of ability Absence of task references	Diligence
Overestimation	Teacher expectations Teacher hope Teacher emotion Social reference (behaviour) Negative character traits	Teacher expectations Positive remarks Teacher: task reference
Underestimation	Grade level 3 Teacher expectation Teacher hope Effort Social reference: (behaviour) Grade level 3 Grade level 4	Positive remarks Teacher: task reference Task reference: writing	Achievement references (task) Achievement reference: (person) achievement

a growing possibility of failure. This would result in overestimation. It seems reasonable that certain student characteristics have stimulated teachers' implicit theories. Some of the implicit assumptions proved to be empirically evident.

If we distinguish only between proper and wrong estimations, i.e. over- and underestimated marks, there are more teacher thoughts characterising the wrongly estimated students. This result holds for German dictation and German composition. In composition, as opposed to dictation, no negative picture is set up under the condition of proper estimation. The only nomination is 'diligence'. Contrary to this result, over- and underestimated marks lead to many teacher thoughts, e.g. positive remarks, teacher task references and teacher expectations. This leads to the conclusion that thoughts of teachers refer more to students whose results are either uncertain or difficult to calculate. Especially the teacher expectations fit this conclusion because they are – with one exception – frequently used with over- and underestimated marks.

Again, mathematics is the exception. Only two categories are associated with expectation accuracy. As stated at the beginning, only 31.9 per cent of the marks have been estimated properly. Therefore, there is variance enough for speculation about students.

Effort Scope

Effort scope is intended to measure students' effort as perceived by the teacher. It is the difference between the minimum and the maximum mark expectation.

Tallied into the groups is wide, medium and narrow effort scope, within which we looked for relevant teacher thoughts. The results have been summarised in Table 12.4.

Again, Table 12.4 presents the significantly affected teacher thoughts and the direction of influence. With respect to German dictation, and German composition, a wide effort scope is characterised by teachers' thoughts of hope ('teacher hope'). In other words, teachers are more hopeful when the expected fluctuation is large. This was not the case for maths, where a wide effort scope is due to 'character traits, parents and family', and even 'participation'. With respect to German dictation and a narrow effort scope, it is the case that negative thoughts, e.g. 'lack of ability, negative remarks', were dominant. In particular, they must be explained by the low achievement of the group.

Table 12.4.   Effort scope as affected by teachers' thoughts based upon written examinations

	Dictation	Composition	Mathematics
Wide effort scope	Teacher expectations* Teacher hope*	Teacher hope	Character traits Parents and family
Medium effort scope	Grade levels 1 + 2		Participation
Narrow effort scope	Negative remarks	Teacher expectations	Achievement references (task)
	Lack of ability	Effort	
	Achievement reference (person): achievement	Task reference: essay	
	Task reference: writing	Task reference: writing	

*Statistically significant, if effort scope is divided into two groups by the median.

Concerning German composition we find another interesting result. 'Teacher expectation' is associated with a narrow effort scope, whereas 'teacher hope' is associated with a wide effort scope. Hope seems to be a sign of variability in achievement, whose probability is greater under the condition of wide effort scope, whereas expectation reflects a kind of stability, whose probability is greater under the condition of a narrow effort scope.

We expected a narrow effort scope to explain a stable achievement view, and a wide effort scope to explain a variable achievement view. Therefore we expected to find a narrow effort scope associated with thoughts of ability, and a trait-oriented achievement reference, e.g. a good student ('achievement reference: person'), and a wide effort scope associated with thoughts of effort and task-oriented achievement references, e.g. good writing. However, the results are not consistent with our hypotheses. Some results support the hypotheses, like 'lack of ability' and 'achievement references (person)' (German dictation); other results are contradicting, e.g. the task references under the condition of narrow effort scope.

Conclusions

It was the purpose of the pilot study to yield some grounded information about teachers' thoughts before the correcting and assessment process. Therefore, results focus on the thought processes themselves, their frequency of occurrence, their connection to written examinations, school system, and students' achievement.

Results did show that 'task references' (action, due to task, and materials) was the most referred-to thought category, because it is mentioned with reference to two-thirds of the students (N = 1034). About every second student is referred to by 'achievement references (person)', e.g. a good student. About every fourth student is labelled by 'character traits, working habits' and 'positive remarks'. The first 10 of 54 categories have been presented in this chapter.

The 54 thought categories consisted of 20 subcategories, often one-word categories, and 34 broader categories, like those above. They cover about three clusters: general personality, e.g. 'character traits, outer appearance, social references (behaviour), parents and family, development and maturity'; achievement-related personality, e.g. 'effort, ability, school-related interest and motivation, work habits'; and teacher–pupil interaction, e.g. 'teacher expectations, hopes, positive remarks, negative remarks, task references, emotions'.

Teachers' thoughts depend on written examinations. German dictation was characterised to a greater degree by 'concentration', home environment, absence of 'teacher expectations', and other categories. German composition was associated with intellectual traits, and character traits. With respect to both examinations and as opposed to mathematics, teachers reflected more thoughts of 'effort, work habits' and school-related 'interest and motivation'.

Teachers' thoughts depend on the school system, too. In the Hauptschule (vocational track), thoughts focused on 'effort' and 'work habits', whereas in the Gymnasium (university track), the focus was based on general or achievement-related personality traits. Moreover, there was a dominance of thoughts reflecting teacher–pupil interaction. As a whole, thoughts in the Gymnasium were more differentiated than in the Hauptschule, and thoughts in the Realschule (mixed track) were not at all striking. Presumably, the differentiated view is a result of teacher education because teachers in the Gymnasium are trained for eight to 10 semesters, with two semesters every year. On the other hand, the training is less pedagogical and student centred. Presumably, the differentiated view is a result of the student population, because brighter students can be more easily characterised than others.

Finally, teachers' thoughts are associated with students' achievement. Concerning mark expectations, judgement-related thoughts, e.g. 'grade levels 1 + 2; grade level 3', resulted in the corresponding concrete mark expectation, e.g. high or medium respectively. The second judgement policy, which was followed by action, consisted of positive remarks, which corresponded to a high mark expectation. These results were based on mark expectations concerning dictation, composition and mathematics.

Many results were specific to the written examination. With respect to a high mark expectation, 'diligence' is associated with dictation, and 'diligence, character traits, teacher expectations' are associated with composition. With respect to a medium mark expectation, dictation is characterised by 'character traits', and with respect to a low mark expectation, it is again dictation which is referred to as 'lack of ability'.

Second, the most striking results are the differences in favour of German dictation. Teachers reported quite a negative image of their students if the estimation of the mark was proper. If the mark was worse than the expected mark (overestimation), teachers reported, for example, 'negative character traits', and if the mark was better than the expected mark (underestimation), they reported, for example, 'effort'. As thought reports were followed by 'marking' action, it was concluded that teachers reflect student characteristics, which are possible causes for over- and underestimation.

Effort scope was the last variable, and intended to measure students' achievement effort. It was the difference between the expected marks under the condition of minimum and maximum effort. Results show that teachers' thoughts of hope, for example, were restricted to a wide effort scope, i.e. the perceived effort range was large in dictation and composition.

In addition to content of teachers' thoughts, the number of thoughts together with our context and student variables suggested another interesting result. The significant thoughts cumulated at high mark expectations, overestimated as well as underestimated mark expectations, and a narrow effort scope. That means teachers were busy with expected high student achievements, with achievements that were either uncertain or difficult to calculate, and with rather stable achievements.

It is difficult to compare the results of our pilot study with the research literature, because of different goals and methods. However, we can stress some critical remarks.

At first, some teachers did not join our study because they correct and assess written examinations objectively, e.g. without looking at students' names and handwriting. Therefore, our results will be restricted to teachers who were engaged in our research.

Second, we assume a connection between thought categories and thought processes of individuals, though the thought listings were not coded by the teachers themselves. Future research should consider this method, called 'communicative validation' (Lechler, 1982). On the other hand, we did some 'action validation' by linking thoughts to student assessment.

Finally, the method could be criticised. 'Non-nomination' means, on the one hand, that a teacher rejects a thought category although he/she thought of it. It means on the other hand, that a teacher did not think of that category. 'Unidimensionality' of analyses refers to the fact of correlating two variables, whereas the correlation is dependent on a third variable. This is a problem of theory and sample size. 'Computer-based content analysis' is another topic of criticism. It has limitations concerning single words as the unit of analysis.

The pilot study was a first attempt to study teachers' thoughts before the correcting and assessment process. We found some grounded information about complex judgement processes, but more research is necessary on this topic. It ought to improve teachers' judgement competencies for the sake of the students' development.

Author Reflection 2004

The results of this chapter led to the conclusion that teachers' thoughts (a) differentiate between different types of written examinations, (b) depend on the school system, and (c) are associated with students' current achievements.

'Task references' were mentioned with reference to two-thirds of the students. The teachers' thoughts referred to 'achievement references' regarding every second student, and every fourth student was labelled by 'character traits, work habits', etc. From this initial position, we did additional analysis on the structure of thought processes. The main results are as follows (Lissmann, 1987):

Factor analysis revealed four dimensions: (1) teachers' thoughts about general personality and behaviour traits; (2) teachers' thoughts about the teacher–student interaction; (3) teachers' thoughts about ability-referenced work habits; (4) teachers' thoughts about effort-referenced achievement behaviour. Moreover, a cluster analysis based on similarity coefficients led to five clusters of teachers, which were different in quantity and quality. Types 1 and 2 were mainly characterised by one thought category, while type 4 was marked by many categories, and the other types took a middle position. With regard to quality aspects, type 1 is dominated by achievement-referenced associations, whereas type 2 is characterised by task-referenced associations. The third type emphasises achievement- and task-referenced associations, plus character traits and positive remarks. The fourth type is marked by achievement, task, social and family references as well as character traits. The salient thought category of the fifth type, apart from other categories, is the frequent use of expectations. The explorative character of our study restricted further interpretations.

Research interest in teachers' thought processes has decreased over the past two decades. First, the ERIC thesaurus term 'thought processes' was dropped in 1980 and the term changed to 'cognitive processes'. Second, our study was based on a 'thinking-aloud protocol', but the emphasis has shifted to 'protocol analysis' recently. Third, the research literature relating to 'teachers' thinking' dropped continuously.

Restricting analysis to the ERIC database, journals and a two-year interval, the number of published articles declined as follows: 26 (1989/90), 23 (1991/92), 19 (1993/94), 21 (1995/96), 9 (1997/98), 14 (1999/2000), 5 (2001/02). A closer look at the thesaurus term 'teacher thinking' in combination with 'assessment', which is our topic, reveals the following numbers (same array as before): 4, 7, 7, 3, 4, 4, and 3. Although less distinct, the trend is comparable to the citation frequency of 'teacher thinking'.

We suppose research interest in teachers' thinking regarding assessment has turned to teachers' cognitions of assessing students and more general thinking skills, e.g. evaluative, critical, creative and communicative skills.

Chapter 13

Teachers' Causal Attributions in Problematic Situations

Karin van Opdorp, Paul den Hertog,
Theo Bergen and Lucie Vreuls

Introduction

Teachers are confronted with many problematic situations during their teaching practice (Veenman, 1984; Peters, 1985). Their behaviour in these situations is substantially influenced by their thought processes (Clark and Peterson, 1986). One aspect of this teacher thinking is the interpretation of such problematic situations; an important part of this judgement process concerns the search for a causal explanation. How could this situation occur? What are the causes of it?

This causal attribution process for experiences or observed events is believed to be a basic cognitive process; analysing the causal structure of events facilitates control over the environment. As such, causal attributions are important determinants of future behaviour, affects and expectations (Kelley and Michela, 1980; Harvey and Weary, 1984; Ross and Fletcher, 1985).

In education, a major part of the research on causal attributions focuses on causal explanations by students for their success or failure in school tasks. Attributional theories of motivation have stimulated this line of research (e.g. Weiner, 1979).

It seems reasonable to assume that causal attributions which teachers make for performance and behaviour of students, but also for their own performance, will have a profound influence on their teaching behaviour and motivation. In fact, a number of theorists mention (causal) attributions as a factor in their models of teacher behaviour (e.g. Bar-Tal, 1979; Shavelson, 1983). Moreover, a number of studies actually found a relationship between teachers' causal attributions for success or failure of their students and their teaching behaviour towards these students, e.g. praise and criticism (cf. Peterson and Barger, 1984; Clark and Peterson, 1986).

Causal Attributions by Teachers

Most of the research on causal attributions by teachers has concentrated on attributions for student performance. Teachers are asked for causal explanations for the successes or failures of their students (e.g. Ross, Bierbrauer and Polly, 1974; Ames, 1975;

Bar-Tal and Guttmann, 1981; Darom and Bar-Tal, 1981). Although the results of these studies are not conclusive, teachers tend to attribute success of students to students' ability and effort, as well as to their own teaching. Failure is attributed to several causes, mostly external to the teacher.

Furthermore, a limited number of studies have been carried out to investigate teachers' causal attributions for (problem) behaviour of students. Vernberg and Medway (1981) found that teachers, when interviewed, mention family circumstances and pupil factors as the most important explanations for problem behaviour of pupils in elementary schools. School factors, or more specifically, teacher or teaching factors, are seldom mentioned. Guttmann (1982) asked elementary schoolteachers to rate the importance of 26 causes for described problem behaviour of a fictitious student. Teachers tended to blame the misbehaving child and his parents, but played down the importance of reasons associated with other children in the class and reasons associated with themselves. Brophy and Rohrkemper (1981) investigated teacher thinking about and strategies for coping with problem students. They found that elementary school-teachers attributed problem behaviour of a fictitious student external to themselves, mainly to pupil factors. Furthermore, they suggest that teachers' attributions are influenced by the kind of problem and are related to the coping strategies that the teachers mention.

It is remarkable that teachers' attributions for their own behaviour and teaching performance have received so little attention in research on causal attributions in education. Only one study was found concerning these attributions. Guskey (1982) asked teachers to judge the importance of four possible causes as an explanation of a situation in which they were 'particularly successful or unsuccessful with a group or class of students'. Teachers attributed their successful performance more to their own ability and effort – failure more to the difficulty of their task.

To summarise the results of research on causal attributions by teachers, it can be stated that problem behaviour of students is mostly attributed to external causes (e.g. student factors and family circumstances). It should be noted that most of this research is done with elementary school teachers. The only study concerning teachers' causal attributions for their own performance suggests that teachers are inclined to ascribe their failures to external factors.

The overview of the literature shows the lack of research into teacher attributions for student behaviour and for their own behaviour or performance in secondary education (cf. Bergen and den Hertog, 1985). Another point that can be made in relation to the research discussed is that the effect of method used seems profound. Open questions seem to lead to more attributions that are external and to disregard of school and teacher factors. With structured questionnaires, teachers tend to attribute to internal aspects. Elig and Frieze (1979) have compared open-ended and structured response measures. They conclude that the latter are preferable. However, preceding a structured response measure it is necessary to make a selection of relevant causes. Free response methods seem the best way to collect relevant causes in a new domain of situations or a new group of respondents.

Research Questions

As far as we know there are no studies using free response methods to collect the causes teachers give for the occurrence of problematic situations during their teaching. We set up an open inventory study as a first step in our research on teachers' causal attributions with respect to problematic situations they encounter in their teaching practice.

The research questions of this inventory study are:

1. What kind of causal attributions do teachers make in problematic situations?
2. Is there any relationship between certain teacher characteristics (sex, teaching experience) and the kind of causal attributions made?
3. Do teachers give different causal attributions for teacher–student situations using an open-ended interview versus an open-ended questionnaire?

Subjects

Twenty-six teachers (13 men and 13 women) from five schools for secondary education in the area of Nijmegen (the Netherlands) participated in the interview study.

The questionnaire was sent to 201 teachers of secondary education in the Netherlands. Seventy-one teachers (35.3 per cent) completed the questionnaire and returned it (49 men and 22 women).

Material

In the interview study as well as in the questionnaire study, we wanted to confront teachers with problematic situations. The selection of relevant problematic situations was based on Peters (1985) who distinguished six clusters of problematic situations within the teaching profession.

For the interview study we formulated four brief 'situation indications' relating to two clusters of Peters (1985), but that lie within the core of the teaching profession. The situation indications all emphasised the interaction between student(s) and teacher. The indications referred to situations within versus outside the classroom and with one student versus several students. In the interview study, we chose these brief indications rather than full descriptions because during the interview teachers should be able to describe problematic situations of their own, situations they had actually encountered themselves.

The interview was semi-structured. The interviewees were confronted with the four indications in a random order. Following each description, they were asked to recall a problem situation they had encountered in their teaching that corresponded to the given description. Having explained the problem situation the subject then answered eight questions. Here we only discuss the following two questions:

1. 'What are the causes for the occurrence of this situation?' (If necessary: 'Can you give any more causes?')
2. 'How problematic is this situation to you?' (Four-point scale from hardly problematic to very problematic.)

For the questionnaire study ten situation scenarios were written; these are complete descriptions of situations, also based on Peters' inventory (1985). The ten descriptions all include a problematic situation between the teacher and another person: teacher–student (cluster I), teacher–colleague (cluster II) and teacher–principal (cluster III). In the questionnaire, the ten scenarios were also presented in random order. After each situation, respondents were asked 'What are the causes for the occurrence of this situation?'

In addition to this open question, they were asked to judge every situation in terms of its problematicity (5-point scale: from 'not problematic' to 'very problematic'), its recognizability (5-point scale: from 'not recognizable' to 'very recognizable') and its frequency of occurrence (5-point scale from 'never' to 'very often').

Procedures

Interview Study

The twenty-six interviews were conducted by two interviewers, who were well-informed about the purpose of the study. All interviews were recorded on tape, except for two (these two teachers refused to be tape-recorded, so the interviewer had to take notes during the interview.) The average duration was 1 hour.

Every interview tape was processed by both interviewers independently. This resulted in two preliminary protocols. A third, definitive protocol was compiled afterwards. The reason for this procedure was that it proved difficult to determine the exact number of causes given by a subject in the course of an interview. Respondents were inclined to give long answers in which the causes were not always clear-cut. Therefore, the two interviewers independently defined the number of causes given in each interview and afterwards the two protocols were compared. Differences were discussed and the definitive number of causes was then fixed in consultation with both interviewers, resulting in a definitive protocol for each interview.

Questionnaire Study

The questionnaires were sent directly to the teachers' home addresses. In the instructions, teachers were specifically asked to identify themselves with the teacher in the situation described, in order to guarantee that the respondent would put him/herself in the position of the teacher in a problematic situation.

The causes written down at the first question were often put in longer sentences. As in the interview study, we had to define the number of causes. After two practice sessions on a small number of situations, the answers to the first question were divided in meaningful units, by two independent judges not involved in the interview study. The degree of agreement was computed, with the formula of Osgood, Saporta and Nunnally (1956): $2 \times O_{12} / O_1 + O_2$ (where O_{12} is number of agreed causes between judge 1 and judge 2: O_1 and O_2 are the number of causes of judges 1 and 2, respectively). This agreement was 0.96. Again, the differences were discussed and the definitive number of causes agreed on in consultation.

Procedure of Categorising the Causes

In order to categorise the causes of the interview study (223) and the questionnaire study (1367) we developed a category system. This whole procedure is described by den Hertog, van Opdorp, Vreuls and Bergen (1986). The definitive category system comprises nine main categories: Teacher, Student(s), Colleague(s), Principal(s), School, Policy of education, Parents and family situation, Combination of teacher and others, Other external aspects. Within each main category, several subcategories are identified; in all, there are 64 subcategories.

All causes were first categorised independently by two persons. At the main category level they agreed on 200 causes (89.6 per cent) in the interview study and

1143 causes (83.5 per cent) in the questionnaire study. At subcategory level, they agreed on 151 (67.7 per cent) and 858 (62.7 per cent) of the causes respectively. The causes that could not be classified in one subcategory unanimously were judged by a third person who was unaware of the previous judgements. In that way most of the causes were classified: at main category level 99.1 per cent and 98.9 per cent of the causes in the interview and questionnaire study respectively, at subcategory level 88.3 per cent and 87.7 per cent respectively. In the interview study two causes could not be classified at main category level, in the questionnaire study 28 causes. These causes were excluded from further analysis, leaving 221 and 1339 causes respectively.

In order to check the stability of the classification process a sample of causes (55 of the interview study, 305 of the questionnaire study) were classified according to the same procedure after a period of 2 months. The percentage of agreement at the level of main categories was 96 per cent for the interview study and 81 per cent for the questionnaire study; at the level of subcategories it was 71 per cent and 73 per cent respectively.

Results

Situations

In the interview study, the 26 teachers formulated 100 problematic situations. (In four cases, it was not possible for the respondent to formulate a situation that fitted the situation indication.) The mean value of how problematic the situations were rated was 2.15 (score 1 to 4 from hardly problematic to very problematic) in the interview study. In the questionnaire study the ten situation descriptions were judged on three scales, namely 'how recognizable', 'how problematic' and 'how often'; the mean scores are shown in Table 13.1. The situations in cluster I (with reference to teacher–student interaction) are judged most recognisable, and most likely to occur. The situations in cluster III (with reference to teacher–principal interaction) are judged most problematic, but unlikely to occur and less recognizable.

Causes

In the interview study, a total number of 223 causes were gathered. In this number 15 causes are included that were given to the added question 'Can you give any more causes?' Because this question may have raised different answers from the original question for causal attributions, we excluded these 15 causes from further analysis. Thus, the average number of causes per situation per respondent in the interview study is 2.08.

Table 13.1. Mean scores for 'how recognizable', 'how problematic' and 'how often' per cluster of situations in the questionnaire study (N = 71)[a]

Cluster	How recognizable	How problematic	How often
I Teacher–student	3.6	3.0	2.7
II Teacher–colleague	2.9	2.9	2.2
III Teacher–principal	2.3	3.4	1.5

[a]All scores range from 1 (= not recognizable; not problematic; never) to 5 (= very recognizable; very problematic; very often).

Table 13.2. Percentages of causes in the nine main categories (MC) for males, females
and total sample for the interview[a] (N = 26) and the questionnaire study[b]
(cluster I) (N = 71)

MC	Interview			Questionnaire cluster I		
	Male	Female	Total	Male	Female	Total
Teacher	25.2	24.3	24.7	33.5	47.5	38.0
Student(s)	48.5	51.5	50.0	43.0	32.6	39.7
Colleague(s)	-	3.9	2.0	5	-	0.4
Principal(s)	-	1.0	5	1.3	1.1	1.2
School	5.8	12.6	9.2	4.4	4.4	4.4
Policy of education	1.0	1.0	1.0	4.6	7.2	5.4
Parents	7.8	1.9	4.9	5.7	2.8	4.7
Combination	1.0	1.9	1.5	1.0	1.7	1.2
Other aspects	10.7	1.9	6.4	5.9	2.8	4.9

[a]Total number of causes is 206. Number of causes for both males (N = 13) and females (N = 13)
is 103.
[b]Total number of causes for cluster I (4 situations): 569. Number of causes for males (N = 49)
and females (N = 22): 338 and 181 respectively.

In the questionnaire study, a total number of 1367 causes were gathered. The
average number of causes per situation per respondent is 1.94 over all situations, and
for each cluster I, II and III, 2.04, 1.88 and 1.79 respectively.

Categorisation in Main Categories
Table 13.2 gives the percentages of causes for the nine main categories for all subjects
of the interview study and questionnaire study (cluster I). It also shows the percentages
for males and females. In the interview study, most of the causes fall in the main
category 'Student(s)' (50 per cent) and in category 'Teacher' (24.7 per cent). There are
no noticeable differences between male and female teachers. For the questionnaire
study (cluster I, 'teacher–student interaction'), most of the causes also fall in the main
category 'Teacher' and 'Students' (38.0 per cent and 39.7 per cent respectively). A difference between male and female teachers can be discerned here: Male teachers attribute more to students than to themselves; for female teachers this is reversed: they
attribute more to themselves than to students. The results of cluster I of the questionnaire and the results of the interviews can be compared, because they both refer to
teacher–student interactions. Most striking is that the above effect for male and female
teachers in the questionnaire study is not present in the interview study.
        Table 13.3 shows that for cluster II (teacher–colleague interaction) a very large
part of the causes falls in the main category 'Colleague(s)' (62.2 per cent) and only a
small part in main category 'Teacher' (14.6 per cent). In cluster III (teacher–principal
interaction) a large part of the causes can be seen in the category 'Principal(s)' (45.6 per
cent) and almost a quarter of the causes falls in category 'Teacher' (23.3 per cent).
        Table 13.3 also shows that teachers are more likely to attribute the situation
to their interaction-partner in a problematic teacher–colleague situation than in a problematic teacher–principal situation. The influence of sex that appears in cluster I does
not appear in clusters II and III.

Table 13.3. Percentages of causes in the nine main categories (MC) for males (N = 49),
            females (N = 22) and total sample (N = 71) for clusters II and III of the
            questionnaire study[a]

	Cluster II			Cluster III		
MC	Male	Female	Total	Male	Female	Total
Teacher	14.0	15.9	14.6	23.0	23.9	23.3
Student(s)	1.1	1.5	1.3	7.0	4.3	6.2
Colleague(s)	62.3	62.1	62.2	1.2	2.6	1.6
Principal(s)	1.5	1.5	1.5	44.5	47.9	45.6
School	11.3	14.4	12.3	10.9	11.1	11.0
Policy of education	1.9	0.8	1.5	0.8	-	0.5
Parents	-	-	-	2.0	1.7	1.9
Combination	4.2	1.5	3.3	5.9	7.7	6.4
Other aspects	3.8	2.3	3.3	4.7	0.9	3.5

[a]Total number of causes for cluster II (3 situations): 397. Number of causes for males and
females: 265 and 132 respectively.
Total number of causes for cluster III (3 situations): 373. Number of causes for males and
females: 256 and 117 respectively.

Table 13.4. Percentages of causes over the nine main categories (MC) for teachers with
            0–4 years, 5–10 years and 11 or more years of experience, in the interview
            study[a] and the questionnaire study[b]

	Interview			Questionnaire cluster I		
MC	0–4 years	5–10 years	≥11 years	0–4 years	5–10 years	≥11 years
Teacher	20.3	27.5	27.6	42.5	38.2	36.9
Students	48.1	52.2	50.0	37.0	39.7	40.3
Colleague(s)	1.3	2.9	1.7	1.4	-	0.3
Principal(s)	-	-	1.7	1.4	1.4	1.1
School	10.1	7.2	10.3	2.7	5.1	4.4
Policy of education	1.3	-	1.7	8.2	5.1	5.0
Parents	3.8	5.8	5.2	5.5	3.7	5.0
Combination	2.5	1.4	-	-	2.9	0.8
Other aspects	12.7	2.9	1.7	1.4	3.7	6.1

[a]0–4 years: N = 10, 79 causes; 5–10 years: N = 8, 69 causes; >11 years: N = 8, 58 causes.
[b]0–4years: N = 8, 73 causes; 5–10 years: N = 19, 136 causes; >11 years: N = 44, 360 causes.

The question whether there is a relation between teaching experience and
causal attributions is treated in Table 13.4. For the questionnaire study, we confine
ourselves to cluster I (teacher–student interaction) for reasons of comparability.

In the interview study, hardly any difference can be noticed, except for the
main category 'Other aspects', in which the teachers with little experience (0–4 years)
have more causes than the teachers with more years of experience.

In the questionnaire study there is a slight tendency that, with increasing years of experience, teachers increasingly attribute the situations to student factors and less to themselves.

Comparison between the two studies shows that a similar tendency is not found in the interview study.

Categorisation in Subcategories

The results at subcategory level are presented in Tables 13.5 and 13.6. It appears that if teachers attribute problematic situations to themselves (see Table 13.5) in the interview study, then it is mostly the 'approach' in that situation or in the lesson (35.3 per cent) that is seen as the cause.

However, there is a difference between male teachers and female teachers within this main category. Female teachers attribute the situations almost equally to 'approach' and to own 'character' (28 per cent and 24 per cent respectively), whereas male teachers attribute them mostly to 'approach' (42.3 per cent) and less to their own 'character' (11.5 per cent). Other minor differences can be seen for the subcategories 'role conflict', 'personal circumstances' and 'effort'. As to cluster I of the questionnaire study, it is evident that if teachers attribute a situation to themselves it is to the 'approach' in that situation (81.0 per cent). In this study, there are no appreciable differences between men and women. A comparison of the results of the two studies shows that although 'approach' is the largest subcategory in both studies, the percentages of the two studies differ substantially (35.3 per cent vs. 81.9 per cent). In relation to this difference, it should be noted that in the interview study the causes are more evenly distributed over subcategories (e.g. character 17.6 per cent, personal circumstances 11.8 per cent, affects 11.8 per cent) than in the questionnaire study. Furthermore, the sex differences found in the interview study are not present in the questionnaire study.

Table 13.5. Percentages of causes within category Teacher, per subcategory (SC) for male, female and total sample, for both the interview[a] and the questionnaire study (cluster I)[b]

SC Teacher	Interview			Questionnaire (cluster I)		
	Male	Female	Total	Male	Female	Total
a. Ability	-	-	-	10.0	5.8	8.3
b. Character	11.5	24.0	17.6	3.1	3.5	3.2
c. Effort	-	8.0	3.9	-	1.2	0.5
d. Approach	42.3	28.0	35.3	83.8	76.7	81.0
e. Personal circumstances	19.2	4.0	11.8	-	1.2	0.5
f. Role conflict	3.8	12.0	7.8	-	-	-
g. Task load	-	4.0	2.0	-	4.7	1.9
h. Affects	11.5	12.0	11.8	-	1.2	0.5
i. Various	-	-	-	-	1.2	0.5
z. Indefinable	11.5	8.0	9.8	3.1	4.7	3.7

[a]Male: N = 13, 26 causes; female: N = 13, 25 causes.
[b]Male: N = 49, 130 causes; female: N = 22, 86 causes.

Table 13.6.   Percentages of causes within category Student(s) per subcategory (SC)
              for male, female and total sample, for both the interview[a] and the questionnaire
              study (cluster I)[b]

	Interview			Questionnaire cluster I		
SC Student(s)	Male	Female	Total	Male	Female	Total
a. Ability	6.0	9.4	7.8	6.6	15.3	8.8
b. Character	24.0	41.5	33.0	32.9	16.9	28.8
c. Effort	14.0	9.4	11.6	18.6	18.6	18.6
d. Behaviour	20.0	13.2	16.5	6.0	3.4	5.3
e. Personal circumstances	14.0	3.8	8.7	5.4	6.8	5.8
f. School background	8.0	7.5	7.8	4.2	11.9	6.2
g. Solidarity	-	-	-	10.8	15.3	11.9
h. Task load	2.0	-	1.0	2.4	-	1.8
i. Effects	2.0	-	1.0	-	-	-
j. Various	-	1.9	1.0	1.2	-	0.9
z. Indefinable	10.0	13.2	11.6	12.0	11.9	11.9

[a]Male: N = 13, 50 causes; female: N = 13, 53 causes.
[b]Male: N = 49; 167 causes; female: N = 22, 59 causes.

If teachers attribute the situations to student- characteristics (see Table 13.6)
in the interview study then it is especially to 'character/personality' (33 per cent) and
to 'disturbing behaviour' (16.5 per cent). For male teachers it can be seen that attributions are almost equally divided between the subcategories 'character' and 'behaviour'
(24 per cent and 20 per cent respectively). For women these percentages are: 41.5 per
cent to 'character' of students and 13.2 per cent to 'disturbing behaviour'. Men also
give more weight to 'personal circumstances' of the student as a cause for problem
situations than do women.

The percentages of the questionnaire study show that if teachers attribute the
situations to student aspects this is mainly to 'character' of the student (28.8 per cent)
and to 'effort' (18.6 per cent). However, a difference between male and female teachers
can be noticed: female teachers attribute situations almost equally to 'character' and
'ability' of students (16.9 per cent and 15.3 per cent respectively), whereas male teachers
attribute them more to 'character' of students (32.9 per cent) and less to 'ability' (6.6 per
cent). Comparison of the two studies for this main category leads to the following
remarks. The results are similar for most of the subcategories for the total samples.
However, subcategory 'behaviour' has more causes in the interview study than in the
questionnaire study (16.5 per cent vs. 5.3 per cent) and 'solidarity' gets no causes in
the interview study versus 11.9 per cent of the causes in the questionnaire study.
Furthermore, it is striking that in the interview study the subcategory 'character' of the
student is filled mostly by causes mentioned by females and less by causes mentioned
by males (41.5 per cent vs. 24 per cent), whereas the questionnaire study shows the
reverse trend (men give more 'character' causes than women).

The results at subcategory level for clusters II and III of the questionnaire study
show that if teachers attribute problematic teacher–colleague situations to themselves
then it is mostly to their own 'approach' (62.1 per cent); this also applies to teacher–
principal situations (cluster III: 67.8 per cent in subcategory 'approach'). If teachers

attribute the situations to their interaction-partner in the teacher–colleague cluster it is mostly to the 'relationship between colleagues' (21.5 per cent) and to 'character' of the colleague (19.8 per cent). In cluster III (teacher–principal situations) if teachers attribute the situation to their interaction-partner, it is mainly to the 'approach' of the principal (34.7 per cent). Furthermore, the subcategory 'character/personality' of the principal is important (24.7 per cent).

There are no relevant differences between men and women, except in one case: in teacher–principal interactions male teachers are more likely to attribute the situation to their own 'ability' than to their 'character' (13.6 per cent vs. 7.1 per cent). For female teachers, this is reversed (7.1 per cent vs. 14.3 per cent).

Discussion

Looking at the results of these studies we see that the causal attributions teachers make for problematic interaction-situations are mainly aspects of both interaction-partners in that situation. In the context of these studies this means: aspects of the teachers themselves and aspects of a student, a colleague or a principal. More generally, this suggests that the explanation for an occurring event (e.g. a problematic interaction) is sought mainly in the interaction-partners and less in non-personal factors.

In both studies, it is clear that teachers are inclined to attribute the situations mostly to the interaction-partner and less to themselves. This result suggests a 'defensive' causal attribution pattern: a problem situation (perhaps comparable to a situation of failure) is attributed to factors external to the teacher.

Research on causal attributions for success and failure (as reviewed by Zuckerman, 1979) shows that attributions for success are usually relatively internal and attributions for failure are usually external (cf. Kelley and Michela, 1980).

In our review of research on teachers' causal attributions, we noticed that pupil (problem) behaviour is mainly attributed to factors external to the teacher; for student performance, we see results that are more mixed. However, in our questionnaire study we found in cluster I (i.e. problematic teacher–student interactions) that teachers attributed the situations almost equally to themselves and to their students, despite the fact that our problem descriptions mostly reflected problematic behaviour of a student.

One can speculate that the result found in cluster I is caused by the fact that in these situation descriptions the problematic behaviour of students is embedded in a larger situational context together with information about teacher behaviour. Moreover, sex differences seem to play a role in these results; we will return to this later.

The results at subcategory level show that if teachers attribute a situation to themselves, then this is due mainly to 'approach'; if teachers attribute it to their interaction-partners then it is often due to 'character'. This resembles an attribution bias described in the literature: if events are attributed to other persons, this is mainly done in terms of qualities of these persons, thereby underestimating the influence of situational effects; when attributing to oneself, one tends to overestimate these situational aspects and to play down one's own stable qualities (Jones and Nisbett, 1972). In our studies, 'character' can be seen as representing more stable qualities and 'approach' can be seen as more situation-dependent.

We must be cautious in interpreting the findings at subcategory level because the categorisation procedure showed that it was more difficult to classify causes at this level.

A possible relationship between the sex and the causal attributions of teachers can only be noticed in cluster I of the questionnaire study; there, women are more likely to ascribe situations to themselves than to students; for men the reverse is the case. In more general research on causal attributions sex differences are also described: women are more likely to attribute failure to aspects of their own, men are more likely to attribute failure to external aspects (cf. Frieze, 1980; Zuckerman, 1979). In our study this relationship was only found in cluster I of the questionnaire study; possibly such an effect is related to the kind of interaction situation. No other relevant differences between male and female teachers can be deduced from the results. For the teacher characteristics 'teaching experience', no convergent tendencies are found.

In all, there are (relatively) substantial differences between the results of the interview study and the questionnaire study. This seems to be the consequence of a number of differences between the methods used in these studies.

First, in the interview study the teachers gave their attributions orally (and were also asked orally to do so by the interviewer). In the questionnaire study, situations were presented on paper and teachers gave their attributions likewise. Thus, in the interview study attributions were given more spontaneously, whereas in the questionnaire study teachers had more time for reflection on their answers. The more spontaneous response seems to lead to fewer internal attributions (i.e. to aspects of the teacher him/herself). Other studies that made use of open-ended (or more specifically oral interview) questions also found that teachers seldom mentioned themselves or their teaching as a factor explaining student performance or student behaviour.

Second, in the interview study teachers were able to formulate their own situations. Possibly these personally experienced and memorised situations led to more involvement than the more neutrally formulated situation description used in the questionnaire study, and this greater involvement in a situation may lead to fewer internal (teacher-related) attributions.

A third important difference between the studies is that in the interview study causal attributions were made to one hundred different situations (because of the fact that every respondent formulated his own situations). In the questionnaire study, all respondents were confronted with the same ten situations. This may be the reason that teachers' attributions in the questionnaire study are more influenced by special features in the formulated situations, whereas this effect is 'averaged' in the interview study. Moreover, this influence of the situation features means that when other features in the descriptions were given a more prominent place this could lead to other causal attributions.

Although these differences limit the comparability of the results of the two studies, the procedure with different designs for the two studies contributed to the main aim of this inventory, namely to obtain a broad collection of causes for problematic situations.

It is difficult to compare the results of our studies with previous research on teachers' causal attributions because most of this research concentrates on causal attributions for student performance or uses structured questionnaires with a limited number of causal elements. Cooper and Burger (1980) also collected causal attributions with an open-ended question. However, their causal attributions were made for student performance, not for interaction situations; this leads to other categories and another distribution of causes.

As we have described, very little research is done on causal attributions of teachers for their own behaviour and performance. Future research should focus on these attribution patterns of teachers and their relationships with motivational and behavioural consequences. More specifically, it would be practically and theoretically interesting to explore the possibilities of applying Weiner's (1979) achievement motivation theory on teachers' attributions for success and failure in their teaching task.

Our future research will use the causal attributions collected in this study to develop a structured response-questionnaire. Making use of the advantages of such a structured instrument (cf. Elig and Frieze, 1979) we will further explore teachers' causal attributions for different interaction situations in their teaching practice and the consequences for teacher behaviour, work satisfaction and stress.

With respect to the research questions of this study, we can conclude that:

1. Teachers attribute problematic interaction situations mostly to aspects of themselves and of their interaction-partners, less to non-personal factors; furthermore they attribute situations more to aspects of the interaction-partner, than to themselves;

2. No systematic relationships were present between the teacher characteristics of sex and teaching experience;

3. Differences in results between the interview and the questionnaire study are due to a variety of differences between the two methods used.

Chapter 14

Teachers' Need for Pupil Information in Special Education

Sip J. Pijl and Stephen F. Foster

Introduction

Students having trouble in regular education sometimes get additional assistance and attention consisting of a few hours of remedial teaching; or they are held back a grade. If learning and/or behavioural problems cannot be solved or diminished, the student can be referred to special education.

The special education school the student is referred to subjects him/her to a compulsory test. This test gives family background, medical and psycho-educational assessment data. Results establish if the student meets the criteria for admission. If so, he/she is admitted to the school for special education; if not, the student is referred back to regular education (for an overview see Meyer, Pijl and Rispens, 1986).

The entrance test data on the child are considered a powerful source of information for the special education teacher. The test provides a basis on which to decide on instructional goals, short-term objectives, strategies, methods, materials, etc. Yet, several research studies (Pijl and Rispens, 1981; McCann and Semmel, 1983; Ysseldyke, 1983) show that special education teachers only make sparse use of the available assessment data on the newly admitted student. Somehow, the data do not make much impact on decisions about teaching. Pijl, Voort and Algra (1985) give three possible explanations for teachers not using the available assessment data: (1) assessment data are hard to translate into decisions on goals, objectives, etc.; (2) teacher training in translating assessment data into decisions on teaching is insufficient and diagnostic reports are not user friendly; and (3) teachers are not interested in detailed and precise information on new students gathered by others. In this paper, we go into the last explanation in detail, asking: Why would teachers be uninterested in potentially helpful data?

Teacher Judgements

The extent to which teachers use the available information about a newly admitted student depends on their need for information in this situation. Teachers' need for information is defined by the decisions on teaching that teachers have to make. To make these decisions information is needed not only on the new student but also on the other pupils in class, the available materials, space, programme, resources, etc. Teachers integrate and (if necessary) reduce all these data to a manageable amount and then make decisions.

Shavelson (1983) developed a model including the factors contributing to forming a judgement and making decisions on teaching (Figure 14.1). It becomes clear from the model that student information leads to forming a judgement, which is in turn the basis for a decision.

Teachers, particularly in special education, have a lot of information on their students. Because of restrictions in the amount of data they can handle, teachers tend to reduce the overload. They integrate available information into a limited number of judgements about students (Borko, Cone, Russo and Shavelson, 1979).

In selecting and integrating information into a judgement, attributions and heuristics play an important role (Figure 14.1). Teachers' attributions for the causes of student achievement in education may explain why teachers form particular judgements, such as judgements on ability, on classroom behaviour, etc. (Borko and Shavelson, 1978). It may explain the dimensions in the judgements about students. In general, attributions for student achievement may be to student ability, background, task difficulty or to teachers' own ability (self-efficacy). Aspects of student ability and student background are especially important in studying the dimensions in teachers' judgements about students. Heuristics are rules to select information, to judge the importance of information, to classify persons or to revise initial judgements (Shavelson, 1983).

Leach (1977) and Borko and Cadwell (1982) showed that teachers differ in the types of judgements used to describe students. Teachers even differ in types of judgements when provided with strictly identical information about a student

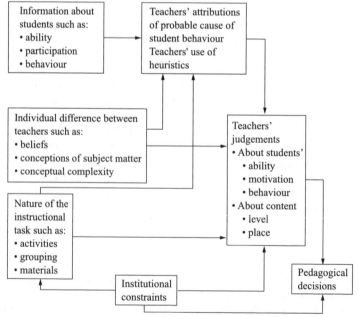

Figure 14.1.   Making pedagogical decisions.

(Cooper, 1979). Despite the differences, attempts have been made to describe the types of judgements teachers make. Shavelson and Stern (1981) found that teachers construct judgements about achievement, classroom behaviour, social skills, independence, work habits and self-concept. Kleber (1978) gives as the types of judgements: work habits, dominance, social withdrawnness, social behaviour and talents. Leach (1977) reports as judgement categories: vividness, behaviour, studiousness, naiivety, stability, responsibility, talents and social background. Hofer (1969) concludes from his research that teachers judge their students on five bipolar dimensions: disciplined versus not disciplined, mentally slow versus mentally fast, modest versus assertive, open versus closed and sensible versus insensible.

The sources of information for the forming of a judgement have a very different nature. The research of Leach (1977) and Kleber (1978) shows that often unreliable and invalid sources are used, e.g. high forehead as an indication for talents or neat schoolwork as an indication of intelligence. Shavelson and Stern (1981) found that teachers' judgements about the students' ability are based on achievement data and to some extent on eventual problem behaviour. In judging motivation, teachers rely heavily on information about achievement, problem behaviour and work habits. Judgements on behaviour are based on information about classroom behaviour and, to some extent, on achievement. Shavelson and Stern (1981) conclude that in forming judgements teachers use a limited number of information sources. For the different judgements, the combination of sources and relative weight of the sources differ, but judgements are in the end a fairly simple sum of a limited number of information sources. Teachers generally are unaware of the nature of their judgement policy. They report using more information in more complex ways than is suggested by the statistical (regression) model of their policies.

Teacher Planning

Teachers' judgements on students, together with information on the nature of the instructional task and institutional constraints, are inputs into (teaching) decisions (Figure 14.1). By making decisions on teaching in the preactive phase of teaching, teachers in fact develop a plan. Planning lastly is any activity of teachers concerned with preparing a framework for guiding future action (Hill, Yinger and Robbins, 1983). In special education, such plans are known as Individual Education Programmes (IEP). To make this plan the teacher has to decide on goals, objectives, teaching methods and materials, evaluation ways, means and dates, etc. Day by day actions in teaching are in principle deductions from the IEP. Evaluation data on student achievement are used as feedback to the plan and lead eventually to a revision of the plan.

From research on teacher thinking and teacher planning, we know that teachers (as yet) do not work that way. Teachers do not plan by stating goals and objectives and then explicitly choosing methods and materials to match them (Clark and Yinger, 1979a). Teacher planning is dominated by choosing actions (Shavelson, 1983). In daily practice, teachers keep the action in classrooms going and that – the action – is their angle of incidence. Action is working with learning contents and materials in a certain order and a certain speed (Shavelson and Stern, 1981). These actions will lead to a goal. Teachers do not think of goals as concrete future pupil behaviour or acquired skills, but of vague, global indications of where activities might lead. With vague goals, evaluation loses its specifiable criteria. Teachers largely do not seem to be very interested in long-term evaluation of pupil achievement gains. They evaluate teaching more in terms of pupil interest, involvement and being active (Hill *et al.*, 1983). Their first concern is 'in having a successful day', not in reaching long-term goals for their pupils (Huberman, 1983).

Planning has to do with choosing actions. How actions are formed is as yet unknown. It is supposed that from teacher education and through years of experience, a repertoire of actions is formed. The question here is how many alternative actions teachers have in a given situation. Brophy (1982) says that teachers depend on the structure of the teaching method and the manual that goes with it, which means that they do not have many alternative actions. Morrissey and Semmel (1975) presumed that teachers do have some alternatives (3 to 4). It is suggested that these alternatives do not deviate much from each other (Peterson and Clark, 1978). This lack of alternatives could explain in part why making individual plans is so difficult for teachers.

One more remark should be made on teacher planning. Teachers assemble groups of pupils in the classroom. A common criterion in forming groups is achievement level. Once the group has been formed, it is the group (and not the individual) that becomes the planning unit (Huberman, 1983; Shavelson, 1983). Planning education may be thought of as being on an individual base, but execution of the plan is certainly not. That in turn makes it understandable that teachers like to make group plans and then assign a newly admitted pupil to one of the groups (Blaauboer and Pijl, 1986). The group plan becomes the pupils' educational plan. It is of course easier and more efficient to make different group plans and to assign pupils to the groups than it is to make individual plans and try to combine the individual plans to a couple of groups with rather similar plans within each group. This preference for group plans and group instruction may subvert the goal of establishing plans most suitable for any individual child.

Some Extensions from Theory

The collection of student information is guided by a teacher's anticipation of the necessity to teach the student. The transformation from student data into teacher judgements about a student is therefore more than simplifying and recording the raw data. Forming of judgements is in the service of deciding which actions will be taken. This implies that elements or dimensions in the judgements on students have a direct link to the choice between actions or teaching alternatives.

In the preceding paragraphs, it was shown that teachers plan by choosing and arranging actions. Actions or activities are central in teacher thinking and judgements on students are probably linked to actions. Teachers know by experience, or by intuition, which student characteristics are contra-indications for a certain action. Student information is then not used to choose an activity per se. Rather the teacher uses student information as a check against the appropriateness of existing teaching programmes. Student information is important to a teacher because the information makes clear if the available teaching action might be workable. If it does not look workable, the teacher checks which alternative actions may be workable.

This requires that the teacher have an image of the students he or she is able to work with. For each available alternative action, the teacher has an image of the characteristics of the students with which the action will be workable. This is probably a major part of the teacher's implicit instructional theory (Schwarzer and Lange, 1979).

Therefore, the first piece of information a teacher needs about a newly admitted student is whether the new student fits into one of the existing (sub) groups. This is in accordance with the findings of Shavelson (1983) and Huberman (1983) that teachers tend to think of groups as units for planning. The teacher matches, as it were, the new student against the teacher's stereotype of an existing group in class. (This is in fact a small extension of the research of the ideal-type student: Leach, 1977). If the student is close to a stereotype, some small adjustments in the educational offering to the group suffice. From research by Peterson and Clark (1978) and Blaauboer and Pijl (1986), it is known that teachers often work with a standard approach in which small adjustments are carried out.

To summarise: At the entry of a new student into the class the teacher checks the fit of the student to an existing student group and an existing educational offering. Next the teacher checks to see if there is a need for 'fine tuning' the educational offering and which adjustments ought to be conducted. This second check might well be done in the interactive phase of teaching. Teachers probably prefer this.

The need for information about a newly admitted student therefore might be limited to a few student characteristics, important in establishing the link to an existing group of students and an existing educational offering.

Research Questions

1. What data are available to teachers about a newly admitted student?
2. What information is essential to teachers before the actual entry into class of the new student?
3. Is it possible to explain teachers' need for information by their attributions for students' learning and/or behavioural problems?
4. What decisions on teaching are made by the teacher at the entry of a new student?

Method

To find out the student information available to teachers we developed a checklist to analyse students' files. The checklist covers the tests used, the scores reported, the information from others (former teacher, parents, etc.) and the conclusions and suggestions made. With this checklist, we analysed the files of existing students with reading problems recently admitted to a school for special education.

Next, a teacher interview was done. In the interview we asked the teacher about: the information needed about a new student, the eventual existence and contents of a group plan, the decision on teaching the new student, the parts in the entrance test file therefore relevant, etc. A separate part of the interview was devoted to teachers' attributions for reading problems of students. The attribution part in the interview consists of 16 statements on the prevalence of, e.g., reading problems caused by low intelligence or, e.g., reading problems caused by inadequate former schooling. Teachers were asked to estimate the percentage of pupils to which each statement is applicable. We presume that if teachers think that a certain cause for reading problems (for example) is rare, the cause would not become a serious attribution. Formulated in another way: attributions are formed by frequently perceived causes.

We interviewed the teachers of all the students whose files had been analysed. We analysed 75 files and interviewed 75 teachers of schools for students with mild mental impairments and schools for students with learning difficulties.

Results

The Available Student Information

Very often (60–85 per cent), the students' files include information on the appearance of the student, their work habits (concentration, motivation, work speed, independence), social skills (contacts with grown-ups and children, behaviour at home and adaptation to group rules) and the social/emotional functioning of the student (e.g. withdrawn, hyperactive, childish, aggressive, anxious). Also included in the files is information on the former school career of the student, the occupation of the parents, the family of the student, the medical records and the reason for referral to the school for special education. Data on the student's achievements make up a large part of the entrance test and the student's file. The backwardness and learning problems of the student in reading, spelling, arithmetic and language are established. To gather these assessment data several diagnostic devices are used. The presentation of the results is fairly precise and detailed. Conclusions and suggestions for further teaching though are on a global level: e.g. 'give more structure', 'stimulate the student'.

The psychologist, as a member of the entrance team, gathers data on intelligence, personality and abilities. The most commonly used IQ test is the WISC-R (in 71 per cent of the files). A description of the personality of the student is based on drawings, sentence completion tests and tests like the CAT, TAT or Rorschach. In approximately half of the files attention was given to abilities of the students. Tests used for this purpose are the Bender, the Beery, the Benton and the ITPA. Results of the psychological section in the entrance test files are presented separately for each test. An integration of results into a diagnosis is given in half of the files. Consequences for further teaching are given in 25 per cent of the files. Here too the suggestions are on a global level: e.g. 'the student needs support and security in teaching'.

The Reported Need for Information by Teachers

In our research, we asked teachers several times and in different ways what they want to know about a newly admitted student. We found that teachers are most interested in educational assessment data to do with present levels of functioning in reading, spelling, language and arithmetic, and information on work habits and on specific learning problems.

Many teachers (approximately two-thirds) are also interested in data on the social/emotional functioning of the student. In fact, they want to know if the student is anxious, hostile, withdrawn, timid, etc. Teachers do not express a need for additional information. Less than one-third of the teachers wanted to have information on the social skills or on the family background of the student. Almost none of the teachers paid attention to available data such as the medical records, the intelligence scores or the description of the weak and strong abilities of the student.

To summarise: teachers report a need for concrete, educational assessment data and for information on the work habits of the student, supplemented with data relevant to their personal interaction with the student.

Teachers' Causal Attributions and Information Need

Depending upon a teacher's pattern of attributions for student success or failure one can predict a highly selective need for information. For example, for a teacher who attributes (potential) student success to ability or prior educational experience one would predict that data concerning these factors (IQ, past teacher's comments) would be sought and other data ignored, or at least given less importance. Task difficulty (a common attribution according to Weiner, Graham, Taylor and Meijer, 1983) requires more information about how the student is performing at present than at previous times. Other sorts of attributions to motivations (effort), physiological factors (health) or chance are related to different types of data with the last being unrelated to most information about the child.

Of course, it may be expected that different attributions be given to success than to failure. A teacher who is very high in the traits of personal attribution or self-efficacy (Bandura, 1972) could ignore much data and rely on their own skills as a teacher to serve the student's needs. If the pupil nevertheless were to fail, one would expect the teacher to externalise the attribution in this case. McArthur (1972) showed that the type of information available to persons influences their pattern of attributions. It is still an open question whether people (teachers) seek data to support pre-existing attributions in natural settings.

We asked teachers to consider students with reading disabilities and to estimate the percentage of students for whom the disability was caused by one (or more) of six factors: (1) intelligence, (2) former schooling; (3) social/emotional aspects; (4) family background; (5) physical aspects and (6) developmental aspects. In the questionnaire, we gave teachers the possibility of avoiding a direct answer by adding a seventh alternative, namely: 'cause is uncertain'. We then performed a cluster analysis on the results of 45 teachers to see if teachers could be grouped according to their choices. The cluster analysis resulted in five different groups (see Table 14.1).

Fourteen (25 per cent) of the teachers reported that intelligence and developmental aspects were important causal factors as much as 70 per cent and 52 per cent of the time. Another fourteen reported developmental aspects (together with former schooling) had a major (62 per cent) role. Two clusters of teachers respectively considered family background (56 per cent) and physical aspects (60 per cent) as important causes for reading disabilities. A small group of teachers stated that it was impossible to select one or more causes for reading disabilities.

In the clusters 1, 2 and 4 teachers give quite a lot of attention to the developmental aspects. In each of these clusters, however, this causal attribution is linked to another attribution: in cluster 1, to intelligence, in cluster 2, to former schooling and in cluster 4, to physical aspects. This suggests that teachers interpreted the attribution to developmental aspects in three different ways, namely developmental backwardness related to intelligence development, as caused by years of inappropriate schooling,

Table 14.1.   Teacher clusters by attribution

	Cluster				
Attribution to	1	2	3	4	5
Intelligence	70.4	21.4	24.2	20.0	15.0
Former schooling	20.4	41.4	21.7	7.5	23.3
Socio-emotional aspects	10.7	12.5	18.3	11.9	5.0
Family background	35.0	32.1	55.8	36.2	18.3
Physical aspects	23.9	18.6	15.8	60.0	46.7
Developmental aspects	52.1	62.5	22.5	46.2	15.0
Uncertain	3.6	17.1	13.3	9.4	60.0
N	14	14	6	8	3

or linked to backwardness in physical development. From this (hypothetical) point of view one might label the first four clusters as teachers attributing reading problems to: (1) intelligence, (2) former schooling, (3) family background and (4) physical aspects.

We had hypothesised that teachers' reported need for data could be predicted from the attributions they made. This prediction was not borne out as teacher ratings of the causal factors were relatively uncorrelated with the reported need for information (see Table 14.2). We planned to test a simple LISREL model in which each attribution causes a need for information (e.g. the attribution to intelligence causes the need for intelligence data and no other information needs). From Table 14.2 it is clear that there is no need to test the LISREL model on these data, since almost none of the reported correlations on the diagonal exceed the other (off-diagonal) correlations.

The educational offering

The entry of a new student into class does not introduce a completely new situation to the teacher. The new student enters an existing class that has a more or less fixed order and organisation, with a way to instruct, with certain subgroups, with teaching methods and materials used, and with certain (implicit) goals. This whole complex of existing habits and routine ways of acting can be regarded as contributing to a group plan. This plan is often not written down and is fairly implicit but it exists nonetheless.

In our research we established that, though there are large differences in content, fixity and elaboration, almost every teacher has some kind of a group plan. Because of its weak rational character, it might be better to speak of a set of routine guidelines for the group of students rather than of a plan. 35 per cent of the teachers had goals for reading and arithmetic instructions to the group and 14 per cent formulated goals for language and spelling instruction. The formulation of the goals is general, e.g. 'reading level end fourth group regular education'. A minority of the teachers were able to formulate more concrete goals for the group. Teachers' group plans (or guidelines) also consist of the forming of subgroups of students especially for reading instruction (80 per cent) and to a lesser extent for arithmetic and language instruction (48 per cent and 40 per cent). Further we found that in teaching reading, spelling and arithmetic approximately 55 per cent of the teachers used a sole, fixed teaching method, 20 per cent of the teachers had a fixed teaching method with some additional material and the others used different methods for different students as necessary.

In addition to the group guidelines for reading, spelling, etc. teachers also have guidelines for the more educational aspects of teaching. A majority of the interviewed teachers (80 per cent) have fairly fixed group rules, ways to reduce fear of failure,

Table 14.2. Attributions and need for information

| Attribution to | Need for information about | | | | | |
	IQ	FS	SE	FB	PhA	DA
Intelligence (IQ)	−0.26	0.05	−0.09	−0.05	−0.04	0.04
Former schooling (FS)	−0.01	0.06	0.06	0.16	0.05	0.06
Socio-emotional aspects (SE)	0.30	−0.09	0.14	−0.07	0.14	0.15
Family background (FB)	0.12	0.01	−0.12	−0.12	0.02	0.06
Physical aspects (PhA)	−0.20	−0.09	0.00	0.01	0.01	0.20
Developmental aspects (DA)	−0.21	0.03	−0.17	0.26	0.06	0.09

increase independence, offer security, and learn to understand each other or learn to have good relations with others.

An interesting question, given this fairly fixed group plan, is to what extent teachers are prepared to change (elements of) the group plan for a newly admitted student. About 70 per cent of the teachers state that they regularly do change it if a student has atypical, individual problems. This percentage is in concurrence with the percentage of teachers in our research (namely 60 per cent) who in actuality did change one or more elements of their group plan for the newly admitted student we discussed with them. The majority of the adjustments concern aspects of both social behaviour and work habits, such as handling conflicts, not using pressure, rewarding good behaviour, giving small tasks, etc.

We checked if teachers who changed the group plan also changed the teaching method. About two-thirds of the teachers who changed the group plan kept strictly to their original teaching method and followed each step in it. Teachers who do change the teaching method delete small sections of the method or the workbooks, replace them by additional material or use a different order compared to the method. Decisions about their adjustments are based on informal progress evaluation (correction of set work and observation while working). If progress slows down, the teacher takes action. To summarise: small adjustments of the group guidelines to the needs of a particular student occur frequently. These adjustments are both in ways of teaching and in ways of handling behavioural problems.

Discussion

Results from our research indicate that special education teachers have a fairly fixed educational offering for their students, at least regarding the teaching method and materials, the division into subgroups and the pedagogical group rules given. Teachers tend not to deviate from this offering.

We presumed that teachers at the entry of a new student to the class check if the available, current educational offering will be workable considering the student characteristics. Student characteristics (formulated as reasons for failure), however, did not correlate with the teachers' need for information. Teachers are mainly interested in the student's present level of functioning, the work habits of the student and some data useful to help them initially interact with the new student.

These data suggest that teachers want some information essential for teaching the new student in the first days. After some experience with the new student, they are able to form their own judgements and make their decisions accordingly.

Our results point out that teachers look to available information for a 'handle' on the first schooldays. All other important information is collected while working with the student directly.

Author Reflection 2004

Over the past 15 years, the inclusion into regular education settings of pupils with special needs has become a central theme (Dyson, 1999). Special needs pupils no longer are 'automatically' referred to segregated special schools, but are educated increasingly in their own local 'regular' school. Compared to 15 years ago, today many teachers are faced with an even wider variety of pupil needs in their classes. Teachers in regular education are expected to adapt their teaching to all of their pupils. Research (Peschar and Meijer, 1997; Houtveen *et al.*, 1998; Edelenbos and Meijer, 2001) has shown that despite a growing awareness of the differences between pupils, teachers still have trouble adapting their teaching to these differences. This is partly because they find it difficult to link pupil characteristics to established ways of teaching and partly because a high degree of individualisation is regarded as synonymous with difficulties in class organisation and management. These two causes hinder effective development towards more inclusive schools.

Pijl and Foster's (1989) study showed that teachers actually work with fairly fixed teaching methods and materials, divisions into subgroups and class rules. Because of this 'teaching standardisation' they expressed a rather limited need for information about newly admitted pupils. In the past 15 years, the trends towards inclusion and society's demands for more adaptive teaching have developed faster than teachers' abilities to achieve adaptive teaching. The gap between what we demand of teachers and what they are able to offer only seems to have widened. Paradoxically this has taken place at the same time as the flowering of pluralistic student-centred concepts such as Generative (Wittrock, 1992) and Multidimensional Intelligence (Gardner, 1993).

Section D

Teacher Thinking
and Teacher Education

This section opens with a chapter by Clark, entitled: 'Asking the right questions about teacher preparation: contributions of research on teacher thinking'. In this he addresses and confronts the issue first raised in Chapter 1 by Berliner, that of how research on teacher thinking can influence teacher practice to realise the practical promise of each. Having discarded two of his posited relationships between research and practice, Clark proceeds to propose a third, one in which researchers act as consultants to teacher educators. He delineates how a good consultant in this role could develop it to useful effect and what had been achieved to the date of his chapter in this respect. In so doing, he provides a wealth of examples from research on: preconceptions and implicit theories; planning and reflection; dilemmas and uncertainty, all of which provide a stimulating resource to novice researchers or those looking for new areas to research. He concludes his treatise by noting the advances that have been made but also urges more collaboration between teachers, teacher educators and researchers (one of the goals of ISATT). He refers to this point again in his Author Reflection 2004, with an additional plea for teacher educators to become more engaged in questioning their own programmes – before others do, perhaps less constructively.

A specific example of such research on teacher education follows in Chapter 16 by Loewenberg-Ball and Feiman-Nemser. Chapter 16, Using textbooks and teachers' guides: what beginning elementary teachers learn and what they need to know, reports on a particular section of an indepth, longitudinal investigation of six undergraduates embarked on teacher education programmes, and three in each of two contrasting programmes for comparison purposes. A wide range of documents from each programme are analysed to determine their central messages with respect to the use of textbooks and how to make curricular decisions. The students were followed through their teaching practicum, with revelations from the data being amply illustrated through the use of case study material. The authors discuss their findings and particularly focus on the difficulties that the student teachers face in using their course learning to inform their teaching practice. From this they provide suggestions to improve teacher education, much in the spirit advocated by Clark in the previous chapter.

In Chapter 17, 'Supervision conferences and student teachers' thinking and behaviour', provided by Broeckmans, another aspect of teacher education is put under the spotlight. Following a review of the relevant literature, a study is described that aimed to illuminate the reflections that student teachers engage in with supervisors following a practice lesson and how those reflections impinge on future lessons.

By distilling 302 reflective processes through three analytic dimensions, eight typical patterns of reflection were identified. These were used in conjunction with case histories that delineated changes in lesson planning and interactive teaching to produce a convincing, if concerning, set of results which are by no means reassuring about the depth of reflection engaged in by many students or about the value of supervision conferences to them. It is clear that this remains a topic worthy of further investigation if teacher education is to be improved.

Morine Dershimer and Oliver present their paper 'Examining complexity of thought in secondary student teachers' as Chapter 18. These authors provide a rationale for and detailed description of research that investigates the degree of complexity of thought exhibited by a particular group of eighteen student teachers. Within this group were some who majored in science/maths, the rest majoring in English/social studies, so that comparisons could be drawn. Two methods, innovative at the time, were used to explore their thinking. At the beginning and end of the course, students were engaged in concept mapping activities whilst, following a videotaped practice lesson, stimulated recall was employed as part of an interview. The authors helpfully provide considerable detail in explaining their measures of complexity of thought before presenting their results. While there was no significant difference in complexity of thought between the students studying different majors, the descriptive analysis reveals some intriguing tendencies. The authors discuss other patterns, related to consistency in complexity of thought, emerging from the data as well as providing their own reflections on the methodological improvements included in their investigation. The Author Reflection 2004 confirms their original view that this exploratory study would be productive in terms of research stimulation and the development of practice.

The final chapter, Chapter 19, was contributed by Feiman-Nemser and Buchmann, who titled it 'Knowing, thinking and doing in learning to teach: a research framework and some initial results'. This continues the theme of exploring and evaluating the development of pedagogical thinking and how it relates to the practice of pre-service teachers. The aim of the paper is to establish the background to research in that area and how such research can be framed to inform and develop teacher education, as urged by both Clark and Berliner. Four poignant case studies from two contrasting teacher education programmes are included in the chapter to illustrate the value of the proposed framework for evaluating learning outcomes in teacher preparation activities. In their conclusion, and also reinforced in their present-day reflections, the authors point out that realities in teacher education are not self-evident, nor is learning to teach a straightforward process, unadulterated by prior experience, so that a framework and focus are required to make sense of issues in teacher learning.

The last authors also suggest in their Author Reflection 2004 that if readers, rather than seeking useful theories about teacher learning and thinking, are intent on finding generalisable results, then they will be disappointed. This caveat applies to most of the chapters in this book. Rather than presenting averages, norms and rules of engagement, the contributors have described their forays into a complex arena, in doing so sharing their triumphs and disappointments. They have also produced an invaluable resource for those intending following in their footsteps: a resource of literature references and varied methods but, most importantly, of stimulating ideas.

Chapter 15

Asking the Right Questions about Teacher Preparation

Contributions of research on teacher thinking

Christopher M. Clark

The field of research on teacher thinking is thriving and growing. But what is not so clear is how (or whether) this research can be informative and useful to teacher educators. What conditions must be satisfied in order to move from the literature on teacher thinking to more thoughtful practice of teacher education? What first steps have already been taken to realise some of the practical promise of teacher thinking research? This paper addresses these questions within the larger framework of the relationship between research and practice in education.

There are three ways to characterise the relationship between research on teaching, on the one hand, and teacher education, on the other hand. In the worst case, research on teaching has no relationship at all to the practice of teacher education. Researchers pursue their own narrow and parochial interests, publish in obscure language in obscure journals, and avoid all discussion of practical implications of their work. For their part, teacher educators see this kind of research as irrelevant and impossible to understand, and continue to use unexamined habits and traditional ways of preparing teachers.

A second and better kind of relationship between research on teaching and teacher education follows from research in the process-product tradition. Teacher effectiveness researchers see the role of research as to discover those behaviours, skills, patterns and strategies that lead to improved student learning and achievement. In this framework, the implications for teacher education are rather direct: train prospective teachers to behave in the ways that research has shown to be most effective

The work reported here is sponsored by the Institute for Research on Teaching, College of Education, Michigan State University. The Institute for Research on Teaching is funded primarily by the Office of Educational Research and Improvement, United States Department of Education. The opinions expressed in this paper do not necessarily reflect the position, policy, or endorsement of the Office of Educational Research and Improvement (Contract No. 400-81-0014).

in producing achievement gains in students. The principal role of the teacher educator in this relationship is that of trainer of students in the skills and strategies documented by the research community. Researchers and the knowledge they produce govern the content and practice of teacher preparation in this essentially top-down model.

In this second kind of relationship between research and practice there are teacher educators who have read one or two reviews of the literature of teacher thinking, who have attended conference presentations of this research, or who have colleagues who are engaged in studies of teacher thinking. These teacher educators may have a felt sense that there is some potential in this work for affecting their conduct of teacher preparation, but may not know quite what to do about it. Some are awaiting a hypothetical 'Phase 2' of research on teacher thinking, when researchers move from description of the ways teachers think to quasi-experiments and other tough-minded designs from which prescriptions will flow for how teachers ought to think, plan and decide. In my opinion, these teacher educators wait in vain. Research on teacher thinking will never provide a scientific basis for prescribing how teachers ought to think.

I want to propose a third kind of relationship between research on teaching (particularly research on teacher thinking) and the practice of teacher education. In this relationship, members of the research community behave as *consultants* to the community of teacher educators. As you know, to work well as a consultant one must come to see the client's (teacher educator's) problems from the perspective of a sympathetic insider. A good consultant has expertise and a perspective different from that of the client, and engages this expertise in the service of the client's own short- and long-term ends. A consultant seldom solves major problems, but often contributes important pieces to the client's own solutions. The best consultants are those who leave us with something interesting and provocative to think about as we continue to wrestle with the complexities of our own local problematic situation. What I am calling for here is a more humble and service-oriented role for research on teaching in relation to teacher education; a relationship in which researchers provide food for thought responsive to the perceived needs of teacher educators. It is in this kind of a relationship that I see great promise for research on teacher thinking as a source of valuable assistance in the thoughtful preparation of teachers.

In this third kind of relationship we have teacher educators who have learned a bit about research on teacher thinking, who have experienced the felt sense that something ought to be done with this work, and who have begun to think about their teaching of novices in light of new descriptions of the way teaching is. These teacher educators are not waiting for researchers to tell them what to do next. Some have begun applied research programmes of their own. Others have begun to make small changes in the content of their teaching and in the ways that they teach. Still others have begun the demanding and politically complicated process of reorganising whole teacher preparation programmes to reflect their collective and emergent sense of what constitutes progress in teacher education. These are the leaders and risk takers in teacher education to whom research on teacher thinking can be most useful.

Four General Claims

Given this way of thinking about the relationship of research and practice, I have four general claims to make about the promise of research on teacher thinking for influencing teacher education:

1.   Research on teacher thinking has small but important contributions to make to the practice of teacher education. I do *not* see in research on teacher thinking

the grounds for *radical* revision of the form and content of teacher preparation. Some of the most important contributions to teacher education may take the form of rationalising, justifying and understanding practices that have long been in place in teacher education. Furthermore, many contributions of research on teacher thinking will not make teacher education easier, but they may make teacher preparation more interesting.

2. The study of the thoughts, knowledge and dispositions of *experienced* teachers (important as this is) does not answer the questions of what novices should be taught and how they should be prepared. There are two interrelated problems here: (a) most of this research describes teacher thinking, planning and decision-making without taking an empirically-supported position on the effectiveness or desirability of these forms and patterns of teacher thinking; and (b) even if these forms of teacher thinking are shown to be desirable for teachers, it remains to be discovered how one might best help start inexperienced prospective teachers moving in these directions.

3. Particular changes and improvements made in the content and process of teacher preparation ought to be invented, tested and adapted by teacher educators themselves. Research on teacher thinking can provide examples of concepts, methods and food for thought for teacher educators, but *not* well-defined prescriptions for how to educate teachers. (The ideal situation, from my point of view, is when researchers on teacher thinking themselves become practising teacher educators and learn how to apply their research to their own teaching.)

4. Fourth, and finally, I believe that research on teacher thinking has already begun to affect the ways we think and act as we prepare novices for the teaching profession. Teacher educators are asking thoughtful questions about the content and process of their work and, in the last five years, a number of interesting and encouraging programme innovations have been started with still more in the planning stages. To date, research on teacher thinking has perhaps affected the ways in which teachers are prepared more visibly than it has affected the ways teachers teach in classrooms.

Thinking from the Research

Suppose that a researcher on teacher thinking is invited to consult with a faculty on teacher educators. What could he or she offer as food for thought to these teacher educators as they think about strengthening their own teacher preparation programme? I want to describe a handful of ideas from research on teacher thinking that such a consultant could offer in response to the teacher educators' needs. I group these ideas under three headings: preconceptions and implicit theories, planning and reflection, and dilemmas and uncertainty.

Preconceptions and Implicit Theories

Research on teacher thinking has documented the fact that teachers develop and hold implicit theories about their students (Bussis, Chittenden and Amarel, 1976), about the subject matter that they teach (Ball, 1986; Duffy, 1977; Elbaz, 1981; Kuhs, 1980) and about their roles and responsibilities and how they should act (Ignatovich, Cusick and Ray, 1979; Olson, 1981). These implicit theories are not neat and complete reproductions of the educational psychology found in textbooks or lecture notes. Rather, teachers' implicit theories tend to be eclectic aggregations of cause – effect propositions from any sources, rules of thumb, and generalisations drawn from personal experience, beliefs, values, biases and prejudices. Teachers are subject to the full range of insights and errors in human judgement (described by Nisbett and Ross, 1980), just as all humans are when faced with complex, real time, consequential, and occasionally emotion-laden social judgements and action situations. Moreover, teachers' implicit theories about themselves and their work are thought to play an important part in the judgements and interpretations that teachers make every day.

As the term 'implicit theory' implies, these systems of thought are not clearly articulated or codified by their owners, but are typically inferred and reconstructed by researchers on teacher thinking. The study of implicit theories employs various methods including stimulated recall interviews, linguistic analysis of teacher talk, paragraph completion tests, responses to simulation materials such as vignettes describing hypothetical students or classroom situations, and concept generation and mapping exercises such as the Kelly Repertory Grid Technique. Research designs also vary considerably from ethnographic case studies of one or two teachers (Elbaz, 1981; Kroma, 1983) to standardised administration of a belief inventory, judgement task, or stimulated recall protocol to several teachers (e.g. Conners, 1978; Marland, 1977; Munby, 1983). Variability in researchers' methods, designs, contexts and interpretive frames of reference leads to great variability in how teachers' implicit theories are described.

Leaving teachers and their implicit theories for a moment, let me turn to research that is primarily about students learning science. Studies of the teaching and learning of science (e.g. Roth, Smith and Anderson, 1983; Roth, 1985) indicate that students come to a science lesson or course with preconceptions about the phenomena and processes in the science curriculum. For example, fifth graders come to a lesson on photosynthesis with their own ideas about how plants get nourishment or to a physics unit on light and vision with preconceptions about how we see. Often, these preconceptions are incomplete, flawed, and in conflict with currently accepted scientific explanations. Moreover, usually, students' preconceptions are robust, that is, students continue to hold and think from flawed but familiar preconceptions about the world even after having been taught scientifically correct explanations (Roth, 1985). Researchers advocating an approach to teaching called 'teaching for conceptual change' (Posner, *et al.* 1982; Roth, 1985), have demonstrated that students' preconceptions can be revised or replaced with scientifically correct conceptions only if considerable teaching time and energy are devoted to unmasking and incontrovertibly confronting students' misconceptions before proceeding with instruction.

So, back in our consultant role, what do we have to work with, in the service of teacher educators? Teachers have implicit theories, students have preconceptions. Both are robust, idiosyncratic, and sensitive to the particular experiences of the holder, incomplete, familiar, and sufficiently pragmatic to have taken the teacher or student to where they are today. Neither are likely to read like a textbook or to be quickly and thoroughly replaced by the usual lecture, reading, discussion, practice, and evaluation methods typically employed in teacher preparation programmes. Implicit theories and preconceptions affect perception, interpretation, and judgement and therefore have potentially important consequences in what teachers and students do and say.

In the context of teacher education, I believe these claims and information about implicit theories and preconceptions have some interesting and provocative implications. Students begin teacher education programmes with their own ideas and beliefs about what it takes to be a successful teacher. These preconceptions are formed from thousands of hours of observation of teachers, good and bad, over the previous 15 or so years. Undoubtedly, students' conceptions of teaching are incomplete, for they typically see and hear only the performance side of classroom teaching. With this in mind, a thoughtful teacher educator might ask: What are the preconceptions about teaching and learning by our students? How should we take account of what our students know and believe as we help them prepare to be teachers? How might we structure field observations early in a teacher preparation programme to make visible important aspects of teaching not usually obvious to primary school or high school students? What do prospective teachers believe about the integration of subject-matter knowledge with pedagogical skills, and what does our preparation programme offer to support or challenge and replace these preconceptions? Notice that these are not questions to which research on teacher thinking offers answers. Rather these are potentially useful questions that might not otherwise have been asked in the absence of research on teacher thinking.

Beyond pursuing answers to questions about prospective teachers, this research can stimulate introspective questions about teacher educators themselves. What do we, as teacher educators, believe about teaching and learning, individually and as a faculty? How consistent are our espoused beliefs with our methods of teaching and evaluation? (That is, do we practise what we preach?) Are the implicit and explicit theories of teacher educators who supervise practice teaching likely to dominate and wash out what has been taught earlier in a teacher preparation programme? How does variability in implicit theories among supervisors of practice teaching influence and bias their judgements and evaluations of our students? Asking questions like these has led a number of teacher educators to take the risky and exciting step of systematically studying their own practices. For example, a few studies of the influence of implicit theories and belief systems of clinical supervisors on their judgements of student teachers were completed in the 1980s (Niemeyer and Moon, 1986; Rust, 1986). These studies have contributed to deliberation about who should be doing clinical observations (i.e. should this usually low-status task be delegated to inexperienced graduate assistants, to experienced teachers hired for these purposes, to experienced teacher educators, experts in the academic disciplines, or teams from two or three of these groups?), how clinical observations should be done, what kinds of evidence might be used in student teacher evaluation, and how clinical supervisors might prepare themselves for their important and demanding work. This research has also begun to contribute to an enhanced sense of professional identity among teacher educators who specialise in clinical supervision, insofar as it has demonstrated the complexity and intellectual demands of this aspect of teacher education and drawn attention to the potentially pivotal role of the clinical supervisor in the process of teacher preparation.

Planning and Reflection

Research on teacher planning consists of a score or more of studies every bit as variable in method and design as the work on implicit theories. Two distinctive features, however, set planning apart from implicit theories. First, virtually everyone involved with education agrees that planning is a real phenomenon, that is, all teachers do something they call planning at some times. Second, many now see teacher planning as the instrumental linking process between curriculum on the one hand and the particulars of instruction on the other.

Psychologically, to understand teacher planning is to understand how teachers transform and interpret knowledge, formulate intentions, and act from that knowledge and those intentions. From the curriculum theorist's point of view, the study of teacher planning can help explain why and how curriculum materials are understood or misunderstood, used, distorted, ignored, or transcended in classroom instruction. Politically and administratively, to control teacher planning is to control, in large measure, the content, pace, emphasis and process of instruction. From the practising teacher's point of view, the study of teacher planning can enhance appreciation of the genuinely professional (as distinct from technical) aspects of teaching. That is, the study of teacher planning can and has documented the many heretofore-unappreciated ways in which the practice of teaching can be as complex and cognitively demanding as the practice of medicine, law or architecture.

I know that those of us who began to do research on teacher planning 10 or 12 years ago did not anticipate that this work had potential for being so central to the concerns of so many audiences. It has only been in hindsight that I have come to believe that to understand teacher planning is to understand teaching; that the study of how teachers prepare for instruction can reveal a great deal about which features of subject matter, students, and of the physical, psychological, administrative and political environments actually influence classroom instruction. We can theorise with the best of intentions about how teaching and school learning could be optimised, but our finest ideas and proposals must still pass through the funnel of teacher planning.

After this big build-up, I am a bit embarrassed to admit that research on teacher thinking has made only modest beginnings in the study of teacher planning. We know, for example, that experienced teachers do several different types of planning in the course of the school year (Clark and Yinger, 1979b), that the time-honoured rational model (moving from learning objectives, through generating alternatives, to choice of an optimal alternative) is not used regularly by experienced teachers (Morine-Dershimer and Valiance, 1976; Yinger, 1977) (Although experienced teachers do claim that the rational model ought to be taught to novices: Neale, Case and Pace, 1983.) Teachers do attend to learning outcomes, sometimes before teaching (while planning), sometimes during teaching, and sometimes only after interactive teaching is over (McLeod, 1981). Teachers also attend to goals, issues and concerns other than learning outcomes in their planning. And the teacher planning process serves immediate personal purposes for teachers, such as study of content, anxiety reduction and confidence building, as well as longer range instrumental purposes, determining the content and structure of classroom interaction (Hill, Yinger and Robbins, 1981; Carnahan, 1980; Peterson, Marx and Clark, 1978).

Psychological models of the planning process have been proposed and, to some degree, tested against the realities of practice (e.g. Yinger, 1977, Clark and Yinger, 1979b). Moreover, styles of planning used by experienced teachers such as 'incremental planning' and 'comprehensive planning' (Clark and Yinger, 1979b) have been described. Curriculum planning has been shown to vary with the subject matter under consideration and with the degree of novelty or familiarity of the material, students and teaching setting (Clark and Elmore, 1981). North American elementary teachers report spending relatively large amounts of time planning (10 to 20 hours per week), but also report that relatively little time or support for planning are officially sanctioned or encouraged (Clark and Yinger, 1979b). An important product of the planning process is routines (Yinger, 1979) or structured patterns of teacher and student behaviour. The first weeks of the school year have been shown to be a particularly important period for teacher planning, inasmuch as many of the routines, rules, relationships and expectations that influence classroom interaction during the remainder of the year are planned, negotiated, re-planned and established during that time (Anderson and Evertson, 1978; Buckley and Cooper, 1978; Clark and Elmore, 1979; Shultz and Florio, 1979; Tickunoff and Ward, 1978).

In the process of reviewing the literature of research on teacher thinking several times (e.g. Clark and Yinger, 1977; Clark, 1983; Clark and Peterson, 1986), I have come to both bless and curse a distinction made by Philip Jackson almost two decades ago – the distinction between preactive teacher behaviour and interactive teaching (Jackson, 1968). On the side of blessings and gratitude, this distinction serves me well as an analytic tool for defining the boundary between studies of teacher planning (preactive teaching) and studies of teacher interactive thinking and behaviour. If no students are physically present, we are dealing with preactive teaching, and if students are present, we are dealing with interactive teaching. The distinction is clear, simple, and has great face validity – the empty classroom is clearly a different place from the classroom populated with teacher and students engaged in the business of teaching and learning.

However, more recently this distinction has given me pause, and even trouble. For, while much of teacher planning begins and ends in the empty classroom, I have come to believe that planning does not stop when students arrive, that teachers can plan and revise plans 'on their feet', and that reflection on plans and on classroom experiences can be an important influence on teacher planning, no matter when that reflection takes place. Teacher thinking is both messier and more integrated (in the person of the teacher) than Jackson's neat distinction suggests. The iterative and social nature of teaching allows and encourages revision, postponement, elaboration, or abandonment of yesterday's plan in response to today's experience in the classroom. The distinctions between planning and teaching, between proactive and interactive thinking, begin to blur and become fuzzy. There is a danger of forcing the phenomenology of teaching to fit models and categories of researchers, possibly distorting and misunderstanding the essential richness and dynamism of teacher thinking. The study of reflection, post-hoc analysis, and response to apparent failures, interruptions, negotiations, teaching disasters and desperate inspirations of the moment may have as much to contribute to understanding both planning and teaching as does the direct study of teachers preparing for instruction in the empty classroom.

One of the side effects of doing research on teacher thinking has been the discovery and elaboration of techniques and procedures for promoting reflection and analysis by teachers of their own thinking and behaviour. These techniques include journal keeping, clinical interviewing, stimulated recall procedures in which teachers view videotape recordings (or sometimes listen to audiotapes) of their teaching and respond to questions about their thinking, perceptions, decisions, and intentions, and concept generation and conceptual mapping tasks. To study teacher thinking researchers must depend on teachers to think aloud, either while in the act of thinking and deciding, or retrospectively; we cannot observe thought directly.

Hand in glove with these technical developments is the development of a commitment to including teachers themselves as full partners in the study of teacher thinking. To some degree, this change in the role that teachers play in the research process from experimental subject to colleague and collaborator follows from the invisible nature of teacher thinking and from the model role of the 'informant' in ethnographic studies of societies linguistically and culturally different from that of the anthropologist. In part, the enhanced role of teachers in research on teacher thinking reflects ideological and political commitments to share power more equitably between the communities of research and of practice. In any case, teachers have found themselves thinking aloud, reflecting, raising and refining questions about their knowledge and practice, writing, analysing data, making formal presentations of research in which they have been involved, and publishing for audiences of researchers and teachers. A great deal of this has happened since the late 1970s and these developments are due largely to the advent of research on teacher thinking (Porter, 1986).

In my experience working with teachers on research projects in these ways, a recurring theme in our conversations concerns the powerful effects on teachers of reflecting on their own practice. Experienced teachers report that describing their plans and intentions, explaining their reasons underlying action and decision, and responding to the questions and presence of an informed, non-judgemental adult seems to breathe new life and meaning into their teaching. Usually, teaching is an action-oriented, operational, 'don't look back, they may be gaining on you' profession. But the intervention of researchers describing planning, thinking and decision-making has required that teachers stop and think, find words and reasons for their thoughts and beliefs, and to take a second look at themselves and their teaching. While not intended by the researchers as professional development activities, the journal keeping, clinical interviews, stimulated recall sessions, and articulation of beliefs and implicit principles of practice have instigated a new awareness among a few teachers. These techniques and the genuine human interest in understanding that accompany their use may constitute professional development activities of the broadest kind. That is, they may enable teachers to see and appreciate what is genuinely professional about their work; to kindle or revive the idealism, freshness and commitment to self-improvement that we often see in the best first-year teachers, but this time, with a difference: the difference that years of accumulated practical wisdom brings. In sum, reflection by teachers makes a difference, albeit a difference expressed in many different ways.

Now, what does this mix of fact, theory, and opinion say to our consultant, trying to be helpful to teacher educators? He or she might bring questions like these to deliberations about teacher preparation: When and how do prospective teachers learn about and practise planning? How many kinds of planning do they practise? To what extent does their practice planning take account of the structural and practical differences between school subject matters (e.g. the concept of 'guided practice' may be realised in quite different ways in the contexts of essay writing or maths problem solving)? Is the theory and practice of planning as expressed in university courses consistent with the procedures and criteria for successful planning built into the practice teaching experience? What do our approaches to training teachers reveal about our implicit theories of teaching (e.g. teaching as literal implementation of curriculum materials, teaching as imitation of experienced models, teaching as curriculum building and adaptation, teaching as behaviour management)? If planning during the first days and weeks of the school year is so important, do our prospective teachers ever get to see and participate in this kind of planning? To what extent do our teacher education students have opportunities to plan, teach, re-plan and re-teach, thus learning about the limits of foresight and about improvement-oriented self-observation? Do we include techniques and opportunities for reflection and professional communication among teachers in our training programmes? And how do we, the teacher educators, show that we value and practise reflection and self-examination about our own teaching? Again, our researcher-consultant brings no crisp and prescriptive answers to these questions. Nevertheless, they are questions worth pursuing, and the pursuit must be framed by the all-important context of particular professional preparation programmes.

Teacher planning and reflection are not the whole of teaching, but research on teacher thinking suggests to me that they deserve explicit and creative attention throughout a sound teacher education programme.

Dilemmas and Uncertainty

The third set of contributions of research on teacher thinking to discourse about teacher preparation concerns the very nature of the teaching situation itself. Not 'what works', but 'what it is really like out there', as seen through the eyes of teachers themselves. In three words, teaching as experienced is *complex, uncertain* and peppered with *dilemmas.*

The research on teacher planning alluded to above speaks eloquently to the complexity and uncertainty inherent in interactive teaching.

Indeed, a great deal of teachers' planning energy goes into trying to predict and anticipate potential problems, guess and estimate what students already know and how they might respond, and to forming plans and routines that are robust to the interruptions and distractions that assault most teachers most of the time.

Researchers have also studied the thinking and decision-making that teachers do during the act of teaching. This research has explored the extent to which teachers make on-the-spot decisions that change their plans or behaviour in the classroom, and attempted to identify the cues used by teachers in reaching these interactive decisions. A few studies have explored the relationships between patterns of interactive decision-making and student achievement, and some compare thinking processes of experts with those of novices in the same situations. Like the literature on teacher planning, the number of studies available is small, and the teachers studied are mostly experienced elementary school teachers.

Research on interactive decision-making indicates that teachers encounter decision situations at two-minute intervals while teaching – literally hundreds of decision points per day. This research also indicates that the greatest proportion of teachers' interactive thoughts is about students (between 39 per cent and 50 per cent), followed by instructional behaviour and procedures, content, materials and learning objectives (Peterson and Clark, 1978). Marland (1977) categorised teachers' interactive thoughts as perceptions, interpretations, anticipations and reflections. There is some evidence to support the idea that teachers consider improvising major changes in instructional process primarily when their teaching is going poorly, i.e. when the myriad adjustments and small changes that teachers make in the ongoing classroom process prove insufficient in maintaining the flow of the lesson (Peterson and Clark, 1978). This is consistent with findings from studies of the cognitive processing of professionals in other fields who are described by Simon (1957) as pursuing a strategy of 'satisficing' rather than optimising. Research by Doyle (1979) also indicates that it is 'adaptive and efficient for a teacher to direct conscious processing primarily to discrepancies or anomalies. By specializing in discrepancies, a teacher can anticipate disruptions and reduce the effects of immediacy and unpredictability on task accomplishment' (Doyle, 1979, pp. 62–63).

Leinhardt and Greeno (1984) describe the cognitive structures that teachers use to move back and forth between implementing pre-planned routines and adjusting their actions to new information that becomes available in the course of a lesson. They found experienced teachers to be distinguished by their ability to obtain and retain new information in interaction with students while continuing to maintain control of their agenda. Others have compared the schema that experienced teachers use to understand what is happening in the classroom with the way novices understand the same situation (Calderhead, 1983; Housner and Griffey, 1983).

Three studies examined the relationship between interactive decision-making and student on-task behaviour or achievement (Peterson, Marx and Clark, 1978; Doyle, 1977; Morine and Valiance, 1975). The interactive decision-making of effective teachers is characterised by rapid judgement, 'chunking' of many events and cues into a few categories, differentiation of cues and events as to their importance, and a willingness to change the course of classroom interaction when necessary.

The studies of teacher planning and decision-making tell us a great deal about the task demands of teaching as well as about how particular teachers cope with those demands. The task environment of the classroom has been characterised by Shulman (1984) as more complex than that faced by a physician in a diagnostic examination. This complexity has been described by Clark and Lampert (1986) as follows:

> The teacher encounters a host of interrelated and competing decision situations both while planning and during teaching. There are no perfect or optimal solutions to these decisions. A gain for one student or in one subject matter may mean a foregone opportunity for others. A motivationally and intellectually profitable digression may reduce time devoted to the mandated curriculum.
>
> Such conflicts among teachers' multiple commitments lead to practical dilemmas (Berlak and Berlak, 1981; Lampert, 1984) that must be managed in interaction with students. Conflicting goals, combined with endemic uncertainty about how to achieve desired outcomes can lead to 'knots' in teachers' thinking (Wagner, 1984). Often these entanglements can only be sorted out as the teacher experiments with action and observes outcomes (Lampert, 1985). By such experimentation, teachers build a store of personal practical knowledge about how to get their job done (Connelly and Clandinin, 1984, p. 28).

Therefore, research on teacher thinking has made an empirical case that the practice of teaching is complex, uncertain and dilemma-riddled. In addition, this research has described how some teachers see, feel and cope with the greyness. What questions might our hypothetical consultant raise with teacher educators that follow from seeing teaching thus? First, one might ask how thoroughly and persuasively a teacher preparation programme informs its postulants that there is more to teaching than meets the eye; that expertise in teaching is less a matter of knowing all the answers than a matter of making the most of the unexpected. While the system of education in China supports the role of the teacher as a virtuoso who creates, practises and polishes exquisitely set pieces of pedagogical performance (Paine, 1986), the teacher in North American schools is faced with a mind-boggling array of mutually incompatible expectations and imperatives. Do prospective teachers hear this, come to believe this, and consider it in forming their emergent expectations and implicit theories? Do methods courses, microteaching and other preparatory experiences reflect the intrinsic uncertainty of teaching? Or do teacher education programmes control, oversimplify and distort practice teaching and field observation experiences to such a degree that our students' practice time is wasted or misdirected in irrelevant and unrepresentative test-like activities? Do the teachers of teachers have the courage to think aloud as they themselves wrestle with troubling dilemmas such as: striking a balance between depth and breadth of content studied, distribution of time and attention among individual students, making inferences about what students know and what grades they should be assigned, or with how to repair errors, teaching disasters, and the human mistakes that even distinguished professors make from time to time? Do we claim to be graduating fully functioning teachers or novices well started? How might teacher preparation programmes be sowing the seeds of learned helplessness and incompetence by advocating practices that simply do not work for novices? For example, teacher educators in two otherwise exemplary preparation programmes (studied by Ball and Feiman-Nemser, 1986) taught their students that good teachers do not use published textbooks or basal readers, they create their own materials. This well-intentioned advice set up students for failure and embarrassment during practice teaching because the teacher preparation programme did not equip these beginners to create original materials of high quality and practicality, and because their experienced cooperating teachers typically relied on textbooks and basal readers quite heavily. Here we have a case of unintentional sabotage of a potentially crucial learning experience.

I will say one final time that research on teacher thinking does not promise to discover a generically effective method or set of techniques for dealing with uncertainty, complexity, or dilemmas. By their very natures, these qualities defy the quest for a technical fix. But I do claim that the teacher educator who tells it like it is, who abandons the fiction that teaching can become a technically exact scientific enterprise, and who has the courage to reveal how he or she agonizes over real dilemmas and contradictions – that teacher educator is likely to be successful at helping prospective teachers to prepare themselves for uncertainty. That teacher educator is likely to minimize the boredom and burnout that plague our profession. That teacher educator is asking the right questions about teacher preparation.

Conclusion

Teacher preparation is already being affected, to some degree, by research on teacher thinking. Thoughtful teacher educators are learning about this research, thinking from it, and asking questions about the ways in which they help their students become well-started and thoughtful novice teachers. Research on teacher thinking has helped us to appreciate in some detail the complexity, artistry and demandingness of classroom teaching. This work now serves as rich food for thought (and action) for colleagues who have chosen the challenging work of influencing the knowledge, skills and dispositions of those who would teach. I hope that this great conversation broadens and continues, with researchers, teacher educators and those who play both roles pursuing answers to the big question: How can we help our students to *prepare themselves* to think and act in ways that will eventually become good teaching?

Author Reflection 2004

Twenty years is a respectable half-life for a discussion of the relationship between research and the practice of teacher education. Research on teaching has changed and developed during the past two decades; so have the political and social contexts in which we prepare new teachers and support veterans in career-long learning.

Accountability pressures fall more and more heavily on the shoulders of teachers and local education agency leaders. In my judgement, teachers and teacher educators are in even more need of positive partnership and support from the research community than was the case in 1986. If I had to focus on just one proposal from my 1986 chapter that has great currency today this is what it would be: Teacher educators themselves should become more heavily engaged in studying their own practice and programmes. Researchers and scholars have developed designs, instruments, models and techniques useful in understanding teaching, learning and teacher education. However, truly useful knowledge is ultimately and intimately local – the product of thoughtful examination of big ideas in small settings by the very teacher educators who design and work within these settings. Now more than ever, I urge teacher educators everywhere to ask and pursue answers to challenging questions about the dynamics and effects of our teacher preparation programmes. For if we do not question our own practice, others will be quick to do so, in much less constructive ways.

Chapter 16

Using Textbooks and Teachers' Guides

What beginning elementary teachers learn and what they need to know

Deborah Loewenberg-Ball and Sharon Feiman-Nemser

Introduction

> I keep hearing this over and over again - get away from the textbooks, you know, the textbooks are just a tool. They're a teaching tool, the actual teaching comes from up here (taps her forehead), from you...
>
> (Janice)[1]

> They said, um, don't rely so much on the textbook, just go out and do your own things and experiment...
>
> (Linda)

This chapter examines what prospective elementary teachers are taught and what they learn about the role of textbooks and teachers' guides in teaching. This emerged as an important issue in our longitudinal study of learning to teach and the preservice curriculum, conducted between 1982 and 1984 at a large Midwestern American university.

In this study, we followed six elementary education students through two years of undergraduate teacher education. Our student informants were enrolled in two contrasting programmes which are part of an effort to reform preservice teacher preparation. The Academic programme emphasised the importance of theoretical and subject matter knowledge in teaching and provided limited field experiences before

This work is sponsored in part by the Institute for Research on Teaching, College of Education, Michigan State University. The Institute for Research on Teaching is funded primarily by the Program for Teaching and Instruction of the National Institute of Education, United States Department of Education. The opinions expressed in this paper do not necessarily reflect the position, policy, or endorsement of the National Institute of Education. (Contract No. 400-81-0014).

student teaching. The Decision-making programme emphasised generic methods of teaching and research-based decision-making. Much of the programme took place in an elementary school where teacher candidates spent considerable time in classrooms, aiding, observing, and teaching lessons. We thought that structural and ideological differences between the two programmes might help account for differences in the student teachers' thinking and learning.

Each term we interviewed our student informants about what they were learning and how they thought that would help them in teaching and learning to teach.[2] We also attended and documented courses, field experiences, and each student's experience in student teaching.

As we sat in on courses, we were struck by the fact that both programmes seemed to promote the idea that good (i.e. 'professional') teachers did not use textbooks and teachers' guides but developed their own curriculum instead. In this chapter, we explore this theme of textbooks and learning to teach by addressing four questions:

1.   What did the teacher education programmes convey about textbooks, planning and curricular decision-making?
2.   What did the prospective teachers come to believe about the use of textbooks, about planning and curricular decision-making?
3.   What did the student teachers do with textbooks and teachers' guides during student teaching?
4.   What should preservice elementary teacher education programmes teach beginning teachers about textbooks and their role in planning and teaching?

What did the Teacher Education Programmes Teach about Curriculum Materials?

To understand what teacher candidates in each programme were taught about textbooks and their role in teaching, we analysed field notes from six courses.[3] We examined explicit statements about textbooks and planning, as well as messages implied in particular assignments. We also looked at opportunities that students had to plan or work with curricular materials (e.g. critiquing textbooks, constructing units, teaching reading lessons). Our informal and formal interviews with the student teachers helped us understand how they were thinking about textbooks and teaching and how they were interpreting what they encountered in their programmes. Below we summarise the central messages about textbooks that came through in each programme.

Academic Programme: 'Use Textbooks as Resources, But Don't Follow Them'
The Academic programme promoted a view of teaching in which teachers focus on student thinking and teach for understanding – referred to in the programme as 'conceptual change teaching'. According to this view, teachers should identify and seek to change students' naive conceptions about subject matter. Key instructors in the programme stressed that good teaching requires much more than following teachers' guides[4].

Several courses emphasised the deficiencies of textbooks and teachers' guides. The teacher candidates heard repeatedly that textbooks often do not fit with the teacher's goals, priorities or theories of learning. A teacher may not like the way a textbook treats a particular topic or may not think that everything in the book is equally important to learn. One instructor said that teachers make these judgements based on their understanding and conception of the subject matter. In the curriculum course, the teacher candidates were told that science texts are often based on an 'additive' view of learning, meaning that they focus on 'filling up' students with knowledge, without attention to how students learn or what their misconceptions might be. In two different courses, students were assigned to critique textbooks, examining the content, the implicit assumptions about learning, and the information provided for the teacher.

The bad news about textbooks was reinforced in the reading methods courses where students were told that basals were bad because they placed too much emphasis on phonics and word identification skills. Finally, except for a brush with basal readers in their reading methods practicum, students in the Academic programme did not confront the use of textbooks in actual classrooms until student teaching since they had almost no field experience.

Academic programme students got the message that textbooks had serious deficiencies and that if they wanted to be good teachers, they should not rely on teachers' guides, but use them only as resources. Danielle, one of our focal students, said she understood she 'should get away from the basal as much as possible'.

Overall, Academic programme students learned to critique textbooks from a conceptual change perspective and developed some general concepts about what good teaching entails (e.g. attention to students' preconceptions). They also developed the strong impression that they should avoid relying on published materials. They did not, however, acquire the knowledge and skill to begin to *adapt* textbooks appropriately.

Decision-making Programme: 'You Are a Professional Teacher Deciding for Yourself'

The Decision-making programme projected an image of the good teacher as a 'professional' who makes systematic data-based decisions and determines for herself why she is doing what she does. 'Text-bound teachers', who rely on teachers' guides for what to teach and how to teach it, were portrayed as 'mere technicians'.

The emphasis on professional decision-making was reflected in a major emphasis on 'generic' planning skills, introduced in the educational psychology course. The instructor told the prospective teachers that he would show them the steps for making instructional decisions. He taught them a formula for writing behavioural objectives and presented structured formats for daily and unit lesson plans.

In this programme, students were explicitly told to avoid following basal readers. In their first reading methods course, the instructor said they should not follow basals, but could use them as a resource or 'instructional tool'. The second reading methods course taught that basal readers, although undesirable, are often inescapable. While new teachers are likely to be required to use a basal series, they should not 'get into a lockstep in that basal'. The instructor said that basal readers do not provide a total language arts programme because they lack variety and she introduced other activities and strategies that could be used 'hand in hand' with the basal (e.g. language experience approach, individualised reading). She did not, however, address how these activities might be integrated with any basal work.

The other methods courses did not deal directly with textbooks. In mathematics methods, students were shown how to teach unusual topics such as probability, and were given activities for teaching more conventional concepts such as place value. There was no opportunity to examine or work with standard maths curricular materials. The same was true in the social studies methods course.

Decision-making programme students developed the impression that following textbooks and teachers' guides was not 'professional' teaching, in reading or in any other subject. The students learned to fill out the planning forms and use technical vocabulary (e.g. 'advance organizers', 'terminal behaviour'). They also formed an impression of the kind of planning that 'professional teachers' do.

Both Programmes: 'Good Teachers Don't Follow Textbooks'

Table 16.1 provides a summary, by course, of the recurring themes within each programme.

While the two programmes differed in the reasons why teachers should avoid textbooks both programmes explicitly communicated that textbooks should be used only as a resource, that following a textbook was an undesirable way to teach. Neither programme showed students alternative ways to use teachers' guides and textbooks thoughtfully (e.g. how to choose from among the many pieces of a curricular programme and modify teaching suggestions and activities appropriately to meet the needs of particular children). The students we followed developed the impression that their own ideas and knowledge were a better source of content than anything in the textbook or teacher's guide; however, in preparation for their role as curriculum developers, they were not helped to think about what counts as a worthwhile learning activity.

What Did The Prospective Teachers Do During Student Teaching?

Even though I was trained to be leery of textbooks, I still found myself falling into that rut for a certain amount of time because I had no other alternative...

(Danielle)

Table 16.1.   Summary of programme messages about textbooks and planning across three courses

Academic programme

1.   *Educational psychology:* Professional teachers are curriculum developers who think for themselves about what to teach and how to teach it. This responsibility cannot be 'abdicated' to a textbook.
2.   *Curriculum:* Teachers must know their subjects well and must understand learning in order to make curricular decisions; textbooks are but one of several sources of information for teachers. A critical examination of textbooks often reveals that they are inadequate to help students learn.
3.   *Science methods:* Good teachers teach for conceptual change in their students. Science textbooks can provide the teacher with helpful information about the activities and the content, but not about student thinking or misconceptions.

Decision-making programme

1.   *Educational psychology:* Making decisions and planning are central tasks of teaching. Good teachers proceed systematically, using scientifically verified principles from psychology as well as their own experience.
2.   *Reading methods:* Basal readers are one of a range of instructional tools for teachers, but professional teachers make decisions themselves about what they are teaching and how they are teaching it; they don't 'simply follow a teacher's guide'.
3.   *Reading methods (second term):* Teachers are usually required to use basal readers. However, basals are not adequate as a total reading-language arts programme for children because the programmes lack variety. Textbooks must be enriched and extended. Good teachers do not inundate students with dittos and workbook pages; they spend time developing their own activities for children.

Confronting Textbooks in Student Teaching

In spite of what they had been taught in their courses, the student teachers in both programmes ended up using basals and teachers' guides. Five out of our six student informants were placed in settings with cooperating teachers who used textbooks as the core of their reading and mathematics teaching. Some of them felt pressed to maintain the established classroom practice. Others, as they assumed responsibility for the entire day, were simply overwhelmed, and resorted to textbooks as a reasonable way to manage, or at least survive, the demands of full-time student teaching.

A surprising finding was that following the text presented unexpected problems for the student teachers. Some discovered that they were unprepared to use textbooks and teachers' guides to teach subject matter. Others followed the teachers' guides rather mechanically, moving through activities without really understanding what they were doing. Because they did not know how to adapt what was in the teachers' manuals, their modifications sometimes distorted the point of the lessons. The following vignettes illustrate some of these reactions to textbooks and teachers' guides [5].

Going through motions. Janice found planning and teaching all subjects all day long for her second grade class an overwhelming task. She relied heavily on textbooks and teachers' guides as a way of managing, although she said she felt guilty about doing so.

Janice often followed the suggested dialogues in the reading and maths manuals almost as scripts. She tried to 'do *everything*' (plan, teach groups, keep track of everything, control the children, etc.), but confessed that she did not think through or understand the lessons very thoroughly. Especially in maths, Janice did not always get the point of the lesson she was teaching directly from the teacher's guide. Although she managed to keep things moving along, Janice reflected:

> Sometimes I just feel like I am going through some motions and
> I don't know what it is all about.

What do the teachers' guides mean? Although the kindergarten maths teacher's manual contained detailed scripts, Linda, another student teacher, found it confusing and insufficient:

> The math lessons – they're so *short*. It says like 'Objective – to get
> the kids to know about representing length' – okay what's that sup-
> posed to mean? And it says, 'You will need these materials' – okay,
> I've got the materials, now what am I supposed to *do* with them?
> 'Procedure You will, um, distribute the chains and they will meas-
> ure their necks and see whose is longer or shorter' or something,
> you know. 'Other suggested activities', you know, it doesn't tell you
> hardly *anything*. I'm not sure what they *mean by* all this stuff...

Linda's problems in understanding the teaching suggestions in the guide stemmed from lacks in knowledge about the subject, about pedagogy and children, not surprising for a beginner. A more experienced teacher, who understood measurement as a mathematical topic, who knew something about how kindergarteners make sense of it, and who could visualise ways of orchestrating such activities, would probably not find these teaching suggestions mysterious or underdeveloped.

Modifying textbook lessons. Trying to modify what was in the teachers' guides turned out to be more complicated than expected. Danielle commented to the researcher that, in writing lessons plans for course assignments, she would routinely add a line, 'Adapt for the needs of individual students'. That was a sure way to get extra points! In student teaching, though, she realised how difficult it really was to 'adapt lessons':

> In our program, we were never told how to use the basal. We were told a basal isn't all that great and there's a lot of other things you could do.

Janice occasionally modified her maths lessons interactively. When an idea occurred to her that seemed related to the topic at hand, she would go off on a tangent. Janice was proud of herself for doing this, because she thought it made the lesson more interesting and allowed her to put more of herself into her textbook teaching. However, her lack of knowledge of mathematics sometimes produced misleading or incorrect digressions. One day, for example, she could not recall how to write a number sentence for 'one-fourth of 100 equals 25' and finally settled on: $1/4: 100 = 25$ (instead of $1/4 \times 100 = 25$ or $100:4 = 25$).

Getting Away From Textbooks in Student Teaching

Students in both programmes had got the idea that good teaching consists of departing from the textbook and developing their 'own' lessons and units. Some said they felt most 'motivated' when they created their own curriculum and that their teaching was most 'meaningful' to students when they did their own things. Others were pushed by their university supervisors to do their 'own' lessons. The cooperating teachers also praised the student teachers when they did something 'creative', reinforcing the students' belief that departing from the textbook was desirable in and of itself. Unfortunately, when student teachers tried to plan outside of textbooks, they often revealed the limits of their own knowledge and experience.

Getting away from the basal: Susan's bookmaking project. Around the middle of student teaching, Susan had her fourth and fifth graders make their own books as a way of motivating them to write stories. Following a procedure she had learned in her children's literature class, Susan spent an entire school day having students cut cardboard, iron the material onto the cover, and sew the pages together. Once the books were made, Susan told the students they could write anything they wanted in their books 'as long as it has an idea behind it'.

While Susan was competent in the technique of bookmaking, she did not know how to structure the writing phase nor did she seem to appreciate the academic possibilities of the project. Students worked on their stories in class and at home. In her comments to students about their work, Susan only noted misspelled words; she did not discuss their underlying ideas. When the children were finished writing in their 'beautiful' books, Susan felt the project was over. It did not occur to her to actually read the books, or to have the student authors read one another's books.

'Make up your "own" plans'. Sarah's university supervisors put pressure on her to do 'real planning' during student teaching: that meant writing her own lesson plans, not following the book or the way her cooperating teacher did things. Sarah puzzled,

> They always tell us, you know; don't use the textbook, but why not? I mean, it's there.

Sarah saw making up her 'own' plans outside of textbooks as unnecessary and very time-consuming. She also recognised that doing her 'own' plans meant getting inside of the subject matter, something she was not always well prepared to do. In planning a social studies unit, she reflected,

> I want (the children) to understand what a 'culture' is, but I am
> having a hard time understanding it myself.

It was not clear how pushing Sarah out of the textbook was supposed to help her learn to teach subject matter.

Beginning Teaching: Trying to See the 'Point of It All'

Whether student teachers used textbooks or departed from the manuals to create their 'own' lessons, they often did not understand the content they were teaching and did not seem to get the point of the lesson. In a few instances, however, the teaching suggestions in the guides seemed to provide a scaffold for student teachers' efforts, helping them understand more about the topic and how it is learned. The guides showed some ways of organising content for instruction and offered activities and questions that helped these novices know how to proceed. In these instances, the student teachers were able to get a handle on both content and pedagogy by following some of the suggestions and reflecting on what happened. Sarah's story is an example of this.

Sarah: Learning to teach place value. Near the beginning of student teaching, Sarah's university supervisor required her to rewrite a text-based unit she had written on place value. The supervisor urged her to incorporate bundling sticks and chip trading,[6] activities to which Sarah had been exposed in her maths methods classes. She told Sarah to focus on 'content, not tasks'.

This was hard for Sarah, who understood neither place value nor the tasks used to teach it. She observed, 'I don't know maths that much'. Sarah incorporated bundling sticks and chip trading into her unit plan as she had been pressed to do, which satisfied her supervisor's concern that she do her 'own' planning. In fact, nothing had changed. Substituting an idea learned in a methods class for pages in a maths textbook was neither more her 'own' nor more focused on content. Indeed, Sarah found it very difficult to teach anything about place value using these activities. The class became loud and hard to manage and she never really got beyond teaching them how to do the chip trading activity. Sarah returned to the maths textbook.

Sarah spent a long time – over three weeks – teaching place value (just ones, tens, hundreds) to her fifth graders. For them, it was review, but for Sarah it was the first time through. At the beginning of the unit, she saw no reason for students to know that 70 meant '7 *tens*': 'They're never going to say it like that', she reasoned. However, by the end of working through the textbook unit on place value, Sarah felt she was beginning to understand the concept better than she had at the beginning. She reflected,

> I had to really think about what place value *is*. Last week, if you'd
> asked me what place value was, I don't *know*... (But) like today, I
> thought of that example of 1263 and 2136 on the spot to get them
> to see about *places*...

She found another textbook which she thought gave better explanations of place value and regrouping than the one she had been using and she talked at length about specifically how she would teach place value another time, including where she would start and what questions she would ask. She seemed to understand the concept better and to appreciate what was complicated about teaching it. This enabled her to appraise another textbook lesson to see how it could help her. She said, 'the next time I teach place value, I'll understand it more and be able to teach it better, faster than this'.

A Sensible Goal for Teacher Education

Why shouldn't we follow the textbook? I mean, it is helping me along and the kids are learning the things they need to be learning. I mean, if it works, why should you be worried about making up your own plans for every single thing?

(Linda)

The difficulties encountered by our six elementary student teachers as they tried to teach with and without textbooks suggest that the goals as well as the methods of teacher education in this area need to be reconsidered.

Justifying decisions in teaching. It is not enough to tell prospective teachers who lack knowledge and experience that they should not follow teachers' guides, but should be curriculum developers and decision makers who create their own plans. Beginning teachers must learn to think about appropriate bases for curricular and instructional decisions.

Whether they use textbooks or not, novice teachers need help in seeing that decisions about what to teach to which students have important consequences (Goodlad, 1984; Scheffler, 1958). Without direct instruction in these matters, such choices may be based merely on individual preferences, (Cusick, 1983; Buchmann, 1986), commonsense views of what was meaningful or 'fun' (Dewey, 1977; Floden and Buchmann, 1984), or stereotyped notions of what particular students 'need' or 'can' learn (Anyon, 1981; Brophy, 1983). When our student teachers made curricular decisions, no one helped them pay attention to these considerations. Moreover, they often lacked a conception of what constitutes a worthwhile learning activity.

A surprising finding in our study was that neither programme dealt with the policy dimension of curricular decision-making. Many of the students were placed in classrooms where district policy mandated the use of a basal series and where curriculum was controlled through objectives and standardised testing. Still, the teacher education programmes conveyed the impression that teachers should be autonomous professionals who make their own curricular decisions. The rhetoric of 'professional decision-making' often conflicts with the fact that many curriculum decisions are made at the district level. Although the justification 'the district mandated it' is not necessarily defensible in some broader sense, prospective teachers need to be prepared to understand, interpret and work with district curriculum policies. This is a dilemma they will have to face. What do the policies mean? What is their intent? What should be the relationship between testing and the curriculum? Why do school districts try to control curriculum? Issues such as educational equity and teacher autonomy must be explored. Ignoring external influences on curricular decision-making seems a serious and misleading omission in preservice teacher education.

In order to help prospective teachers learn to justify their decisions carefully, they need to learn how to think deliberatively and responsibly about curricular planning. Ben-Peretz (1984a) suggests that student teachers may profit from collaborative participation in curriculum development projects. Such experiences can provide a deeper understanding of curricular decision-making, including how choices about content, instructional strategies, scope and sequence are made, in some absolute sense and under external constraints. This kind of experience is different from the individual unit planning which our students did, for it affords the opportunity to work with and learn from other, more expert curriculum planners.

Textbooks as sources of subject matter and pedagogical knowledge. Developing 'one's own' plans requires a flexible understanding of the topic to be taught and ideas about how children can be helped to learn about it. Teacher educators often assume that intending teachers know their subjects better than they do. Since the prospective teachers we followed lacked subject matter knowledge, using textbooks and teachers' guides to guide and strengthen their teaching would have been a more defensible starting point.

Implementing curriculum. Teaching well even from a highly prescriptive curriculum is more complicated than many seem to appreciate.[7] Our students had trouble visualising or understanding the numerous teaching suggestions and follow-up activities listed in the teachers' guides and adapting them to meet the needs of particular students. Beginning teachers must be helped to use textbooks and teachers' guides appropriately by learning how to get inside the curriculum as well as how to realise it in a specific setting (Joyce, Showers, Dalton and Beaton, 1985).

Ben-Peretz (1984a) argues that teachers must *understand* curriculum materials in order to be able to use them appropriately. She outlines specific areas of focus for teacher education to help beginning teachers take a reflective and deliberative stance toward curriculum implementation. Based on our study, two of these areas seem especially important. First, she argues that teachers must have an 'awareness of theoretical "choice points" in the materials – the deliberate choices made by curriculum developers'. Using materials thoughtfully requires an understanding of the meaning and possible consequences of the way they are designed and what they include.

Ben-Peretz (1984a) proposes that beginning teachers should learn to analyse curriculum using both internal and external frames of reference and points out that multiple frames of reference can help teachers uncover the educational potential as well as the limitations of a set of curriculum materials. Our students learned to critique textbooks using only external frames of reference – the lens of conceptual change learning in one programme, and lesson plan formats in the other programme – and they tended to recognise only deficiencies in the textbooks they examined.

Besides helping prospective teachers learn how to get at the orientation and rationale underlying curriculum, teacher education should give intending teachers guided practice in implementation. They need opportunities to plan and teach from teachers' guides and to supplement them appropriately (Joyce *et al.*, 1985).

Learning to learn from curriculum materials. Finally, and perhaps most important, preparing prospective teachers to use curriculum materials well should not be the ultimate goal. Preservice teacher education must prepare teachers to go on learning from their teaching experience. Teachers' guides may provide a helpful scaffold for learning to think pedagogically about particular content, considering the relationship between what the teacher and students are doing and what students are supposed to be learning.[8,9] This kind of thinking about ends and means is not the same as following a teacher's guide like a script. Beginning teachers must be oriented toward learning from teacher's guides and other curriculum materials, so that they can move toward being able to build their own units of study that are responsible to subject matter goals and responsive to their students. This is a reasonable goal for teacher development, not a starting point for beginners.

Appendix

Academic Programme
Educational psychology. This was the first course in the programme. It began with cognitive psychology (e.g. short- and long-term memory, cognitive networks,

schemata) and emphasised a constructivist view of learning. The second part of the course focused on epistemology; it dealt with the nature and kinds of knowledge and ways to think about what children should learn. The course concluded by drawing parallels between children's learning and the growth of knowledge in the disciplines. We examined this course for its messages about teaching, the teacher's role and subject matter.

Curriculum. This was the next course in the programme. It was divided into four segments: teachers as curriculum decision-makers, constructing a spiral curriculum, alternative perspectives on curriculum and controversies over the curriculum. Students analysed textbooks, planned lessons and worked on building a spiral curriculum. We looked closely at the course messages about curricular materials and curricular decision-making and the practical experiences that students had with textbooks.

Science methods. This was the first course in the second year of the Academic programme and occurred the term before student teaching. The instructor emphasised the value of teaching for conceptual change and criticised the alternatives – 'didactic' teaching and 'activity driven' teaching. This course included microteaching: students teaching short science lessons to groups of elementary children. The teacher candidates also analysed science curricular materials and were taught about planning for science instruction. This course conveyed strong messages about science teaching and the appropriate role of textbooks and teachers' guides in planning and teaching.

Decision-Making Programme

Educational psychology. As in the Academic programme, this was the first course that students took. The content of the course was designed to encourage students make systematic decisions about instruction. The emphasis was on application of knowledge derived from educational psychology (e.g. Piagetian stages, theory of motivation, concept, principle, and skill learning). Students were taught to write behavioural objectives. They were given a format to use for daily and unit planning and they practised writing lesson plans. This course set the stage for the overall programme emphasis on planning and decision-making.

Reading methods/field 1. This was the next course in the programme. It was taught in a local elementary school where the teacher candidates were also observing and teaching in classrooms. The course emphasised what the instructor called the 'big theory of reading' – essentially that reading instruction should emphasise reading for meaning. Students learned about teaching sight words, use of context and the language experience approach. This course gave distinct messages about the nature of basal textbooks. 'Professional' teachers do not follow basals. In light of this, we were especially interested in the fact that the prospective teachers were in classrooms where teachers relied on basal programmes for reading instruction.

Reading methods/field 2. This was another field-based course in the second year of the programme. Course objectives were for students to gain specific knowledge about grouping practices, materials selection, language development, word recognition, recreational and 'content area' reading, and comprehension. The general goal was to be able to make 'effective and appropriate instructional decisions'. Students taught a reading group and one 'special needs' student all term in conjunction with this course, and 65 per cent of their course grade depended on their application of course concepts and strategies in their teaching. In this course, the instructor dealt directly with the issue of basal textbooks, stating that these materials, although often mandatory, are insufficient. The course offered students several approaches and activities to be used in conjunction with basals.

Acknowledgement

The authors gratefully acknowledge Margret Buchmann, Beth Lawrence, and Karen Noordhoff Hagstrom for their valuable comments on drafts of this paper, and for their assistance with data analysis.

Notes

1. Pseudonyms are used for all names of persons, programmes, and schools.
2. The six teacher education students were chosen from candidates nominated by programme coordinators and matched based on survey data collected on all students at Michigan State University.
3. The appendix provides a summary of the content and structure of these courses. We developed a set of questions to help us explore what each programme communicated explicitly about textbooks, curricular decision-making and the teacher's role. Based on our course and student teaching observations, we began with questions logically connected to issues of curriculum and to beginning teachers. Our concurrent review of empirical and conceptual-analytic work about curricular materials and curricular decision-making suggested other topics. These questions, grouped under four headings, served as a framework for scrutinizing what a set of courses in each programme taught:

    (a) *The nature of textbooks and other curricular materials*
    How were textbooks portrayed? What were they said to be good for or not good for? Were students encouraged to evaluate curricular materials and on what bases (e.g. implicit conception of learning, content coverage, quality of explanations, appropriateness to level, ethnic bias, etc.)?

    (b) *Curricular decision-making: the teacher's role, other influences on curriculum*
    What should be taught and how should it be taught? Who should decide? Are teachers supposed to decide what to teach? How to teach it? If so, how should they decide? Are they supposed to 'adapt' what is in the text or curriculum guide, and, if so, what does 'adapt' mean? What else influences the curriculum and how should teachers respond to external pressures or policies (e.g. district curriculum guidelines, testing, state competency objectives, federal legislation, colleagues, principals, parents)?

    (c) *Planning*
    How was planning presented? What is the role of the textbook, teacher's guide, other curriculum materials in teacher planning?

    (d) *Practical experiences*
    What kinds of experiences did students have with curricular materials and curricular decision-making? How were these structured (e.g. textbook critiques)? What kinds of experiences did the teacher candidates have in planning, in either courses or field experiences? Did the prospective teachers have chances to develop curriculum? Did the students have opportunities to 'adapt' materials? How were these practical experiences supervised or evaluated?

4.   Doyle (1985) argues that the tasks teachers assign have important conse-
     quences for what students learn, and since the same content can be repre-
     sented by different learning tasks, any investigation of curriculum requires
     more than a cursory examination of topics covered.

5.   Ball and Noordhoff (1985) provide case studies of what two of our focal student
     teachers (Danielle and Sarah) did with curricular materials during student
     teaching and what they learned from their experiences.

6.   Bundling sticks and chip trading are activities that are used to explore funda-
     mental concept of place value and numeration with elementary children.

7.   People often underestimate the task of implementing curriculum. For exam-
     ple, Harste (1985) claims, "you don't need to study reading in college to
     be able to teach a basal reading lesson" because such materials are "teacher-
     proof."

8.   Vygotsky's (1979) notion of "instructional scaffolding" has interesting
     possibilities for thinking about how to help novices learn the tasks of teach-
     ing. Instructional scaffolding is a process in which a novice's performance is
     supported in a way that enables him or her to participate in the entire task.
     Usually this support is provided through collaboration with another, more
     expert, person, who initially assumes much of the responsibility for getting
     the task done. Gradually the beginner takes over an increasing share of the
     tasks until he/she is able to perform independently.

     Rogoff (1982) asserts that a novice "learns the skills involved in a activity
     through exposure to the tools and procedures others have developed for such
     situations" (p. 160). In learning to teach, therefore, we are suggesting that if
     teachers were oriented to learning *from* curricular materials, a teacher's guide
     might be able to provide a kind of external support which could help the
     beginning teacher learn to think pedagogically about particular content.

     See Griffin and Cole (1984), Vygotsky (1979), and Wood (1980) for further
     discussion of instructional scaffolding in children's learning. Ball and Noordhoff
     (1984) discuss the applications of this concept to teacher education.

9.   Feiman-Nemser and Buchmann (1986) elaborate what we mean by 'pedagogi-
     cal thinking.'

Chapter 17

Supervision Conferences and Student Teachers' Thinking and Behaviour

Jan Broeckmans

Introduction

Student teaching and supervision are often labelled the core of teacher training. Research could assist teacher educators in optimising this part of training by clarifying what and how student teachers learn during the experience. Interesting perspectives for meeting these expectations are offered by teacher thinking research. According to this approach (changes in) overt teaching behaviour rely on (developments in) teachers' cognitions during planning and interactive teaching (Clark and Peterson, 1986). Although some studies have been done on student teachers' 'concerns' (Fuller and Bown, 1975) and 'teacher perspectives' (Tabachnick and Zeichner, 1983), the cognitive mechanisms underlying learning to teach remain a largely unexplored domain of research.

It seems also appropriate for research on student teaching to apply the mediating process paradigm that Doyle (1978) suggested for teacher effectiveness studies, that is, to investigate processes in prospective teachers that mediate between features of a student teaching programme and its effects. Few data are available on these processes (Popkewitz, Tabachnick and Zeichner, 1979). Regarding student teacher supervision, for instance, verbal interactions during supervision conferences have been studied by means of category systems (e.g. Barbour, 1971; Weller, 1971; Zeichner and Liston, 1985). However, student teachers' cognitive processes that result from such conferences and that enable them to acquire or to change teaching behaviour have not been investigated (Finlayson, 1975; MacLeod, 1976). Data about such processes are needed because supervision can influence teaching in different ways that are not equally desirable. For instance, a student teacher may apply suggestions made by his supervisor because he approves of them or because he wants to get a good grade. Presumably, most supervisors prefer the former effect of conferences.

Aims of this study were to describe (a) student teachers' lesson planning and interactive teaching, (b) their reflections during supervision conferences and afterwards, and (c) changes in planning and interactive teaching that result from these reflections. Furthermore, relations were explored between (d) types of reflections and types of changes in teaching, and (e) types of reflections and features of supervision conferences and supervisor behaviour. The concept of 'reflection' is used in a broad sense. By reflections are meant all student teachers' thoughts, feelings and actions during and resulting from supervision conferences.

The study was restricted to changes in teaching over a short period. It was assumed that the processes by which supervision conferences influence teaching are best manifested in short-term developments.

This chapter is limited to the processes resulting from supervision conferences and their influence on teaching. Other parts of the study are reported elsewhere (Broeckmans, 1984, 1986a, 1987).

Collection of Data

Research Sample and Design

Eighteen first year student teachers and eleven supervisors of three Belgian colleges for elementary school teachers participated in the study on a voluntary basis. Before the study, the students had less than ten hours of teaching practice. The lessons studied were 'practice lessons', that is, a form of teaching practice in which students teach one or more weekly lessons in a school that is attached to the training college.

Twelve student teachers taught two lessons. Immediately after the first lesson, a supervision conference took place. The second lesson was taught one week after the first. For six student teachers, the study lasted four weeks. They taught one lesson every week. Supervision conferences took place after the first lesson and after the second or third.

All 48 lessons were in grades 3 or 4. Lesson subjects were reading (n=27), other aspects of language teaching (grammar, creative writing, spelling; n=8), maths (n=11) and social studies (n=2).

Methods

Each student teacher filled up a planning logbook for each lesson. In these logs, students reported discussions about the lesson (e.g. with cooperating teachers or peers), sporadic thoughts about it, and the train of thought while actually planning. The logbooks also contained a written lesson plan, provisional versions thereof, incidental notes, 'cribs', lesson materials chosen and prepared, and references to documents consulted (e.g. textbooks, manuals, curricula). During interviews after the lessons, the students were asked to reconstruct the course of planning by clarifying and completing the logbook.

Lessons and conferences were recorded on videotape. Additionally, the researcher observed the lessons and constructed narrative descriptions. During stimulated recall sessions, the student teachers tried to remember and to report their thoughts while teaching and while participating in the conferences.

Immediately after each lesson and each supervision conference, the student teachers wrote on a sheet of paper the thoughts concerning the lesson and the conference that went through their heads at that moment. During interviews afterwards, these notes were clarified.

In the week between two lessons, the students also filled up a logbook on their further reflections. In this log, the students reported discussions about the past lesson, as well as their thoughts and feelings about it. Written lesson critiques were added to the logs. These further reflections were also clarified and completed during interviews.

According to the Ericsson and Simon (1980) self-reporting model, questions with a restricted focus may lead to incomplete and inaccurate verbal data. Therefore, the only instruction given to the students in the logs, interviews and stimulated recall sessions was to remember and report all their thoughts and actions.

The Ericsson and Simon model also pointed out a problem in the design of the study. It can be assumed that interviews and stimulated recall lead to reflections that influence later teaching. Retrospections that take place before the end of the study threaten external validity. Delaying these interviews until the end of the study, however, jeopardises internal validity. After two or four weeks, retrospections probably are very incomplete and inaccurate. For this dilemma, the following compromise was found. For the student teachers that were followed for two weeks, all retrospections were grouped into one interview. This took place immediately after the second lesson and lasted about four hours. The students who were followed during four weeks were interviewed after each lesson. Each interview concerned the further reflections about last week's lesson, as well as the planning and execution of this week's lesson. Each interview lasted about two hours.

Different kinds of data were available (logs and interviews on planning, videotapes, observations, and stimulated recall data on interactive teaching, etc.). Before starting the analysis, these different data were rearranged into chronological order, so that they could be read as one case history. This rearrangement is described by Broeckmans (1984).

Hereafter data analyses and results are discussed concerning (a) reflections during and after supervision conferences, (b) resulting changes in teaching and (c) relations between types of reflections and types of change in teaching.

Patterns of Reflection Resulting from Supervision Conferences

Analysis of the Data

It was assumed that the effects of a supervision conference depend on all students' reflections, rather than on elementary processes at one moment. It was apparent from the data that reflections were organised around aspects of the lesson that were discussed during conferences. Therefore, it was decided to describe 'patterns of reflection', that is, sequences of all the reflective process about one aspect of a lesson.

First, types of 'elementary reflective processes' were distinguished. These processes are the smallest units of thinking and talking about a lesson or supervision conference. For all student teachers' action, verbal utterances, thoughts during, and resulting from conferences, descriptions were given of (a) the 'object' of reflections (that is, the aspect of teaching concerned), and (b) the 'operation' performed by the students. By comparing descriptions, categories for reflective processes were developed. The scope of this chapter does not permit discussion of this extensive category system.

To identify patterns, reflections were divided into 'content units'. Such units contain all the actions, utterances and thoughts about one aspect of teaching that occur at the same time. For example, a student and a supervisor first discussed the suitability of having pupils working in groups during a part of the lesson and next discussed errors in subject matter. The content units 'working in groups' and 'correctness of subject matter' were distinguished. Next, elementary reflective processes in the content units were coded with the categories developed. For each content unit, overviews were drafted of all the reflections immediately after the lesson, during and immediately after the conference, and later. Patterns of reflection were identified by investigating how the successive processes in each overview built on each other.

Results: Eight Patterns of Reflection

In all, 302 overviews of reflective processes were drafted. These overviews were classified on the following three dimensions.[1]

The first distinction was between 'open' and 'closed' reflections. In open reflections students explicitly intended to learn something for later lessons or for their development as teachers. In closed reflections, the content of conferences was considered information about a completed task. Students mainly rated the value of the past lesson.

Second, some reflections concerned aspects of teaching that were important to students. They identified solutions for problems experienced or evaluated lessons with criteria that they considered important. Other reflections concerned supervisors' criticism. Students thought about supervisors' evaluations or looked for solutions for their criticism.

The third distinction was between 'analytical' and 'global' reflections. Students' evaluations were labelled analytical when they referred explicitly to norms or principles. Analytical solutions for problems or criticism were identified by looking for causes of difficulties. Global evaluations referred implicitly to norms or principles. Global solutions were developed without identifying causes of problems or criticism.

The combinations on these dimensions formed eight typical patterns of reflection.[1] These eight patterns are presented in Table 17.1. There were four open patterns. 'Problem analyses' and 'problem-solving patterns' concerned problems experienced by students. In 'analyses of faults' and 'corrective' patterns students tried to remedy supervisors' criticism. Problem analyses and analyses of faults were analytical, that is, solutions were developed by looking for causes. In problem-solving and corrective patterns, solutions were 'global'. The four other patterns were closed. These patterns were labelled 'analytical self-evaluations', 'global self-evaluations', 'analytical assessments of criticism' and 'global self-appreciations of criticism'.

Table 17.1 also gives the frequencies of dimensions and patterns. Student teachers' reflections were aimed mainly at rating the value of past lessons. Only 41 per cent of the patterns were aimed at learning something for later lessons. Furthermore, most reflections concerned supervisors' criticism. Only 15 per cent of the patterns were about problems experienced by students or were self-evaluations. Moreover, student teachers' thinking was mainly global. Only 23 per cent of the patterns were labelled analytical.

Table 17.1.   Classification and frequencies of patterns of reflection

		Open (n=124)	Closed (n=178)
Emphasis on problems or self-evaluations (n=46)	Analytical (n=20)	Problem analyses (n=11)	Analytical self-evaluations (n=9)
	Global (n=26)	Problem-solving patterns (n=22)	Global self-evaluations (n=4)
Emphasis on supervisors' criticism (n=256)	Analytical (n=50)	Analyses of faults (n=15)	Analytical assessments of criticism (n=35)
	Global (n=206)	Corrective patterns (n=76)	Global appreciations of criticism (n=130)

Two patterns occurred frequently. Global appreciations of criticism accounted for 43 per cent of all the patterns and for 73 per cent of the closed ones. Corrective patterns were 25 per cent of all the patterns and 61 per cent of the open ones. Of the other patterns, only analytical assessments of criticism reached the 10 per cent level. Problem-solving patterns accounted for 7 per cent, analyses of faults for 5 per cent and problem analyses for 4 per cent. Analytical and global self-evaluations occurred only a few times.

Resulting Changes in Lesson Planning and Interactive Teaching

Analysis of the Data

The 48 case histories on lesson planning were repeatedly compared, as were the 48 case histories on interactive teaching. This led to the development of two extensive category systems. Because both systems contain more than 100 categories, they are not discussed here. By coding all the lessons and by comparing the coded lessons, descriptions of planning and interactive teaching were generated. Changes in teaching were identified by comparing the lessons of each student. All the changes in planning and interactive teaching, occurring in one lesson and concerning the same aspect of teaching, were considered as one 'case of change'. In the 30 lessons concerned, 139 cases of change were observed. (For 18 lessons, that is, for the first lesson of each student, changes in teaching were not investigated.) Seventy-one of these cases of change were ascribed to the supervision conferences studied. By comparing these cases, types of change in teaching resulting from supervision conferences were identified.

Results

The 71 cases of change that were ascribed to supervision conferences were divided into four main types. Three types consist of student teachers' attempts to meet supervisors' criticism or to remedy problems discussed during conferences. These three types of change correspond to the orienting, executive, and controlling components that were distinguished in planning and interactive teaching.[2] Executive components of planning are thoughts and actions by which student teachers construct a lesson plan, memorise it or practise teaching behaviour. Executive components of interactive teaching are verbal and non-verbal interactions with pupils in the classroom. Orientations and controls are subordinated to the executive ones. Orientations 'pave the way' for executive components. Student teachers identify principles and directives that must be respected in lesson plans and classroom interaction; they determine planning procedures, read useful information, etc. Controlling components are students' assessments of lesson plans, simulated or real teaching behaviour, pupils' answers, cooperation, behaviour, etc. (Broeckmans, 1984, 1986a, 1987). In the types of change that correspond to these components of teaching, student teachers try to meet criticism or problems experienced: by inserting orienting components into planning and interactive teaching, by inserting controls, and by changing executive components of planning. The fourth main type of change consisted of reductions of the planning process. Hereafter, the four types of change are further described.[3]

Insertion of Orienting Components (n=46)

Student teachers tried to remedy problems or criticism by identifying planning procedures, principles and directives. The solutions that were identified through these orienting components of planning or interactive teaching were next applied in lesson plans and in classroom interactions. Sometimes, orientations also led to controlling components of teaching. Principles identified were first applied in lesson plans and classroom interaction and were used later as explicit criteria for judging these plans and interactions. This type of change was divided into three subtypes:

1.   *Analyses of problems or faults during planning (n=10)*. As with the patterns of reflection that were labelled problem analyses and analyses of faults, students tried to remedy problems or criticism by looking for causes. In four cases, students decided to change planning procedures. One student teacher, for instance, who had experienced problems in defining difficult words in a reading text, attributed his problem to a lack of planning and decided to define difficult words in advance and to look up definitions in a dictionary. In five occurrences, students identified principles and directives that next were applied in the choice and elaboration of teaching learning activities (n=5). A lack of pupil cooperation in a former lesson, for instance, was attributed to the method of lecturing used. Therefore, the student decided to apply the principle of discovery learning. One analysis led to the identification of a norm for teacher speech. The student teacher attributed undesirable pupil reactions to her nervous behaviour and decided to avoid this by lowering her speech pace.

2.   *Judgements of supervisors' advice (n=6)*. Student teachers judged the desirability and practicality of solutions that had been suggested by their supervisors. 'Desirability' did not concern teaching in general, as in some reflections, but applied specifically to the next lesson. 'Practicality' involved the difficulty for student teachers and pupils, as well as a number of practical considerations (e.g. time, space, classroom arrangement). In five cases, students assessed the desirability and practicality of principles like 'learning by doing' and 'discovery learning'. One student teacher judged the practicality of planning more in detail, as was suggested by his supervisor.

3.   *Recalling supervisors' advice (n=30)*. Students identified solutions for problems or criticism by merely remembering supervisors' prescriptions. These were next applied in the lesson plan or in interactive teaching without being reflected upon. In seventeen cases, orientations took place only during planning. In seven occurrences, recalls of supervisors' advice were repeated during the lesson. In six cases of change, orientations occurred only during the lesson. Most prescriptions that were recalled during planning concerned features of teaching-learning activities (n=11) and teacher speech (e.g. pronunciation and speech pace; n=12). Once, a suggested planning procedure was recalled. Prescriptions recalled during interactive teaching primarily applied to teacher speech (n=9). Principles regarding teaching–learning activities were concerned less frequently (n=4).

Insertion of Controlling Components (n=10)

In this type of change, conferences led student teachers only to control whether the lesson plan and the lesson course met supervisors' prescriptions. These prescriptions were merely recalled and used as criteria for judging lesson plans or teaching behaviour. Negative judgements led student teachers to attend to criteria that were not met. In one case, control took place only during planning. In two occurrences, students not only judged the lesson plan, but also the lesson itself. In these three cases, criteria were principles regarding teaching–learning activities. In the remaining cases of change, controlling components were inserted in interactive teaching or took place immediately after the lesson. Criteria concerned lesson pace (n=2), teacher speech (n=2) and teacher-pupil interaction (e.g. 'acting friendly'; n=3).

Changes in Executive Components of Planning (n=4)
Student teachers met supervisors' criticism also by changing executive components of planning. In two cases, students used teaching–learning activities that were suggested by supervisors. These suggestions were merely remembered and applied in the lesson plan. In the two other cases, principles that were communicated during a conference functioned as implicit criteria in the choice of teaching–learning activities. Students met these criteria without consciously representing them.

Reductions of the Planning Process (n=11)
Because of supervisors' positive evaluations, lesson planning became less laborious than before. Two types of reduction of planning were distinguished.
1.   *Gradual reductions (n=6)*. The construction of a lesson plan gradually became less laborious because the identification and elaboration of activities were more 'condensed' or 'abbreviated' than before. Less thinking was required to achieve the same degree of planning detail. Gradual reductions also applied to 'memorising or practising'. In this part of planning, students memorised lesson plans or practised teaching behaviour (Broeckmans, 1986a). Extensive procedures were replaced by less extensive ones. One student, for example, first role-played lessons with an imaginary audience. Later she only read written lesson plans. Gradual reductions could be ascribed to student teachers' acquaintance with a repertoire of teaching strategies and to their growing self-confidence. This implied that supervisors' positive evaluations were not the only prerequisite for these reductions. Other indications of 'success' were also needed.
2.   *Immediate reductions (n=5)*. These reductions applied to the construction of a lesson plan. Students used activities that they had developed for a former lesson of the same type. Development of these activities had required an extensive planning process. After an activity had succeeded and after a supervisor had approved of it, students used it again without any form of reflection.

Two changes in executive components of planning were preceded by corrective patterns. Another case of change resulted from a corrective pattern and an analytical assessment of criticism. In these three cases, student teachers merely applied formerly approved procedures or norms. The fourth case of change was preceded by a global appreciation of criticism. The norm that was implied in supervisors' criticism was used as an implicit criterion to choose teaching–learning activities.

Reductions of planning resulted mainly from global appreciations of criticism. Mere reception of positive evaluations apparently strengthened students' self-confidence or their trust in teaching–learning activities used. Consequently, constructing a lesson plan and memorizing it became less laborious than before. The other reductions resulted from corrective patterns and from analysis of faults, that is, from students' resolutions to apply norms implied in supervisors' positive evaluations.

Table 17.2 also shows that the patterns of reflection had different effects on teaching. Proportionally, open patterns led to changes in teaching almost twice as often as closed patterns. Reflections concerning problems experienced by students influenced teaching more often than patterns concerning supervisors' criticism. Between analytical and global patterns, there were no large differences. Problem-solving

Table 17.2.   Relations between types of change in teaching and patterns of reflection

Types of change		Patterns of Reflection							
		PA (n=11)	PS (n=22)	AF (n=15)	CO (n=76)	AS (n=9)	IS (n=4)	AC (n=35)	IC (n=130)
Insertions of controls (n=10)			1 0	1 —	3 |—0 |		1	3	2
Changes in executive components of planning (n=4)					3 | X —0			1	1
Reductions of planning	Gradual (n=6)			1	2				4 0--X
	Immediate (n=5)				1				4 X
TOTALS n		3	11	6	21	2	1	9	19
(%)		(27)	(50)	(40)	(28)	(22)	(25)	(26)	(15)

PA, Problem analyses; PS, problem-solving; AF, analyses of faults; CO, corrective patterns; AS, analytical self-evaluations; IS, intuitive self-evaluations; AC, analytical assessments of criticism; IC, intuitive appreciations of criticism.

The cell frequencies indicate how much patterns in the column contribute to the cases of change in the row.

X--X = one of these patterns leads to two cases of change of the row(s) concerned.

0--0 = two patterns of the columns concerned lead to 1 of these cases of change.

X--O = idem; the pattern of the column with the X leads to a second case of change X.

patterns and analyses of faults led to changes in teaching most frequently. Global appreciations of criticism influenced later teaching least frequently.

Open patterns were related primarily to insertions of orientations. With problem analyses and analyses of faults most of these orientations consisted of recalling norms. With problem-solving patterns, the three types of orientations were about equally frequent. Corrective patterns led to all types of change. Only two cases of change resulted from self-evaluations. Two analytical self-evaluations contributed to a problem analysis during planning. One global self-evaluation led to the insertion of controls into interactive teaching. The most frequent effects of analytical assessments were orientations by recalling norms and insertions of controls. Global appreciations of criticism led most frequently to orientations by recalling norms and reductions of planning.

Discussion

Because this is an exploratory study results cannot be generalised. Some findings, however, are worthy of mention. Student teachers' reflections, resulting from supervision conferences, were aimed more at rating the value of past lessons than at learning something for later. Furthermore, most reflections concerned supervisors' criticism.

Self-evaluations by student teachers and reflections about problems experienced occurred infrequently. Most solutions for difficulties were identified without looking for causes. Most evaluations referred to criteria only implicitly.

Most cases of change resulting from supervision conferences were attempts to remedy shortcomings in former lessons. Mere applications of supervisors' advice (that is, orientations by recalling norms, controls and changes in executive components of planning) occurred more often than changes in which students had a more active role (that is, analyses of problems or faults and judgements of supervisors' advice). As far as supervisors' positive evaluations influenced teaching, they led to reductions of lesson planning. Most changes occurred during planning. Insertions of orientations and controls in interactive teaching were less frequent. Moreover, all the changes in overt teaching behaviour in the classroom could be ascribed to changes in planning and to orientations and controls in interactive teaching. Finally, changes in planning concerned teaching–learning activities, planning procedures and teacher speech. Changes in interactive teaching applied mainly to teacher speech and to teacher–pupil interaction.

As to relations between patterns of reflection and changes in teaching, no firm conclusions can be drawn. Most types of change resulted from various patterns of reflection and most patterns led to various types of change. Only some trends can be mentioned. Patterns of reflection influenced teaching most frequently when they were aimed at learning something for later lessons. These 'open' reflections led most frequently to insertion of orienting components in teaching. 'Active' types of change, that is, orientations consisting of analyses or judgements, resulted mainly from reflections in which 'global' solutions for problems or criticism were identified, that is, from problem-solving and corrective patterns. Most reductions of planning resulted from students' mere reception of supervisors' positive evaluations.

In spite of the lack of firm conclusions, the present results have some importance for teacher education. According to Clark and Peterson (1986), there is no clean-cut border between post-interactive teaching behaviour (including 'reflections') and planning. Relations between patterns of reflection and changes in teaching can be considered different sequences of the processes resulting from a supervision conference. Sometimes processes during planning and interactive teaching were continuations or 'applied' reiterations of reflections. In other cases, reflections and processes in later teaching were very different. These various sequences can be viewed as different ways in which student teachers learn from conferences. Striking differences were: (a) the degree to which each lesson was considered a separate task or a part of the larger task of learning to teach; (b) the relation of changes in teaching to problems experienced or to criticism; (c) the more analytic or the rather 'intuitive' way in which changes came about. These ways of learning from supervision conferences can be valued differently for intrinsic reasons. Provided teacher educators clarify which ways of learning they prefer, the present results can offer a basis for prescriptions.

The theoretical and practical meaning of this study is limited for at least four reasons. First, results only apply to eighteen first-year students, three training colleges, one type of Belgian teacher education, and one form of teaching practice. Second, the use of verbal reports probably influenced the reflections and changes in teaching that were distinguished. It can be assumed that unobtrusive processes were not reported. Third, only short-term developments were covered. Their ultimate meaning can only be known by relating them to changes over a longer period. Fourth, what remains to be investigated is which situational factors, characteristics of student teachers and features of supervision conferences are related to the patterns of reflection and the types of change in teaching. This investigation is needed for theory building, as well as for the practice of teacher education. The first three limitations are unavoidable in a study of this scope. The fourth, however, can be remedied by further analyses of the present date.

Notes

1.   Two additional dimensions concerned the 'degree of autonomy' in student teachers' thinking, and the 'criteria' used. Broeckmans (1986b) gives a description of the patterns of reflection on these two dimensions.
2.   The distinction of components with orienting, executive and controlling functions in planning and interactive teaching is one of the basic features of the action-oriented interpretation of teaching that was the theoretical framework of this study. (For a discussion of this interpretation see Broeckmans, 1984, 1986a, 1987.)
3.   The types of change described here are combinations of changes in lesson planning and in interactive teaching. They may differ from the short-term developments in planning described by Broeckmans (1986a).

Chapter 18

Examining Complexity of Thought in Secondary Student Teachers

Greta Morine Dershimer
and Bernard Oliver

Background

The cognitive abilities that appear to characterise effective, experienced teachers (Calderhead, 1981a; Corno, 1981; Doyle, 1977; Leinhardt and Greeno, 1986; Morine and Vallance, 1975) might be summarised as 'complexity of thought'. These teachers focus on salient information and organise that information into categories rather than dealing with many discrete details. This organised structure of information enables them to be attentive to a variety of aspects of the lesson. Schroder, Karlins and Phares (1973) theorised that individuals with well-developed information processing skills would exhibit just such a combination of focus (which they called *depth* of information) and distribution of attention (which they called *breadth* of information).

Procedures for investigating complexity of thought related to interactive teaching were developed for use in a prior study of experienced secondary school teachers, conducted at the University of Texas at Austin Research and Development Center for Teacher Education (Morine-Dershimer, 1983), and explored in more detail in a later paper (Morine-Dershimer, 1984). This paper reports on the application and extension of these procedures in a two-year study of secondary student teachers. Methodological improvements attempted in this study included: examining interactive thinking in closer relation to interactive behaviour; examining complexity of thought about interactive teaching in relation to complexity of thought about teacher planning; and identifying quantitative measures of complexity of thought. Questions addressed in this study were: (1) Do student teachers vary in the complexity of their thinking about teaching? (2) Is student teachers' complexity of thought about interactive teaching related to their complexity of thought about teacher planning? and (3) Do student teachers who differ in subject matter major also exhibit differences in complexity of thought, or in patterns of thinking about interactive behaviour?

Procedures

Subjects

Subjects were 18 student teachers in the undergraduate secondary education programme at Syracuse University; six completed student teaching in autumn 1984 and
12 in autumn 1985. Nine were majoring in science/maths education and nine in
English/social studies education. Five were male (three in the sciences) and thirteen
were female (six in the sciences). All subjects had been students in a generic methods
course on Models of Teaching (Joyce and Weil, 1972), taught by Morine Dershimer
just before their entry into student teaching. All undergraduate majors in these four
subject areas who took the methods course were invited to participate in the study.

Data Collection

During the methods course, students engaged in a concept mapping exercise in which
they were asked to graphically display their ideas about teacher planning. A sample
concept map is presented in Figure 18.1. All subjects were asked to develop these concept maps at the end of the methods course, following several experiences in planning
and peer teaching lessons. Subjects in autumn 1985 prepared these concept maps at
both the beginning and the end of the 7-week course. All subjects were assigned to
student teaching in middle schools or high schools in nearby urban or suburban
public school districts. Towards the end of the 7-week student teaching experience,
each subject was videotaped teaching one lesson to one of the classes to which he or
she was assigned. The class, the instructional procedure and the lesson topic were all
determined by the student teacher, with the agreement of the cooperating teacher.

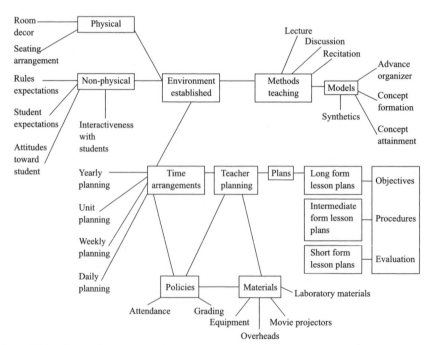

Figure 18.1.   A sample concept map.

Shortly after the lesson ended, the videotape was played back to the student teacher, and a stimulated recall interview was conducted. Subjects were instructed to stop the videotape at any point where they were aware of making a decision or noticing something particular during the lesson. Each time the videotape was stopped, the interviewer (who had also videotaped the lesson) asked: 'What were you thinking at that point in the lesson?'

All interviews were recorded on audiotape, including the audio portion of the full playback of the videotape, so that the lesson event triggering each student teacher comment was recorded on the audiotape. Transcripts of the audiotapes were made for purposes of coding student teacher comments.

Data Analysis

The analysis of transcripts from the stimulated recall interviews was based on a descriptive category system developed for a prior study (Morine Dershimer, 1983). Comments of student teachers were categorised as referring to Goals, Evaluation, Pupil Characteristics, Pupil Behaviour, Explanation of Strategy, or Principles of Teaching. Each of these major categories was subdivided to indicate whether comments were about Instruction or Management.

In commenting about a single lesson event, a subject might refer to several different categories, or aspects of the lesson. The sequencing of thoughts in these instances was considered useful evidence about complexity of thinking. To examine these sequences, or 'chains' of thought, a Flanders-type matrix was used (Morine Dershimer, 1983, 1984).

A matrix was prepared for each student, recording all the sequences of thought exhibited in reporting on interactive thinking during the stimulated recall interview. Frequency counts in each cell were transformed into proportional frequencies for purposes of comparing patterns of sequencing across individuals and groups. These matrices provided the bases for further analyses, which included the quantification of complexity of thought and the graphic representation of patterns of thought sequences.

In an extension and improvement of procedures used in prior studies (Morine Dershimer, 1979, 1983), interactive behaviour was examined in close relation to interactive thinking. A qualitative analysis was made of interactive events preceding each point in the lesson that was discussed in the interactive interview. (This analysis was carried out only for the 12 students who were interviewed in autumn 1985.) Based on the qualitative analysis, descriptive categories were developed to identify the types of events that triggered student teachers' comments about their interactive thinking.

Three major categories or sets of interactive events were identified, focused on actions of the teacher, actions of students, or interaction between the teacher and a student. Events focused on the teacher included: teacher *explanations* of concepts and content to students; teacher *directions/procedures;* and *other* teacher actions (mainly non-verbal). Events focused on interaction included; *teacher questions* to individual students or to the class; and *student question/responses* to the teacher. The third category involved classroom events focused on *student behaviour.*

Analysis of concept maps considered the number of major categories generated, the number of levels of categories identified (e.g. major categories, subcategories and distinctions within subcategories were considered to be three different levels within a concept hierarchy) and the total number of terms generated (procedure based on a prior study of undergraduate education majors at Syracuse) (Beyerbach, 1985). This initial analysis was expanded to provide a measure of complexity of thought as exhibited in the concept mapping exercise.

For all three of the types of data considered (comments about interactive thinking, events triggering those comments and concept maps of teacher planning), responses of science/maths majors were compared to those of English/social studies majors. In addition, possible relationships between complexity of thought as exhibited on the two different tasks (reporting on interactive thinking and constructing a concept map of teacher planning) were examined.

Quantifying Complexity

An important methodological issue in this study was the identification of quantifiable measures of the complexity of thought exhibited in the stimulated recall interviews and the concept maps. The ground rules established in the search for appropriate measures were that: a single best measure should be identified for each task; the measure should distribute responses to the task along a continuum from lower to higher complexity; the measure should reflect the theoretical view that complexity of thought involves a combination of breadth and depth (Schroder, Karlins and Phares, 1973); the measure should reflect prior research on teacher thinking, indicating that less effective teachers attend to more details than more effective teachers (Morine and Vallance, 1975); and the measure should define complexity of thought as distinct from fluency in production of ideas (a factor in measures of creativity). The measure identified for each task satisfied all these requirements.

Degree of cell development. Complexity of thought exhibited in stimulated recall interviews was measured by the degree of 'development' of cells in the matrix that was used to tabulate the sequences of comments made in reporting on interactive decisions. When the proportion of instances recorded in a given cell exceeded 0.085 (two standard deviations above the mean for all cells for all subjects), that cell was said to denote a 'major sequence' of thought exhibited by the particular subject. The formula for degree of cell development was:

$$\text{Degree of cell development} = \frac{\text{No. of cells denoting a major sequence}}{\text{No. of cells containing recorded instances}}$$

A subject whose matrix showed greater cell development in effect exhibited both depth (tendency to frequently associate two particular aspects of the lesson in his/her thinking) and breadth (tendency to exhibit several such association).

The degree of cell development was negatively correlated ($r = 0.87$, $df = 16$, $p < 0.001$) with the proportion of cells used. A matrix with recorded instances in a large number of cells indicated that a student teacher noted a greater variety of aspects of the lesson, or attended to more 'details' of the lesson. Thus, a measure of attention to detail was negatively correlated with the measure of complexity of thought. Neither the measure of complexity nor the measure of attention to detail was significantly related to what might be termed measures of 'fluency' (the number of lesson events in which decisions were reportedly made and the number of 'chains' of thought that occurred in the transcript of the interview).

Degree of category development. Complexity of thought exhibited in the concept maps was measured by the degree of 'development' of new categories. At each level in the category hierarchy depicted on a concept map, any number of elements could be identified in describing aspects of a given category considered important in teacher planning. Any one of these elements could then become a new, subordinate category, if it in turn was 'developed' by noting the elements or subunits that it encompassed (e.g. in Figure 18.1, 'models' is an element in 'Methods of Teaching' that becomes a new, subordinate category with four elements identified). At each level in the concept hierarchy a proportion was calculated based on the elements developed into categories at the next lower level in the hierarchy. The mean of these proportions over all levels of the hierarchy was termed the degree of category development, and was used as the measure of complexity of thought exhibited in constructing the concept map. Development of a single element into a new category was considered evidence of depth of understanding of that particular element of teacher planning. Development of a variety of elements into new categories was considered evidence of breadth of understanding about several aspects of teacher planning.

The degree of category development was negatively related (Spearman Rank Order Correlation, $t = 3.758$, df $= 16$, $p < 0.01$) to the degree of detail (mean number of elements generated per category). Students who generated larger numbers of elements were attending to a greater number of details related to each category. Thus, the measure of complexity of thought for the concept map task was also negatively associated with a measure of attention to detail. Neither degree of category development nor degree of detail was significantly related to what could be considered a measure of fluency on this task, the number of total items included on the concept map.

A further check on fluency versus complexity was conducted. The twelve students participating in this study in autumn 1985 had constructed concept maps at both the beginning and the end of the course on Models of Teaching. The pre–post comparison of measures on these maps showed a significant increase in the number of elements included ($t = 2.09$, df $= 11$, $p < 0.05$). The pre-test mean was 38.7 and the post-test mean was 49.3. There was no significant change in the number of major categories, the number of hierarchical levels or the degree of category development, suggesting that complexity of thought (as measured by response to the concept mapping task) remained stable while fluency of ideas associated with teacher planning increased.

Categorising responses. Responses of students to the two tasks were quantified using the measures of degree of cell development (stimulated recall interviews) and degree of category development (concept maps). For each measure a mean and standard deviation were calculated, and students who scored more than 0.5 standard deviations below the mean were categorised as exhibiting less complexity of thought on that particular measure or task. For degree of cell development ($n = 18$, $X = 0.244$, $SD = 0.201$), seven students were categorised as exhibiting less complexity of thought. For degree of category development ($n = 18$, $X = 0.252$, $SD = 0.149$), eight students were categorised as exhibiting less complexity of thought.

Graphic Representation

In addition to identifying quantitative measures of complexity of thinking, procedures were developed to produce graphic representations of patterns of responses. For the stimulated recall interview the graphic representation showed the most prominent (frequently used) sequences of movement from commenting on one category or aspect of the lesson to commenting on another category or aspect. The graphic displays were designed to reflect and complement the quantitative measures, so that patterns of response identified as less complex were visually less complex in the graphic representation, as well as scoring lower on the quantitative measure.

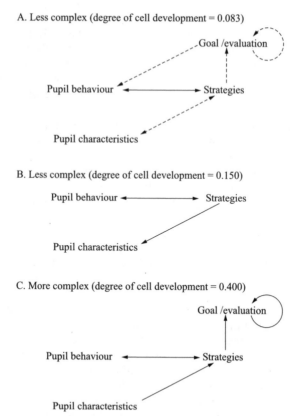

Figure 18.2.   Graphic representation of more and less complex.

Thinking in Reporting Interactive Decisions

Three graphic representations of sequenced thinking are presented in Figure 18.2. Major sequences are denoted by continuous lines and minor sequences by dotted lines. The first illustration displays a pattern of response that is less complex because attention is diffused over many minor categorical sequences ('breadth' but very little 'depth'). The second displays a pattern of response that is less complex because it is highly focused on a few major categorical sequences ('depth' but very little 'breadth'). The third displays a pattern of response categorised as more complex. It shows strong focus (depth), as indicated by the existence of major sequences, and it also shows some distribution of attention over several category sequences (breadth), as indicated by the number and variety of these major sequences.

Measures of Complexity

As reported earlier, two quantitative measures were developed for the purpose of categorising students as exhibiting more or less complexity of thought (degree of cell development and degree of category development). A direct statistical test showed no significant correlation between these two measures ($r = 0.418$, $df = 16$, $p < 0.10$).

Sequences of thought (degree of cell development)	Concept mapping (degree of category development)		
	Less complex		More complex
Less complex	E-2B-F E-4B-M SS-IA-F	Sc-IA-F M-IB-F M-3B-F	SS-IB-F
More complex	E-3B-F SS-2B-M		E-1A-F Sc-2A-M E-2A-F Sc-3A-M E-1B-F M-IB-M Sc-2B-F Sc-3B-F M-2B-F

Figure 18.3.   Categorical grouping of students by two measures of complexity of thought. E, English; SS, social studies; Sc, science; M, maths; A, autumn 1984; B, autumn 1985; F, female; M, male.

When the two measures were used, as intended, for the purpose of categorising students by level of complexity of thought, a second comparison was made, based on categorical grouping of students. Figure 18.3 presents the information on categorical grouping, noting the subject matter major, the year of participation in the study and the sex of each student. A chi-square test of this table was significant ($X = 7.92$, df = 1, $p < 0.005$, contingency coefficient = 0.553). Students tended to be categorised similarly on the two measures.

Table 18.1 presents information on the interactive events that prompted student teachers' comments during stimulated recall interviews, organised to highlight differences between students exhibiting more and less complexity of thought on this task. Student teachers categorised as less complex tended to stop the videotape more frequently, and were heavily focused on the major category of teacher action and on the subcategory of teacher explanations to students about lesson content. Student teachers categorised as more complex distributed their attention fairly equally across three types of lesson events: teacher explanations; teacher directions; and teacher questions.

Table 18.1.   Lesson events prompting thinking: comparison by complexity of thought (mean percentages)

Group	Mean no. video stops	Focus on teacher action			Focus on interaction		
		Explanation	Direction/ procedure	Other	Teacher question	Student question/ response	Focus on student behaviour
More complex (n = 7)	14.5	28.0	20.6	5.7	27.0	12.1	6.9
Less complex (n = 5)	22.6	44.6	14.6	8.6	16.0	9.6	7.2

The first two categories involved a focus on teacher actions, and the third involved a focus on teacher–student interaction.

Subject Matter Majors

Figure 18.3 is constructed to permit a visual comparison of complexity of thought by subject matter major. It is immediately obvious that more science/maths majors than English/social studies majors are categorised as exhibiting more complexity of thought on both measures. Because of the small number of subjects involved, no statistical test of significance was made of this distribution by subject matter major.

There were no significant differences by subject matter major on any of the several measures of performance for either of the two tasks. However, some interesting descriptive differences were noted. Science/maths students tended to move from comments on Goals/Evaluation to comments on Strategies. English/social studies majors reversed this pattern, moving more frequently from comments on Strategies to comments on Goals/Evaluation. In addition, science/maths majors exhibited a major sequence of thought moving from Pupil Characteristics to Strategies, while this was just barely strong enough to be rated a minor sequence for English/social studies majors. These differences in pattern suggest that science/maths majors were more apt to move from reason (Pupil Characteristics or Goal/Evaluation) to action (Strategy) in discussing their interactive decisions, while English/social studies majors were more apt to report the action before giving the reason for the action.

Table 18.2 shows some group differences in the types of lesson events prompting comments about interactive decisions. English/social studies majors were most apt to stop the videotape to make comments related to their explanations to students about lesson content. Compared to English/social studies majors, science/maths majors were more apt to stop and make comments related to their questioning of students. Science/maths majors focused on interactive events much more frequently than English/social studies majors did. The English/social studies majors were heavily focused on teacher actions.

Another interesting difference between students grouped according to subject matter major was exhibited in response to the concept-mapping task. In constructing

Table 18.2.   Lesson events prompting thinking: comparison by subject matter major (mean percentages)

Group	Mean no. video stops	Focus on teacher action			Focus on interaction		
		Explanation	Direction/ procedure	Other	Teacher question	Student question/ response	Focus on student behaviour
Sciences/ maths (n = 6)	19.8	27.0	14.3	9.5	26.3	16.7	7.2
English/ social studies (n = 6)	15.8	42.8	22.1	4.3	18.5	5.5	6.8

these maps, it was possible for students to denote relationships between coordinate categories (i.e. those on the same level on the concept hierarchy) by drawing connecting lines. For example, if first-level categories included both Objectives and Evaluation, a student might draw a line from Evaluation to Objectives, indicating the cyclical nature of teacher planning. The first-level categories in Figure 18.1 are interconnected in this way. This aspect of concept mapping was not discussed when directions were given for the task, but six of the eighteen students did display such interconnections on their concept maps. Five of the six science majors drew these interconnections, as compared to one of the six English majors, and none of the maths majors or social studies majors.

Discussion

Student teachers in this study showed variation in the complexity of their thinking about both interactive teaching and teacher planning. Students categorised as exhibiting more complexity in their reports of interactive thinking tended also to be categorised as exhibiting more complexity in their conceptions of teacher planning. Similarly, students categorised as exhibiting less complexity in their reports of interactive thinking tended to be categorised as less complex in their conceptions of teacher planning.

Students majoring in different subject areas did not differ significantly in complexity of thought on any quantified measure of thinking about either interactive teaching or teacher planning. However, descriptive analyses showed some interesting tendencies. More science/maths majors than English/social studies majors were categorised as complex in their thinking about both interactive teaching and teacher planning. Science/maths majors focused on interactive events (particularly teacher questioning) during stimulated recall interviews more frequently than English/social studies majors. The latter group focused more on teacher actions, particularly teacher explanations of lesson content. Science/maths majors tended to move from comments about purpose to comments about action in discussions of their interactive decisions, while English/social studies majors tended to reverse that sequence. Finally, science majors were much more likely than any of the other students to construct concept maps that indicated relationships among conjunctive categories (i.e. categories at the same level in the concept hierarchy).

These differences are interesting in light of Leinhardt and Greeno's (1986) references to the importance of subject matter knowledge as a basis for skill in teaching. Leinhardt and Greeno emphasise the importance of subject matter *content* knowledge, but these findings suggest that the *thinking processes* typically associated with the subject matter may influence the processes used to think about teaching. The science/maths majors in this study displayed patterns of thought generally associated with logical reasoning more frequently than the English/social studies majors' reason. For example, they phrased their comments about interactive decisions as if the goals or conditions (pupil characteristics) determined the strategies or procedures to be followed. In addition, they demonstrated greater awareness of the logical relationships in a concept hierarchy by their tendency to identify interconnections among conjunctive categories. The evidence here suggests a possible relationship between patterns of thought about subject matter content and patterns of thought about teaching. This question deserves further study with a larger sample of subjects.

The general patterns of response in this study support findings from prior studies. These student teachers discussed pupils and instructional strategies most frequently in reporting on their interactive thinking. In this, they were similar to experienced teachers (Clark and Peterson, 1986) and other prospective teachers (Norton, 1985). What this study has demonstrated in addition is that these two categories are tightly intertwined in the thinking of these student teachers. Observations of pupil behaviour lead regularly to explanations of strategies applied, and explanations of strategies used are followed by references to associated pupil behaviour. Thus, for these prospective teachers pupil behaviour appears to be regarded as both an antecedent and a consequent of interactive decisions. Unlike the experienced teachers in prior studies (Clark and Peterson, 1986), these student teachers also referred to pupil characteristics and goals/evaluation as antecedents of their interactive decisions. Comments about these aspects of interactive teaching also follow as well as precede comments about instructional strategies.

The methodological improvements attempted in this study produced some interesting findings. This was particularly true of the effort to identify the lesson events that prompted these student teachers to report on interactive decisions and observations. These events were mainly instructional activities, with teacher explanations and teacher questions precipitating more than half of the stimulated recall comments. Yet, in reporting on their thinking associated with these events, the student teachers discussed managerial aspects of the lesson as often as instructional aspects. This suggests that even when teacher behaviour seems on the surface to be directed toward instruction, teacher thinking may be distracted by other issues. Like Leinhardt and Greeno's (1986) novices, these student teachers lacked the routines and lesson structures that would enable them to concentrate most productively on the immediate activity.

The data on lesson events also supplemented the information on complexity of thought in an interesting way. Students who displayed more complexity in patterns of sequenced thinking also distributed their attention over a wider variety of lesson events. Thus, their tendency to consider several aspects of the lesson in discussing interactive decisions was complemented by their tendency to make these decisions in relation to several types of classroom events.

Perhaps the most interesting finding of this study was the fact that students categorised as exhibiting more complexity of thought in stimulated recall interviews also exhibited more complexity in their concept maps of teacher planning. This suggests that complexity of thought about teaching is a characteristic that maintains some consistency across different situations.

It remains to be seen whether complexity of thought as measured in this study is associated with effectiveness of teaching. Prior studies of the thinking of more effective teachers would lead us to expect that this might be the case, but the observation of a single lesson for each student teacher in this study provided too limited a data base for judgements of the effectiveness of these prospective teachers. The next test of the measures of complexity of thought developed in this study should be to determine whether they are related to teacher effectiveness.

Author Reflection 2004

There are several different measures that one might use to determine how well a study 'holds up' 15 to 20 years after its results were originally reported. We might ask: Are the issues addressed still of interest to the field? Did any later studies build on the results or methodology of this work? Did the study methodology or results suggest any useful or effective practices in teacher education? I tend to think that the second question is the most important, particularly for an exploratory study such as this was. An important issue that even today needs increased emphasis in research on teacher thinking was suggested in the final sentence of this 1989 paper: the need to explore more fully how aspects of teacher thinking might be related to teacher effectiveness. As we were completing this study, my co-author, Bernie Oliver, persuaded me that any follow-up study should examine pupil responses in relation to teacher actions and thinking, for pupil responses to a lesson could be seen as an 'immediate' measure of pupil learning and teacher effectiveness. That prodding prompted a series of studies conducted in cooperation with colleagues and graduate students at Syracuse University and the University of Virginia. We collected pupil responses to interactive lessons ('key idea statements' and 'what was heard being said') together with observational or stimulated recall data from prospective and experienced teachers who taught the lessons. These pupils' written responses were closely associated with observable indicators of pupil engagement in the lessons. We also found interesting relationships between pupil responses and both instructional strategy and teacher experience (Morine-Dershimer, 1991, Learning to think like a teacher, *Teaching and Teacher Education,* 7(2), 159–168). Perhaps more importantly, we also found that collecting and analysing pupil response data was a simple and effective way to move prospective teachers toward greater awareness of pupil thinking, learning and engagement in lessons. Therefore, in a round-about way, this study also led to a useful teacher education practice. Given these productive follow-up activities, I consider that this early exploratory study could be judged to 'hold up' rather well.

Chapter 19

Knowing, Thinking and Doing in Learning to Teach

A research framework
and some initial results

Sharon Feiman-Nemser
and Margret Buchmann

Without systematic descriptions of what is taught and learned in formal preparation and field experiences, we cannot understand what professional education contributes to teachers' learning or the ways that teachers' learning can best be fostered. That means we need to understand (1) what teacher educators teach; (2) how opportunities for learning in the preservice curriculum are structured; (3) what prospective teachers make of these opportunities to learn over time; (4) what happens when student teachers take their learning from the university setting into the classroom; and (5) how these different experiences do or do not measure up as a preparation for teaching. These questions shape the 'Knowledge Use in Learning to Teach' study that looks at the ways personal biography interacts with the preservice curriculum to influence opportunities to learn and learning outcomes during teacher preparation. We began the study with grounded assumptions about the preservice phase of learning to teach (Feiman-Nemser, 1983). Teacher preparation is a brief period of formal study preceded by a long period of informal learning through teacher watching and classroom participation as a pupil and succeeded by another period of informal on-the-job learning. Effective teacher preparation needs to pay attention to the prior beliefs of candidates and prepare them to learn from their teaching in ways that go beyond the typical trial-and-error approach and reliance on personal preference. The possibility that teacher education can make a difference implies that what candidates bring to their studies by

Preparation of the chapter was supported by the Institute for Research on Teaching, College of Education, Michigan State University, funded primarily by the Office of Educational Research and Improvement, United States Department of Education (Contract No. 400-81-0014).

way of personal beliefs and dispositions may not be adequate and can be altered. It also suggests that teacher educators have worthwhile knowledge and skills to impart.

One goal of the study is to *describe* and *analyse* what prospective teachers learn in relation to what they are taught, both at the university and in the field. A second goal is to *appraise* the content and import of the lessons learned and consider if and how they add up as preparation for teaching.

To accomplish these goals, we have developed a framework that allows us to relate empirical realities of teacher preparation and learning to teach with a view of worthwhile ends and defensible means in teacher education. The framework integrates empirical description and analysis with questions of value. In this chapter we set out the framework, briefly describe our study and then show what the framework allows us to see by presenting illustrative findings from our research.

Framework of the Study

The framework rests on a conception of the central tasks of teaching based on the distinctive work of teachers. This starting point leads us to posit a major goal for preservice preparation – helping prospective teachers make a transition to 'pedagogical thinking'. The sorts of changes involved in this transition go beyond the acquisition of subject matter knowledge and technical skills. We also describe major sources of influence on teacher learning during formal preparation and how they help or hinder that transition. These sources of influence include the personal capacities, temperaments and entering beliefs of teacher candidates and their opportunities to learn in professional courses and field experiences, especially student teaching.

Central Tasks of Teaching and Teacher Preparation

What distinguishes teaching from other helping professions is a concern with helping people learn worthwhile things in the social context of classrooms. Whatever else teachers do, they are supposed to impart knowledge and see that pupils learn (Wilson, 1975; Peters, 1977; Buchmann, 1984). To promote learning, teachers must know things worth teaching and find ways to help students acquire skills and understandings.

Since teachers cannot observe learning directly, they must learn to detect signs of understanding and confusion, feigned interest and genuine absorption (Dewey, 1964). Because teachers work with groups of students, they must also consider the learning needs of many individuals as they orchestrate the social and intellectual sides of classroom life. Good teachers at their best moments manage both sides together whereas novices usually cannot give them equal attention at the same time. By concentrating on the interactive side of classroom teaching, however, student teachers may learn to manage pupils and classrooms without learning to teach (Dewey, 1964).

Pedagogical thinking and acting. Although the lengthy personal experience of schooling provides teacher candidates with a repertoire of beliefs and behaviour to draw from, it does not prepare them for the central tasks of teaching. Looking at teaching from the perspective of a pupil is not the same as viewing it from the perspective of a teacher. Prospective teachers must learn to look beneath the familiar, interactive world of schooling and focus on student thinking and learning.

There is a big difference between going through the motions of teaching – checking seatwork, talking at the board, assigning homework – and connecting these activities to what pupils should learn over time and checking on what they have actually understood. Helping prospective teachers recognise that difference and laying the groundwork for the orientations and skills of pedagogical thinking are central tasks of teacher preparation.

Teaching in a multicultural society. Puzzling about what is going on inside the heads of young people is difficult enough when teachers and students share a culture; it becomes even more complicated when they do not. Yet, teachers must assume some responsibility for equal access to knowledge. This requires that they examine their own beliefs about the capacities and needs of different pupils and pay attention to the effects of various teaching strategies on them.

Prospective teachers are not likely to approach their teacher education with these orientations. Consider the qualities they think are important for teaching and their expectation about what they will learn from their professional studies. Elementary education majors typically cite warmth, patience and a love of children as personal qualities that will make them effective teachers. They expect to teach youngsters like themselves in schools that are like the ones they attended. Often they think that common sense and memories from their own schooling will supply the subject matter necessary to teach young children. They mostly hope to learn instructional techniques and methods of classroom control through formal preparation.

Teacher educators cannot ignore the expectations and personal qualities of candidates but must relate them to a view of teaching and learning to teach in which student understanding is central. They must help prospective teachers connect their reasons for teaching to the central tasks of teaching and help them see that their decisions about content and pedagogy have social consequences.

Sources of Influence on Teacher Learning During Teacher Preparation

Most models of learning to teach emphasise the role of a single source of influence on teacher learning. For example, theories of teacher development focus on individual teachers' capacities and concerns that presumably unfold in a succession of stages through experience over time (e.g. Fuller, 1969). Theories of teacher socialisation emphasise the impact of the school setting where teachers are influenced by colleagues, pupils and the work itself (e.g. Waller, 1932). Theories of teacher training highlight a process of practice and feedback meant to equip teacher with a repertoire of skills and strategies (e.g. Joyce and Showers, 1980).

These models have no clear connection to the central tasks of teaching and teacher preparation. The developmental and socialisation accounts do not accord much of a role to teacher educators, focusing, instead, on the teacher as a person and the workplace as a setting. The training model presupposes a limited idea of teacher performance and treats learning to teach as an additive process that largely bypasses person and setting. None of the models illuminates the role of prior beliefs or 'preconceptions' in teacher learning. Nor do they take into account the 'ecology' of teacher education – the influence of programme features, settings and people as they interact over time (Hersh, Hull and Leighton, 1982).

In the 'Knowledge Use in Learning to Teach' study, we examine the *thinking* of future teachers in relation to the *content* of the preservice curriculum and the *context* of the schools in which they work as student teachers. Because opportunities to learn and learning outcomes result from the interactions of persons, programmes and settings, we focus our work on describing and analysing the patterns of interaction and influence over time. We briefly describe each source of influence in what follows.

Persons. Prospective teachers perceive and interpret the preservice curriculum in terms of their preconceptions about teaching and learning to teach. Although many aspects of the 'apprenticeship of observation' (Lortie, 1975) may be common, teacher candidates also have personal dispositions, orientations and experiences relevant to teaching. Qualities such as social and intellectual skills and expectations about life and work affect the way they approach their preparation and influence what they learn from it.

Programmes. Typically, teacher education programmes rely on the arts and science faculty to provide teachers with general education and subject matter knowledge. In teacher education courses, future teachers are exposed to knowledge presumed to be relevant to teaching. Foundations courses generally draw their content from the disciplines undergirding education (e.g. psychology, sociology, philosophy) and, more recently, from research on classrooms and teaching (Smith, 1980). Methods courses focus on approaches to teaching different school subjects. Some courses have associated field experiences during which teacher education students 'apply' the knowledge they are learning to teaching situations. What teacher candidates learn in their education courses, however, depends not only on the knowledge they encounter but also on the way those encounters are structured.

The 'field'. As a model of classroom life and an arena of practice, the 'field' influences the boundaries and directions of what can be learned. Cooperating teachers set the affective and intellectual tone in classrooms and demonstrate ways of working with pupils. They can also influence what student teachers learn by the way they conceive and carry out their roles as teacher educators (e.g. by the responsibilities they assign and the feedback they offer). The ethos of the school and the norms that govern faculty interactions are other potential sources of influence on teacher learning. Teachers often regard student teaching as the most valuable part of their formal preparation.

By conceptualising central tasks of teaching and teacher preparation and by identifying sources of influence on teachers' learning, our framework gives us a way to study the preservice phase of learning to teach. It focuses attention on the extent to which future teachers become oriented to the distinctive work of teaching during teacher preparation and begin to develop the understandings and practical skills that their work requires.

The Knowledge Use in Learning to Teach Study

Between 1982 and 1984, we followed six elementary education students ('focal students') through two years of undergraduate teacher education. The students were enrolled in two contrasting programmes. The Academic Programme emphasised theoretical and subject matter knowledge in teaching. Many of the courses stressed teaching for understanding and conceptual change. Students had limited field experiences before student teaching. The Decision-making Programme emphasised generic methods of teaching and research-based decision-making. Instructors stressed procedures for planning. Much of the programme took place in an elementary school where students spent time in classroom aiding, observing and teaching lessons.

Each term we interviewed the focal students about what they were learning in their courses and field experiences and how they thought that would help them in teaching and learning to teach. Our interviews probed specific features of the courses in each programme and the teacher candidates' thinking about what they were learning. Each term we observed a 'core' course in each programme (e.g. a foundations or methods course developed especially for this programme), taking field notes about the content, activities and interactions. We focused on comparable components (e.g. a pair of educational psychology courses, pairs of methods courses). Besides providing a common referent for the interviews, the observational data were used to describe and analyse the preservice curriculum (see, e.g. Ball and Feiman-Nemser, 1986).

During student teaching, each of our focal students was paired with one researcher who visited weekly to observe and document the student teacher's activities in the setting. We kept notes of informal conversations with the student teachers, their cooperating teachers and university supervisors; we also conducted two more formal interviews with the teacher candidates before and after student teaching.

Illustrative Findings

To show how our framework allows us to describe and appraise opportunities to learn and learning outcomes in teacher preparation, we present two sets of illustrative findings. In each set, we focus on a particular issue in the context of a particular occasion for learning to teach. The issues – equity and the teaching of academic content – derive from our conception of the central tasks of teaching. The occasions – education courses and field experiences – become opportunities to learn through the interaction of programme, person and setting.

The first illustration pairs Janice, a student in the Academic Programme, with Sarah, a student in the Decision-Making Programme. It illustrates how personal history influences the way beginning education students make sense of their professional courses (see Feiman-Nemser and Buchmann, 1986a). The example shows how two students from different programmes form ideas about teaching related to issues of equity.

The second illustration pairs Susan, a student in the Academic Programme, with Molly, a student in the Decision-Making Programme.

Drawing on our case studies of student teaching (Feiman-Nemser and Buchmann, 1986b), we consider one teaching episode that elicited considerable pride in each student teacher. The issue there is the teaching of academic content.

Janice: Bringing Things Home

Like most people, Janice already had a sense of what teaching was all about when she began her preparation. Her preconceptions derived from her own school memories and from being an older sister in a large family. In her first interview, Janice spoke with pride about helping her brother and sister of 12 and 13 years learn how to drive the family tractor.

> I really got into showing 'em and explaining it to 'em so that when they were all done, they would be able to do it as well as I and it made me, I was really pleased, I liked doing it, you know... And that made me think, 'Well, I can, I can keep going, I can do this, it won't be that hard'.

Janice's mother wanted her girls to go to school so that they could support themselves if anything happened to their husbands. Her mother pushed her to read and to go to college even though Janice did not feel ready or interested. The academic orientation of Janice's programme reinforced her personal concerns about readiness and reading.

For instance, the Academic Programme required difficult reading during the first year and Janice could not understand why, nor see how, the reading would help her learn to teach. The lack of opportunities to link key ideas in the programme to classroom experiences was hard for Janice, who needed to see things to understand them.

When asked by an interviewer to describe an assigned reading that particularly stood out for her, Janice selected an article by Jean Anyon (1981) that critiques the inequitable distribution of school knowledge by social class and school location. She summarised Anyon's argument as follows:

> She dealt with class structures and the different social settings in schools. Some schools are like a working class; some are middle... It was interesting, you know, the aspects of what, what each school wanted for their students and the way they learned.

Janice connected the article to a reading assignment for another class on the topic of student motivation:

> I was reading that low class people are...from like ghettos and urban areas. They, their goals are really present-oriented, so you have to work out the success, so it's every day they are achieving immediate type of success.

In the same interview, Janice talked at length about Mexican migrants who worked on the family farm:

> One thing I always noticed that, when I was going to school and everything, the kids, you know, they weren't all that interested in going to school. A lot of times they wouldn't show up, 'cause they would just turn around and like, maybe a couple of weeks go back to Texas and so even the parents didn't seem to pressure 'em into going to school here.

Janice's experiences as a youngster made what she heard in her education classes ring true. For her, the experience with migrant children vividly exemplified the apparent lack of interest in school and learning that she expected some groups of children to have.

Finally, Janice integrated discussion questions from her curriculum class with her thoughts about minority children. In doing so, she *equated* school location, social class and low achievement, as well as the importance and meaning of poetry, with the use poetry may have for some people:

> One of the things Kelly was mentioning to us, 'What is the importance of poetry to a low class kid that is from the ghetto?'... A low achiever and things like that, poetry maybe doesn't mean anything to him. Is it that important to him? How is he ever gonna use poetry in the class structure he's in?

This is a hard pedagogical question. Janice wavered between pursuing the problem and dismissing poetry as unimportant in some schools:

> Is it really necessary, you know, how would you stress the importance of teaching poetry to somebody that didn't want to learn it? It was really hard, just to put that into words...You can do poetry with cars and things like that. But, it just made me think that, maybe, some things maybe aren't important and maybe we should stress

other things. Certain things should be stressed in certain schools, depending on where they're located.

This example shows how Janice put together past experience with things she picked up in her formal preparation – reinforcing earlier beliefs that conflict with equality of educational opportunity and reversing the intended message of her assigned reading on the inequitable distribution of school knowledge.

Sarah: Helping Children in Need

Sarah, by contrast, had always liked to read. Black herself, she grew up in a small Midwestern city and was inspired to become a teacher because of all the stories she had read about teachers who had helped 'poor black kids in the ghetto' to make it. Somewhat older and more experienced than other students in her programme, Sarah believed that her maturity and ability to help others would be an asset in teaching. To her, teaching was 'kinda like being a social worker... 'cause you're shaping that child's life'.

One of the more serious challenges for Sarah during her first year was trying to 'teach comprehension' to a black pupil in her reading group. Before her first reading course, Sarah said she 'didn't even know what comprehension was'. After extensive reading on the subject, she learned that 'comprehension is understanding what you are reading, getting some meaning out of it':

> If a child reads the story to you out loud, if he doesn't read every single word or if he reads a 'this' for a 'that', it's not a big deal. The child would know that word when it came up in context...

Sarah had learned in her programme that comprehension has to do with the thought processes in a child's mind, but teaching comprehension posed a real challenge. Sarah confronted this difficulty directly while working with her focus pupil, who could recognise words and read books from the library but could not talk about what she was reading. The day Sarah's pupil was supposed to give her book report was a day when the reading methods instructor observed Sarah. Following the advice of her instructor, Sarah had abandoned the basal reader and given students a chance to read books of their own choosing. She assumed this would motivate them to read for meaning and write stories on their own. But her student did not respond and Sarah did not know how to motivate her.

> I take them to the library and they've gotten books that they want to read and I just threw away my whole lesson. I said all we're going to do is enjoy reading and we're going to write about it and you're going to tell me about a story you've read and you're going to write a story 'cause I wanted to see if the student, given a chance to write about a story, would be able to tell me about it.

Disappointed that her actions did not seem to improve the motivation or comprehension of this student, Sarah blamed herself. 'I don't think I helped her at all'. She suspected that the child had special problems but also recognised that she, as a beginning teacher, 'didn't have the background or the knowledge to test her right'.

By her own testimony, Sarah had a personal interest in the educational advances of black children that shaped her commitment to teaching. When confronted with the kind of student she wanted to work with, however, she did not know how to help her as a teacher.

Equal Access to Knowledge: Comparing Sarah and Janice

Sarah may seem closer than Janice in connecting issues of equity and diversity to the responsibilities of teaching, but actually both candidates relied on personal experience that is limited and subject to bias. Janice's home experiences shaped how she made sense of what she read in her education courses. Putting pieces together based on unquestioned assumptions prevented her from seeing unequal access to knowledge as a problem teachers need to address. Clearly she did not understand the main point of Anyon's article. Because no one challenged her interpretation, her stereotypes were elaborated and legitimised. Sarah was personally disposed towards helping children in need, but general ideas about comprehension promoted by her reading methods instructor did not go far enough. Sarah needed specialised knowledge to analyse the problems and necessary skills to implement alternatives under guidance. Her own good intentions and general advice from the programme were not enough.

Susan: Doing 'Meaningful' Things in the Classroom

Like Janice, Susan was enrolled in the Academic Programme, where she was regarded as one of the more capable students. Even before student teaching, she began incorporating key programme ideas into her thinking about teaching. For example, in describing her work with a reading group, she revealed concerns and expectations about student thinking and learning:

> I'm trying to make the kids connect what they're doing with something they should be learning. I don't want them to just read and then sit down and close the book without thinking about 'Why did we read this story? What did I get out of it? What's it saying to me? What good has it done me?' – that sort of thing.

Susan's goals and expectations for student teaching revealed that she saw her responsibilities in terms of the central tasks of teaching. She said she wanted a chance to plan lessons in all the content areas and be responsible for pupils' learning over time. She described her ideal classroom as a place where pupils were busy and happy learning through 'fun' activities and where the teacher was liked and respected.

Susan's notion of learning through 'fun' activities reflects her interpretation of an important message in the Academic Programme: Good teachers do not rely on textbooks. She translated this message into a dichotomy between 'meaningful' learning activities, usually created by the teacher and 'boring' seatwork, usually based on workbooks and dittos.

Susan's cooperating teacher exemplified many of the commitments of the Academic Programme. Bob involved his third and fourth graders in challenging projects and was especially skilful at giving clear explanations, asking questions and probing students' thinking.

Overall, he gave Susan a lot of responsibility. Unfortunately, Susan did not perceive Bob as a model because his approach to discipline was, in her words, 'too laissez-faire'.

Susan's Prideful Occasion

Of all the things Susan did during student teaching, she was most proud of her book-making project. She thought that having students make their own books would motivate them to write because then their writing would be personally meaningful.

To initiate the project, Susan had students write letters to their parents saying that they would be making books in reading and asking if they could bring a piece of material for the cover. An entire school day was devoted to cutting cardboard, ironing the material into the cover and putting the books together.

Once the books were made, Susan told the students that they could write anything they wanted 'as long as it has an idea behind it'. Without explaining what this requirement meant or giving examples, Susan changed the formula, stressing, 'every story has a problem and a solution'.

Students worked on their stories in class and at home without getting criticism or advice. Susan did not discuss with students possible problems and solutions in their stories nor make any effort to identify and clarify students' ideas. Spelling was the only standard applied to the final product and even that was left to the children, who were supposed to check each other's work. Even before all the students had finished their stories, Susan turned the class back to Bob. As far as she was concerned, the project was over.

Bob, however, saw a way to carry it farther. Pulling a chair up to the front of the room, he asked those who had finished to put their books on a side table so that others could read them. Meanwhile, he invited one of the students to sit beside him and read his story aloud. During the reading, Bob noticed a misspelling and sent the student to the dictionary saying, 'This is really great, but can we make it better?'

Molly: Being a 'Creative' Teacher

Molly calmly looked forward to student teaching. In her programme, she had a reputation for being 'creative' and being 'her own person'. The Decision-Making Programme had provided her with ample and varied classroom experiences that she expected to build on. She hoped to bring together all the things she had learned in her programme, from all the different sources – classroom experiences, ideas and concepts from courses. To Molly, being able 'to put it all together' was the test of what she really knew. Her learning goals during student teaching were compatible with her programme's emphasis on 'knowledge use' and 'teacher decision-making'.

Molly's cooperating teacher, Suzy, was a skilful manager and Molly was impressed with her ability to anticipate what might happen and step in immediately when things got out of hand in class. At the beginning of the year, Suzy gave a lot of attention to 'grooving' her second graders, expecting them to sit still and upright with their eyes on the teacher and to listen attentively. She was concerned that children follow directions, follow them when given and follow them completely. These goals fit with the ethos of control that characterised her school.

Right from the start, Molly took on an equal share of the classroom routines in maths drills, spelling tests and reading skill instruction. Within these contexts, she developed a teacherish persona, mirroring her cooperating teacher's bland and authoritarian comportment. She spoke in a slow and wooden manner, demonstrating little evidence of thought or involvement on her part. Molly was not happy giving skill instruction 'when kids can't immediately see the application'. She felt that the children were 'skilled to death in reading'.

Molly's Prideful Occasion

Molly was most animated teaching an elections unit she developed herself. To decide on content, she drew on her everyday knowledge, illustrated by the vocabulary words and definitions that she got 'out of her own head'. For instance, she defined 'power' as 'when you can do things your way'; 'voting' as 'giving your support'; 'opinion' as 'what you yourself believe'.

Aiming for a tangible outcome to give her a sense of completion and to help the children remember what they had studied, Molly decided to have the children make a book with a ditto sheet for every lesson. The dittos, for instance, required colouring the American flag and matching words to definitions.

Molly drew on her dramatic talents to plan the unit. She came up with the idea of using puppets for candidates and picked 'issues' that she thought would be meaningful to the children. She realised that what she was teaching about presidential elections was simplified and not true to reality, but she believed the students could transfer what they learned to other elections.

A description of the last lesson in the unit conveys what Molly did and the way that the children responded. To start the lesson, Molly pretended that one of the fuzzy blue puppets, President Richard, was calling, 'Hey, take me out of the closet'. She took the puppet out, saying 'Hello everybody'. The children called back, 'Hi, President Richard'. The puppet said, 'I hope you'll vote for me'. When Molly got the other puppet out, the children greeted it, too.

The children were noisy and excited and Molly interjected a few warnings. 'Does anyone know what the word "votes" means?' One girl said, 'If you pick one person and they are 35, that means you vote.' Molly let this confused response pass and put down the right answer: 'Vote is the way you support the candidate.'

When it was time to vote, Molly said, 'I am looking for two people with good behaviour who can go to the voting booth. Who knows what a voting booth is?' She wrote the definition on the board: 'Voting booth is where you vote.' Then she pantomimed stepping into a booth, closing the curtains and stepping out. Watching her, the cooperating teacher spontaneously remarked: 'Isn't she fun to watch?'

Teaching Academic Content: Comparing Molly and Susan

Both Susan and Molly responded to the character and content of schoolwork but in different ways. Susan aimed for meaningful activities and she tried to transform schoolwork into something personally involving for students. She saw the book-making project as a substitute for 'boring seatwork' and reading from the basal. To work toward meaningful activities, Susan drew from the messages of the Academic Programme and her own limited academic knowledge. Molly responded to the character of the setting as well as the character and content of schoolwork by finding ways to enliven activities for herself and her students. To develop the elections unit, she drew from common sense and her personal talents.

Molly and Susan both stopped short of serious engagement with academic content. Intent on getting away from texts, their substitutions were not successful. Susan structured activities that students liked without knowing how to carry them forward to produce worthwhile learning. Book-making never became transformed into serious story-writing. Molly tried to do 'creative' things that often centred on displaying her own talents. In doing her elections unit, however, she lacked a grounded understanding of the political process or children's interests.

Both Molly and Susan were ready to learn, but no one used student teaching to help them see how to promote understanding or figure out what counts as a 'worthwhile learning activity'. Both received glowing recommendations from their cooperating teachers that reinforced their sense of being successful as teachers. They did not go very far in developing their capacities to teach academic content, nor were they helped to acquire the capacities and skills of pedagogical thinking that mark the transition to the teacher role. Both were hampered by lack of subject matter knowledge but neither they, their programme, nor their cooperating teacher seemed to notice.

Conclusion

As these illustrative findings demonstrate, realities in teacher education are not self-evident. Researchers, teacher educators and policy-makers need a framework to help them focus on important aspects of teacher learning, such as the interaction of programme features, settings and personal characteristics. Since curriculum defines valued capacities to be developed, a framework in teacher education must consider worthwhile aims and standards for appraisal in order to provide direction for enquiry and curriculum development.

Author Reflection 2004

This chapter describes one of the earliest efforts to frame the problem of teacher education as a 'learning' problem. Aiming to replace the language of 'teacher training' with a normative concept of 'teacher education', researchers followed six preservice students through two years of courses and field experiences in order to understand how prospective teachers make sense of their formal preparation and how that learning is mediated by biography and school culture. The researchers – a philosopher interested in teacher education and a teacher educator with a philosophic bent – had a second, conceptual goal: to assess how well the programmes added up as serious preparation for teaching. Thus, the research combined conceptual/analytic enquiry into the central tasks of learning to teach during preservice preparation with empirical investigation of learning opportunities and outcomes. Looking back at this study from the vantage point of twenty years, one sees both enduring contributions and shortcomings.

  In the current climate of accountability, when policy-makers want to know whether teacher education makes a difference, this study demonstrates that learning to teach is not a linear, straightforward process. By showing how preservice teacher learning (and mislearning) result from a complex interaction of personal characteristics, programme features and school settings, the study lays some groundwork for thinking about the outcomes question while helping teacher educators reflect on their programmes and practice. Clearly, we cannot account for the impact of teacher education without knowing something about the process. By focusing on proximate outcomes and relying on fine-grained description and analysis, however, the study will disappoint those seeking generalisable findings regarding pupil learning rather than useful theories regarding teacher learning.

About ISATT

What is ISATT?

The purpose of ISATT is to promote, present, discuss and disseminate; to carry out research on teachers and teaching; to contribute to theory formation in this field – all in order to gain more insight into these aspects of education, add to knowledge, and enhance the quality of education through improved teaching and forms of professional development at all levels of education. Research on teachers and teaching in schools and higher education encompasses several perspectives. These include:

- Teachers' purposes, beliefs, conceptions, practical theories, narratives, histories, stories, voice.
- Teachers' intentions, thought processes and cognitions, personal practical knowledge.
- Teachers' emotions, thinking and reflection as aspects of professional actions.
- Teachers' thinking and action as influenced by contextual factors in their structural, cultural and social environments including the workplace of teaching and learning.

A central intention for this research is to focus on the way teachers themselves understand teaching and their own roles in it. Research is not limited to studying what teachers do but tries also to understand how they think and feel about what they are doing and the cultural contexts in which their work is embedded. Consequently, research is individually as well as socially, psychologically and culturally based.

There is an increasing acceptance of the value of research carried out by researchers from complementary research traditions. Researchers from different disciplinary backgrounds at all levels of teaching have come to study such diverse phenomena as teacher planning, decision-making, reflection, teacher understanding of subject matter and of curricula, their judgement of students' work, their beliefs, attitudes, conceptions, implicit theories and thought processes as well as their principles of action, criteria and dilemmas of teaching. Insights from this wide variety of studies have informed teacher education programmes and curriculum development, contributed to teachers' self-reflection and professional awareness, and provided a growing data bank from which educational policy makers may draw.

The growing interest in research from Teacher Thinking and Action Perspectives is an international trend. As an organisation, ISATT is at the forefront. It draws its membership from teacher-researchers worldwide at every academic level and from a range of disciplines publishing in several countries and in their respective languages.

Activities and Publications

ISATT offers a biennial Conference with leading researchers as keynote speakers presenting state-of-the-art frontline contributions in the field. Parallel groups for paper presentations provide participants with stimulating discourses of their work, and symposia, workshops, round tables and poster sessions offer possibilities for interactive work on methodological innovations or theory application. The ISATT conferences are known to have developed an atmosphere of intellectual stimulation combined with an amicable collegial climate. ISATT publishes its own international journal *Teachers and Teaching:-Theory and Practice* in cooperation with CARFAX. There are four issues per year. This refereed journal offers an interesting selection of new research reports and theoretical contributions.

ISATT Membership Directory

The Directory is an effective means of establishing contact with research colleagues working on similar problems or using similar methods.

ISATT Newsletter

The Newsletter provides information of the activities and plans of the association and is published 2 times a year and is also available at www.isatt.org

The ISATT Publication Series

The series consists of a volume of selected papers from each of the conferences including the keynote speeches.

Ben-Peretz, M, Bromme, R. and Halkes, R. (eds) *Advances of research on teacher thinking.* ISATT, Lisse/Berwyn: Swets and Zeitlinger/Swets North America, 1986.

Lowyck, J. and Clark, C. M. (eds) *Teacher thinking and professional action.* Leuven University Press, 1989.

Day, C., Pope, M. and Denicolo, P. (eds) *Insights into teachers' thinking and practice.* Falmer Press, 1990.

Day, C., Calderhead, J. and Denicolo, P. (eds) *Research on teacher thinking: towards understanding professional development.* Falmer Press, 1993.

Carlgren, I., Handal, G. and Vaage, S. (eds) *Teachers' minds and actions: research on teachers' thinking and practice.* Falmer Press, 1994.

Halkes, R. and Olson, J. K. (eds) *Teacher thinking: a new perspective on persisting problems in education.* ISATT, Lisse: Swets and Zeitlinger, 1984.

Kompf, M., Boak, R. T., Bond, W. R and Dworet, D. H. (eds) *Changing research and practice: teachers' professionalism, identities and knowledge.* Falmer Press, 1996.

Kompf, M., and Denicolo, P.M. (eds) *Teacher thinking twenty years on; revisiting persisting patterns and advances in education.* Lisse: Swets and Zeitlinger, 2003.

Lang, M., Olson, J., Hansen, H. and Bunder, W. (eds) *Changing schools/changing practices: perspectives on educational reform and teacher professionalism.* Garant, 1999.

Sugrue, C. and Day, C. (2001) (eds) *Developing teachers and teaching practice: international research perspectives.* London: Routledge/Falmer Press.

Please visit **isatt.org** for further information.

References

Adams, R. S. and Biddle, B. J. (1970). *Realities of teaching. Explorations with videotape.* New York: Holt, Rinehart and Winston.

Adams-Webber, J. R. (1979). Personal construct theory: concepts and applications. New York: John Wiley and Sons.

Allport, A. (1987). Selection for action: Some behavioural and neurophysiological considerations of attention and action. In H. Heuer and A. F. Sanders (Eds.), *Perspectives on perception and action* (pp. 395–419). Hillsdale, NJ: Erlbaum.

Ames, R. (1975). Teachers' attribution of responsibility: Some unexpected non-defensive effects. *Journal of Educational Psychology, 67,* 668–676.

Angell, J. R. (1907). The province of functional psychology. *Psychological Review, 14,* 61–91.

Angyal, A. (1969). A logic of systems. In F. E. Emery (Ed.), *Systems thinking.* Harmondsworth: Penguin.

Anyon, J. (1981). Social class and school knowledge. *Curriculum Inquiry, 11,* 3–42.

Argyris, C. and Schon, D. (1974). *Theory in practice: Increasing professional effectiveness.* San Francisco: Jossey Bass.

Bagnato, S. J. (1981). Developmental diagnostic reports: Reliable and effective alternatives to guide individualized intervention. *The Journal of Special Education, 15,* 65–76.

Ball, D. L. (1986). Unlearning to teach mathematics. Paper presented at the 8th annual meeting of the North American chapter of the International Group for the Psychology of Mathematics Education. East Lansing, Michigan.

Ball, D. and Feiman-Nemser, S. (1986a). *Using textbooks and teachers' guides: What beginning teachers learn and what they need to know* (Research Series No. 174). East Lansing: Michigan State University, Institute for Research on Teaching.

Ball, D. and Noordhoff, K. (1984). Toward conceptual change about teachers' cognitive development and teacher education. Unpublished paper, Michigan State University, East Lansing, MI.

Ball, D. and Noordhoff, K. (1985). *Learning to teach by the book: The influence of persons, programme, and setting on student teaching.* Paper presented at the annual meeting of the American Educational Research Association, Chicago.

Ball, D. L. and Feiman-Nemser, S. (1986b). *The use of curricular materials: What beginning elementary teachers learn and what they need to know.* Paper presented at the annual meeting of the American Educational Research Association, San Francisco.

Bandura, A. (1972). Self-efficacy mechanism in human agency. *American Psychologist, 37,* 122–147.

Bannister, D. and Fransella, F. (1971). *Inquiring Man: the psychology, of personal constructs.* Malabar Florida: Krieger.

Barbour, C. (1971). *Levels of thinking in supervision conferences.* Paper presented at the annual meeting of the American Educational Research Association, New York (EDRS, No. ED 049 186).

Bar-Tal, D. (1979). Interactions of teachers and pupils. In J. H. Frieze, D. Bar-Tal and Carroll, J. S. (Eds.), *New approaches to social problems* (pp. 337–358). San Francisco: Jossey Bass.

Bar-Tal, D. and Guttmann, J. (1981). A comparison of teachers', pupils' and parents' attributions regarding pupils' academic achievements. *British Journal of Educational Psychology, 51,* 301–311.

Baumeister, A. (1986). Subjektive Leistungsbeurteilungstheorien von Lehrern im Sonderschulbereich. *Psychologie in Erziehung and Unterricht, 33*(1), 46–52.

Bender, M. P. (1974). Provided versus elicited constructs: an explanation of Warr and Coffman's anomalous findings. *British Journal of Social and Clinical Psychology, 94,* 281–285.

Ben-Peretz, M. (1984a). Curriculum theory and practice in teacher education programs. In L. Katz and J. Raths (Eds.), *Advances in teacher education,* Vol. 1 *(pp. 9–27).* Norwood, NJ: Ablex.

Ben-Peretz, M. (1984b). Kelly's theory of personal constructs as a paradigm for investigating teacher thinking. In R. Halkes and J. Olson (Eds.), *Teacher thinking, a new perspective on persisting problems in education* (pp. 103–111). Lisse: Swets and Zeitlinger.

Ben-Peretz, M., Katz, S. and Silberstein, M. (1982). Curriculum interpretation and its place in teacher education programs. *Interchange, 13*(4), 47–55.

Ben-Peretz, M., Bromme, R. and Halkes, R. (Eds.) (1986). *Advances of research on teacher thinking.* Lisse: Swets and Zeitlinger.

Bereiter, L. (1985). Toward a solution of the learning paradox. *Review of Educational Research, 15,* 201–226.

Berger, P. and Luckmann, T. (1967). *The social construction of reality.* New York: Anchor.

Bergen, Th. C. M. and den Hertog, P.C. (1985). Attributies door docenten tijdens hun onderwijs (Attributions by teachers during their teaching). In J. von Grumbkow, D. van Kreveld and P. Stringer (Eds.), *Toegepaste sociale psychologie,* Vol. 1 (pp. 83–99). Lisse: Swets and Zeitlinger.

Berkowitz, L. and Donnerstein, E. (1982). External validity is more than skin deep. Some answers to criticism of laboratory experiments. *American Psychologist, 37,* 245–257.

Berlak, A. and Berlak, H. (1981). *Dilemmas of schooling: teaching and social change.* London: Methuen and co..

Berliner, D.C. (1986). In pursuit of the expert pedagogue. *Educational Researcher, 15*(7), 5–13.

Berliner, D.C. (1969). *Microteaching and the technical skills approach to teacher training.* (Technical Report No. 8.) Stanford, CA: Stanford University, Stanford Center for Research and Development in Teaching.

Berliner, D.C. and Carter, K. J. (1986). *Differences in processing classroom information by expert and novice teachers.* Paper presented at the meeting of the international Study Association on Teacher Thinking (ISATT), Leuven, Belgium.

Berliner, D.C. and Rosenshine, B. (1977). The acquisition of knowledge in the classroom. In R.C. Anderson, R.J. Spiro and W.E. Montegue (Eds.), *Schooling and the acquisition of knowledge* (pp. 375–396). Hillsdale, NJ: Erlbaum.

Berliner, D.C. and Tikunoff, W. J. (1976). The California Beginning Teacher Evaluation Study: Overview of the ethnographic study. *Journal of Teacher Education, 27,* 24–30.

Beyerbach, B. (1985). *Concept mapping as an approach to assessment of students'*
representation of structural knowledge. Unpublished doctoral dissertation,
Syracuse University, Syracuse.

Blaauboer, S. A. A. and Pijl, S. J. (1986). Beslissen over het onderwijsaanbod.
In C. J. W. Meijer, S. J. Pijl and J. Rispens (Eds.), *Beslissen over verwijzen*
en toelaten (pp. 99–113). Lisse: Swets and Zeitlinger.

Block J. H. and Burns, R. B. (1976). Mastery learning. In L. Shulman (Ed.), *Review*
of research in education, Vol. 4 (pp. 3–49). Itasca, IL: F. E. Peacock.

Borg, W.R. and Ascione, F. R. (1982). Classroom management in elementary
mainstreaming classrooms. *Journal of Educational Psychology, 74,*
85–95.

Boring, E.G. (1957). *A history of experimental psychology.* New York:
Appleton-Century-Crofts.

Borko, H. and Cadwell, J. (1982). Individual differences in teachers' decision
strategies: An investigation of classroom organization and management
decisions. *Journal of Educational Psychology, 74,* 598–610.

Borko, H. and Shavelson, R.J. (1978). Teachers' sensitivity to the reliability of
information in making causal attributions in an achievement situation.
Journal of Educational Psychology, 70, 271–279.

Borko, H. and Shavelson R.J. (1983). Speculation on teacher education:
Recommendations from research on teachers' cognitions. *Journal of*
Education for Teaching, 9, 210–225.

Borko, H., Cone, R., Russo, N. A. and Shavelson, R.J. (1979). Teachers' decision
making. In P. L. Peterson and H. J. Walberg (Eds.), *Research on thinking*:
Concepts, findings and implications (pp. 136–161). Berkeley: McCutchan
Press.

Bransford, J.D. and Franks, J. J. (1971). The abstraction of linguistic ideas.
Cognitive Psychology, 2, 331–350.

Brehmer, A. (1984). *Betygsattning i textilslojd. I. En strukturerad intervjumed*
20 textillärare (Technical Report No. 9.). Uppsala: Uppsala University,
Sektorn for Undervisningsyrken.

Brehmer, A. and Brehmer, B. (1986a). *Self-selected and experimental selected cues*
in policy-capturing. Manuscript, Uppsala University, Department of
Psychology, Uppsala.

Brehmer, A. and Brehmer, B. (1986b). *Insight into judgment processes.* Manuscript,
Uppsala University, Department of Psychology, Uppsala.

Brehmer, A. and Carnmark, A. (1984). *Betygsattning i textilslojd. I. En strukturerad*
intervjumed 20 textillärare (Technical Report No. 9). Uppsala: Uppsala
University, Sektorn for Undervisningsyrken.

Brehmer, A. and Lindfors, L. (1986). *Effect of recommendations about grading:*
A comparison between the grading policies of Swedish and Finnish
handicraft teachers. Manuscript, Uppsala University, Department of
Psychology, Uppsala.

Brehmer, B. (1987). Social judgment theory and forecasting. In G. Wright and
P. Ayton (Eds.), *Judgmental forecasting.* Chichester: Wiley.

Broadbent, D. H. (1971). *Decision and stress.* London: Academic Press.

Broeckmans, J. (1984). An attempt to study the process of learning to teach from an
integrative viewpoint. In R. Halkes and J. K. Olson (Eds.), *Teacher*
thinking. A new perspective on (persisting problems in) education (pp.
210–219). Lisse: Swets and Zeitlinger.

Broeckmans, J. (1986a). Short-term developments in student teachers' lesson planning. *Teaching and Teacher Education, 2,* 215–228.

Broeckmans, J. (1986b). Supervision conferences and student teachers' thinking and behaviour. In J. Lowyck (Ed.), *Teacher thinking and professional action.* Proceedings of the third ISATT conference (pp. 558–575). Leuven, Belgium: University of Leuven.

Broeckmans, J. (1987, April). *Orienting and controlling functions of student teachers' interactive thoughts.* Paper presented at the First Joint Conference of the Arbeitsgruppe fiir Empirisch Padagogische Forschung (West Germany) and the Onderzoeksthemagroep Onderwijsleerprocessen (The Netherlands), Dusseldorf, West Germany.

Bromme, R. (1981). *Das Denken von Lehrern bei der Unterrichtsvorbereitung.* Weinheim: Beltz.

Bromme, R. (1983). 'Understanding texts' as heuristics for the analysis of thinking aloud protocols. *Communication and Cognition, 16,* 215–231.

Bromme, R. (1984). On the limitations of the theory metaphor for the study of teachers' expert knowledge. In R. Halkes and J. K. Olson (Eds.), *Teacher thinking* (pp. 43–57). Lisse: Swets and Zeitlinger.

Bromme, R. (1987). Teachers' assessment of students' difficulties and progress in understanding in the classroom. In J. Calderhead (Ed.), *Exploring teachers' thinking.* Eastbourne: Holt, Rinehart and Winston.

Bromme, R. and Brophy, J. E. (1986). Teachers' cognitive activities. In B. Christiansen, G. Howson and M. Otte, (Eds.), *Perspectives on mathematics education* (pp. 99–139). Dordrecht: Reidel.

Brophy, J. E. (1982). How teachers influence what is taught and learned in classrooms. *Elementary School Journal, 83,* 1–13.

Brophy, J. E. (1983a). Research on the self-fulfilling prophecy and teacher expectations. *Journal of Educational Psychology, 75,* 631–661.

Brophy, J. E. (1983b). Classroom organization and management. *Elementary School Journal, 83,* 1–13.

Brophy, J. E. and Evertson, C. M. (1981). *Student characteristics and teaching.* New York: Longman.

Brophy, J. E. and Good, T. L. (1974). *Teacher–student relationships: Causes and consequences.* New York: Holt, Rinehart and Winston.

Brophy, J. E. and Good, T. L. (1986). Teacher behaviour and student achievement. In M. C. Wittrock (Ed.), *Handbook of research on teaching,* 3rd edn (pp. 328–375). New York: Macmillan.

Brophy, J. and Rohrkemper, M. (1981). The influence of problem ownership on teachers' perception of and strategies for coping with problem students. *Journal of Educational Psychology, 73,* 295–311.

Brown, A. F. (1957). The self in interpersonal theory: the relationship between attitudes referring to self and significant others. *Alberta Journal of Educational Research, 3,* 138–148.

Brown, A. F. (1986). Professional literacy, resourcefulness, and what makes teaching interesting. In M. Ben-Peretz, R. Bromme, R. Halkes (eds), *Advances in Research in Teacher thinking.* Lisse, Holland: Swets and Zeitlinger.

Brown, J. S. and Burton, R. B. (1978). Diagnostic models for procedural bugs in basic mathematical skills. *Cognitive Science, 2,* 155–192.

Brown, J. S. and VanLehn, K. (1980). Repair theory: A generative theory of bugs in procedural skills. *Cognitive Science, 4,* 379–426.

Brown, J. S. and VanLehn, K. (1982). Towards a generative theory of 'bugs'. In T. P. Carpenter, J. M. Moser and T. Tomberg (Eds.), *Addition and subtraction. A cognitive perspective* (pp. 117–135). Hillsdale, NJ: Erlbaum.

Brunner, E. J. (1986). *Grundfragen der Familientheraphie. Systemische Theorie und Methodologie.* Berlin: Springer.

Brunner, E. J. and Huber, G. L. (1982). Lehr-Lern-Forschung als Erforschung von Interdependenzen in Lehrer-Schuler-Systemen. *Unterrichtswissenschaft, 11,* 296–308.

Buchmann, M. (1984). The priority of knowledge and understanding in teaching. In L. Katz and J. Raths (Eds.), *Advances in teacher education,* Vol. 1 (pp. 29–50). Norwood, NJ: Ablex.

Buchmann, M. (1985). Improving education by talking: Argument or conversation? *Teachers College Record, 86,* 441–453.

Buchmann, M. (1986). Role over person: Morality and authenticity in teaching. *Teachers College Record, 87,* 529–544.

Buckley, P. K. and Copper, J. M. (1978). An ethnographic study of an elementary schoolteacher's establishment and maintenance of group norms. Paper presented at the annual meeting of the American Educational Research Association, Toronto: Canada.

Burton, R. B. (1982). Diagnosing bugs in a simple procedural skill. In D. Sleeman and J. S. Brown (Eds.), *Intellectual tutoring systems* (pp. 157–183). London: Academic Press.

Bussis, A. M., Chittenden, F and Amarel, M. (1976). Beyond surface curriculum. Boulder Co: Westview Press.

Calderhead, J. (1981a). A psychological approach to research on teachers' classroom decision making. *British Educational Research Journal, 7,* 51–57.

Calderhead, J. (1981b). Stimulated recall: A method for research on teaching. *British Journal of Educational Psychology, 51,* 211–217.

Calderhead, J. (1983, April). Research into teachers' and students' cognitions: exploring the nature of classroom practice. Paper presented to the annual meeting of the American Educational Research Association, Montreal, Canada.

Calderhead, J. (1984). *Teachers' classroom decision making.* London: Holt, Rinehart and Winston.

Calderhead, J. (1986). Developing a framework for the elicitation and analysis of teachers' verbal reports. Paper presented at the annual meeting of the American Educational Research Association, San Francisco.

Carnahan, R. S. (1980). *The effects of teacher planning on classroom processes* (Technical Report No. 541). Madison, WI: University of Wisconsin, Wisconsin Research and Development Center.

Carr, W. and Kemmis, S. (1986) *Becoming critical.* London: Palmer Press.

Carroll, J. B. (1963). A model of school learning. *Teachers College Record, 64,* 723–733.

Champagne, A. B., Gunston, R. F. and Klopfer, L. E. (1983). *A perspective on the differences between expert and novice performance in solving physics problems.* Pittsburgh: University of Pittsburgh, Learning Research and Development Center.

Chase, W. G. and Simon, H. A. (1973). Perception in chess. *Cognitive Psychology, 4,* 55–81.

Chi, M. T. H., Feltovich, P. J. and Glaser, R. (1981). Categorization and representation of physics problems by experts and novices. *Cognitive Science, 5,* 121–152.

Clandinin, D. J. and Connelly, F. M. (1986). Rhythms in teaching: The narrative study of teachers' personal knowledge of classrooms. *Teaching and Teacher Education, 2*(4), 377–387.

Clark, C. M. (1983). Research on teacher planning: an inventory of the knowledge base. In D. C. Smith (Ed.), *Essential knowledge for beginning educators.* Washington, D. C.: American Association of Colleges for Teacher Education.

Clark, C. M. and Elmore, J. L. (1979). Teacher planning in the first weeks of school (Research Series No. 56) East Lansing: Michigan State University, Institute for Research on Teaching.

Clark, C. M. and Elmore, J. L. (1981). Transforming curriculum in mathematics, science and writing: a case study of teacher yearly planning (Research Series No.99). East Lansing: Michigan State University, Institute for Research on Teaching.

Clark, C. M. and Lampert, M. (1986). The study of teacher thinking: implications for teacher education. *Journal of Teacher Education, 37(5),* 27–31.

Clark, C. M. and Peterson, P. L. (1986). Teachers' thought processes. In M. C. Wittrock (Ed.), *Handbook of research on teaching,* 3rd edn (pp. 255–296). New York: Macmillan.

Clark, C. M. and Yinger, R.J. (1979a). Teachers' thinking. In P. L. Peterson and H. J. Walberg (Eds.), *Research on thinking: Concepts, findings and implications* (pp. 231–263). Berkeley: McCutchan Press.

Clark, C. M. and Yinger, R.J. (1979b). *Three studies of teacher planning* (Research Series No. 55). East Lansing: Michigan State University, Institute for Research on Teaching.

Clark, C. M. and Yinger, R.J. (1987). Teacher planning. In D. C. Berliner and B. V. Rosenshine (Eds.), *Talks to teachers* (pp. 342–368). New York: Lane Akers. Cooper H. M. and Good, T. L. (1983). *Pygmation Grows Up.* New York: Longmans, 1983.

Cohen, A. R. (1961). Cognitive tuning as a factor affecting impression formation. *Journal of Personality, 29,* 235–245.

Collingwood, R. G. (1946). *The idea of history.* Oxford: University Press.

Common, R. W. (1984). PRAISE. *Canadian School Executive, 4*(2).

Corno, L. (1981). Cognitive organizing in classrooms. *Curriculum Inquiry, 11,* 359–377.

Connelly, F. M. and Clandinin, J. (1984). Personal practical knowledge at Bay Street School: Ritual, personal philosophy and image. In R. Halkes and J. Olson (Eds.), *Teacher thinking: A new perspective on (persistent problems in) education* (pp. 134–148). Lisse: Swets and Zeitlinger.

Conners, R. D. (1978). *An analysis of teacher thought processes, beliefs, and principles during instruction.* Unpublished doctoral dissertation, University of Alberta, Edmonton, Canada.

Cooper, H. M. (1979a). Pygmalion grows up: A model for teacher expectation communication and performance influence. *Review of Educational Research, 49,* 398–410.

Cooper, H. M. (1979b). Some effects on performance information on academic expectations. *Journal of Educational Psychology, 71,* 375–380.

Cooper, H. M. and Burger, J. M. (1980). How teachers explain students' academic performance: A categorization of free response academic attributions. *American Educational Research Journal, 17,* 95–109.

Cooper, H. M. and Good, T. L. (1983). *Pygmalion grows up.* White Plains, NY: Longman.

Cronbach, L. J. (1949). *Essentials of psychological testing.* New York: Harper.

Cusick, P. (1983). *The egalitarian ideal and the American high school.* New York: Longman.

Daniels, L. (1971). *The justification of curricula.* Paper presented to the American Educational Research Association, New York.

Daniels, L. (1975). What is the language of the practical? *Curriculum Theory Network, 4*(4), 237–261.

Darom, E. and Bar-Tal, D. (1981). Causal perception of pupils' success or failure by teachers and pupils: A comparison. *Journal of Educational Research, 74,* 233–239.

Davis, L. (1979). *Theory of action.* Englewood Cliffs, NJ: Prentice-Hall.

Davis, R. B. (1984). *Learning mathematics: The cognitive science approach to mathematics education.* London: Croom Helm.

De Corte, E. and Verschaffel, L. (1985). Beginning first graders' initial representation of arithmetic word problems. *Journal of Mathematical Behaviour, 4,* 3–21.

Denham, L. and Liebermann, A. (Eds.). (1980). *Time to learn. A review of the beginning teacher evaluation study.* Sacramento: California State Commission for Teacher Preparation and Licensing.

Denicolo, P.M. (1985). *Figurative language: An investigation of its value in the teaching and learning of chemistry.* Unpublished PhD thesis, University of Surrey, Guildford.

Denicolo, P. M. and Pope, M. L. (2001). *Transformative professional practice - Personal construct approaches to education and research.* London: Whurr.

Dewey, J. (1896). The reflex arc concept in psychology. *Psychological Review, 3,* 357–370.

Dewey, J. (1916). *Democracy and education.* New York: Macmillan.

Dewey, J. (1939). *Theory and Valuation.* Chicago: University of Chicago Press.

Dewey, J. (1963). *Experience and Education.* New York: Collier (reprint of Collier Macmillan, 1938).

Dewey, J. (1964). The relationship of theory and practice in education. In M. Borrowman (Ed.), *Teacher education in America: A documentary history* (pp. 140–171). New York: Teachers College Press (Originally published in 1904).

Dewey, J. (1977). *Experience and Education.* New York: Collier. (Original work published 1938).

Diamond, C. (1982). Teachers can change: A Kellyian interpretation. *Journal of Education for Teaching, 8*(2), 163–173.

Diamond, C. T. P. (1985). Becoming a teacher: An altering eye. In D. Bannister (Ed.), *Issues and approaches in personal construct theory.* London: Academic Press.

Dobbert, M. (1982). Ethnographic research: Theory and application for modern schools and societies. New York: Praeger Publishers.

Douglas, J. (1985). *Creative interviewing.* Beverly Hills, CA: Sage Publications.

Doyle, W. (1977). Learning the classroom environment: An ecological analysis. *Journal of Teacher Education, 28,* 51–55.

Doyle, W. (1978). Paradigms for research on teacher effectiveness. In L. S. Shulman (Ed.), *Review of research in education*, Vol. 5 (pp. 163–198). Itasca: Peacock.

Doyle, W. (1979). Making managerial decisions in classrooms. In D. L. Duke (Ed.), *Classroom management* (Yearbook of the National Society for the Study of Education, vol. 78, Pt 2, pp. 42–74). Chicago: University of Chicago Press.

Doyle, W. (1985, June). *Content representations in teachers' definitions of academic work.* Unpublished paper, Research and Development Center for Teacher Education, University of Texas, Austin, TX.

Doyle, W. and Ponder, G. (1977). The practicality ethic and teacher decision-making. *Interchange, 8*(3), 1–12.

Dray, W. (1957). *Laws and explanation in history.* Oxford: University Press.

Duffy, G. (1977). A *study of teaching conceptions of reading.* Paper presented at the National Reading Conference, New Orleans.

Dyson, A. (1999). Inclusion and inclusions: theories and discourses in inclusive education. In: H. Daniels and Ph. Garner (Eds), *Inclusive education* (pp. 36–53). London: Kogan Page.

Edelenbos, P. and Meijer, W. (2001). Pedagogisch-didactische consequenties van diagnosticeren. Groningen: GION.

Edmonds, R. R. (1979). Effective schools for the urban poor. *Educational Leadership, 37,* 15–27.

Elbaz, F. (1981). The teacher's 'practical knowledge': Report of a case study. *Curriculum Inquiry, 11,* 43–71.

Elbaz, F. (1983). *Teacher thinking: A study of practical knowledge.* London: Croom Helm.

Elig, T. W. and Frieze, J. (1979). Measuring causal attributions for success and failure. *Journal of Personality and Social Psychology, 37,* 621–634.

Ericsson, K. A. and Simon, H. A. (1980). Verbal reports as data. *Psychological Review, 87,* 215–251.

Evertson, C. M. and Emmer, E. T. (1982). Effective management at the beginning of the school year in junior high school classes. *Journal of Educational Psychology, 74,* 485–498.

Feiman-Nemser, S. (1983). Learning to teach. In L. Shulman and G. Sykes (Eds.), *Handbook on teaching and policy* (pp. 150–170). New York: Longman.

Feiman-Nemser, S. and Buchmann, M. (1986a). The first year of teacher preparation: Transition to pedagogical thinking? *Journal of Curriculum Studies, 18*(3), 239–256.

Feiman-Nemser, S. and Buchmann, M. (1986b). *When is student teaching teacher education?* (Research Series No. 178). East Lansing: Michigan State University, Institute for Research on Teaching.

Finlayson, D. (1975). Self confrontation: A broader conceptual base? *British Journal of Teacher Education, 1,* 97–103.

Fisher, C. W. and Berliner, D.C. (Eds.). (1985). *Perspectives on instructional time.* New York: Longman.

Floden, R. and Buchmann, M. (1984). *The trouble with meaningfulness.* (Occasional Paper No. 82). East Lansing: Michigan State University, Institute for Research on Teaching.

Frieze, J. (1980). Beliefs about success and failure in the classroom.
    In J. H. Macmillan (Ed.), *The social psychology of school learning*
    (pp. 39–78). New York: Academic Press.

Fuller, F. (1969). Concerns of teachers: A developmental characterization. *American
    Educational Research Journal, 6,* 207–226.

Fuller, F. F. and Bown, O. H. (1975). Becoming a teacher. In K. Ryan (Ed.), *Teacher
    education* (Yearbook of the National Society for the Study of Education,
    vol. 74, Pt. 2, pp. 25–52). Chicago: University of Chicago Press.

Gadamer, H. G. (1975). *Truth and method.* New York: Seabury Press.

Gage, N. L. (1963). Paradigms for research on teaching. In N. L. Gage (Ed.),
    Handbook of research on teaching (pp. 94–141). Chicago:
    Rand McNally.

Gage, N. L. (1985). *Hard grains in the soft sciences. The case of pedagogy.*
    Bloomington, IN: Phi Delta Kappa.

Galperin, P. J. (1974). Die geistige Handlung als Grundlage für die Bildung von
    Gedanken and Vorstellungen. In P. J. Galperin, A. N. Leontjew *et al.* (Eds.),
    Probleme der Lerntheorie. Berlin: Volk und Wissen.

Gardner, H. (1993). *Multiple intelligences: The theory in practice.* New York:
    Basic Books.

Good, T. L., Grouws, D. A. and Ebmeier, H. (1983). *Active mathematics teaching.*
    New York: Longman.

Goodlad, J. (1984). Access to knowledge. In *A place called school: Prospects for
    the future* (pp. 130–166). New York: McGraw Hill.

Griffin, P. and Cole, M. (1984). Current activity for the future: The Zoped.
    In B. Rogoff and J. Wertsch (Eds.), *Children's learning in the 'zone of
    proximal development'.* San Francisco: Jossey-Bass.

Grundy, S. (1982). Three modes of action research. *Curriculum Perspectives,*
    2(3), 23–34.

Guskey, T. R. (1982). Differences in teachers' perception of personal control of
    positive versus negative student learning outcomes. *Contemporary
    Educational Psychology, 7,* 70–80.

Guskey, T. R. (1986). Staff development and the process of teacher change.
    Educational Researcher, 15, 5–20.

Guttmann, J. (1982). Pupils', teachers' and parents' causal attributions for problem
    behaviour at school. *Journal of Educational Research, 76,* 14–21.

Haber, R. N. (1966). Nature of the effect of set on perception. *Psychological Review,*
    73, 335–351.

Halberstam, D. (1986). *The reckoning.* New York: William Morrow.

Halkes, R. (1985). Teacher thinking: A promising perspective into educational
    processes. *ISATT Newsletter,* No. 3, 8–13.

Halkes, R. and Deyker, R. (1984). Teachers' Teaching criteria. In R. Hales and
    J. K. Olson (Eds.), *Teacher thinking* (pp. 149–162). Lisse: Swets and
    Zeitlinger.

Halkes, R. and Olson, J. K. (Eds.). (1984). *Teacher thinking, a new perspective on
    persisting problems in education.* Lisse: Swets and Zeitlinger.

Hammond, K. R. (1982). *Principles of organization in intuitive and analytical
    cognition* (Technical Report No. 226). University of Colorado: Center for
    Research on Judgment and Policy.

Hammond, K. R. and Brehmer, B. (1973). Quasi-rationality and distrust:
    Implications for international conflict. In D. Summers and L. Rappoport

(Eds.), *Human judgment and social interaction* (pp. 338–391). New York: Holt, Rinehart and Winston.

Harnischfeger, A. and Wiley, D. E. (1977). Kernkonzepte des Schullernens. *Zeitschrift für Entwicklungspsychologie und pädagogische Psychologie, 9,* 207–230.

Harre, R. (1982). *Social being.* Oxford: Oxford University Press.

Harste, J. (1985). *Excellence: Multiple realities.* Paper presented at the annual meeting of the Political Issues Affecting Literacy Interest Group of International Reading Association. Forthcoming in B. Altwerger and G. Pinnell (Eds.), *The politics of literacy.* Portsmouth, NH: Heinemann.

Hastorf, A. H., Schnieder, D. J. and Polefka, J. (1970). *Person perception.* Reading, Massachusetts: Addison-Wesley

Harvey, J. H. and Weary, G. (1984). Current issues in attribution theory and research. *Annual Review of Psychology, 35,* 427–459.

Hayes-Roth, B. and Hayes-Roth, F. (1978). *Cognitive processes in planning.* Report prepared for the Office of Naval Research, R-23660-ONR. Santa Monica, CA: Rand Corporation.

Heckhausen, H. (1976). Relevanz der Psychologie als Austausch zwischen naiver and wissenschaftlicher Verhaltenstheorie. *Psychologische Rundschau, 27,* 1–11.

Heckhausen, H. (1980). *Motivation und Handeln.* Berlin: Springer.

Heiland, A. (1984). Methodologie pädagogisch-psychologischer Forschung. In G. L. Huber, A. Krapp and H. Mandl (Eds.), *Pädagogische Psychologie als Grundlage pädagogischen Handelns.* Munich: Urban and Schwarzenberg.

Hellmann, Th. (1976). *Die Psychologie und ihre Forschungsprogramme.* Gottingen: Hogrefe.

Helmke, A. and Fend, H. (1981). Wie gut kennen Eltern ihre Kinder und Lehrer ihre Schiller? In G. Zimmer (Ed.), *Persönlichkeits-entwicklung und Gesundheit im Schulalltag. Gefahrdung und Prevention.* Frankfurt: Campus.

Herrmann, Th. (1979). *Psychologie als Problem.* Stuttgart: Klett-Cotta.

Hersh, R., Hull. R. and Leighton, M. (1982). Student teaching. In H. Mitzel (Ed.), *The encyclopaedia of educational research,* 5th edn (pp. 1812–1822). New York: Free Press.

den Hertog, P.C., van Opdorp, C. A. W., Vreuls, L. M. and Bergen, Th. C. M. (1986). De ontwikkeling en evaluatie van een categorieensysteem voor het indelen van causale attributies van docenten (The development and evaluation of a category system for causal attributions of teachers). In W. J. Linden and J. M. Wijnstra (Eds.), *Ontwikkelingen in de methodologie van het onderwijsonderzoek* (pp. 100–114). Lisse: Swets and Zeitlinger.

Hidi, S. and Klaiman, R. (1983). Note taking by experts and novices: an attempt to identify teachable strategies. *Curriculum Inquiry, 13,* 397–418.

Hill, E. A. (1986). Understanding the disoriented senior as a personal scientist: the case of Dr. Rager. In Fransella and Thomas (eds): *A book of readings in personal construct psychology.* London: Routledge and Keegan Paul.

Hill, J., Yinger, R.J. and Robbins, D. (1981). *Instructional planning in a developmental preschool.* Paper presented at the annual meeting of the American Educational Research Association, Los Angeles.

Hill J., Yinger R.J. and Robbins, D. (1983). Instructional planning in a laboratory preschool. *Elementary School Journal, 48,* 182–193.

Hofer, M. (1969). *Die Schülerpersönlichkeit im Urteil des Lehrers.* Weinheim: Beltz.

Hofer, M. (1986). *Sozialpsychologie erzieherischer Handlung. Wie das Denken und Verhalten von Lehrern organisiert ist.* Göttingen: Hogrefe.

Hofer, M. and Dobrick, M. (1981). Naive Ursachenzuschreibungen und Lehrerverhalten. In M. Hofer (Ed.), *Informationsverarbeitung und Entscheidungsverhalten von Lehrern.* Munich: Urban and Schwarzenberg.

Housner, L. D. and Griffey, D.C. (1983). Teacher cognition: Differences in planning and interactive decision making between experienced and inexperienced teachers. Paper presented at the annual meeting of the American Educational Research Association, Montreal, Canada.

Houtveen, T., Pijl, S. J., Pijl, Y. J., Reezigt, G. and Vermeulen, A. (1998). *Adaptief onderwijs. Stand van zaken in het WSNS-proces.* De Lier: Academisch Boeken Centrum.

Huber, G. L. and Mandl, H. (1982). Gedankenstichproben. In G. L. Huber and H. Mandl (Eds.), *Verbale Daten* (pp. 104–118). Weinheim: Beltz.

Huber, G. L. and Mandl, H. (1984). Access to teacher cognitions: Problems of assessment and analysis. In R. Halkes and J. K. Olson (Eds.), *Teacher thinking* (pp. 57–72). Lisse: Swets and Zeitlinger.

Huber, G. L., Krapp, A. and Mandl, H. (1984). Pädagogische Psychologie als handlungsorientierte Wissenschaft. In G. L. Huber, A. Krapp and H. Mandl (Eds.), *Pädagogische Psychologie als Grundlage pädagogischen Handelns.* Munich: Urban and Schwarzenberg.

Huberman, M. (1983). Recipes for busy kitchens: A situational analysis of routine knowledge use in schools. *Knowledge: Creation, Diffusion, Utilization, 4,* 478–510.

Ignatovich, F. R., Cusick, P.A. and Ray, J. E. (1979). *Value/belief patterns of teachers and those administrators engaged in attempts to influence teaching* (Research Series No. 43). East Lansing: Michigan State University, Institute for Research on Teaching.

Ingenkamp, K. (1977). *Die Fragwürdigkeit der Zensurengebung,* 7th edn. Weinheim: Beltz.

Irle, M. (1975). *Lehrbuch der Sozialpsychologie.* Göttingen: Hogrefe.

Jackson, P. W. (1968). *Life in classrooms.* New York: Holt, Rinehart and Winston.

James, W. (1890). *The Principles of Psychology* (Vols 1 and 2). New York: Dover Publications.

Jones, E. E. (1979). The rocky road from acts to dispositions. *American Psychologist, 34*(2), 107–117.

Jones, E. E. and De Charms, R. (1958). The organizing function of interaction roles in person perception. *Journal of Abnormal and Social Psychology, 57,* 155–164.

Jones, E. E. and Nisbett, R. E. (1972). The actor and the observer: Divergent perceptions of the causes of behaviour. In E. E. Jones *et al.* (Eds.), *Attributions: Perceiving the causes of behaviour.* Morristown, NJ: General Learning Press.

Jones, E. E. and Thibaut, J. W. (1958). Interaction goals as bases of inference in interpersonal perception. In R. Tagiuri and L. Petrullo (Eds.), *Person perception and interpersonal behaviour* (pp. 151–178). Stanford: Stanford University Press.

Joyce, B. (Ed.). (1978–79). How teachers think in the classroom. From thought to action. *Educational Research Quarterly, 3,* 4.

Joyce, B. and Showers, B. (1980). Improving inservice training: The messages of research. *Educational Leadership, 37*(5), 379–385.

Joyce, B. and Weil, M. (1972). *Models of teaching.* Englewood Cliffs, NJ: Prentice-Hall.

Joyce, B., Showers, B., Dalton, M. and Beaton, C. (1985, April). *The search for validated skills of teaching: Four lines of inquiry.* Paper presented at the annual meeting of the American Educational Research Association, Chicago, Illinois.

Karweit, N. (1985). Should we lengthen the school term? *Educational Researcher, 14*(6), 9–15.

Keeney, B. P. (1979). Ecosystemic epistemology: An alternative paradigm for diagnosis. *Family Process, 18*, 117–129.

Kelley, H. M. and Michela, J. L. (1980). Attribution theory and research. *Annual Review of Psychology, 31*, 457–501.

Kelly, G. (1955). *The psychology of personal constructs.* New York: Norton.

Kendall, P.C. and Hollon, S.D. (Eds.). (1980). *Assessment strategies for cognitive-behavioural interventions.* New York: Academic Press.

Killian, J. E. and McIntyre, D. J. (1986). *Preservice students' attitudes toward pupil control as they develop throughout the field experiences.* Paper presented at the Annual Convention of the AERA, San Francisco.

Klauer, K. J. (1980). Experimentelle Unterrichtsforschung. *Unterrichtswissenschaft, 12*, 61–72.

Kleber, E. W. (1978). Probleme des Lehrerurteils. In K. J. Klauer (Ed.), *Handbuch der pädagogischen Diagnostik*, Vol. 3 (pp. 582–617). Düsseldorf: Schwann.

Kompf, M. F., Repetory grid adaptations in detecting connotative trends and social behaviour problems in education. Unpublished Master of Education thesis, Brock University, Canada.

Kounin, J. (1970). *Discipline and group management in classrooms.* New York: Holt, Rinehart and Winston.

Krampen, G. (1986). *Handlungsleitende Kognitionen von Lehrern.* Göttingen: Hogrefe.

Kroma, S. (1983). *Personal practical knowledge of language in teaching: An ethnographic study.* Unpublished doctoral dissertation, University of Toronto.

Kuhs, T. (1980). *Teachers' conceptions of mathematics.* Unpublished doctoral dissertation, Michigan State University, East Lansing, MI.

Kusinen, J. (1972). Individual versus supplied constructs, cognitive complexity and extremity of rating in person perception, Stockholm University Psychological Labs (october).

Lampert, M. (1984). Teaching about thinking and thinking about teaching. *Journal of Curriculum Studies, 16*, 1–18.

Lampert, M. (1985). How do teachers manage to teach? Perspectives on problems in practice. *Harvard Educational Review, 55*, 178–194.

Leach, D. (1977). Teachers' perceptions and 'problem' pupils. *Educational Review, 29*, 188–203.

Lechler, P. (1982). Kommunikative Validierung. In G. L. Huber and H. Mandl (Eds.), *Verbale Daten* (pp. 243–258). Weinheim: Beltz.

Leinhardt, G. and Greeno, J. (1984). *The cognitive skill of teaching.* Paper presented at the annual meeting of the American Educational Research Association, Montreal, Canada.

Leinhardt, G. and Greeno, J. G. (1986). The cognitive skill of teaching. *Journal of Educational Psychology, 78*(2), 75–95.

Leinhardt, G. and Putnam, R. T. (1987). The skill of learning from classroom lessons. *American Educational Research Journal, 24,* 557–587.

Leinhardt, G. and Smith, D. (1985). Expertise in mathematics instruction: Subject matter knowledge. *Journal of Educational Psychology, 77,* 247–271.

Leinhardt, G., Weidman, C. W. and Hammond, K. M. (1987). Introduction and integration of classroom routines by expert teachers. *Curriculum Inquiry, 17*(2), 135–176.

Leistikow, J. (1977). Voraussetzungen, Methode und Ergebnisse einer Interaktionsanalyse in der klientzentrierten Kinderpsychotheraphie. In F. Petermann (Ed.), *Methodische Grundlagen klinischer Psychologie.* Weinheim: Beltz.

Libby, R. and Lewis, B. L. (1982). Human information processing research in accounting: The state of the art in 1982. *Accounting, Organizations, and Society, 7,* 231–285.

Lindgren-Rydberg, A. (1982). *Textilslojdens roll i barns utveckling* (Technical Report No. 4). Uppsala: Uppsala University, Sektorn for Undervisningsyrken.

Lissmann, U. (1987). Lehrergedanken zur Schülerbeurteilung. Dimensionalität und Struktur. *Zeitschrift für Entwicklungs- und Pädagogische Psychologie, 19,* 266–284.

Lortie, D. (1975). *Schoolteacher: A sociological study.* Chicago: University of Chicago Press.

Lowyck, J. (1984). Teacher thinking and teacher routines: A bifurcation? In R. Halkes and J. K. Olson (Eds.), *Teacher thinking.* Lisse: Swets and Zeitlinger.

Lundgren, U. P. (1972). *Frame factors and the teaching process.* Stockholm: Almqvist and Wiksell.

MacIntyre, A. (1981). *After virtue: A study in moral theory.* Notre Dame: University of Notre Dame Press. Cited in M. Schilling, (1985). *Practical reason and curricular criticism.* Paper presented to the 1985 American Educational Research Association, Chicago.

MacLeod, G., (1976). Self confrontation revisited. *British Journal of Teacher Education, 2,* 219–228.

Makins, V. (1985). Better than a good idea. *Times Educational Supplement 29*(3587), 21.

Mandl, H. and Huber, G. L. (1983). Subjektive Theorien von Lehrern. *Psychologie in Erziehung und Unterricht, 30,* 98–113.

van Manen, M. (1984). *Action research as theory of the unique: From pedagogic thoughtfulness to pedagogic tactfulness.* Paper presented to the American Educational Research Association, New Orleans.

Marland, P. W. (1977). A *study of teachers' interactive thoughts.* Unpublished doctoral dissertation, University of Alberta, Edmonton, Canada.

Marton, F. (1981). Phenomenography – describing conceptions of the world around us. *Instructional Science, 10,* 177–200.

Marton, F., Dahlgren, L. O., Sveensson, L. and Saljo, R. (1976). *Inlarning och omvarldsuppfattning.* Stockholm: Almqvist and Wiksell.

McArthur, L.A. (1972). The how and what of why: Some determinants of causal attributions. *Journal of Personality and Social Psychology, 22,* 171–193.

McCann, S. K. and Semmel, M. I. (1983). *Are IEP's 'Individualized Education Programs'?* Santa Barbara: University of California.

McIntyre, D. (1987). *Designing a teacher education curriculum from research and theory on teacher knowledge.* Paper presented at a meeting of the British Educational Research Association, Lancaster, England.

McLeod, M. A. (1981). *The identification of intended learning outcomes by early childhood teachers: An exploratory study.* Unpublished doctoral dissertation, University of Alberta, Edmonton, Canada.

Meyer, C. J. W., Pijl, S. J. and Rispens, J. (Eds.). (1986). *Beslissen over verwijzen en toelaten.* Lisse: Swets and Zeitlinger.

Miles, M. B. and Huberman, A.M. (1984a). *Qualitative data analysis: A sourcebook of new methods.* Beverly Hills: Sage.

Miles, M. B. and Huberman, A.M. (1984b). Drawing valid meaning from qualitative data: Toward a shared craft. *Educational Researcher, 13,* 12–30.

Miller, J. G. (1978). *Living systems.* New York: McGraw-Hill.

Mischel, T. (1964). Personal constructs, rules, and the logic of clinical activity. *Psychological Review, 7*(3), 180–192.

Mohler, P.P. and Zuell, C. (1984). *Textpack, Version V, Release 2.* Mannheim: Zentrum für Umfragen, Methoden and Analysen.

Morine, G. and Vallance, E. (1975a). *Special study B: A study of teacher and pupil perceptions of classroom interaction* (Technical Report No. 75-11-6). San Francisco: Far West Laboratory.

Morine, G. and Vallance, E. (1975b). A *study of teacher and pupil perceptions of classroom interaction* (Beginning Teacher Evaluation Study, Special Study B). San Francisco, CA: Far West Laboratory for Educational Research and Development.

Morine-Dershimer, G. (1978–79). How teachers 'see' their pupils. *Educational Research Quarterly, 3,* 43–65.

Morine-Dershimer, G. (1979). *Teacher plan and classroom reality: The South Bay study, Part IV.* East Lansing, MI: Institute for Research on Teaching.

Morine-Dershimer, G. (1983). *Tapping teacher thinking through triangulation of data sets.* Austin, TX: Research and Development Center on Teacher Education, University of Texas.

Morine-Dershimer, G. (1984). *Complexity and imagery in teacher thought: Alternative analyses of stimulated recall data.* Paper presented at American Educational Research Association Meeting, New Orleans.

Morine-Dershimer, G. and Valiance, E. (1976). *Teacher planning* (Beginning Teacher Evaluation Study, Special Report C). San Francisco: Far West Laboratory.

Morrissey, P.A. and Semmel, M. I. (1975). Instructional models for the learning disabled. *Theory into Practice, 14,* 110–122.

Munby, H. (1983). A *qualitative study of teachers' beliefs and principles.* Paper presented at the annual meeting of the American Educational Research Association, Montreal, Canada.

Munby, H. (1984). A qualitative approach to the study of a teacher's beliefs. *Journal of Research and Science Teaching, 21*(I), 27–38.

Munby, H. (1986). Metaphor in the thinking of teachers: Exploratory study. *Journal of Curriculum Studies, 18*(2), 197–209.

Murray, H. J. (1979). Evaluation of university teaching; a selective bibliography. *Labyrinth, 5,* 10–30.

Neale, D.C., Pace, A. J. and Case, A. B. (1983, April). *The influence of training, experience, and organizational environment on teachers' use of the systematic planning model.* Paper presented at the annual meeting of the American Educational Research Association, Montreal, Canada.

Newtson, D. (1976). Foundations of attribution: The perception of ongoing behaviour. In J. H. Harvey, W. J. Ickes and R. F. Kidd (Eds.), *New directions in attribution research* Vol. 1, (pp. 223–247). New York: Wiley.

Niemeyer, R. and Moon, A. (1986, April). *Researching decision-making in the supervision of student teachers.* Paper presented at the annual meeting of the American Educational Research Association, San Francisco, CA.

Nisbett, R. E. and Ross, L. (1980). *Human inference: Strategies and shortcomings of social judgment.* Englewood Cliffs, NJ: Prentice-Hall.

Norton, R. (1985). Interactive thoughts and decisions of preservice teachers: what are the knowledge sources? Unpublished doctoral dissertation, Syracuse University.

Nystrand, M. (ed). (1977). *Language as a way of knowing: a book of readings.* Toronto: OISE Press.

O'Neal, E. and Mills, J. (1969). The influence of anticipated choice on the halo effect. *Journal of Experimental Social Psychology, 5,* 347–351.

Oberg, A. (1987). Using construct theory as a basis for research and professional development. *Journal of Curriculum Studies, 19*(1), 55–65.

Oberg, A. A. and Field, R. (1986). *Teacher development through reflection on practice.* Paper presented at the Annual Convention of the AERA, San Francisco.

Oberg, A. and Field, R. (1987). Teacher development through reflection on practice. *Australian Administrator, 8*(1 and 2) (whole issues).

Oberg, A. and McElroy, L. (1987). *Educational criticism for classroom teachers.* Paper presented at the American Educational Research Association, Washington, D.C.

Oberg, A. and Tucker, P. (1985). *The personal practical knowledge of the practitioner.* Paper presented at the Meadow Brook Symposium on Collaborative Action Research, Rochester, MI.

Oberg, A. A., Chambers, C. and Field, R. (1986). *Discovering the ground of professional practice.* Paper presented at the ISATT Conference, Leuven, Belgium.

Oldenburger, H. (1986). Does a tendency to group pupils or attributes exist within teachers' cognitions/judgements? In M. Ben-Peretz, R. Bromme and R. Halkes (Eds.), *Advances in research on teacher cognitions* (pp. 186–200). Lisse: Swets and Zeitlinger.

Olson, J. (1980). Teacher constructs and curriculum change. *Journal of Curriculum Studies, 12*(2), 1–11.

Olson, J. (1981). Teacher influence in the classroom: A context for understanding curriculum translation. *Instructional Science, 10,* 259–275.

Olson, J. (1982). Dilemmas of inquiry teaching. In J. Olson (Ed.), *Innovation in the science classroom.* London: Croom Helm.

Olson, J. (1984). What makes teachers tick? Considering the routines of teaching. In R. Halkes and J. K. Olson (Eds.), *Teacher thinking* (pp. 35–42). Lisse: Swets and Zeitlinger.

Olson, J. (1986). *Microcomputers in the classroom.* Toronto, Ontario: Ministry of Education, 1986.

Olson, J. (1992). *Understanding teaching: Beyond expertise*. Buckingham, UK: Open University Press.

Osgood, C. E., Saporta, S. and Nunnally, J.C. (1956). Evaluation assertion analysis. *Libera, 3*, 47–102.

Packer, M. (1985). Hermeneutic inquiry in the study of human conduct. *American Psychologist, 40*, 1081–1093.

Paine, L. W. (1986). *Teaching as a virtuoso performance: The model and its consequences for teacher thinking and preparation in China*. Paper presented to the third conference on Teacher Thinking and Professional Action, International Study Association on Teacher Thinking, Leuven, Belgium.

Parkes, V. (1985). Appraisal in F.E.: The professional tutor and 'triangulation'. *Journal of Further and Higher Education, 9*, 3.

Parsons, T. and Shils, E. A. (Eds.) (1954). *Toward a general theory of action*. New York: Harper and Row.

Pennington, R. C. and O'Neill, M. J. (1985). *Appraisal in H.E.: Mapping the terrain*. SRHE *conference paper*, London.

Peschar, J. L. and Meijer, C. J. W. (1997). *WSNS op weg*. Groningen: Wolters-Noordhoff.

Petermann, F., Hehl, F. J. and Schneider, W. (1977). Veranderungsmessung im Rahmen der klassischen Testtheorie. In F. Petermann (Ed.), *Methodische Grundlagen klinischer Psychologie*. Weinheim: Beltz.

Peters, R. S. (1977). *Education and the education of teachers*. London: Routledge and Kegan Paul.

Peters, T. J. and Waterman, R. H., Jr. (1982). *In search of excellence: Lessons from America's best-run companies*. New York: Harper and Row.

Peters, V. A. M. (1985). *Docenten en hun probleemsituaties* (Teachers and their problematic situations). Unpublished dissertation, Katholieke Universiteit, Nijmegen, The Netherlands.

Peterson, P. L. and Barger, S. A. (1984). Attribution theory and teacher expectancy. In J. B. Dusek (Ed.), *Teacher expectancies* (pp. 159–184). Hillsdale, NJ: Erlbaum.

Peterson, P. L. and Clark, C. M. (1978). Teachers' reports of their cognitive processes during teaching. *American Educational Research Journal, 15*, 555–565.

Peterson, P. L., Marx, R. W. and Clark, C. M. (1978). Teacher planning, teacher behaviour, and student achievement. *American Educational Research Journal, 15*, 417–432.

Pijl, S. J. and Foster, S.F. (1989). Teachers' need for pupil information in special education. In J. Lowyck and C. Clark (Eds.), *Teacher thinking and professional action* (pp. 267–281). Leuven: Leuven University.

Pijl S. J. and Rispens, J. (1981). *Handelingsplannen in het buitengewoon onderwijs. Eindrapport*. Haren: RION.

Pijl S. J., Voort, R. and Algra, T. (1985). *Het gebruik van diagnostische informatie*. Groningen: RION.

Polanyi, M. (1958). *The study of man*. Chicago: Chicago University Press.

Pope, M. L. (1978). *Constructive education*. Unpublished PhD thesis, Brunel University, Uxbridge.

Pope, M. L. and Denicolo, P. M. (2001). *Transformative education: Personal construct approaches to practice and research*. London: Whurr.

Pope, M. L. and Keen, T. R. (1981). *Personal construct psychology and education.* London: Academic Press.

Popkewitz, T. S., Tabachnick, B. R. and Zeichner, K. M. (1979). Dulling the senses: Research in teacher education. *Journal of Teacher Education, 30,* 5, 52–61.

Porter, A. C. (1986). *Collaborating with teachers on research: Pioneering efforts at the Institute for Research on Teaching* (Occasional Paper No. 105). East Lansing: Michigan State University, Institute for Research on Teaching.

Posner, G. J., Strike, K. A., Hewson, P. W. and Gertzog, W. A. (1982). Accommodation of a scientific conception: Toward a theory of conceptual change. *Science Education, 66*(2), 211–227.

Prawat, R. S. (1985). Affective vs. cognitive goal orientations in elementary teachers. *American Educational Research Journal, 22,* 587–604.

Prinz, W. (1983). *Wahrnehmung und Tätigkeitssteuerung.* Berlin: Springer.

Purkey, W. W. and Novak, J. M. (1984). *Inviting School Success: a self-concept approach to teaching and learning* (2nd edition). Belmont California: Wadsworth Publishing.

Putnam, R. T. (1985). *Teacher thoughts and actions in live and simulated tutoring of addition.* Doctoral dissertation, Stanford University, Stanford.

Putnam, R. T. (1987). Structuring and adjusting content for students: A study of live and simulated tutoring. *American Educational Research Journal, 24*(1), 13–48.

Putnam, R. T. and Leinhardt, G. (1986). *Curriculum scripts and adjustment of content in mathematics lessons.* Paper presented at a meeting of the American Educational Research Association, San Francisco.

Rapaille, J. P. (1986). Research on assessment process in 'natural' conditions. In M. Ben-Peretz, R. Bromme and R. Halkes (Eds.), *Advances of research on teacher thinking* (pp. 122–132). Lisse: Swets and Zeitlinger.

Resnick, L. B. (1982). Syntax and semantics in learning to subtract. In T. P. Carpenter, J. M. Moser and T. A. Romberg (Eds.), *Addition and subtraction. A cognitive perspective* (pp. 136–155). Hillsdale, NJ: Erlbaum.

Resnick, L. B. (1983). Toward a cognitive theory of instruction. In S. G. Paris, G. M. Olson and H. W. Stevenson (Eds.), *Learning and motivation in the classroom* (pp. 5–38). Hillsdale, NJ: Erlbaum.

Revenstorf, D. and Vogel, B. (1979). Zur Analyse qualitativer Verlaufsdaten – ein Überblick. In F. Petermann and F. J. Hehl (Eds.), *Einzelfallanalyse.* Munich: Urban and Schwarzenberg.

Ritchie, T. (1982). In praise of idiosyncratic study. *Interchange, 13*(4), 31–38.

Rix, E. (1982). Shift and sift effect: A cognitive process in understanding the psychological dynamics of administrators' personnel decisions. *Interchange, 13*(4), 27–30.

Rogoff, B. (1982). Integrating context and cognitive development. In M. Lamb and A. Brown (Eds.), *Advances in developmental psychology*, Vol. 2 (pp. 125–169). Hillsdale, NJ: Erlbaum.

Rogosa, D. (1979). Causal models in longitudinal research: Rationale, formulation, and interpretation. In J. R. Nesselroade and P. B. Baltes (Eds.), *Longitudinal research in the study of behaviour and development* (pp. 263–302). New York: Academic Press.

Romberg, T. A. and Carpenter, T. P. (1986). Research on teaching and learning mathematics: Two disciplines of scientific inquiry. In M. Wittrock (Ed.),

Handbook of research on teaching, 3rd edn (pp. 850–874). New York: Macmillan.

Rosenshine, B. V. (1983). Teaching functions in instructional programs. *Elementary School Journal, 83,* 335–352.

Rosenshine, B. and Furst, N. (1973). The use of direct observation to study teaching. In R. M. W. Travers (Ed.), *Second handbook of research on teaching* (pp. 122–183). Chicago: Rand McNally.

Rosenthal, R. and Jacobson, L. (1968). *Pygmalion in the classroom.* New York: Holt, Rinehart and Winston.

Ross, L., Bierbrauer, G. and Polly, S. (1974). Attribution of educational outcomes by professional and non-professional instructors. *Journal of Personality and Psychology, 29,* 609–618.

Ross, M. and Fletcher, G. J. O. (1985). Attributions and social perception. In G. Lindsey and E. Aronson (Eds.), *Handbook of social psychology,* Vol. 2, 3rd edn (pp. 73–122). New York: Random House.

Roth, K. J. (1985). *Conceptual change learning and student processing of science texts.* Unpublished doctoral dissertation, Michigan State University, East Lansing, MI.

Roth, K. J., Smith, E. L. and Anderson, C. W. (1983). *Students' conceptions of photosynthesis and food for plants.* Paper presented at the annual meeting of the American Educational Research Association, Montreal, Canada.

Rowe, M. B. (1974). Wait-time and rewards as instructional variables, their influence on language, logic, and fate control: Part 1. Wait-time. *Journal of Research in Science Teaching, 11,* 81–94.

Rust, F. (1986). *Supervisors' conceptions of their role: A journal based study.* Paper presented at the annual meeting of the American Psychological Association, San Francisco, CA.

Rutter, M., Maughan, B., Mortimor, P., Ousten, J. and Smith, A. (1979). *Fifteen thousand hours: Secondary schools and their effects on children.* Cambridge, MA: Harvard University Press.

Ryle, G. (1949). *The concept of mind.* London: Hutchinson.

Sacerdoti, E. D. (1977). *A structure for plans and behaviour.* New York: Elsevier-North Holland.

Scheffler, I. (1958). Justifying curriculum decisions. *School Review, 66,* 461–472.

Schmidt, W., Caul, J. Byers, J. and Buchmann, M. (1984). Content of basal text selections: Implications for comprehension instruction. In G. Duffy, L. Roehler, and J. Mason (Eds.), *Comprehension instruction: Perspectives and suggestions* (pp. 144–162). New York: Longman.

Schon, D. (1983). *The reflective practitioner.* New York: Basic Books.

Schroder, H., Karlins, M. and Phares, J. (1973). *Education for freedom.* New York: Wiley.

Schwab, J. J. (1973). The practical: Translation into curriculum. *School Review, 81,* 501–522.

Schwarzer, R. and Lange, B. (1979). Implizierte Unterrichtstheorie von Lehrern. In D. Bolscho and C. Schwarzer (Eds.), *Beurteilen in der Grundschule.* Munich: Urban and Schwarzenberg.

Schwille, J., Porter, A., Belli, G., Floden, R., Freeman, D., Knappen, L., Kuhs, T. and Schmidt, W. (1983). Teachers as policy brokers in the content of elementary school mathematics. In L. S. Shulman and G. Sykes (Eds.), *Handbook of teaching and policy* (pp. 370–391). New York: Longman.

Scriven, M. (1972). Die Methodologie der Evaluation. In C. Wulf (Ed.), *Evaluation.*
    Munich: Piper.

Selvini-Palazzoli, M. *et al.* (1978). *Der entzauberte Magier.* Stuttgart: Klett-Cotta.

Shavelson, R. J. (1983). Review of research on teachers' pedagogical judgments,
    plans, decisions. *Elementary School Journal, 83,* 392–413.

Shavelson, R. J. and Stern, P. (1981). Research on teachers' pedagogical thoughts,
    judgments, decisions and behaviour. *Review of Educational Research,*
    51, 455–498.

Shavelson, R. J. Webb, N. M. and Burstein, L. (1986). Measurement of teaching.
    In M. C. Wittrock (Ed.), *Handbook of research on teaching,* 3rd edn
    (pp. 50–91). New York: Macmillan.

Shaw, M. (1980). *On becoming a personal scientist.* London: Academic Press.

Shelly, A. (1986). *Life after coding – Moving to higher levels of abstraction.* Paper
    presented at the Annual Convention of the AERA, San Francisco.

Shelly, A. and Sibert, E. (1985). *The QUALOG user's manual.* Syracuse, NY:
    School of Computer and Information Science, Syracuse University.

Shroyer, J. C. (1981). *Critical moments in the teaching of mathematics; what*
    makes teaching difficult? Dissertation, Michigan State University,
    East Lansing.

Shulman, L. S. (1984). It's harder to teach in class than to be a physician. *Stanford*
    School of Education News (p. 3). Stanford, CA: Stanford University.

Shulman, L. S. (1986a). Paradigms and research programs in the study of teaching.
    A contemporary perspective. In M. C. Wittrock (Ed.), *Handbook of*
    research on teaching, 3rd edn (pp. 3–36). New York: Macmillan.

Shulman, L. S. (1986b). Those who understand: Knowledge growth in teaching.
    Educational Researcher, 15(2), 4–14.

Shulman, L. S. and Carey, N. B. (1984). Psychology and the limitations of
    individual rationality: Implications for the study of reasoning and civility.
    Review of Educational Research, 54, 501–524.

Shultz, J. and Florio, S. (1979). Stop and freeze: The negotiation of social and
    physical space in a kindergarten/first grade classroom. *Anthropology and*
    Education Quarterly, 10, 166–181.

Sibert, E. and Shelly, A. (1985). *Logic programming: Computer programming that*
    complements qualitative research. Paper presented at the Annual
    Convention of the AERA, Chicago.

Simon, H. A. (1957). *Models of man.* New York: Wiley

Simpson, D. J. and Jackson, M. (1984). *The teacher as philosopher.* Toronto,
    Canada: Methuen.

Slovic, P. and Lichtenstein, S. (1971). Comparison of Bayesian and regression
    approaches to the study of information processing in judgment.
    Organizational Behaviour and Human Performance, 6, 649–744.

Smith, B. O. (1980). *A design for a school of pedagogy.* Washington, DC: U.S.
    Department of Education.

Smith, J. K. and Heshusius, L. (1986). Closing down the conversation: The end of
    the quantitative-qualitative debate. *Educational Researcher, 15,* 4–12.

Snyder, B. (1971). *The hidden curriculum.* New York: Knopf.

Spradley, J. P. (1979). *The ethnographic interview.* Toronto, Canada: Holt,
    Rinehart and Winston.

Stenhouse, L. (1975). *An introduction to curriculum research and development.*
    London: Academic Press.

Stones, E. (1986). Report of the group and plenary discussions. In: *Appraising appraisal*. Report on BERA conference.

Tabachnick, B. R. and Zeichner, K. M. (1983). *The impact of the student teaching experience on the development of teacher perspectives*. Madison: University of Wisconsin Madison, Wisconsin Center for Education Research.

Thorndyke, P. W. (1977). Cognitive structures in comprehension and memory of narrative discourse. *Cognitive Psychology, 15,* 437–446.

Tikunoff, W. J. and Ward, B.A. (1978). *A naturalistic study of the initiation of students into three classroom social systems* (Report A-78-11). San Francisco: Far West Laboratory.

Tobin, K. (1987). The role of wait time in higher cognitive level learning. *Review of Educational Research, 57,* 69–95.

Treiber, B. and Groeben, N. (1981). Handlungsforschung und epistemologisches Subjektmodell. *Zeitschrift für Sozialisationsforschung und Erziehungssoziologie, 1,* 117–138.

VanLehn, K. and Brown, J. S. (1980). Planning nets: A representation for formalizing analogies and semantic models of procedural skills. In R. E. Snow, P.A. Frederico and W. E. Montague (Eds.), *Aptitude, learning and instruction: Vol. 2. Cognitive process analysis and problem solving* (pp. 95–136). Hillsdale, NJ: Erlbaum.

Veenman, S. A. M. (1984). Perceived problems of beginning teachers. *Review of Educational Research, 54,* 143–178.

Vernberg, E. M. and Medway, F. J. (1981). Teacher and parent causal perceptions of school problems. *American Educational Research Journal, 18,* 29–37.

Voss, J. F., Fincher-Kiefer, R. H., Greene, T. R. and Post, T. A. (1986). Individual differences in performance: The contrastive approach to knowledge. In R. J. Sternberg (Ed.), *Advances in the psychology of human intelligence,* Vol. 3 (pp. 297–334). Hillsdale, NJ: Erlbaum.

Vygotsky, L. S. (1979). Mind in Society. In M. Cole, V. John-Steinger, S. Scribner and Souberman (Eds.), *Mind in society.* Cambridge: Harvard University Press.

Wagner, A. (1984). Conflicts in consciousness: Imperative cognitions can lead to knots in thinking. In R. Halkes and J. Olson (Eds.), *Teacher thinking: A new perspective on (persistent problems in) education* (pp. 163–175). Lisse: Swets and Zeitlinger.

Wahl, D., Weinert, F. E. and Huber, G. L. (1984). *Psychologie für die Schulpraxis.* Munich: Kosel.

Waller, W. (1932). *The sociology of teaching.* New York: Russell and Russell.

Warr P. B. and Coffman, T. L. (1970). Personality, involvement and extremity of Judgement. *British Journal of Psychology, 9,* 108–121.

Watson, J. B. (1913). Psychology as the behaviourist views it. *Psychological Review, 20,* 158–177.

Weiner, B. (1979). A theory of motivation for some classroom experiences. *Journal of Educational Psychology, 71,* 3–25.

Weiner, B., Graham, S., Taylor, S.E. and Meijer, W. U. (1983). Social cognition in the classroom. *Educational Psychologist, 18,* 109–124.

Weinert, F. E. (1977). Pädagogisch-psychologische Beratung als Vermittlung zwischen subjektiven und wissenschaftlichen Verhaltenstheorien.

In W. Arnhold (Ed.), *Texte zur Schulpsychologie and Bildungsberatung,* Vol. 2. Braunschweig: Westermann.

Weller, R. H. (1971). *Verbal communication in instructional supervision. An observational system for and research study of clinical supervision in groups.* New York: Teachers College Press.

Wilson, J. (1975). *Educational theory and the preparation for teachers.* Windsor, England: NFER Publishing.

Wittrock, M. C. (1992). Generative learning processes of the brain. *Educational Psychologist, 27*(4), 531–541.

Wood, D. (1980). Teaching the young child: Some relationships between social interaction, language, and thought. In D. Olson (Ed.), *The social foundations of language and thought* (pp. 280–296). New York: Norton.

Yaakobi, D. and Sharan, S. (1985). Teacher beliefs and practices: The discipline carries the message. *Journal of Education for Teaching, 11,* 187–199.

Yinger, R. J. (1977). *A study of teacher planning: Description and theory development using ethnographic and information processing methods.* Unpublished doctoral dissertation, Michigan State University, East Lansing, MI.

Yinger, R. J. (1979). Routines in teacher planning. *Theory into Practice, 18,* 163–169.

Yinger, R. J. (1980). A study of teacher planning. *Elementary School Journal, 80,* 107–127.

Yonemura, M. (1982). Teacher conversations: A potential source of their own professional growth. *Curriculum Inquiry, 12*(3), 239–256.

Yorke, D. (1985). *Construing classrooms and curricula: A framework for research.* Paper prepared for the 1985 Conference of the International Study Association on Teacher Thinking, Tilburg, The Netherlands.

Ysseldyke, J. E. (1983). Current practices in making psycho-educational decisions about learning disabled students. *Journal of Learning Disabilities, 16,* 226–233.

Zadny, J. and Gerard, H. B. (1974). Attributed intentions and informational selectivity. *Journal of Experimental Social Psychology, 10,* 34–52.

Zahorik, J. T. (1970). The effects of planning on teaching. *Elementary School Journal, 71,* 143–151.

Zajonc, R. B. (1960). The process of cognitive tuning in communication. *Journal of Abnormal and Social Psychology, 61,* 159–167.

Zeichner, K. M. and Liston, D. (1985). Varieties of discourse in supervisory conferences. *Teaching and Teacher Education, 1,* 155–174.

Zuckerman, M. (1979). Attribution of success and failure revisited, or: The motivational bias is alive and well in attribution theory. *Journal of Personality, 47,* 245–287.

Index